Making Modern Love

In the series *Sexuality Studies*,
edited by Janice Irvine and Regina Kunzel

LISA Z. SIGEL

MAKiNG
MODERN LOVE

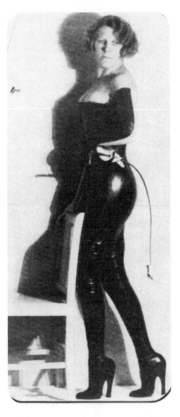

Sexual Narratives and Identities
in Interwar Britain

TEMPLE UNIVERSITY PRESS
PHILADELPHIA

TEMPLE UNIVERSITY PRESS
Philadelphia, Pennsylvania 19122
www.temple.edu/tempress

Library of Congress Cataloging-in-Publication Data

Sigel, Lisa Z., 1965–
  Making modern love : sexual narratives and identities in interwar
Britain / Lisa Z. Sigel.
    p. cm. — (Sexuality studies)
  Includes bibliographical references and index.
  ISBN 978-1-4399-0804-4 (cloth : alk. paper) —
ISBN 978-1-4399-0805-1 (pbk. : alk. paper) —
ISBN 978-1-4399-0806-8 (e-book) 1. Gender identity—Great
Britain—History—20th century. 2. Marriage—Great Britain—
History—20th century. 3. Sex—Great Britain—History—20th
century. I. Title.
  HQ75.6.G3S54 2012
  305.800941—dc23

                                                          2012008894

♾ The paper used in this publication meets the requirements of the
American National Standard for Information Sciences—Permanence
of Paper for Printed Library Materials, ANSI Z39.48-1992

Printed in the United States of America

2 4 6 8 9 7 5 3 1

Contents

Acknowledgments   vii

Introduction: Narratives and Identity   1

1   Reading Matters   17

2   Reading *Married Love*   46

3   Fashioning Fetishism from the Pages of *London Life*   76

4   Mr. Hyde and the Cross-Dressing Kink   125

5   Whipping Stories in the Pages of the PRO   152

Conclusion: Narratives and History   175

Notes   185

Bibliography   223

Index   237

Illustrations follow page 112

Acknowledgments

Since I started this project six years ago, I have accumulated more personal debts than I can remember. Soon I will be reduced to writing names on chits that will fall out of my stuffed pockets as I walk befuddled through my life. In fact, I should have begun that process long ago. If I have lost track of any names along the way, I apologize up front.

DePaul University provided me with both a professional home and support for my research. Though DePaul is first and foremost a teaching institution, it has generously supported the research that allowed me to finish this book. I have benefited from a paid leave and from support through the University Research Council. I am also indebted to the Liberal Arts and Social Sciences Faculty Summer Research Grant program, which has repeatedly supported my scholarship.

The Wellcome Library generously made the Marie Stopes papers available to researchers, and Lesley Hall has provided welcome assistance at that institution. The National Archives, which continues a tradition of open access that enriches historical research regardless of the field, allowed me to locate fascinating documents. The library and archive at the Kinsey Institute for Research in Sex, Gender, and Reproduction—whose staff demonstrated great professionalism and courtesy—are bursting with materials that moved this project forward. Nigel Roche at St. Bride's Library proved to be a wonderful resource and a great source of ideas for researching the history of magazines. The National Archives, the Wellcome Library, and the Kinsey Institute generously allowed me to reproduce images from their collections.

Peter Farrer has become my patron saint of *London Life*. He has been kind, generous, helpful, and unfailingly polite. Without his assistance, I could not have completed this book. David Kunzle is an impeccable scholar who cut the trail for others to follow. He not only carefully noted the origin of ideas in his book *Fashion and Fetishism: Corsets, Tight-Lacing, and Other Forms of Body-Sculpture* but also donated his materials to the Kinsey Institute and took the time to answer my e-mails. When I advise students that researchers should be able to follow in their tracks, I consider David Kunzle the model. Anthony Quinn of MagForum, who knows the history of magazines, has been generous with his time and erudition. I am continually amazed when scholars hang their shingle on the Web and answer questions freely, thoughtfully, and carefully.

Cynde Moya of AltaGlamour.com, who has corresponded with me at length, and Michael Goss of Delectus Books have been great resources on antique materials. The antique book trades reveal more about the circulation of information on sexuality than most historians realize. Frankly, scholars would do well to direct more attention to book dealers.

I have been fortunate to have the opportunity to present various versions of my research at a number of venues—including the Newberry Library Seminar on Women and Gender and the Indiana University Modern European Work Group—and to benefit from the generous feedback from the participants. The Youngstown State University Departments of History and Women's Studies allowed me to present an early version of my materials to a group of thoughtful and committed graduate students and faculty. The British Queer History Conference at McGill University helped me understand the intellectual and methodological stakes between queer scholars and historians of sexuality. That experience has transformed me. A special issue of the *Journal of British Studies* (*JBS*) emerged from that conference, and I was privileged to contribute to that issue an article about my work on *London Life*. I thank Professor Brian Lewis and the anonymous reviewers for helping me make improvements to that article. I also thank *JBS* for permission to reprint portions of the article in this book.

I thank the Department of History at DePaul University for supporting my scholarship. In particular, Benton Williams, Colleen Doody, Eugene Beiriger, Julia Woesthoff, Amy Tyson, Valentina Tikoff, Tom Foster, Tom Mockaitis, and Warren Schultz have been generous with their time, sympathy, and ideas. I am also grateful to Susannah Walker, Michael Embree, Bridget Altenburg, Sam Fenno, and Angela Larson for their willingness to discuss with me any number of events from the 1920s and 1930s.

Peter Stearns and Mary Lindemann taught me how to work. They provided excellent advice that has been crucial to the completion of this project. Even more, they have been role models throughout my career. Tim Haggerty of the Center for the Arts and Humanities of Carnegie Mellon University offered years of assistance and discussion. Tim's editorial eye and willingness to help other scholars makes him the sort of colleague that we would all like to become. I also thank Regina Kunzel, coeditor of the series, and Janet Francendese of

Temple University Press for their commitment to this project and for their suggestions on how to improve it.

I am grateful to Ljubomir Perkovic for being my sounding board, systems administrator, and final reader. Finally, I thank Lena, Ellie, and Muffin for their patience. They kept me grounded in the new millennium when I became lost in the last one.

Introduction

Narratives and Identity

In 1936, Edward VIII, king of the United Kingdom and the British Dominions and emperor of India, abdicated from the British throne to marry the twice-divorced American socialite Wallis Simpson. Edward's explanation seems quite straightforward: In a radio broadcast from Windsor Castle, he said that marrying mattered more than reigning as monarch. As Edward stated, he could not continue as king "without the help and support of the woman [he] love[d]." Edward also declared his brother to be better suited to reign, since he had "one matchless blessing, enjoyed by so many of you and not bestowed on me—a happy home with his wife and children."[1] At that moment, according to this script prepared for public consumption, married love trumped power, privilege, and even dignity as the king brought his private affairs forward to the public. This explanation may well have been a cover for even more questionable associations on the part of the king, including possibly treasonous relations with the Nazi state. Nonetheless, the response from the archbishop of Canterbury indicates a discomfort with the idea that marriage and sexuality mattered so dearly. According to the (London) *Times*, the archbishop stated that "of the motive that has compelled that renunciation we dare not speak."[2] The statement, oddly reminiscent of Lord Alfred Douglas's famous line "The love that dare not speak its name," hints that Edward's public declaration remained suspect not for what it covered up but for what it revealed—a central commitment to a sexual self. As Edward articulated it, love and sex had become essential to life rather than ancillary concerns to the more important matters of state.

Other prominent individuals also put their sexual stories at the center of their identities in interwar Britain. Radclyffe Hall, a well-known author with considerable money and cultural clout, self-consciously martyred herself for the cause of sexual inversion. Not only did she write *The Well of Loneliness* as a plea for recognition of sexual inversion, but she did so believing in the terrible consequences that might result.[3] For Hall, the public recognition of sexual identity was worth a great deal. Quentin Crisp, the acclaimed raconteur and memoirist, offers another example of the interwar commitment to the sexual self. He publicly appeared in high heels, dyed hair, and makeup despite police harassment and violent beatings on the streets.[4] He believed that sexuality mattered, even in circumstances in which repression or circumspection would have made sense.

Less prominent but no less important were the tens of thousands of people who wrote of themselves as sexual subjects in letters to doctors, popular magazines, and each other between the end of the Great War and the beginning of World War II. Men and women—rich and poor, young and old, and in between—wrote such letters. They wrote from major cities and small towns, from England and across the empire and dominions: from Ilford, Glastonbury, Manchester, Glasgow, Sudan, Victoria, and Saskatchewan. When they mentioned occupations, they described themselves as gentleman farmers, intellectuals, laborers, sailors, soldiers, activists, domestics, teachers, workers, engineers, and housewives. They wrote to explain themselves, to describe themselves, to communicate with others, to garner information, and to testify to their own existence. The sheer number of these accounts speaks to the importance that people placed on the articulation of their sexual selves.

Their stories emerged as part of a broader process of identity formation. Modern identities emerged over multiple centuries. Over the course of the late eighteenth century and early nineteenth century, people across Europe began to see themselves according to social class. Instead of being working class and then suddenly realizing it, they *became* working class, as E. P. Thompson's classic volume, *The Making of the English Working Class*, has shown.[5] With the formation of the nation-state, people defined themselves by nationality. Peasants became Frenchmen and Italians became a people.[6] By the end of the nineteenth century, sex and gender became paramount. Sexuality, according to Michel Foucault's account, became a central category, a key way that people began to see themselves as modern subjects with modern subjectivities.[7]

How that happened needs further clarification. A generation of scholars has shown that the Victorian focus on sexuality, the endless articulation of sex, gave rise to multiple streams of language that chattered on about sexuality and gender. These streams of discourse discussed bastardy, prostitution, onanism, hysteria, and other sorts of sexual actions deemed problematic. Coupled with that language of repression came an erotic focus that played out in pornography, ethnology, reportage, popular fiction, and science, to name just a few.[8] The proliferation of discourse saturated society with sexuality, and it was from this saturation that sexual identities began to emerge. Foucault suggests that sexology, the science of sexuality, bore special weight in the creation of new sexual identities.[9] Sexology encouraged the naming of sexual types and the creation of standard sexual stories.[10] According to Foucault's model of identity formation, once codified, these typologies affected how people saw themselves. However, Foucault offers no real agency; instead, according to Rita Felski, "individuals recognized themselves in the interpersonal, medical descriptions of the sexologists and took on these sexual identities as their own."[11] Somehow, people took these theories and remade them into stories they told about themselves; they began to think of themselves in new ways and began to make use of theories to comprehend their inner selves and their own actions.

The question of agency in the dispersal of sexual stories is the core preoccupation of this book. This project suggests that popular culture provided a method for the dispersal of stories about sexuality. Popular culture—sometimes making use of sexological definitions and sometimes influenced by sexological research but often not—allowed people to read about sexual pleasures and to write of themselves as sexual actors. Popular culture became a place to read about sexuality, a place to articulate new stories of the self, and a place to consider the paraphernalia of desire. Magazines, popular science, pamphlets, and cheap triple-decker novels all offered the delights of the modern experience in highly accessible forms. Havelock Ellis, a British sexologist, wrote that women had bimonthly cycles of sexual arousal, but Marie Stopes, the bestselling author, popularized the idea.[12] Richard von Krafft-Ebing, another influential sexologist, coined the term *sadomasochism*, but magazines about sexual whipping flooded into the English market.[13] Sexologists defined *voyeurism* as sexual spectatorship, but the Windmill Theatre offered daily shows that let some ten million patrons look at nude women posed in erotic tableaux.[14] These performances allowed the largely male audience to understand watching as a sexual act.[15] Readers of sexology might have recognized a description of voyeurism and applied it to themselves in a few cases, but experiences at the Windmill made room for millions to consider themselves as sexual subjects even if they did not have a name to put on the act of watching. The importance of the tableaux experience reverberated even further, however, since one could see re-creations of the Windmill's performances in the pages of popular magazines such as *London Life*. The processes of attending a show, looking at magazines, and staring at pinups became methods for the transmission of sexual energy. Popular culture, in its many iterations, could have a multiplying effect. Whether or not popular culture mingled with the sexological, it affected the sorts of stories that people could conceptualize.

This account confirms the work done by Alison Oram in her exploration of cross-dressing women in the popular press. Her survey of stories about cross-dressed women finds few accounts influenced by sexology; instead, for much of the twentieth century, popular culture marveled at the mysterious and astounding cases of women's boldness at crossing the gender divide. While Oram originally expected to find that modern lesbian identities had emerged from sexological case studies, the shift to modern sexual identities did not happen until the 1940s, according to her findings. Instead, she finds "wonderment, oddity, and the irrational" in narratives that circulated in the popular press.[16] This study documents a similar chronology of a delayed impact by sexology and much larger splash made by the circulation of popular culture.

As Lucy Bland notes, many decried the impact of popular culture and grew alarmed about people's engagement with books on the topics of love, romance, and sex; supposedly, popular literature pandered to women who sought cheap thrills.[17] This project takes the idea of impact a step further, past the circulation of narratives in the press, past social reactions to the spread of popular culture, and into the circulation of narratives in people's own responsive iterations. In doing so, this project follows along the lines suggested by Regina Kunzel that "popular texts provide cultural resources" for people's stories of themselves.[18] As Kunzel shows, readers appropriated and remade narratives published in popular culture to speak to their own experiences. Because popular culture gave people a language and a model for their own stories, representations and experience remain inextricably linked.[19]

To make this case, this project starts with the circulation of texts to consider how people consumed writings about sexuality. The generation reaching adulthood in the 1920s and 1930s read at a remarkable rate. As Q. D. Leavis famously wrote in 1923, "In twentieth-century England not only every one can read, but it is safe to add that every one does read."[20] During the period, a profusion of materials fed any number of appetites. Highbrow, middlebrow, and lowbrow books circulated, though as the intellectuals and their allies complained, the lowbrow circulated with an alarming velocity that kept libraries afloat.[21] People met their needs, even their intimate needs, through reading. It is no accident that Marie Stopes's *Married Love* sold two thousand copies within a fortnight of its publication in 1918. Magazines, popular fiction, sexology, and popular science all circulated through British society, creating a reservoir of ideas, metaphors, and narratives about sexuality and gender that allowed people to make sense of the world.

Despite the proliferation of published works, some sorts of information were harder to find than others. Laura Doan suggests that even those who actively looked for information about sexuality often had a hard time finding it.[22] These limitations look particularly true for the area of sexual science. It took years for Freud's first thousand copies of *Three Essays on the Theory of Sexuality* to sell. In contrast, *London Life*, a newsstand magazine, sold tens of thousands of copies a week. While Freud's model might have had a greater impact on a theory of fetishism over the whole of the twentieth century, readers of *London Life* had illustrations of the latest rubber garments and descriptions of how to wear them. To consider the issue of impact, this project starts with the circulation of popular science, sexology, novels, magazines, and ephemera. Chapter 1, "Reading Matters," details distribution mechanisms for sexual materials during the interwar years to consider the question of who read what when. However, the consideration of distribution is just the first step toward understanding how people read.

Even if individuals looked for sexual information and found it, they still needed to make sense of it. How readers read and understand the written word is no simple matter. Current reader-response studies examine how people read through some combination of questionnaires and intensive interviews. In contrast, historical reader-response studies must make use of the evidence that earlier generations of readers left behind. Jonathan Rose, for example, looks at the reception of classic works such as the Bible and *Pilgrim's Progress* to see how workers read and understood them. He provides evidence that historians can go beyond discourse analysis into reader reception through the use of archival documents and memoirs.[23] However, few sources document reading about sexuality, let alone provide evidence to consider how people make use of ideas about sexuality and gender to build identities. There are all sorts of reading about sexuality: Reading is no straightforward process, as Clarissa Smith, the one scholar who has done a reader-response analysis of pornography, has demonstrated.[24]

The question of how people read sexual materials and how their reading affected the self and others remains freighted, given the vehemence and destruction of the so-called porn wars of the 1980s. During that moment, antipornography feminists in the United States and to a lesser degree in the United Kingdom tried to redefine pornography as works that subjugate and degrade women. In doing so, they articulated a position that pornography taught men how to treat women like objects. This position posited a straightforward relationship between reading practices and actions. However, the process of reading and the results of reading seem like two different issues that each deserve their own analysis. There are really two questions embedded here: How do people understand what they read? How does what they read affect them? These questions are both interesting but only tangentially related. Furthermore, neither is as straightforward as it first appears. People can be stupid or lazy readers. They can also subconsciously or consciously focus on certain aspects of a text and ignore others. For example, although Marie Stopes's book *Married Love* was embedded with ideas about who should and should not procreate—she suggested in no uncertain terms that only the fit, healthy, and wholesome should copulate and procreate—people wrote her about marital passion and the desire to have children despite having syphilis and consumption, clear dysgenic disasters. They ignored pieces of her message and emphasized others. This sort of example suggests that the process of reading deserves examination in order to say how people understood and made use of texts.

Then there is the question of how texts affected the reader. Instead of assuming that sexual narratives acted on people in some sort of straightforward way, this project considers how people reacted to narratives. One of the ways it does so is by analyzing how people created their own stories in response to the narratives they read. The comparison between Marie Stopes's best seller, *Modern Love*, and her readers' responses illustrates the ways that they reacted to her ideas. These reactions often speak to something multidirectional; instead of a one-way relationship in which people read Stopes and adopted her ideas, they discarded part of the message, emphasized certain bits, reinvented other pieces, and then reinvented themselves in relation to what they thought they understood. In other words, people rewrote and reinvented sexual ideas as they circulated through society to create new narratives of self.

The recognition of narrativity has been central to the profession of history for a generation and has allowed new and radically different readings of documents. The understanding that people shove their stories into a preexisting narrative framework has allowed for a reinterpretation of the sorts of work that happened in the courts, such as when individuals needed to make themselves explicable to the state; such an emphasis on narrativity has brought historians beyond the reflex to find the truth in the archives and has encouraged us to see that archival documents make use of narrative strategies. The next stage of considering narrativity is shifting the locus to consider not the truth or falsity of these claims but the sorts of work that narrativity does for a sense of self.

Narrative and narrativity have become important in psychological theory to conceptualize self-identity. Oliver Sacks, a neurologist, provides a working definition of the relationship of narrative and identity that deserves attention: "Each of us *is* a singular narrative, which is constructed, continually, unconsciously, by, through, and in us—through our perceptions, our feelings, our thoughts, our actions; and, not least, our discourse, our spoken narrations. Biologically, physiologically, we are not so different from each other; historically, as narratives—we are each of us unique."[25] Sacks sees the story of self as central to the functioning of personality. Without a narrative, people lose their ability to function in the world and, even more important for Sacks, lose the spark of individual identity. This sense of the connection between narrative and identity has been further developed by Marya Schechtman, who uses narrative self-constitution to define personhood: "At the core in this view is the assertion that individuals constitute themselves as persons by coming to think of themselves as persisting subjects who have had experience in the past and will continue to have experience in the future, taking certain experiences as theirs."[26] Schechtman links this narrative self-constitution with identity formation. It is through the story of self that the self is made.

The idea that we create our sense of self through our stories has limits, according to philosophers. What happens when we age and our stories radically change? Are we the same person if we have forgotten the stories of self that we developed as children? What about self-deceptions in our storytelling? Do the stories we tell get to the truth of self? Galen Strawson believes that such storytelling "almost always does more harm than good—that the Narrative tendency to look for story or narrative coherence in one's life is, in general, a gross hindrance to self-understanding: to a just, general, practically real sense, implicit or explicit, of one's nature. It's well known that telling and retelling one's past leads to changes, smoothings, enhancements, shifts away from facts."[27] Strawson believes that the self exists beyond coherent narrative, and I suspect he may be right that there is self beyond identity.

However, the philosopher's objection becomes the historian's objective. Despite Strawson's belief that this telling and retelling creates a problem to knowing oneself, it is just this telling and retelling that becomes central to identity formation in a historical sense. As a historian, rather than a philosopher or a psychologist, I am less concerned that the stories people tell get them to an unchanging truth than the fact that they tell particular stories about themselves at particular moments in time. The truth of those stories seems historically specific in a way that both philosophers and psychologists would find insupportable. If the truth of self can be historically flexible according to current tenets of identity formation, then the problem of identity can be shown to be historically constructed and delimited. Social class dominated the way that people categorized each other and themselves in the nineteenth century; sexual identity dominated in the twentieth century. A man might define himself as a worker in the nineteenth century but a heterosexual in the twentieth. Showing the way that these systems of classification were constituted and the ways that people made use of those systems seems like a historically more relevant concern than distinguishing the truth of people's claims.

This distance between subjectivity and narrativity is the most tantalizing feature of them. When a woman wrote about finding perfect union with her husband but in the next sentence suggested that he was impotent, the historian is given a choice about truth. Do we privilege the first statement about perfection or emphasize the second about failure? Do we focus on the mind or body? Or do we try to find some sort of way to square the two such that they both may be equally true but perhaps suggest that the lack of union met her needs? When a man wrote about being a "loving mother" to his nonexistent children, do we stress his delusions as "mother," or do we privilege his self-construction as "female?" If historians believe in a singular truth, these sorts of claims create a dissonance that insists on winnowing facts from fictions. However, a focus on self-narration and identity suggests an alternative. Understanding these stories as self-narratives allows for an exploration of them as the necessary projections that measure the distance between what was and what writers wanted to be. It is that distance that allowed new forms of identity to emerge. The fantastical mattered acutely during this time of great flux because it created room for people to conceptualize themselves in new ways. Self-delusion was a necessary precondition for self-creation.

These stories of self, for all the urgency of their tellings, remain radically indeterminate. People described themselves and their desires at great length, but few defined themselves according to current definitions of sexual identity or even according to contemporary labels. They occasionally called themselves "queer" or "odd," sometimes labeled their desires as "kinky," but rarely called themselves heterosexuals, homosexuals, straight, gay, sadists, masochists, or voyeurs. Instead, they told complicated stories that remain irreducible.

Queer scholars including Laura Doan, Matt Cook, H. G. Cocks, and Matt Houlbrook have explored the permutations of queer desire before a consolidation of modern gay and lesbian identities. They have charted queer existence in ways that emphasize temporal and geographic variation, and their accounts stress the ways that individuals built a sense of themselves from a variety of cultural and social meanings.[28] Harry Cocks, in his analysis of nineteenth-century London, describes a historical sense of selfhood that remains irreducible to acts or identities. Matt Cook has extended the examination of London forward to the late nineteenth century. As he describes it, London simultaneously functioned as an indecent city, an inverted city, a decadent city, and a Hellenic city. Matt Houlbrook looks to London between the end of the Great War and the publication of the Wolfenden Report as a place that supported "homosex" without necessitating homosexual identities. And Laura Doan has explored sapphic fashioning against and around the emergence of legal and medical wrangling around lesbianism. The dynamic relationships between social meanings, individual experiences, and discourse made meanings not only multiple but multiplying.

If, as these scholars have suggested, individuals in the past saw themselves not as gay or straight, not as committing acts or articulating identities but as telling stories that were labile stories of desire, then the categories of sexual desire can be far wider than currently examined. The exploration of such stories of desire would demand extending the terrain of queer beyond same-sex desire to include a much wider range of longings. That extension of queer would make sense if, as David Halperin suggests, "the prominence of heterosexuality and homosexuality as central, organizing categories of thought, behavior, and erotic subjectivity" remains recent.[29]

During the interwar years, the profusion of erotic desires did not fit within the organizing principles of homosexual or heterosexual. Consider a case of a man who dressed as a woman for its many humiliating pleasures. (The novel *Gynecocracy* [1893] details this sort of character in great psychological depth.) In trying to make sense of such a person, one could consider various sexological categories such as invert, transsexual, transvestite, or masochist. If—rather than spelunking the past for characteristics that speak to identities as we understand them now—we see these states as amorphous and overlapping with no clear line demarcating them, then we can see the ways that telling stories about sameness and difference allowed individuals to articulate themselves. Rather than deciding which identity fits better, one can focus on the story itself.[30] As storytelling itself becomes the focus of the study, tautological trajectories melt away.

And as they do, the clear demarcations that have separated historians of sexuality from scholars of queer studies also diminish. Historians of sexuality have been documenting a broad array of sexual acts and arrangements for a generation.[31] Historians, particularly social historians, have combed the archives and used the sources to reconstruct a diversity of patterns based on lived experience.[32] They have found a wide range of sexual behaviors, models, and ideas, and they have considered a wide range of sex acts. Though queer scholars have chastised historians for choosing archival strength over theoretical sophistication and for a desire to understand the making of the present, historians have found and documented a diversity of patterns and behaviors; they have looked for and found evidence in which masses of subjects testify to their desires. Bringing empirical evidence to the table is no small matter because of the elusiveness of understanding sexual behavior in the past. According to Matt Houlbrook, the inability to know about sex acts in the past comes from the problematic nature of the historical record itself.[33] The examination of behaviors that extend the range of "queer" calls for the merger of archival strength and theoretical vision. If queer theory applies to more than same-sex relations, then it should illuminate a range of relationships including married love, kink, cross-dressing, and whipping.[34] Archival holdings that document the desires of a broad range of people should be open to queer readings. This project demonstrates the overlooked richness of the archival record and extends the sorts of stories that the record tells.

Three sorts of sources form the backbone of this project. Letters to Marie Stopes provide one set of documents. At the end of *Married Love*, Stopes asked for data regarding women's sexual cycles of arousal; thousands of people wrote to her in response. These letters form a remarkable testimony to the ways that men and women explained themselves, their relationships, and their sexual problems during the interwar years. A second group of sources comes from the Public Records Office (PRO) of the National Archives and was entered into the evidence for court cases and as part of government testimony. For example, one man wrote dozens of obscene letters about his desire to whip girls. These letters were collected as part of the police case against him. The police file ran to hundreds of pages. Concomitantly, hundreds of administrators, doctors, governmental officials, and concerned individuals wrote letters, memos, and position papers about whether corporal whipping overlapped with sexual whipping in the Home Office and Colonial Office files. All of these materials spoke to the meanings of whipping at that moment. A third set of materials comes from magazines such as *Bits of Fun* and *London Life*, which published correspondence from its readers. The innumerable letters about rubber wear, stockings, corsets, piercings, tattoos, girl boxing and wrestling, amputees, and more attest to people's diversity of desires.[35] These three sets of sources add up to tens of thousands of stories that people told about themselves and each other. As a group, these letters allow us to make sense of how people saw themselves as sexual beings and how they wrote stories in which they could star. In some sense, these sources answer the logistical problem of how the audience for writings about sex responded. They detail what individuals took away from what they read. They form a sort of reader response to questions that individuals were never asked.

Nonetheless, letters as sources have problems. They are fragmentary, offering little of the depth or breadth of more accomplished memoirs. One cannot learn about a writer by comparing the changes in thinking over time or by comparing passages on a particular topic. Instead, one needs to judge the writer by a series of snippets or by a single snippet in time. Letters are written as mediation between self and other and often organize their accounts for a specific reason. Writers use the conventions of their genre and condense their stories to fit in a few short pages. They are written from a person to another and mediate all the markers of social difference. They organize a life into a coherent framework. They are linear products that flatten life into simple patterns. In all sorts of ways, they are not unmediated self-expressions. Further, there are no guarantees about veracity; sometimes these letters provide a fantasy about what the writer wanted rather than a description about how the writer lived—a problem particularly relevant to accounts of sexuality. The adaption of certain motifs could happen consciously or subconsciously, in a straightforward manner or in a manner more twisted and interesting.

This element of strangeness has allowed historians to write off some of the letter writers used in this book as marginal. However, the qualities that they embodied are less marginal than they first appear because the questions that they considered—including the meaning of sexual unions, the erotics of gender, the problems of corporal punishment, and the impact of consumer pleasures—affected everyone, even if everyone did not follow the same logic or come to the same conclusions. Further, such letter writers are not marginal in terms of numbers. Though part of this project builds on the case file of a single man, for example, that man noted roughly two dozen associates in his address book, and his account correlated with a thousand stories in the ephemeral press. Such magazines were printed in the tens of thousands, and those magazines would be passed from person to person weekly and read by the hundreds of thousands. A case study of one may be marginal, but as those voices add up, their marginality begins to raise questions about the center. The mass of British society struggled with similar issues to these sources as they reacted to the changing character of their world.

This book focuses on the interwar years because it is only during those years that people began to write about sex in mass numbers. In other words, the project simply follows the sources. However, the sources emerged in a specific context, and the historical period between the wars therefore becomes critical to understanding how people came to construct their sexual stories. A particular set of circumstances emerged after the Great War that made letter writing possible, that made sexual lives more fraught, and that encouraged people to tell stories in new ways. The war transformed life in myriad ways, making change possible. The broad realization of changed circumstances after the war demanded the development of new expectations and roles for men and women.[36] New social circumstances began to demand new models of understanding. The repercussions from the Great War continued to affect the populace and mark their lives until the next war swept it away as the defining moment of their times.

During the war, soldiers and civilians began writing letters in astonishing numbers. The Army Post Office saw an increase in the number of letters sent, from 650,000 letters per week in 1914 to 3 million per week in early 1915. By 1916, more than 11 million letters were sent to the troops per week.[37] The war multiplied the culture of letter writing and encouraged people, who had no reason to write letters before the war, suddenly to begin.

Change from the war affected people on a mass scale. Some five million British men, or 22 percent of men, served during the war.[38] More men came from the empire and dominions; Canada and Australia, for instance, had a higher proportion of men in military service than England.[39] The Great War passed a far longer shadow across Britain than in the United States. The war dead numbered 722,000 in the United Kingdom, while in the United States fewer than 120,000 died despite a population more than twice the size. The impact rose accordingly. Virtually every person in Britain saw someone—whether a relative, friend, colleague, lover, spouse, or companion—wrenched out of daily life and sent into service. As a result, daily life on the home fronts suffered from deep disturbances, and soldiers experienced disruptions on a mass scale. Most men and women experienced change in acknowledged and unacknowledged ways.

Men came back from the war changed and sometimes broken. They suffered from impotence, from debilitating pain that affected their sexual function, aroused by strange desires according to their own accounts.[40] Men returned longing for softness, from either women or the clothes that generated memories of women. Prewar gender roles stressed masculinity as virile, rugged, aggressive, and self-contained.[41] The idealization of sacrifice and heroism in adventure stories and poetry encouraged men to volunteer for service in the war but did not prepare men to withstand the horrors of trench warfare.[42] Soldiers experienced mental and psychological trauma in unprecedented numbers. Masculine models of strength and self-control crumbled, and men's will gave way to crippling emotional and mental disorders.[43] Other men rejected models of masculinity and instead valued femininity, especially mothering, welcoming a return to domesticity at the end of the war.[44] Finally, the war had enormous consequences on men's sense of themselves as men and on their ideas of sexuality.[45] As one Lancashire woman wrote in 1926, "Men are so funny these days, since the war, they certainly haven't been the same."[46] She looked for tips on how to keep her husband sexually interested—a problem for which she and her female friends could find no solution.

Women were met with a rising consumer culture that whetted their desires and a society that denounced them for their engagement with those desires at every turn. Commentators blamed women for the inability to return to prewar life and suggested that women's gains came at the expense of men's losses.[47] Women outnumbered men by almost two million after the war, though these numbers were routinely discussed and embellished. Counted among the remaining men were the wounded and maimed who could not resume normal life.[48] In fact, women's gains were often illusionary.[49] Though women made some progress toward equality, including achieving full suffrage in 1928, social and economic inequality between men and women continued and even grew at war's end when women were forced from their jobs as men demobilized.[50] Society focused on the young single girl as a locus of social disorder, and women became a focus for contempt, bitterness, and aggression. There would be few eras when derision and desire so intertwined around a central icon. Supposedly struck with "khaki fever" during hostilities, the young single woman was thought to embody the excesses of the postwar world.[51] Hedonistic, pleasure-seeking boyettes or flappers smoked, drank cocktails, and engaged in sordid love affairs. They were promiscuous, fashion fixated, boyish, and independent; they were unsettled and unformed. They were not even serious enough to be feminists; instead, they embodied sexual frivolity.[52] Anger at them became a way to explicate anger at the changed world. This picture of pained social relations between men and women created a deep reservoir of gender ideas and behaviors for erotic consideration.

The results of the war lingered after the armistice. The landscape of the postwar world remained littered with people who had experienced amputation and trauma.[53] The horrors of trench warfare affected men with fits, faints, paralysis, convulsions, tics, tremors, mutism, hallucinations, and nightmares for decades.[54] Men and women emerged from the war with new tactile and sensory experiences and new needs, sexual and otherwise, that they expressed. Those who could not cope with the return to civilian life were locked in mental asylums across Europe.[55] And those who could work through such experiences flooded the cinemas, the publishing houses, and the art houses with their efforts. Thus, the war as an experience, as a memory, and as a fragment of cultural expression marked the interwar years and contributed to the sorts of stories people told about themselves.

The war changed the tenor of their storytelling. People no longer saw their world as strictly rational or logical, and the methods they used to decipher themselves and the world around them rested on longings and will as much as reason and measure. Modris Eksteins argues that the twentieth century has been essentially ahistorical because "this century has been one of dis-integration rather than integration. The psychologist has, as a result, been more in demand than the historian. And the artist has received more respect than either."[56] Slow and careful reasoning no longer provided the model for understanding the world; instead, dynamism and illegibility became the model for the modern age. New models for writing and representation emerged. The tone of their stories of self changed as well.[57] Paul Fussell's examination of the impact of the war on literature found that the experience of war engendered a deep sense of irony and despair.[58] Modernists such as James Joyce and Virginia Woolf captured stream of consciousness through experimentation in form and structure. Among writers less skilled and polished than Joyce, attempts to speak a truth about sexual subjectivity took a variety of forms. In some cases, sex and aggression exploded onto the page in a hash of words. In others, the form of the carefully wrought case study allowed individuals to organize their accounts. People told new stories and used new methods to tell them.

All of these ideas affected people's sense of themselves and became fodder for people's sexual scripting. Rapid changes during the war years allowed them to rewrite the stories they told. World War I did not start all of these transformations; nor did the war cause them. Instead, the war and its resultant traumas effected change and then marked out the process of change in people's lives. People rewrote their ideas about women and men, marriage, trauma, sex, the future, and the past, not once but repeatedly, sometimes compulsively returning again and again to these fraught concepts until the next great war remade the conceptual world again. They wrote their sexual subjectivity in relationship to these concepts continuously until once-relevant constellations of ideas seemed antiquated, and then those antiquated ideas seemed nostalgic. And then they eroticized that nostalgia.

The moment of people's writing, between the wars, is thus central to this account. The legacy of the war, the ascendence of consumer culture, the habit of writing letters, the enormous conceptual problems regarding sex and gender, the broad social reorganizations that took place, and the popularization of sexual science all contributed to people's sexual stories and all crystallized during this short period. There was no single cause of change or a single change to follow; instead there was a rapid cascade of transformations that affected a wide variety of people. The period saw the shift from industrial culture to a widespread consumer culture replete with ready-made goods, paraphernalia that advertised and celebrated them, and a growing service economy that dealt in them. The period contributed to the development of modernism as a form of expression and as a set of ideas and allowed for the consolidation of modern gender and sexual identities. As Lucy Bland notes, the issues of "crucial importance" after the war included the "adjustment to a postwar economy; blurring of class boundaries; ambivalences towards the spread of mass culture, including the spread of the popular press; and above all, deep anxiety about gender roles and the modern woman."[59] None of these transformations happened easily, and all of them had long-term repercussions for British society and modern sexual relations.

If the chronological markers condense rapid change into a few short years, the geographic limits of this process expand its boundaries exponentially. People wrote their accounts from within an empire that was at once a geographical expression and a conceptual world.[60] Though often forgotten given the rapidity with which it dissolved after World War II, the British Empire reached its apex during the interwar years. It yoked together roughly one quarter of the world's population and controlled roughly a quarter of the earth's total mass. Even the most committed critics at that moment saw it as robust.[61] Ideals of what it meant to be British had salience on people's constructions of themselves, even as groups within the empire continuously reconstructed what that might mean.[62] People constructed the self and the other as part of a process of "mutual constitution" organized, according to Catherine Hall, by "grammars of difference."[63] People wrote themselves according to logics presented in consumer culture with the dominions as a location of a white-settler society full of fit yeoman farmers, the Indian empire as a hierarchy of castes and religions, and the broader empire as featuring a range of exotic peoples and practices.[64] When Laurence Lenton, a Fulham corset maker, sent a photograph of "A Tight-Belted Maori" for publication in the correspondence column of a popular magazine, he not only communicated with other readers about fetish wear; he also let other readers map sexuality onto regions of the empire.[65] He defined himself and others according to "grammars of difference" marked by race and empire.

Individuals across the empire experienced an overlapping consumer culture reinforced by popular culture and advertising. Imperialism pervaded life in the United Kingdom, though often in ways that people never noted. They read and responded to novels that featured an imperial background—whether explicitly, like Margaret Pedler's stories, set in British India, or implicitly, like Sax Rohmer's stories of Dr. Fu Manchu. They used and eroticized imperial products such as rubberized rain gear, and they moved back and forth from England to empire as part of a continuous conceptual world. Reading let people map erotic pleasures onto a variety of geographies. Artifacts and ideas flowed along the lines of the empire; books and ephemera published in London passed to the rest of Britain and onto the dominions and empire, bringing with them conceptions about sexuality that contributed to ideas of race and identity.[66] Marie Stopes's writings about the creation of a fit and healthy race spread to South Africa, Australia, and Canada, and readers in those locales and others saw themselves as sharing a cultural identity. As one couple explained to Stopes, "I suppose to other folk we are a very ordinary pair—but it is something very wonderful in our hearts towards each other."[67] In many ways, the couple was both ordinary and emblematic of a shared set of values and beliefs. Their common conceptual world connected discussions about the importance of fresh air and orgasms from South Africa to England.[68] Shared material goods, patterns of reading, concerns, experiences, and mental practices knit together a common culture across vast distances. Though the ubiquity of imperial ideas and products did not make all Britons imperialists, it contributed to a culture of imperialism that pervaded daily life and common experience.

When the British traveled across the empire, they turned to the London publishing world to stay abreast of culture. Across the empire, popular culture linked modes of thought with the mechanism of the state. Consumers received their magazines though a centralized, organized, and highly efficient system of moving popular culture that included publishers, wholesalers, and agents and that made use of the latest technologies, including ships, boats, rails, and eventually airplanes to deliver information in a continuous stream. Sexually explicit literature appeared in urban areas in South Africa, popular science appeared in Canada, glamour magazines traveled to Australia. Popular books, legal magazines, and even the occasional obscene work followed the spread of consumer culture across the dominions and colonies. There was not one single set of ideas but multiplying, overlapping ideas communicated through a variety of mediums, transmitted inward to the self and outward to others across the empire at the same time.

The consumption of such ideas allowed people to link sexuality with biopolitics.[69] Men and women remade themselves and each other as emblems of the imperial order. The leader of the physical culture movement, Eugen Sandow, promoted bodily perfection as a way to promote cultural regeneration across the empire. His idea of bodily strength and beauty linked 100,000 members of the Health and Strength League by 1931.[70] Magazines such as *Health and Efficiency* and *Health and Strength*, which encouraged this self-fashioning and self-regulation, affected people across the empire. Further, incitements overlapped with discipline in the spread of censorship codes and corporal punishment. Consumers in England and the empire read erotic descriptions of corporal punishment while members of the Foreign Office communicated with local administrators in Africa about the use of corporal punishment for sex crimes. The whip linked sex to the state, illustrating the often covert ways that biopolitics of the empire ramified through the population. By reading the same authors, by writing to each other, by following legal codes derived from the same set of laws, and by breaking legal codes resulting in the same sets of punishments applied to their persons, Britons reconstituted the empire on themselves in sexual terms.

To understand the material culture that formed the basis of their conceptual and cultural world, Chapter 1 considers how writings about sexuality circulated in the interwar world. The chapter details the distribution patterns for magazines, novels, and sexology and examines the specific constraints that affected access to those ideas. The chapter also considers what sorts of ideas circulated in the interwar world, paving the way for the subsequent examination of how people used those ideas in the construction of their sexual stories. The book then follows an overlapping chronology to examine stories about married love, fetishism, cross-dressing, and whipping. Central to each chapter is the consideration of the ways that published materials circulated and the ways that people responded with their own stories of self.

Chapter 2, "Reading *Married Love*," examines the correspondence sent to Marie Stopes after she published her best-selling marriage manual in 1918. It considers how men and women wrote their own stories in response to her book. It asks: How did readers of Stopes's works describe themselves? How did they plot their own stories of love and sexual longing? How did they adopt her vocabulary and adapt her ideas about race, marriage, and sexual satisfaction to their own needs? The comparison between Stopes's prose and readers' responses illustrates the ways that individuals rewrote themselves after the Great War to embody a future defined by health and marital happiness.

Chapter 3, "Fashioning Fetishism from the Pages of *London Life*," examines correspondence columns that ran from 1923 until 1941 in a popular magazine to see how people created their own sense of queer sexuality in the interwar years. The chapter considers the tens of thousands of letters about corsets, amputees, piercing, high heels, water play, tattoos, girl boxing and wrestling, tight gloves, and long hair to examine how people scripted their own desires. In considering how popular culture opened room for people to write queer narratives of desire, the chapter explores the ways that historical transformations created ruptures that played out in sexual and gender transformations.

Chapter 4, "Mr. Hyde and the Cross-Dressing Kink," considers the relationship between the circulation of ideas in the popular press and people's lived experiences. Building on the previous chapter, which looked at the letters from a correspondence column, the chapter ties the distribution of magazines to an identifiable person and his community. Mr. Hyde bought the same magazines and materials and then lived what others wrote. By exploring interwar ideas of male cross-dressing, the chapter demonstrates the ways that cross-dressing responded to the gender and sexual anxieties that emerged in the wake of the Great War before cross-dressing had been dissected into sexological taxonomies.

Chapter 5, "Whipping Stories in the Pages of the PRO," considers the ways that the circulation of stories transformed state policy. It juxtaposes the close study of an obscene-letter writer who accused local girls of all sorts of perverse acts and demanded that their parents whip and cane them, acts described in pornographic detail, with the consideration of officials in the Home Office and Colonial Office who tabulated, assessed, and examined the state's practice of whipping prisoners, largely for sex crimes. Reformers denounced whipping as a sort of state-sanctioned perversion and by 1938 convinced members of the British government that whipping resulted in a range of sexual desires including sadism, masochism, and sexual inversion. The broad assessment of whipping as contributing to sex run amok forced the British state into recognizing the preexisting perversion of its own acts and resulted in changing policies toward corporal punishment.

The progression of chapters does not imply a straightforward linear model, whether along a spectrum of loving to aberrant, liberation to repression, or margins to center. All of the sexual beliefs and desires in this book have been presented as perversions, and all of them embodied a longing for love and completion. Instead of linearity or simple binaries, this volume suggests that people experienced a chaotic mix of emotions, engaged in myriad relationships, and viewed themselves and each other in multiple and often contradictory ways. Each chapter follows the circulation of ideas and details an aspect of the various relationships between production, distribution, and consumption. Most important, each chapter details the impact of reading and writing on the narrative construction of self. People searched for explanations and entertainment, bought materials, read them, and responded with stories of their own. In the process, they wrote a future and struggled to lever themselves away from their own conception of history. Caught between a past from which they were trying to awaken and a modernity of their imagination, people felt electrified by possibilities.

1

Reading Matters

n 1929, a married woman wrote to Marie Stopes, the popular writer on sex and marriage, about an upsetting item that she had read in a news report.

> What, to me, is rather puzzling, and if true, very dangerous, has been detailed to me this week. It is the case of a girl, being pregnant and by her statement and that of her friends having had no connection with a man. The doctor in charge of the case seems to agree to this statement and says he can only ascribe the presence of the male element to the use of a public lavatory.[1]

Another woman wrote to Stopes after reading books about sex in preparation for marriage:

> For though I am 29, my ideas on marriage were the haziest, and as you say in one of your books, it is just one's most intimate relations to whom one can *not* go for information in these matters. Your books have helped me in a very real way + I feel grateful to you.[2]

A third writer, experiencing problems with sexual continence, found himself continually aroused. According to his own descriptions, "even to read a book the least thing excites imagination." He ended his letter with a plea for advice from Stopes.[3]

If this project plans to explore how people told stories about themselves as sexual subjects, then these three examples suggest that the project should begin with the circulation of narratives. After all, these people wrote letters to Stopes after reading books and articles, including hers, about sexuality.

To understand what people wrote and why they did so, this chapter considers reading. Reading about sexuality allowed people to know about a range of desires. Reading provided a mechanism for people to try on ideas. As Matt Houlbrook and Lucy Bland have noted, books offered people a language, a set of emotions and characters, and a set of narratives for understanding themselves and each other.[4] Reading provided the necessary background for people to articulate themselves as sexual subjects by providing style sheets for writing. Readers themselves attested to its importance. They used books to enjoy themselves and to punish themselves. People read to learn, to clarify, and to arouse.[5] A 1947 survey published by Mass-Observation suggested that "only 3 per cent of the general population said they never read anything at all."[6] People made sex books into best sellers and they made mysteries and romances into the mainstays of lending libraries. From all evidence, reading, especially reading about sexuality, affected people in profound ways.

Questions about knowledge production have typically stood in for the orthogonal issue of reading.[7] Literary critics and intellectual historians have focused on books that were published during the period, tracking down sexology and medical science, examining the great novels that faced obscenity campaigns and censorship, and detailing the sorts of messages that circulated in these media.[8] These accounts, though extremely useful in documenting a history of ideas, nonetheless say little about what people knew because few people read James Joyce, Havelock Ellis, or Radclyffe Hall and fewer still read Sigmund Freud or Richard von Krafft-Ebing. Not all people had access to all stories.

To understand what people knew, social historians have turned to people's assessments of their own sexual knowledge during the period and found a population mired in ignorance.[9] Oral histories, memoirs, diaries, and surveys document deep levels of confusion and anxiety.[10] Hera Cook suggests that the degree of ignorance meant that sexual information, even when delivered, was not always understood.[11] Kate Fisher suggests an alternative explanation that the presentation of ignorance remained central to women's identity.[12] She argues that because sexual ignorance signified sexual purity, women were discouraged from stating what they knew, particularly when they feared judgments would be made. A cultural insistence on sexual ignorance should not be dismissed, but neither should it be accepted literally as knowing nothing. Perhaps when people spoke of their own ignorance, they did not mean no knowledge but rather incomplete knowledge or the wrong knowledge. After all, that one could read a newspaper account about impregnation via a toilet seat illustrates that there was a popular source for information, rather than no information at all.

In contrast, this chapter grounds questions of knowledge in issues of access. A consideration of access allows historians to move beyond either erudition or ignorance to see the circulation of narratives in the population. Specific factors, including distribution mechanisms and censorship patterns, affected people's access to ideas, as this chapter shows. As a result, people had the great-est access to magazines and ephemeral materials, considerable access to pop-ular literature and popular science, less access to serious novels on sexuality, and only limited access to sexology. Because each set of materials brought its own conceptions of sexuality, patterns of access affected what people knew. By documenting access, this chapter delineates the available accounts that people used to write their own stories.

Distribution

Simply because a book was published does not mean that it was read by every-one. Books and magazines, especially those about sex, circulated and sold in dis-tinct ways that affected who could find them. By examining the ways that people acquired reading materials, this section suggests that distribution patterns—responding to often obscure censorship laws and practices—had an enormous impact on people's access to knowledge about sexuality. As a result, people often had little choice about what they read; they took what they could get.

Ross McKibbin's work has been central to considering reading as the result of access. He suggests that such factors as "class, sex, age, geography" deter-mined access to literature and the degree of literacy that one would bring to reading matter.[13] However, materials about sexuality complicated an already intricate rubric for understanding reading. While sophistication and social class affected the depth of literacy and the ability to access the written word, other factors, such as gender beliefs, distribution routes, and location, could have a far greater impact on people's abilities to learn about sex. As a result, people had different patterns of access to these materials than to other forms of literature. A wealthy matron from London who was well versed in Shake-speare might be more literate, sophisticated, and comfortable buying books than a working-class man, but she would have had a harder time getting hold of obscene or even explicit wares than a working-class soldier during the war because a trade in such materials had sprung up for soldiers. Explicit materi-als were available on "the streets of Port Said" and "displayed on every kiosk in Paris."[14] Wealth and sophistication were overturned in that case in favor of movable markets for a largely male population. After the war, however, wealth-ier individuals found relatively easy access to Marie Stopes's popular books on marriage, whereas workers might have learned about birth control only from newspaper accounts.[15] Certainly, factors that limited access could be broken down by the desperate need for information, but even that battering ram went only so far. Thus, standard rubrics for gauging access and literacy changed when the topic was sex.

Despite a desire for better sex education, few individuals received one.[16] In "infant schools," a classroom pet would suffice to introduce discussions of sex, biology, and nature.[17] As a result, people were forced to become autodidacts. They turned both to their families and to material culture for information.

People looked for clarity and direction from printed sources about ways to control their bodies and achieve pleasure.[18] They sought out sexual information from a surprising array of places, and they tried hard to make sense of the information they found. Caches of information were saved and circulated, sometimes for generations.[19] Though materials from the late nineteenth century might have appeared hopelessly out of date by the interwar years, the continued circulation of antiquated goods illustrates the depth of the demand.[20]

Reading materials could be found in bookshops, through mail order, through circulating libraries, and at the corner news agent's shop, though none of these venues provided unfettered access to information about sexuality. Circulating libraries allowed patrons to borrow popular works. The number of book titles published rose from 9,000 in 1914 to 14,000 in 1939; public libraries owned more than 247 million books by 1939.[21] According to one cultural critic, however, the library system pandered to the lowest tastes. Supposedly, commercial libraries picked popular books because it paid "to buy (at a substantial discount) three hundred copies of one novel that every one will be willing to read than a few each of a hundred different books that will not circulate throughout the clientele."[22] As a result of these purchasing decisions, one could find out a good bit about romance but less about sexual acts or even sexual hygiene.

Many books were not stocked at all by such libraries, including *Lady Chatterley's Lover* and *Ulysses*, and few circulating libraries stocked sexological literature by Magnus Hirschfeld and Richard von Krafft-Ebing. These decisions could have real impact both on an author's ability to publish serious work and on the circulation of knowledge.[23] Private and public libraries either refused to buy books thought obscene or impolitic or refused to circulate them even if they had been donated or bought. The refusal, especially if part of a coordinated campaign, could put pressure on publishers to avoid the positive portrayal of sexual themes.

Serious sexological studies had to be viewed in such venues as the British Museum Library, where collections such as the Private Case and Cupboard collections were available only to qualified researchers.[24] Such restricted access kept the young and impressionable from perusing articles that might inflame their passions. Such hidden controls occasionally became more overt. Lewis R. Farnell, during his reign from 1920 to 1923 as vice chancellor of Oxford University, attempted to purify Oxford by banning public-speaking engagements by Marie Stopes, Bertrand Russell, George Lansbury, and Maude Royden, all of whom were known to speak about sexuality. Farnell garnered attention by the national press for shutting down a student-controlled publication and expelling the editors of the periodical, the first students to be thrown out of Oxford for political views since Shelley in 1811.[25]

Booksellers tried to stock only legal books, but the borders between licit and illicit remained nebulous though consequential.[26] A clear statement of the law was often hard to find because of the patchwork of laws and practices that had developed over decades.[27] The most relevant laws included the Vagrancy

Act (1824), which called for hard labor for exhibiting indecent prints; the 1853 Customs Act, which prohibited importation of obscene materials; the 1857 Obscene Publications Act, which allowed magistrates to destroy books, prints, typefaces, and plates if the materials were found obscene; and the 1868 Hicklin standard, which established a definition of obscenity based on an object's ability to "deprave and corrupt those whose minds are open to such immoral influences."[28] These acts were joined by the Post Office (Protection) Act of 1884, which made it illegal to send obscene and indecent articles through the mail.[29]

The interwar years provided little new to the structure of state suppression beyond its extension. The Hicklin definition remained standard throughout the United Kingdom, and the courts used the proximity of materials to audience to define obscenity in Britain and the empire. Deana Heath explains that in India "as in Australia, officials, magistrates, and judges drew on the precedents set by English common law for the regulation of the obscene, which meant that the Hicklin test became, once again, the standard common law definition of obscenity in yet another completely different context from which it originated."[30] In Burma, the British Empire built its censorship policies from those in British India.[31] Officials in Capetown and Rhodesia formulated policies about the circulation of obscene goods on the model of the British legal code and then ratcheted up punishments for breaking those laws in response to each other.[32] In 1926, the League of Nations recognized the dependencies' accession to the International Convention for the Suppression of the Circulation of and Traffic in Obscene Publications. As a result, Nigeria, Seychelles, British Honduras, Ceylon, Kenya, Mauritius, British Solomon Islands Protectorate, Gilbert and Ellis Islands Colony, Fiji, Uganda, Trinidad, Zanzibar, the Tanganyika Territory, Leeward Island, Windward Island, Gambia, Nyasaland, Straits Settlement, the Federated Malay States, Brunei, Johor, Kedah, Kelantan, Terengganu, Sierra Leone, Northern Rhodesia, Barbados, Gold Coast, Cyprus, Gibraltar, Malta, Somaliland, Basutoland, Bechuanaland, Swaziland, and Hong Kong agreed to suppress obscenity and report directly to the League of Nations.[33]

These laws allowed the British state to curtail obscene books without calling into question the state's commitment to a free press.[34] According to the Home Office, a free press meant something particular: It implied that there was no prepublication approval of books.[35] In other realms, such as cinema and theater, there were formal censorship boards that preapproved materials.[36] Because there were no such boards for printed matter in Britain, the law allowed full freedom for the press to publish and print as it saw fit. However, once printed, books became subject to the laws of obscenity, sedition, and libel. After publication, the state pursued materials on the basis of how they were displayed, sold, mailed, and shipped in the twentieth century. In other words, the state went after distribution.

Obscenity laws divided the markets in two—the legal market and the obscene market—and then put pressure on both markets to curtail discussions of sexuality at the point of distribution. The obscene market remained a niche marketplace operating off the continent while the legal market operated out of England, most often London, which stood at the center of a vast distribution network that connected English publishers to vendors of magazines and books across the empire. The law's focus on distribution, rather than creation, meant that distributors and vendors were pressured to maintain standards of decency. As a result of these policies, by the late 1930s, most distributors had entered into a voluntary, joint censorship pact to curtail the distribution and sale of obscene materials.[37] Even before that, the high level of organization for sales and distribution of books and magazines meant that curtailing obscenity at the point of distribution became efficient. To try to eliminate obscene materials, the Home Office would notify Customs and the Postal Union about materials coming into the country via mail order, and those offices would seize the materials. The Home Office also coordinated with the Foreign Office to have publishers and distributors pursued abroad.[38]

Distribution as the key place to control the circulation of ideas worked even more successfully in the empire. The close cultural ties between Australia and Britain, the trade networks, and the postal organization encouraged Australian importation of British reading materials. As a result, British publishers controlled the Australian marketplace in books and literature, which by the 1890s was worth more than one million pounds a year. Because of Britain's monopoly, there was virtually no indigenous publishing market until after World War II.[39] The Department of Trade and Customs regulated obscenity after the Australian federation because reading matter came from abroad. To go after obscene books meant to go after imports.[40]

In Britain, materials were subject to another round of inspections if they made it to stores. Voluntary organizations such as the National Vigilance Association and the London Public Morality Council alerted the police to obscene materials, or the police found materials that seemed to contravene the law.[41] In either scenario, the police would seize the materials, sometimes arresting those producing or distributing the materials. Though the courts needed to decide whether an article was obscene, in practice, the police, customs agents, and postal inspectors assumed that certain articles—such as pornographic films, explicit photographs, and novels—that graphically depicted sex would deprave and corrupt any minds that came into contact with them.[42] Other materials became obscene in context. Statues and paintings of nudes that were legally displayed in museums would become illegal if reproduced on the postcards, photographs, and lithographs of the poor.[43] Mass-market novels that described genital excitement would raise the attention of the police, while medical texts that described genital excitement would not. Materials that described sexual intercourse when cross-dressed were confiscated and destroyed; materials that described cross-dressing as a joke were not. The more prone to condemnation the books were, the easier the courts were on them. As Celia Marshik demonstrates, the state went after *The Well of Loneliness* and *Sleeveless Errand*, two sympathetic portrayals of lesbianism, because the authors were earnest; in contrast,

Compton Mackenzie's *Extraordinary Women*, which presented a satire of lesbianism, was allowed to circulate because it "made nasty fun" of lesbians.[44]

Although state offices knew that certain books were outlawed, that certain types of magazines raised alarm, and that certain authors were under suspicion, they did not publicize this information, even to booksellers and news agents who wanted it.[45] Shop owners themselves had little knowledge of the law and unknowingly stocked materials that broke the law. If booksellers were caught by the police with materials considered obscene, the ramifications could be extreme, including confiscations, fines, imprisonment, and hard labor.[46] Thus, while people might look to booksellers for information about sexuality, booksellers tended to err on the side of caution and tried to avoid such publications. To avoid such complications, few offered access to sexological, medical, or racy materials.

Even if readers could find purveyors that dealt in sexual information, they would still have to find appropriate volumes. Consumers trying to find information about sex would need to differentiate between titles that promised more than they delivered and others that sounded rather tame but could get both purchasers and book dealers put on the watch list at Customs. Charles and Company used the ploy of advertising legal materials as erotica.[47] Conversely, books like *Marital Confidences* hid an erotic intent behind a plain blue binding and nondescript name.

If customers found a bookstore that offered a wide range of materials, they would need to steel their nerves to go inside. One army officer described entering "rather an unsavory little establishment which some men and most women would hesitate to enter. I mean the kind of place with a window devoted to cheap rubber goods and pornographic fiction."[48] Customers would have to be able to articulate what they wanted since materials were often hidden away, rather than prominently displayed. Once there he noted "that whilst 'lustful' books with 'passionate' covers and titles [were] freely exposed for sale," Marie Stopes's volume had to be requested.

Certain neighborhoods became centers for bookstores, both legitimate and those that housed illicit materials. The concentration of bookstores at Charing Cross allowed a few less-than-respectable vendors to coexist with legitimate trade until May 1937, when the police decided to clean up Charing Cross Road. The range of materials confiscated indicates the sorts of materials available in such venues. At the Cambridge Bookshop, the police seized *Faradole, Sexology, Sex, Sunbathing Review, La Vie Parisienne, Paravant, Lingeries Libertines, Ici Paris, Paris Music Hall, Nudist Artist, Bagatelle, Nudist, Vive Paris, Paris Plaisirs, Paris, Beaute, Lire a Deux, Sex Appeal, Mon Paris, Honni Soit, Petit Choc,* "Spanking Stories," "Very Naughty Stories," photographs, and the book *Sadism and Masochism* by Wilhelm Stekel [orthography as in original].[49] From another location, the police seized magazines such as *Salon de Beaute, Chic Nus, Etudes de Nus, Petites Amies, French Cancan, Cupids Capers, Gay Parisienne, Tattle Tales, Bedtime Stories, Pep, La Paree, Parasol, Scandale, Almanach, Paris, Lire a Deux, Beaute, Mon Paris, Bagatelle, Pages Folles, Vive Paname,* and *Vive le*

Soleil. In addition, the proprietor had packets of photographs with such titles as "Lingerie Libertines," "Tableaux Nus," "Tableaux Deshabilles," and "Les Nudities."[50] At a third location, *Spanking Stories* and *Very Naughty Stories* as well as photographs of German nudists, photographs of lingerie past and present, and miniature photographs joined the same magazines that had been seized from other shops.[51] In these semilegitimate shops, legal goods rubbed against semilegal and illegal displays; obscenity, nudism, and the occasional work of sexology appeared alongside postcards.[52] Such shops stocked a diversity of goods including rubber goods and images as well as books and magazines. Large cities like London might have a few such bookstores that provided a panoply of illicit or so-called immoral goods—one that would not be obscene but that would raise a shop holder's profile with the police. Residents of smaller towns relied on either mail order or news agents' shops.

People who wanted more explicit goods, whether visual or literary, or who lived in smaller towns in England and across the empire needed to turn to the mail-order trade. Mail order—from both London and the continent—had linked people from across the British Isles to sources of illegal knowledge for more than a generation. Paid for with cash, checks, and stamps, mail-ordered goods would arrive wrapped in a plain brown wrapper. Larger dealers, such as Paul Ferdinando, best known as Charles Carrington, distributed a steady stream of both pornographic and nonpornographic materials to readers in Britain. Orders for materials numbered in the tens of thousands in the 1890s, and he continued the trade well into the 1910s.[53]

Less explicit wares could be bought from Charles and Company, a mail-order business run from a private dwelling in London. The firm sold contraceptives, rubber goods, and "suggestive books and prints," according to the police, from the 1890s until after World War II.[54] Charles and Company routinely advertised in *London Life*, a glamour magazine that became associated with the fetish community in the 1920s. The slowly evolving ads in the magazine featured photo sets that promised more than they delivered; books, particularly reprints of erotic classics; and birth control. A paper-covered copy of *The Awful Disclosures of Maria Monk* would be sent with free postage, for example. That volume, originally published in 1836, offered a risqué and sensational view of convent life in America. It remained a steady presence in the circular trades. *Female Flagellants or the History of the Rod* also appeared in Charles and Company catalogs.[55] A book titled *Exhibition of Female Flagellants* had been first published in 1777, and a volume titled *A History of the Rod* had been first published in 1870.[56] The Charles and Company volume could have been an amalgam of the two, an expurgated copy that had been renamed, or some variation of the two since all of these practices remained standard in the trade. The catalog also featured nude and seminude artists' models in cabinet-size prints (fifty such images could be had for fifty shillings), bathing scenes, and "screaming comic post cards." The wares of mail-order companies like Charles and Company demonstrate the polyglot of materials available through the mail-order trade.

Books, postcards, and magazines remained the main technology for communicating about sexuality. The extent of more explicit materials remains speculative, but confiscations by Customs and the Postal Office suggest both the magnitude and the proportions of books, magazines, and such visuals as postcards and photographs. The 1935–1936 statistics given to the League of Nations stated that the Postal Office seized 733 packets while Customs seized 397 and another office cautioned 31 people. Customs also seized 260 books, 119 photographs, 125 postcards, 142 prints, and more than 20,000 magazines. Additional cases spanned the empire: nine cases in Ceylon, six offenses in Hong Kong, four cases in Mauritius, four cases in Singapore, and one in Tanganyika.[57] Magazines were the most popular, though the state saw books and erotic photos as the most pernicious. Only occasionally did individuals get caught with obscene film—the most cutting-edge technology available.[58] Few pornographic materials fully disappeared; instead they circulated endlessly and illegally before getting seized, pulped, or immolated.[59] Older works that should have lost their appeal continued to circulate and sell for good prices.[60]

Most people had only limited access to bookstores in large and anonymous cities and did not use mail order to access racy materials. Instead, they tried to eke out a sense of sex from materials they had at hand. For many, that meant the news agent's shop. Such shops were everywhere according to contemporaries: "Every district, even the poorest," had a few news agents who sold magazines and newspapers.[61] In 1925, only nine bookstores served a population of 110,000 in South Wales, but eighty-two news agents and stationers served the area. One news agent suggested that he helped shape the reading tastes of the population by finding individuals the right materials.[62] The ubiquity of news agents' shops and their periodicals riled intellectuals to no end. George Orwell offers a compelling description of the place of such shops in the local community. "You never walk far through any poor quarter in any big town without coming upon a small newsagent's shop. The general appearance of these shops is always very much the same: a few posters for the *Daily Mail* and the *News of the World* outside, a poky little window with sweet-bottles and packets of Players, and a dark interior smelling of liquorish allsorts and festooned from floor to ceiling with vilely printed twopenny papers, most of them with lurid cover illustrations in three colours."[63] In retrospect, intellectuals' bitterness over reading matter seems ill advised given later alternatives of no reading, but contemporary writers saw the reading of periodicals as soul-deadening. "The more newspapers people read, the shorter grows their historical memory; yet most people read little else."[64] Intellectuals made complaints about the ubiquity and the quality of periodicals as well as the amount of money spent on them rather than books. They recognized that periodicals shaped tastes and minds the ways that more serious literature could not. "Probably the contents of these shops is the best indication of what the mass of the English people really thinks and feels. Certainly nothing half so revealing exists in documentary form. Best-seller novels, for instance tell one a great deal, but the novel is aimed almost exclusively at people above the £4-a-week level."[65]

The reliance on the news agent for information spread across the British Empire. If anything, imperial wholesalers established a more thoroughgoing control over materials than even agents in the United Kingdom. In Australia, Gordon and Gotch imported most magazines and distributed them to news-stands, stationers, tobacconists, and confectioners. John Gotch, a Liverpudlian bitten and then impoverished by gold fever, joined forces with Alexander Gordon, a Scottish news agent with a stand in Melbourne in the 1850s. Gotch sold newspapers and magazines "on the diggings" or at the gold fields while Gordon sold from his stall. Though two local newspapers were published, the agents primarily imported British magazines that were shipped by boat and then rushed by hansom carriage to readers. As railroads connected Australian territories, the agents extended their domain. The agents gradually solidified their monopoly across areas of the British Empire, joining with other companies, such as the Central News Agency (CNA) in South Africa in 1914. Eventually the company became the major wholesaler for New Zealand, Canada, and Papua New Guinea, while the CNA controlled South African distribution.[66] International distribution transported materials across the empire so that readers in Australia, New Zealand, South Africa, and Canada could read the same magazines as readers in London. The local newsstand, with its copies of glamour magazines, fashion news, movie magazines, and sporting magazines, including bodybuilding and sunbathing magazines, provided an education of sorts to the vast majority in Britain and the empire.

Censorship laws did not eliminate access to materials about sexuality, but they did shape the market in distinct ways by making booksellers leery of stocking and selling materials that might contravene the law. Libraries also curtailed the spread of explicit works. As a result, people had little choice of what they could read. They took what was available. Most people across Britain had access to magazines that were cheap and easily available at news agents, organized by a highly efficient system of moving materials from printers to buyers via the latest shipping methods. Popular novels were also widely available at booksellers and lending libraries, and popular science became available during this period in record numbers.

These methods delivered sexual knowledge to the population during the interwar years, but each sort of material brought with it its own culture of ideas. By looking next at the ideas available in each category of print culture, we can get a better idea of what people read and therefore what they used to develop their stories of themselves as sexual subjects.

Magazines

Though often overlooked as a source of information, magazines provided the mass of people with sexual information across Britain and the empire. Some magazines explicitly concerned themselves with sex and bodies, while others approached the topic more obliquely.[67] The range of magazines at a news agent's shop included humorous papers, such as *Punch*; illustrated magazines, such as *Hush* and *World Stories of Thrills and Adventure*; women's magazines, such as *Modern Woman* and *Woman and Beauty*; film magazines, such as *Reel Screen Humor, Real Screen Fun*, and *Screen Romances*; magazines that emphasized fiction, such as *Love Stories* and *Peg's Paper*; paper-covered fiction, such as *Ranch Romances* and *Love Romances*; and bodybuilding and naturist magazines, such as *Health and Efficiency* and *Health and Strength*. Other magazines, such as *Silk Stockings, High Heels*, and *Gay Book*, served both fetishist and fashion-oriented audiences. Some of these magazines offered little more than photo series of women dressing and affecting highly sexualized but nonetheless legal poses. In one, for example, a woman disrobes backstage with the caption "A very intimate glimpse of what goes on backstage—or should we say, goes off?"[68] Such publications delivered little more than sly innuendo; illustrations of legs, cleavage, and bare arms offered a certain pleasure for buyers interested in glimpses of nudity. Cartoons illustrated an occasional indiscreet nipple. Formalized gaping continued in such magazines as *The Man about Town* (1939), which promised "Sexational Questions" and "the Truth about Nude Models." Despite its lurid promise in a three-tone cover, its stories offered little in the way of sexual "truth." Instead of revealing the sex life of models as the title promised, the article suggested that nude models had no interest in sex. The magazine offered little concrete in the way of sex advice. Instead, it proffered a cosmopolitan leer by the man about town.

Paris Sex Appeal offered a variety of racy features, including "conversations about love," Western adventures, and historical stories about Rome. For readers not fluent in French, the text still offered a wealth of information in its photographic imagery. (Advertisements in English for English books, photos, and films suggest that the readership may well have relied on such visual cues.) Nude models on almost every page offered life lessons on the female form. Stepping out of lingerie, sunbathing, climbing, and dancing, the nude model allowed the reader to visualize the female body in motion as it moved through a variety of eroticized postures. Nude photos, supposedly sent by readers, included back shots of men and women. These images added to the risqué appeal of the magazine and may have functioned as a sexual forum for visual exhibitionism. The relation between the sexuality and photography was made even more explicit by advertisements that offered film developed with discretion guaranteed; the developer, in Nancy, promised to keep no copies.

Others magazines offered stories of love and passion. In *Ranch Romances: Love Stories of the Real West*, the hero finally finds love and hangs up his holster. In such love stories, men become the focus of erotic longing. "A gun in the hand of Jim Harlan is like a living poem. He is the personification of red-blooded Western manhood. He glorifies the wind-swept plains with flaming guns raised only for honor and justice."[69] Red-blooded men found love in the arms of good women, but these stories offered little information of what that love might look like beyond the obligatory ending clinch. The popularity of these magazines and their ubiquity suggests that many women enjoyed a nebulous sense of sex in which romantic tension stood in for sexual intercourse and that saw union embodied in the kiss.

Magazines could be used in more than one way and served more than a single audience. Film magazines could inform young women about the latest styles and gossip from Hollywood (most such magazines were imported from the United States), but they could also be used as pinups for those interested in masturbatory images. *Movie Merry-Go-Round*, for example, offered glamour shots of movie starlets and chorus girls; these shots lingered on the women's lingerie and heels, making the line between glamour rag, star copy, and fetish source unclear. Men's magazines, if read by boys, could serve as models on how to be men; if read by gay men, could allow men to think about other men's erotic longings; and if read by women, could allow women access to the mysterious (if entirely fictitious) world of masculine sexuality.

Nudist magazines served as a conduit for information about nudism as a practice, for notices about club activities, and for articles about the body in general. The best known in Britain, *Health and Efficiency*, gained newsvendors status. Despite the girlie cover that featured a well-endowed woman carefully inhaling for the camera, the magazine maintained its reputation as a quasi-legitimate channel for physical fitness and naturism in the United Kingdom. Other magazines—such as *Sun Bathing Review*, published by the Sun-Bathing Society; *Gymnos*, published by the Gymnic Association of Great Britain; and *Nudelife*—focused more directly on the so-called sport of nudism. Magazines such as *Health and Strength: The National Organ of Physical Fitness* used the images of the sunbather and the nude athlete as ways to promote their model of physical fitness.[70] All of these magazines served nudist communities, but the ratio of nudists to magazines suggests that they had other purposes as well. As Brian Hoffman demonstrates of nudist magazines in the American context, the range of content allowed these magazines to be read multiple ways and serve a variety of sexual identities.[71] Thomas Waugh suggests that such physical fitness magazines served as "beefcake" imagery for other men. No doubt, ubiquity of the image of the partially nude male athlete made it a powerful motif for erotic longings.[72] The interspersing of images of male and female nudists and athletes across these magazines suggests that such magazines served as reservoirs for sexual ideas for and about both sexes.

Such magazines allowed a wide variety of people to see bodies supposedly stripped of artifice. Physical fitness and nudist magazines capitalized on the desire to see nudity in order to compare and assess one's own body against those of others. Thus, such venues not only fed desire; they could also add to or alleviate anxieties about the body. One article explained how fashion hid men's flaws: "By wearing the right type of clothes the weak and under-developed man is able to conceal nearly all his physical defects. Well-cut sleeves hide his scrawny arms; padded shoulders mask his feeble deltoids; there are patterns to suggest the illusion of height and designs to suggest slenderness. Only one part of his body is beyond the range of the tailor's artifice: the neck." To illustrate a well-developed neck, the magazine used a photograph of a bodybuilder whose neck appeared in all its bullish strength. Such magazines exposed bodies for visual confirmation of health and fitness and for comparisons that might not be available otherwise.[73] Furthermore, ads for men's physical fitness programs appeared in women's magazines, suggesting that women bought such programs for their loved ones or that men read women's magazines as well. In ads like "What Do Women Want Most?" which featured the half-naked torso of muscle builder Earle Liederman, the answer would seem to be a man with a swell physique. These sorts of images served multiple purposes in creating anxiety and promising to allay it, in feeding desire and in offering ways to sublimate it through physical fitness.

Visual images circulated internationally both with and without attribution. The fondness for German bodybuilding and nature photos meant that such images popped up with great regularity. Despite attempts by certain vehement national elements in Germany to stress the uniqueness of German nudist culture, these images spoke to the higher ideals of physical reform. The Life-Reform Movement in Germany channeled both right-wing and left-wing energies toward transforming society through reforming the body. Thousands of nudists in Germany saw nude bathing and sun worship as a way to wash away the stains of industrial capitalism, and individuals across Europe and America saw Germany as the center of the movement.[74] The spread of images from the German nudist and body publications into new contexts contributed to a proliferation of meanings; what might be read as life affirming in Germany could easily be reread as prurient in another locale.[75] Thus, nudist images appeared in girlie magazines and stories of "life among the nudists" became a popular feature in books and magazines.

The proliferation of meanings allowed for the circulation of materials that might not otherwise pass the censors. *London Life*, for example, functioned at the intersection of glamour magazine, sex column, and fetishist correspondence center. According to David Kunzle, before the Great War its circulation stood at more than fifty-five thousand and rose throughout the interwar years. He notes that advertisements for the magazine graced "1,000 cinema screens throughout Britain" in 1928 and that it was available in railway stations all the way to India.[76] In one way of reading the magazine, it seemed only slightly racier than other glamour publications. Whereas other glamour magazines might feature chorus girls, *London Life* photos, for example, of the Revue belles at the Windmill Theatre showed women's breasts barely obscured by a panel of transparent fabric. Whereas other magazines might feature an inside-page advertisement for women's medicine, this publication featured a back cover ad for birth control in the July 29, 1933, issue. However, the magazine could be read in multiple ways, and it played off that multiplicity quite knowingly. The headline of the September 15, 1934, issue read, "Some Queer Stories and Some Queerer Letters." "Queer" in that context might have been understood as "odd" but could also be understood as inverted, especially given the lengthy story about a male pedicurist with a "swaying walk and babyish lisp" and others about boys who liked needlework in that issue. Even more revealing were the advertisements for high heels—six inches or more—in all sizes (an important feature for male cross-dressers) that could be sent anywhere. Photographs of black leather shoes show that these were no ladylike pumps; instead, these strappy super-high heels embraced severe and distorted lines. The magazine also featured stories about tattooed ladies and cross-dressed men. Central features of the magazine were its correspondence columns (see Chapters 3 and 4 for further discussion, and see the gallery of illustrations for examples) and advertisements for corsets for men and women, rubber goods, and naughty books. Magazines such as *London Life*, *New Photo Fun*, and *Bits of Fun* could pass as innocent of sexual content for those unfamiliar with the sexual symbols of fetishism. For those in the know, such stories spoke to more specific fantasies.

The wide range of magazines and cheap ephemera provided a sex education, though one that disguised itself as an innocent interest in glamour, health, fitness, and romance. The wide circulation and the easy availability of these sorts of materials suggest that most individuals would have at least a passing acquaintance with them. While the mental framework that one brought to such publications mattered at least as much as the materials featured, such publications offered a wide sense of sexuality that hinted at a range of desires. Nonetheless, the sort of education one could garner from most of these materials focused on emotion, rather than technique. That is, such works might eroticize the cowboy but wouldn't offer explicit advice about what to do with him; magazines showed stockings but not stockings used as sex aids. These magazines emphasized erotic symbols, romantic ideals, and potent visual cues but offered little in the way of concrete advice.

Novels

Three books stand out as signaling the arrival of a literature that engaged sexuality in the interwar years: *Lady Chatterley's Lover* by D. H. Lawrence, *The Well of Loneliness* by Radclyffe Hall, and *Ulysses* by James Joyce. However, most of the population did not read these books. Most people turned to novels available in public and private libraries, such as those that operated out of Boots and W. H. Smith. The latter had a stock composed of half romances, one quarter adventure stories, and one quarter crime stories.[77] Although reviled by literary elites, popular novels provided a bank of ideas about sex, marriage, and romance from which people could make sense of the sexual world.

The list of best sellers during the interwar years included novels by Edgar Wallace, Sax Rohmer, Zane Grey, Agatha Christie, Ethel M. Dell, E. M. Hull, May Christie, William Le Queux, Margaret Pedler, Kathlyn Rhodes, and Olive Wadsley. Not all of these authors wrote romantic fiction, but most included romantic relationships in their fiction. Ethel M. Dell's writings made her one of the wealthiest authors in Britain, and her fiction earned her the title "the house-maid's choice," though Rebecca West labeled her work as "tosh."[78] E. M. Hull, a pig farmer's wife from Derbyshire, wrote *The Sheik*, which was later made into a Rudolf Valentino film.[79] These novels circulated in commercial libraries and were available in cheap paperback form. Just as intellectuals denigrated magazines as soul-deadening, they considered such novels mere escapism for middle-class housewives, female office workers, and seaside vacationers, a sort of fiction tailored toward escapism.[80] The two most popular genres at the beginning of the twentieth century were the same as the ones at the end: detective stories and romances.[81]

The combination of sex and death formed the bedrock of the contemporary mystery. In Agatha Christie's *Death on the Nile* (1937), for example, romantic love works as a plot device as a jilted girlfriend haunts the honeymoon of new-lyweds. In *Murder in Mesopotamia* (1936), the murder of a much loved arche-ologist's wife throws questions on the relations of the whole crew.[82] Even spy thrillers used romance to provide narrative tension, as in William Le Queux's *The Doctor of Pimlico* (1919). Le Queux's hero, Walter Fetherston, longs for Enid Orlebar, whose "fresh face, betraying as it did, her love of a free, open-air life, was one of those strangely mysterious countenances met only once in a life-time."[83] Only after foiling an international ring of forgers and saving her step-father from humiliating exposure can Fetherston claim her love, her hand, and her happiness. What the novel lacks in explication, it makes up for in frustrated longing and mutual mistrust. The lovers neither kiss nor caress; instead, they spend much of the novel speculating about each other's motives while travel-ing across international borders to cozy country estates. Fetherston, Le Queux's hero, is a sophisticated world traveler with a taste for particular brands of suits and cigarettes. The popularity of such novels suggests aspirational desires as well as a willingness to believe that true love made its way on mystery and distrust.

Other heroes had a rugged masculinity, like the men in H. Rider Haggard's and Jack London's novels. Margaret Pedler's *The Barbarian Lover* (1923) de-scribes a master marksman and outdoorsman who camps rough in India and England. He is imbued with the "untamable love of freedom . . . the call of the wild."[84] He renounces civilization and his claims to the landed gentry to become the titular barbarian lover. Pedler's novel treats conflicts between her hero and heroine as emblematic of romantic tension. The heroine, Patricia, rec-ognizes, "with sudden unerring consciousness, that he was again asserting his mastery over her, just as he asserted it a dozen times. . . . Always there had been a sense of struggle between them—of cool dominance on his part, of reluctant yielding on hers."[85] To be forced into yielding is the essence of feminine falling in love in such romances.

These novels celebrated modern women, rather than Victorian throw-backs, and their modernity added to their allure. In *The Girl from Scotland Yard* (1926), the heroine rises from stenographer to detective because "she thinks quick and she's lucky."[86] Also of note are her lovely violet eyes and trim

figure. In *The Doctor of Pimlico*, William Le Queux marks out his heroine's allure by her modernity. "Austerely simple in dress, with a face which betrayed a
spiritual nobility, [she was] the very incarnation of modern womanhood, alive
with modern self-knowledge, modern weariness and modern sadness."[87] In *Silk
Stocking Murders*, a novel first published in 1928, Anne Manners, the vicar's
daughter, is "one of those capable girls whom the emergency seems so often to
produce; and unlike most capable girls, she was good to look at as well."[88] Such
modern heroines were willing to engage in subterfuge if necessary but showed
themselves as wholesome, levelheaded women in the end. They had come to
embody the "pluck" of Victorian boys, the unshockable sophistication of the
modern, and the wholesomeness of the English sweetheart.[89] They traveled
through a cosmopolitan world but valued straight dealing and simple pleasures.

These romances and mysteries use sex to add to the narrative twists and
turns and see romantic love as a way to resolve them. In Olive Wadsley's *Possession* (1916), the heroine, Val, marries Blaise even after she realizes she is
pregnant by another man. Blaise willingly acts as father to the child but re-
jects Val for her dishonesty. The many plot twists untangle with her confession
and his acceptance: "They clung together desperately, their tears mingled with
the driving rain; only the wind heard the words they whispered between their
broken kisses."[90] The final clinch also resolves doubts about character. As May
Christie wrote, "Thus they remained in each other's arms, their two true hearts
beating in unison, their kisses mingling, their twin souls united in the first
moments of their newly-found ecstasy of perfect love."[91] *Love's Miracle* (1930)
ends with Jim pacing back and forth in the hospital while his wife, Jane, gives
birth. As he embraces his wife and son, his thoughts are revealed: "Here was the
whole meaning of life. Here was his heaven."[92] The ending embrace signals the
resolution to all sorts of sexual confusions and dilemmas.

Despite the centrality of marriage and love, these popular novels do not
eschew sexual and social problems but use them to create a more fraught and
therefore a more adventurous world. Sexuality forms the chaotic background
that calls for love and marriage to provide a sense of clarity. *Silk Stocking Murders* built on the sexual chaos of the London nightlife scene; in case the charged
nature of the atmosphere was lost on the reader, the detectives explicitly reference Jack the Ripper and Thomas Neill Cream, another well-known mass murderer. When someone kills a series of women, detectives decide the murderer
must be a "homicidal maniac of the sexual type."[93] As in a true-crime proce-
dural, the detectives build up a psychological profile of the criminal as a "lust-
murderer" based on Krafft-Ebing's sexual taxonomy.

In *The Girl from Scotland Yard*, a number of shady characters cross-dress
to elude identification. The butler—Arthur Druze—is really the cross-dressed
woman Alice Druze. His sister, Annie Druze, also takes a false identity. Going
by a false name, Annie embodies all of the features of the emerging sapphist
stereotype: "There was a certain ruthless strength in every line, every feature.
She was something more than fifty and just under six feet in height. The mas-

culinity of the powerful face was emphasized by the gray hair, cut close in an Eton crop, and the rimless monocle which never left her eye."[94] These cross-dressed and sexually suspect members of the Druze family blackmail and baby-farm their way across the country. Olive Wadsley's *Possession* uses the problems of bigamy, premarital pregnancy, and illegitimacy to test the love of Blaise and Val. Ethel M. Dell uses the ruse of a fraudulent first marriage that wrecks the virtue of an otherwise honorable woman in *The Lamp in the Desert* (1919). Not for nothing did Robert Graves and Alan Hodge suggest that "the most compelling popular fiction of the day was sex-problem fiction."[95]

For the more "serious" reader, D. H. Lawrence's works provided a sexual education of sorts. More than 10 percent of students surveyed from the London Workers Education Association listed Lawrence as their favorite novelist, one whose works they "read frequently and enjoy."[96] Lawrence, during the inter-war years, was considered a modernist who belonged alongside James Joyce and Virginia Woolf, though his focus on relationships made him a more accessible writer, according to the readers.[97] Graves and Hodge placed Lawrence in the sex problem camp of writers and suggested that "Lawrence's sex-ridden men and women were weighed and compared even in Suburbia."[98] His most famous book about sex, *Lady Chatterley's Lover* (1928), was not legally available in Britain and not subject to the full protection of copyright. The suppression and piracy of the book befoul any estimate of publication numbers.[99]

Lawrence, whose name became synonymous with sexuality in the inter-war years,[100] saw sexual passion as creating transcendent bonds between men and women but only if done right. His works created more standards for doing sex wrong than right, and they read like a road map to the sexual travesties that ruin relationships. There are inadequate unions of weak men and strong women.[101] There are men who lost virility: "You say a man's got no brain, when he's a fool: no heart, when he's mean; and no stomach, when he's a funker. And when he's got none of that spunky wild bit of a man in him, you say he's got no balls."[102] There are whorish women who long for sexual stimulation.[103] And finally, there is the lesbian: "When I'm with a woman who's really a Lesbian, I fairly howl in my soul, wanting to kill her."[104] In *Lady Chatterley's Lover*, sex ultimately allows the main characters, Connie and John Thomas, to transcend their stations in life—she as a wife and he as a gamekeeper—by forcing them to disentangle themselves from their failing relations. According to Lawrence, sex provided dynamism to life by offering a productive energy. In Lawrence's account, sex done wrong cheapened and demeaned the human spirit, while sex done right provided the "living and re-vitalizing connection between man and woman."[105] Lawrence sketched out a map of liberated sexuality followed by later generations, one that emphasized sexual naturalness and passion over practice and calculation.

Despite the novel's reputation as salacious, few outside the intelligentsia actually read *Ulysses* (1922). Although its reputation has been growing ever since its publication, as Steven Kellman suggests, "it is a book more venerated than read." First editions of the book have gone unopened and unread, and copies, including Hemingway's, went uncut.[106] The lack of "accessibility" in Joyce's case made it the "most unlikely of dirty books."[107] If one persevered, the volume contained a language that made use of obscenity, moments of defecation unrelated to farce, affirmations of adultery, and scenes of cross-dressing and whipping that might well have been modeled on those in *London Life*.

The final volume in the "trilogy of literary dirt," according to Anthony Burgess, is Radclyffe Hall's *The Well of Loneliness*.[108] Hall saw her work as the first serious attempt to look at female sexual inversion. The book, published by Jonathan Cape, originally received largely positive reviews; reviewers suggested that its challenging relationships might not be for everyone, but in general they noted its delicacy and beauty. According to Laura Doan, by the time the state began proceedings against the publisher, the book was a tolerable seller with roughly five thousand copies in circulation.[109] As Elisabeth Ladenson makes clear, *The Well of Loneliness* differed from most obscene books in that the state defined it as obscene because of its earnest treatment of the subject matter, rather than for a particular scene or series of scenes. Hall wrote *The Well* as a plea for understanding of inversion; she created a world of women who exist largely without men. Rather than questioning the roles of men, Hall divided her characters along sharp gender lines but peopled both roles with women. Masculine women take on male roles as ambulance drivers, horsewomen, and writers, while their feminine counterparts act as lovers, nurses, governesses, and companions. Stephen Gordon, the protagonist, is a virile man caught in a woman's body, and he shares a love for horses, fast cars, cigarettes, and soft women with other virile men. Stephen loves Mary but ultimately renounces the relationship to protect Mary from the world's censure. The book offers very little in the way of sexual content. Outside a series of kisses between Stephen and his amours, the scene that implies a sexual relationship between women reads, "Stephen bent down and kissed Mary's hands very humbly, for now she could find no words any more . . . and that night they were not divided."[110]

Thus, whether popular or more erudite, novels created a world charged with sexual energy and romantic love. They elaborated beliefs about gender in great and compelling detail. They showed how to admire a man's rough physicality and a woman's tender care. They suggested an importance for physical intimacy. They hinted at the variety of sexual types and suggested that chorus lines and cocktail parties might be places to find them. Such novels were favorites among lending libraries and booksellers. Novels, especially popular novels, circulated wide and far and therefore taught a great number of people about sex and love. Novels introduced the many problems of sex: crossdressers, illegitimacy, sex done wrong, and villainous murderers of the sexual type. Novels reinforced ideals of romance and emphasized the emotional work necessary to form romantic unions. They provided descriptions of dashing heroes and sweet-faced young heroines and the occasional dashing heroine as well. However, such materials provided little in the way of how-to information.

In other words, novels, though widely available and widely read, gave cultural cues about the emotional work of sex but provided little technical information. Even the raciest novels, those outlawed by the state for obscenity, offered little concrete advice on what to do "when not divided." Because of this, few individuals counted novels as sources of information when asked. Nonetheless, the circulation of novels, like that of magazines, pervaded society with sexual energy and emphasized the importance of sex for a large part of the population.

Sexology and Its Popularizers

In some sense, the highly charged eroticism in novels and magazines may well explain the simultaneous saturation of sexual culture and continued sexual ignorance. When participants were asked how they learned of sex, the first results of the Mass-Observation study found that one in four said they "just picked it up," while others believed that knowledge "just came"—that they learned from other children or from a parent.[111] The ubiquity of sexual materials may account for people's ability to just "pick up" sex because it meant that the culture was saturated with sexual symbols that went unarticulated and were therefore only partially explained or understood.

At the same time, books had an outsized importance. When people thought about their sexual education, they referred to books, particularly nonfiction books. Just over half of the individuals surveyed as part of the Mass-Observation's National Panel mentioned books as a source of sexual knowledge. According to the report, the "most frequent authors mentioned by name are Havelock Ellis and Marie Stope [sic]." Participants of the study mentioned the following books and authors as having the greatest impact on their sexual knowledge:

Havelock Ellis	[Sigmund] Freud
Norman Haire	Kenneth Walker
[T. H.] Van de Velde	Illustrated Medical Dictionary
Dictionaries	L. M. Fowler
Encyclopedias	Bible
Books on Sex Hygiene, Sex Instruction Manuals	The Home Doctor
	Max Hodam
Aristotle	[William] Shakespeare
Marie Stopes	"Grown up novels"
W. Bowen-Partington (writing in Health and Strength)	A. S. Neill
	[Richard von] Krafft-Ebing
Red Light	Magnus Hirschfeld
Health Manuals	Dr. Gray "Men, Women and God"
The Household Family Doctor Book	[Aldous] Huxley
Physiology Books, Natural History Books, Biology Books	Bertrand Russell[112]

In part, this emphasis on books resulted from the middle-class bias of the Mass-Observation study. However, it also resulted from people's memory. Books were given a place of importance since they seemed like the most serious and legitimate forums for sexual information. Whether this was true or not, the information in books seemed to have a factuality and an importance that made them memorable and worth noting as a source of information.[113] They provided a venue for individuals to seek out answers to embarrassing questions about health, fitness, and bodies. They appeared scientific, giving them a veneer of respectability. The standard ways of guaranteeing that a book would be sold as science rather than prurience was to give it a name in Latin, such as Krafft-Ebing's *Psychopathia Sexualis*, or to include a foreword with a statement like the following: "This monograph was prepared for circulation amongst the clergy, the lawmakers, the judiciary, and the doctors."[114] This ploy allowed authors, publishers, and printers to argue that their work went only to sophisticates who would not be corrupted according to the Hicklin standard, but of course, people could read it for nonscientific reasons as well.

By far the most widely sold nonfiction author of the period was Marie Stopes, whose books *Married Love* and *Wise Parenthood* were best sellers. Stopes liked to emphasize her own early ignorance of sexuality; according to her own telling, she had a miserable first marriage to Reginald Ruggles Gates. She had no idea why the marriage foundered, not realizing until she studied materials in the British Museum Library that her marriage had never been consummated. She argued that she herself was not a connoisseur of sexual pleasures but a victim of ignorance. "In my own marriage I paid such a terrible price for sex-ignorance that I feel that knowledge gained at such a cost should be placed at the service of humanity."[115] (This explanation ignored an earlier relationship with Kenjiro Fujii, a Japanese botanist with whom Stopes was in love. Stopes followed Fujii back to Japan, though he was married and had a child. It also ignored evidence from her husband that they had a normal sexual relationship.)[116] Whether innocent of sexual congress or not, Stopes used this version of her life history to underscore the necessity of sexual information. Armed with a Ph.D. in botany and an inquiring mind, she fashioned herself as a conduit for scientific information. At the British Museum, she read Edward Carpenter, Havelock Ellis, and Ellen Key, among others. She also worked with the Cupboard collection of the British Museum, which housed obscenity.[117] On the basis of her studies, Stopes wrote *Married Love*, dedicated to "young husbands and all those who are betrothed in love," and offered a blend of biology, race theory, self-help, and romance.

Major publishers would not handle the volume. A smaller firm, A. C. Fifield, agreed to print it but demanded a subsidy to offset costs. Humphrey Verdon Roe, a wealthy supporter of the eugenics and birth control movements, supplied the money to pay printing costs and later married Stopes. According to Ross McKibbin, *Married Love* sold two thousand copies in a fortnight and went through six printings before the year was out.[118] By 1925, the book had sold more than half a million copies, outstripping best-selling fiction in volume of sales.[119] That volume was followed by others, including *Wise Parenthood* (1918), also a best seller; *Radiant Motherhood* (1920); and *Enduring Passion* (1928). Stopes's writing style and explicit instructions allowed her to become a phenomenally popular writer. For working-class readers, Stopes wrote a series of short articles in *John Bull*, priced at two pence.[120] While all of her books were successful by most standards, *Married Love* remained the public's favorite. By 1955, it had sold more than a million copies.[121] Though her earliest books sold best, Stopes continued to publish throughout the interwar years, allowing her views on sexuality to remain influential.

The married couple formed the mainstay of society, according to Stopes's ideas. She was not concerned with how one marries or attracts a partner (as many novelists were); nor was she concerned with variation, deviation, or primitive customs (as were anthropologists and sexologists). Instead, her focus throughout her career was on the British couple. As she explained, "I do not touch upon the many human variations and abnormalities which bulk so largely in most books on sex, nor do I deal with the many problems raised by incurably unhappy marriages."[122] Stopes looked after the normal and left agitation over inequalities to others. For Stopes, information about sexuality would strengthen the marriage and save the couple. Rather than revolutionize society, Stopes sought to save it.

Though Stopes remained the most popular writer about sexuality during the interwar years, others also served as intermediaries between sexologists and the public. Dr. Eustace Chesser's (1902–1973) intellectual path illustrates the trend toward popular sexual education. Chesser's *Love without Fear*, first published as two separate volumes in 1941, built on the writings of sexologists and demonstrated the sorts of dispersals of information taking place in the 1930s. Chesser, who anglicized his name from Isaac Chesarkie, was a British psychiatrist and social reformer who underwent psychoanalysis during the 1930s before returning to private practice on Harley Street.[123] In *Love without Fear*, his best-known marriage guide, Chesser cited the writings of Havelock Ellis, Stella Brown, Norman Haire, Dr. Alice Stockham (*Karezza*), Magnus Hirschfeld, Freud, Owan [Ivan] Bloch, and Theodoor Van de Velde, thus demonstrating one way that knowledge circulated.[124] Chesser's marriage guide emphasized emotional work, self-improvement, and sexual techniques. His sexual program was quite explicit, and he emphasized sexual variety including erotic kissing; multiple positions, including standing, kneeling, and lying down; and genital stimulation including cunnilingus and fellatio. He even favored erotic tattooing. As long as both partners regarded a practice as arousing, as long as the final aim remained intercourse, and as long as neither partner was a pervert, Chesser suggested that the practice could be incorporated into a satisfying sexual life. *Love without Fear* was tried but acquitted for obscenity in 1942, in part because Chesser's medical qualifications made him appear authoritative, rather than merely prurient.

Another popular educator, Kenneth Walker, also emerged from a medical background.[125] From early work on male sexual disorders, Walker broadened his focus to sexual health and marital happiness through such primers as *Physiology of Sex*. His background in urology, combined with his grounding in sexology and his "psychological leanings" according to one reviewer, gave Walker a "birds and the bees approach."[126] Walker saw sex as a physiological imperative for reproduction, and his works defined sexual failures as a failure of the reproductive urge. He built his claims from sexologists, particularly from Ellis, but where Ellis organized his work for the medical community and concerned professionals, Walker wrote for medical professionals and the patients whose sexual problems had not been addressed by them. As Walker and his reviewers made clear, although such sexual disorders as impotence, homosexuality, masturbation, sterility, and promiscuity might be regarded by doctors as minor ailments, to the patient these conditions mattered a great deal.

Complementing Walker was *Ideal Marriage* by the Dutch gynecologist Theodoor H. Van de Velde. Whereas Walker emphasized male sexual function and dysfunction, Van de Velde stressed female satisfaction. According to Angus McLaren, Van de Velde's book became a "world-wide romantic best-seller."[127] His approach began with anatomy and the function of organs, rather than minds. Nonetheless his description of sexual intercourse retained room for considerable experimentation. He suggested, for example, that loveplay could also involve a wide range of body parts. Men should pay attention to the breasts, nipples, and clitoris; however, women should be wary of direct penile stimulation lest men reach orgasm too quickly. His instructions included extended foreplay—including cunnilingus—so that men could sufficiently rouse levels of desire in their female partners and the two could reach satisfactory communion. He charted various sexual positions including the benefits for men and women and contraindications for each. To make use of such technical advice would necessitate a certain level of education, however. Terms such as "attitudes of flexion," "equitation," and "anterior-lateral" required a sophisticated vocabulary and strong ability to visualize the placement of bodies.[128] For Van de Velde, the problem of how to match divergent sexual rhythms remained paramount, but he offered little to the single man or woman and even less to those whose desires resisted that pairing.

Freudian theory made its way to the British public through a number of intermediaries. Arthur Tansley's *The New Psychology and Its Relation to Life* offered an introduction to Freud's ideas and threw in a bit of Jung's as well. The immense popularity of the volume suggests the level of interest in these ideas. The volume, first published in 1920, was reprinted "ten times in four years" and sold more than ten thousand copies in the United Kingdom and more than four thousand in the United States within three years of its publication.[129] Tansley's version of Freudian theory was remarkably sexless. He spent quite a bit of time showing that when Freud spoke of sex, he meant, for example, "human tenderness and love at large."[130] His shepherding of Freud's ideas in England received assistance from Ernest Jones and Melanie Klein, who successfully popularized their own variants on ideas during the 1920s and 1930s. The publication of the *International Journal of Psycho-Analysis* contributed to the circulation of Freudian ideas, as did Freud's own flight to the United Kingdom in 1938 with the assistance of Jones and the British state.

Sexuality, for most of these writers, meant intercourse between a man and woman, preferably when married and during childbearing years. Helping men be successful at union became the key to the sex book. Men were instructed on how to be better partners to their wives by bringing them to orgasm. These books conceptualized men as worldly and authoritative; their leadership roles meant that they would teach their wives about the physical side of marriage. Furthermore, sexual intercourse became a way to ensure the success of the marriage. The improvement of sexual pleasure within marriage would strengthen the bonds of matrimony and therefore society as whole.

More serious works of sexology had a far more limited circulation, though ultimately they could have an enormous impact. Havelock Ellis (1859–1939) set the standard for erudition and detail. Almost everyone who mentions Ellis's work, then as now, does so with a nod to the size of his volumes. Graves and Hodge refer to them as "massive," and one British officer from the period called them "Ellis's elephantine work."[131] His literary output included more than forty books, hundreds of articles, and innumerable letters. As Ivan Crozier makes clear, few innovations in the human sciences happened without his input and comments.[132] For example, Marie Stopes cribbed her ideas of periodicity, or the theory of women's sexual arousal cycle, from his work, and his influence could be felt across writings about sexuality. By the interwar years, Ellis had established himself as the grand old man of sexology in Britain, and he provided a model of scholarly thoughtfulness and detachment.

Ellis made his reputation with the monumental *Studies in the Psychology of Sex*, an expensive, limited-edition series meant for serious scholars or members of the medical profession. The first volume of the set, *Sexual Inversion* (1897), was cowritten with John Addington Symonds, who died before the text was completed and whose literary executor removed his name from the project. *Sexual Inversion* was subject to seizure in 1898; despite its prosecution for obscenity, that volume allowed Ellis to cement his reputation as a serious scholar.[133] This original volume was published first in German and kept in the separate region of the uncataloged (and therefore unreachable) collection in the British Museum.[134] After the furor of the obscene libel trial died down, Ellis found a publisher in America who would put out the work in English. In 1928, Ellis republished his volumes in a four-volume set known as *Studies in the Psychology of Sex*. The set remained cordoned off from the public by price, length, and limited availability and functioned more as a textbook than a self-help manual; in fact, it was recommended for medical students by the 1930s.[135] (Norman Haire, the first sexologist on Harley Street, first read Havelock Ellis's work in the State Library in New South Wales, reading from morning until the library closed at night.)[136]

The series became foundational for sex psychology, an alternative to the psychoanalytical approach to sexuality. Sex psychology was built from a natural-history perspective that saw human behaviors as an extension of animal activities.[137] According to this model, variations in behavior among people did not signify degeneration or perversion; instead, they followed the natural variability within the animal kingdom.[138] For example, Ellis linked human masturbation with the masturbatory tendencies found in higher animals and suggested that only excessive masturbation was a problem. He argued that the laws against homosexuality made people victims of social hostility and should thus be abolished: "It is better that a man should be enabled to make the best of his own natural instincts, with all their disadvantages, than that he should be unsexed and perverted, crushed into a position that he has no natural aptitude to occupy."[139] Ellis provided a biological rationale for sadomasochism that tied these practices to primitive courtship patterns.[140] His scholarship attempted to place the wide variety of sexual desires and behaviors within a biological framework that legitimated sexuality.

His intellectual method emphasized the collection of a wide assortment of materials to understand sexuality in all its variety. He made use of medical texts, anthropological writings, biologists' papers, literature, and autobiographical disclosures.[141] On one hand, he saw the human family quite broadly and believed that natural variation within that family should be acknowledged and understood. This method had the great benefit of making his work appear depoliticized and scientific. On the other hand, it encouraged him to incorporate materials of dubious value into his scholarship. As a result, his work was built on specious claims and offered evidence for almost anything one might want to say. (For example, Ellis saw women's reliance on the corset as a symptom of the inability to adapt to the evolutionary shift to bipedalism.)[142] Ellis provided an alternative framework to Freud's model of sexuality—one continued by Alfred Kinsey after Ellis's death, according to Ivan Crozier.[143] Whereas Ellis based his model of sexuality on biology and natural history, Freud cemented his conception on trauma and the unconscious. Furthermore, Ellis remained a progressive reformer throughout his lifetime, while Freud emphasized introspection and individual transformation rather than social change. Though Ellis's importance was well established during his lifetime, acclaim and respect for his work waned after his death, while Freud's reputation continued to rise.

The texts of other sexologists circulated in smaller numbers in Britain, though some of their ideas were popularized and thereby gained name recognition. According to Lesley Hall and Roy Porter, the British medical community remained suspicious of continental writers, such as Ivan Bloch (1872–1922), Magnus Hirschfeld (1868–1935), Krafft-Ebing (1840–1902), and Freud (1856–1939). That mistrust limited the circulation of the works of these prominent sexologists. However, references to their works did occasionally appear. Chesser mentioned Bloch, Hirschfeld, and others in his popular marriage guide. Correspondents in *London Life* name-dropped Krafft-Ebing as well as Ellis.

Radclyffe Hall's *The Well of Loneliness* used Krafft-Ebing's work as a significant source of information. Freud's work developed a certain cachet among educated laymen.[144]

Krafft-Ebing wrote the first medical volume to classify sexual disorders. His
background as a mainstream psychiatrist who directed asylums in Graz and
Vienna allowed him to identify and write about sexual disorders. His model incorporated internal (or psychological) symptoms as well as external (physical)
criteria.[145] Krafft-Ebing's volume provided case histories of masochism, sadism,
sexual anesthesia, impotence, perversion, *lustmord*, fetishism, homosexuality,
and hermaphroditism. Krafft-Ebing gleaned these stories of sexual pathology
from literature (for example, from Leopold von Sacher-Masoch's description
of masochism embedded in *Venus in Furs*), oral histories, court records, and
patient letters.[146] As he learned more about sexual suffering, he continually revised his volume and his own position on sexuality. His book, which began as
a study of 45 cases, grew to 238 case studies and almost quadrupled in length
by 1902.[147] English translations of Krafft-Ebing's work by the American Charles
Gilbert Chaddock appeared as early as 1892, though Havelock Ellis noted that
he did not think that early edition circulated in Britain. The Englishman F.
J. Rebman translated the tenth edition and then the twelfth edition and published them in Britain, and no doubt these editions had a greater impact.[148] This
model of sexuality based on disorders provided the groundwork for the English
medical community to see continental writers as morbidly inclined and unfit
for the general reader.

Freud's work took the problem of sexual morbidity even further by suggesting that all disorders had a sexual origin and that no matter how properly bodies
might function, disorder could still lurk in the mind.[149] Freud, in the estimation
of Graves and Hodge, gained popularity during the 1920s, and the impact of
Freud was made later than publication figures may suggest. *The Interpretation of
Dreams*, finished in 1899 and published in 1900, did not appear in English until
1913. In the United Kingdom, the sale of that volume was limited to the legal,
medical, scholastic, and clerical professions, a common practice for books too
frank for the general public but too important for censorship.[150] The thousand-
copy initial printing of *Three Contributions to the Theory of Sex*, first published
in German in 1905, took four years to sell. The A. A. Brill translation of that
volume became available in English in 1910; however, the definitive edition that
incorporated Freud's revisions waited until 1949, a decade after his death. *A
Child Is Being Beaten*, written in 1919, was translated into English and appeared
in the first issue of the *International Journal of Psycho-Analysis* in 1921.[151] Thus,
during the 1910s, 1920s, and 1930s, much of Freud's work was available only in
German, and translation lagged behind his lifelong habit of revision.

The extent to which the lay public was conversant with Freud's work remains debatable. According to Graves and Hodge, Freudian theory became
more popular than psychoanalysis, and the language of Freudian analysis became the most popular of all. "Freudian gospel . . . filtered down into people's

minds, through translations, interpretations, glosses, popularizations, and general loose discussion. 'Intriguing' new technicalities were bandied across tea-cups or the Mah-Jong table: 'inferiority complex,' 'sadism,' 'masochism,' 'agoraphobia,' 'sublimation' (which got mixed up with 'sublimation'), 'id,' 'ego,' and 'libido.'"[152] The language of Freudian theory percolated into general conversation without the full adoption of Freudian theory.

Porter and Hall think that Freud's work took a backseat to the biological conceptions of sexuality offered by Ellis, Stopes, and Walker. In comparison, Jeffrey Weeks believes that Freud's ideas spread in Britain but in a much diluted form. Jonathan Rose's analysis of readership suggests that Londoners were more accepting and included Freud, H. G. Wells, Bernard Shaw, and A. S. Neill among their favorite nonfiction writers. In contrast, northern readers found modernism and psychology far less compelling.[153] Dean Rapp suggests that the English public's early acceptance of psychoanalytical theory was based on the expurgation of its sexual contents.[154]

Though these writers had radically different models of sexuality, they shared a model of sexuality at the center of human nature and saw the couple as foundational for civilization. Even Havelock Ellis, who championed sexual variety, in *Studies in the Psychology of Sex* argued that the loving couple had become the foundation for society. "Without the factor of mutual love the proper conditions for procreation cannot exist; without the factor of procreation the sexual union, however beautiful and sacred a relationship may in itself be, remains in essence, a private relationship, incomplete as a marriage and without public significance."[155] In Ellis's formulation, a couple's sexual love performed the greatest social good. Well-joined couples ameliorated alienation and tied individuals to society. The orgasmic marriage made a stronger society according to Stopes, Ellis, Chesser, and Van de Velde. How-to directions for achieving sexual pleasure varied by author (Stopes and Ellis believed in timing while Van de Velde and Chesser, for example, stressed foreplay); regardless of the method, however, the well-joined couple would create a well-joined marriage, according to these accounts.

In these books, sexuality as a vital force meant that it would erupt if not properly channeled. Celibacy, considered as outmoded and irregular, represented the denial of life's vital forces. As Chesser explains, "We know that sex is part of all our lives. We know that none can escape it. We know that to try to escape from it is harmful."[156] Caresses, effective for achieving arousal, were not valued as an end to themselves; intercourse was instrumental in strengthening marriage, rather than for its own pleasures. Across the board, marriage became the path for an individual to acquire a sexual identity. Thus, sex among the young became premarital sexuality, though even that received little notice. Most authors maintained the pretense that sexual exchanges began on the wedding night, though some talked about "love-affairs," which may have meant dating or extramarital flirtations. Part of this practice of emphasizing marital sex may well have been an attempt to stay on the right side of the law; certainly, most of these writers understood that desire could strike outside the marital union. (Van de Velde's marriage was wrecked by an affair, Stopes fell in love more than once and may well have fallen out of the marriage bed, Kenneth Walker divorced and remarried in the 1940s, Bertrand Russell had numerous affairs and marriages, and Ellis's sexual predilections remained unconventional.) Thus, the assumption that sex in marriage could provide the glue for couples and for society as a whole spoke either to savvy political instincts or to wish fulfillment. Men and women needed to recognize its explosive potential and work toward directing sex.

Many of these authors advocated for tolerance of sexual inversion, though with a wide variety of justifications and rationales. Significantly, Marie Stopes did not. Her view of sex was so grounded in the marital couple that she could not present herself as champion of female "inverts" despite being begged to do so.[157] Other writers showed themselves as more supportive of homosexuals, though lesbians were less often addressed.[158] Ellis saw sexual inversion and homosexuality as part of natural variation that should be addressed with aesthetics rather than the law. Continental writers such as Krafft-Ebing and Hirschfeld advocated for the reform of laws that discriminated against homosexuals and detailed the suffering that such discrimination caused.

Sadomasochism received surprisingly positive consideration by most sexologists. Most accounts stressed its gendered dimensions; that is, most sexologists saw sadism as natural to men but perverse in women and masochism as natural to women but perverse in men. Few saw it as having a sexual etiology unrelated to gender, though Freud, who saw a distinct trajectory for boys and girls, nonetheless believed it had a similar origin in childhood fantasies of being beaten. Havelock Ellis, for example, saw in men a primitive thrill in the hunt and capture of women and believed that male cruelty toward women functioned as an extension of that brutality. Women's masochism, in this model, merely elaborated their cultural submission.

Together sexologists detailed a wide range of sexual practices including heterosexuality, inversion, fetishism, sadism, masochism, cross-dressing, and transvestitism. Thus, sexologists offered a broad sexual education for people who could access the full range of materials. But most readers could not. Instead, people read what they could find, and with the exception of a few individuals with either a large personal library or access to the British Museum's research collection, most could find only one or two such works. Nonetheless, access to sexological writings could have a profound impact on people's lives, and people remembered what they read. For those searching for an understanding of their own desires, sexological writers, sometimes through their own publications and sometimes through popularizers such as Stopes and Chesser, offered legitimacy and understanding. As a result, sexology left indelible impressions even as other media shaped sexuality in hidden and often forgotten ways.

Conclusion

Despite censorship policies that tried to curtail the spread of obscenity, the interwar world was replete with ideas about sexuality. Materials circulated through mail order and semilegitimate bookstores, in tourist locales and city centers, through circulating libraries and news agents' shops. Men and women found novels, magazines, popular science, obscenity, and sexology through these mechanisms, and each of these sets of materials taught people about sexuality. Magazines offered a visual education based in symbolic erotics, novels made the world fraught with romance, marriage guides offered a how-to program on sex, and sexology offered a program on sexual variation.

Though all sorts of materials circulated between the wars, their relative numbers affected their impact. Truly pornographic works—those that described genital excitement, penetration, and orgasm—were published in runs of five hundred copies. Sexological works, such as Freud's *Three Contributions to the Theory of Sex*, might double those numbers. *The Well of Loneliness* was considered a brisk seller; its print run measured five thousand. In comparison, the circulation figures for certain works, such as *Married Love, Wise Parenthood, Ideal Marriage*, and *Love without Fear* (measured in the tens and hundreds of thousands of copies), allowed these books to reach across the population rather than remain limited to the professional classes. Few read sexology, but the ideas of sexology began to affect the population through the work of such popularizers as Stopes and Chesser. The world of cheap ephemera reached even further across society. For every copy of *Married Love* in circulation, the corner newsstand carried a dozen pulp magazines and the circulating library carried the latest popular novel.

The array of mediums was crossed by a jumble of messages from the cliché d that "love conquers all" to the clinical that declared the clitoris as a seat of female pleasure. Interwar ideas provided no single coherent framework to understand sexuality. If the full range of materials is considered, it would offer a broader sexual education than may be immediately apparent. Reading across genres would offer a wide range of sexual attitudes, gender roles, and behaviors. Between sexological studies, marriage manuals, magazines, and novels, diverse sexual identities were articulated in the interwar years. Thus, one could learn about sexual fetishes from such novels as *Silk Stocking Murders*, from such magazines as *Silk Stockings* and *London Life*, from Freud's *Three Essays on the Theory of Sexuality*, and from Havelock Ellis's "Erotic Symbolism." All of these works dealt with the erotic excitement generated by stockings and footwear, and readers could develop a rather substantial body of images, ideas, and theories about a stocking fetish by mixing materials on the topic. The same holds true of sadomasochism, which had an even more developed pedigree. One could begin by rereading *Uncle Tom's Cabin*, then turn to the obscene book trades for *Spanking Stories* or *The History of the Rod*, glance at the correspondence columns for discussions of birch discipline, and then join in a debate over whether penal reform should remove whipping as a method of punishment. Interwar materials offered ideas about sexual diversity to the savvy reader that would appear more explicit the more one knew. If put together, these mediums might have created a saturated world of sexual possibility; however, few people could access a full range of materials. Most people did not have the privilege of consulting research collections and bought materials at the local news agent or borrowed them from a lending library. They made do with the materials they found.

As a result, although people read, they did not put together messages about sexuality or mediums in a straightforward way. As one woman quoted in Jonathan Rose's account explained, "I even read Radclyffe Hall's classic story of lesbianism, *The Well of Loneliness*, without having the faintest ideas what it was about."[159] One man said that he did not connect romance with sex: "I read about love in the romantic novels—I would read anything—without ever suspecting it had anything to do with sex."[160] Although a wide range of materials circulated in the interwar years, people's understandings of the sexual messages that these materials provided could remain partial or fragmented. As a woman wrote to Marie Stopes, "I knew, of course, that a union took place, but quite how it took place I did not know, but I supposed my husband would know. In theory he seems to understand, as he studied Biology at Cambridge, but in reality he knows no more than I do."[161] Cultural knowingness as much as availability of information affected what people understood about sex.[162] Realms of information functioned simultaneously, only sometimes addressing each other or affecting each other, often creating disjunctions and gaps in a culture that nonetheless felt saturated with sexuality.

The popularity of shoddy romances and smutty magazines, of popular works that sold cheaply and circulated widely, certainly saturated the interwar world with sexual narratives. But the process of reading narratives and the impact of reading on the formation of identity deserves further explication. Just as the publication of certain books did not mean the wide circulation of them, the circulation of materials did not imply a particular method of reading or understanding them. How people responded to those narratives and made sense of the materials takes a different set of methods and sources. The consideration of reading as a set of practices and writing as a method of response are addressed in the remaining chapters of this book, which examine how people scripted their own sexual stories in response to what they read.

2

Reading *Married Love*

Marie Carmichael Stopes's 1918 marriage manual, *Married Love*, included a short note calling for evidence to support her theory of women's periodicity. It read:

> While I believe that the charts I give of the Law of Periodicity of recurrence of desire truly represent the fundamental rhythm of average healthy women, it must be remembered that my theory is new, and every well-authenticated case for or against it will be valuable. I invite letters from those who can confirm, qualify, or correct my views from their own experience. To obtain scientific knowledge the largest possible number of individual cases must be studied. All communications will be treated with the strictest confidence.
>
> Dr. M. C. Stopes c/o Mr. A. C. Fifield, 13, Clifford's Inn, London EC4.[1]

The call for information about women's cyclical nature was widely misconstrued as a call for information about sexuality in general. Readers saw the invitation as a sincere interest in their sexual lives, and they responded.

Women wrote Stopes with questions about their husbands' sexuality and tendered queries about birth control, spacing pregnancies, and learning to orgasm. Couples—both men and women—wrote of joint desire and mutual failure. The young on the cusp of marriage asked her advice about their unions. Older men and women wrote about the appropriateness of coitus, the problems of menopause, and the issue of flagging libidos. People across the class structure wrote to Stopes about sexuality and queried her for more information.[2]

Individuals wrote from within Great Britain and across the empire. Occasionally, South Asians wrote, but most often her correspondents were white and often Protestant.

Their letters, in a wide variety of styles, on an assortment of papers, in a diversity of hands, came in such numbers that they quickly overwhelmed Stopes. Though she originally replied to all the letters herself, by 1919 her husband, Humphrey Verdon Roe, intervened. According to the notes sent out to readers, he had to insist that she no longer answer all the letters because of health concerns.[3] Roe and Stopes's secretary began to send out form letters for common problems, and Stopes postscripted additional points.

The letters, perhaps numbering ten thousand, written over multiple decades, are unique in terms of quantity and date.[4] As Ruth Hall makes clear, "Marie Stopes was the first person to whom large numbers of men and women wrote freely about their sexual problems."[5] These letters were written for a specific reason—for (legal) birth control,[6] for (semi-illegal) abortions,[7] for sexual advice, and for a sense of how one's behaviors fit into the scale of normality—so they are not unself-conscious productions of people's sexual histories. Instead, people organized their accounts by what they needed from Dr. Stopes. As Angus McLaren notes of these letters, "these apparently candid confessions have to be used with care, however, because the writers unconsciously knew what they had to say."[8] Nonetheless, they are still an extraordinary valuable way of seeing how individuals fashioned themselves as readers and writers, how they understood their histories and futures, and how they tried to explain their bodies and its sensibilities to others.

These letters have been an extremely valuable source for any number of historians working on the issues of fertility control,[9] sexual behaviors,[10] and gender anxieties.[11] In this chapter, I continue the work started by previous scholars who examined the construction of narrativity in the Stopes correspondence. In particular I follow up the insights of Lesley Hall, who explored Stopes's rhetorical strategies, and Ellen Holtzman, who examined the ways that correspondents couched their appeals to Stopes.[12] Hall considered Stopes's narrative constructions and in particular her use of romantic and scientific metaphors, while Holtzman considered the ways that readers used those narrative strategies in their letters. My work builds on these considerations of storytelling to think about the ways that letter writers constructed stories of their own sexuality.[13] If identity emerges from stories of self, as narrative theorists suggest, then perhaps Stopes's readers constructed a coherent sense of the self as having a sexual identity when they wrote to her. In making claims and in asking for advice, men and women organized their own sexual stories and set themselves out as sexual agents—as individuals both acted against and as acting, as responding to information and creating it. By telling stories, they showed that they conceptualized themselves as individuals whose sexuality mattered. These letters demonstrate how people explained themselves as sexual beings.

In particular, this chapter considers the ways that men and women invested in a particular form of modern, sexual couple by exploring ways that individuals conceptualized their past, their futures, and their bodies.

Stopes's Model of *Married Love*

Marie Stopes wrote at a moment when compassionate marriage had begun to transform men's and women's lives, especially among the middle classes.[14] For the generations that came of age during the interwar years, marriage became a matter of partnership and cooperation. The newer model of married life stressed mutuality and the ways that men and women could find pleasure in their union. They developed their model of marriage in opposition to their notions of Victorian life and the disservice it had supposedly done to marriage.[15]

Supposedly, the Victorian family had been dominated by the father and his authority. A lack of education, legal rights, and property rights forced women into unequal marriages that perverted the sex instinct, according to modernist ideas of the past. In this model, men dominated sex as they had all else, and women submitted out of desperation but found no real pleasure in sexual union. According to this model of the Victorian world, the differences between men and women went soul deep, and men and women had separate distinct natures that garnered them distinct characters and values. Of course, this model exaggerated the horrors of the Victorian past in order to reenvision the present. Even while decrying the Victorian model of sexuality, modernists retained the ideals of men's and women's separate natures and sought to remake a model of male and female difference into a complementarity that would benefit both. Radical intellectuals and sexologists began to envision ways that reformed marriage would allow men's and women's lives to be mutually supportive.[16]

The radical program of modernists was helped along by broader social changes. Falling birth rates contributed to shifting ideals of marriage.[17] Patterns of family limitation began among the middle classes in the 1880s and became noticeable by the 1890s.[18] Having fewer children allowed men and women to develop new expectations, while changes in daily life made room for new models of togetherness. Middle-class men and women who met in a youth culture defined by madcap parties, cocktails, and the latest fashions could move into married culture with Sunday picnics, crossword puzzles, and radio broadcasts.[19] According to these new ideals, men and women would come together as equals.

Marie Stopes contributed to new ideals by providing a model of modern marriage for the masses. Further, Stopes popularized the ideas that modern marriage could help the British race and the British Empire. She had emerged from the intellectual communities of feminism and eugenics, and she bridged those communities' commitments to birth control. Feminists had been arguing that birth control would strengthen women's control of their own bodies, while eugenicists thought that population control and sexual procreation were matters of state concern, particularly after the Great War.[20] Not only had the birth rate been slowing down since before the war; fewer able-bodied men returned from the war, leaving the disabled and the unfit to produce an unhealthy population, according to the alarmed rhetoric of the day.[21] These ideas came together in Stopes's belief that voluntary reproduction would allow the British couple to raise healthier babies for the race and empire. According to Stopes and other birth control advocates, planned births by the best of society could help restore the population. Birth control would thus strengthen both the nation and the race. The overlapping set of concerns contributed to the passage of such welfare laws as the British Maternal and Child Health Act of 1918 and allowed birth control clinics, including Stopes's Mothers Clinics, to gain legitimacy in Britain.[22]

Stopes stood at the radical edge of eugenics and was a life member of the Eugenics Society, though many in that society wished she would quiet her commitment to sterilization and birth control.[23] By the 1920s, the radical program of social control among eugenicists had been muted into one more palatable for a democratic age. Sacrifices across British society during the war and the shift toward full adult democracy made the class implications of many eugenics recommendations unseemly, particularly regarding questions of sterilization.[24] However, Stopes remained committed to both positive and negative eugenics programs, those that encouraged the best to breed and that sought to limit the reproduction of the unhealthy. She recommended the cervical cap, tellingly named the Pro-Race, as the best method of birth control to help couples choose when to bear children. Further, she thought that "one third of men in Britain should be sterilized, 'starting with the ugly and unfit.'"[25] In her own mind, questions of "race suicide" and racial advancement justified radical measures.

Stopes's concerns with race stressed cultural ideas of British fitness. Stopes's idea of race emphasized wholesome, beautiful, well-fed, exercised, medically sound bodies, a set of qualities that have little to do with skin color and a great deal to do with culture.[26] This idea of race remained persuasive for supporters of British eugenics whose mapping of cultural qualities onto people of the empire conflated race with certain ideals of the British nation. Though eugenics could be crudely racist, more often in the British context it was crudely classist, and supporters and detractors fought over legislation about the poor, rather than legislation about the empire.[27] The idea that the residuum of British society—the feeble, criminal, alcoholic, and mentally defective— were a separate race who would outbreed the meritocratic middle class galvanized British support for eugenic measures throughout the 1910s and 1920s. Stopes placed herself at the more radical edge of eugenicist ideas and suggested that involuntary sterilization would be appropriate for many. In fact, Stopes disinherited her son for marrying a woman with imperfect vision.[28] However, the eugenic impulses behind the establishment of birth control clinics by Stopes and her supporters did not translate into eugenic practices or beliefs among working-class women who visited those clinics. Even fervent supporters of Stopes picked certain aspects of Stopes's program and ignored others that did not suit.[29] Stopes herself, in the face of misery, would alter her message, seeing an end to suffering as more important than ideological consistency. Thus, though Stopes had a deeply ingrained sense of the British race that tied in with her beliefs about birth control and eugenics, her sense of race was broadly cultural and wildly malleable.

According to Stopes's model, sexuality was central to the modern couple, and the modern couple was central to the future of the race. "These prophetic dreams . . . are yet true of the race as a whole."[30] Her emphasis on race and eugenics and her goal of elevating the couple contributed to her acceptance by the British state and British society.[31] In her model, healthy and well-made couples would produce healthy and fit children who would people the British nation. In her published works, Stopes followed the arc of the married couple as they moved through the stages of life; *Married Love*, concerned with union, was followed by *Wise Parenthood*, which discussed birth control in the context of voluntary parenthood, and *Radiant Motherhood* (1920), which discussed pregnancy, newborns, and the health of the race.[32] As the couple aged, husband and wife could turn to *Enduring Passion* (1931) and *Change of Life in Men and Women* (1936), which would help them through the process of shifting patterns of desire and menopause.[33] The couple could then invest in *The Human Body* so that their children could develop a proper appreciation for sexuality and bodies.[34] Couples would be prepared for a lifetime of dealing with sexuality in a modern style that emphasized education.[35]

Married Love began with the explanation that marital sexuality functioned as the cement for marriage as a partnership. According to Stopes, marital happiness required sympathy and understanding. Without a fundamental understanding of the sexual differences between male and female, couples would fall prey to antagonisms, and the sexual intercourse that promised to unite the couple would instead become acrimonious and one-sided. In her account, men and women have different biological patterns of receptivity and arousal (called *periodicity*). Men's continually imminent arousal interfered with their ability to read cues about women's monthly cycles. Men needed to watch women closely and press for intercourse only during women's period of arousal. By explaining periodicity, Stopes hoped to smooth relations between married couples to strengthen the physical bonds of marriage. In her chapters "The Broken Joy" and "Woman's Contrariness," Stopes detailed the path toward failure, while "Fundamental Pulse" and "Mutual Adjustment" suggested how couples can avoid misunderstood cues and failed expectations.

Stopes welded popular idioms with technical information to create a highly accessible form of writing. She wrote with the linguistic vehemence of novelists at the same time that she incorporated the vocabulary and technical information used by sexologists. The closing to her book quite literally promises couples the stars and the heavens if they appropriately organize and manage their sexual relations. "When knowledge and love together go to the making of each

marriage, the joy of *that new unit, the pair* will reach from the physical foundations of its bodies to the heavens where its head is crowned with the stars."[36]
Stopes's language, including her strange amalgam of modern sensibilities, scientific conceptions, and metaphoric excess, created a way to talk about bodies
that emphasized sexuality as transformative.[37] By emphasizing the beauty, purpose, and spiritual nature of sex, Stopes stressed that sex could be both a physical state and a metaphysical one. To give another example of her prose and her
process: "The bodily differences of the two, now accentuated, become mystical,
alluring, enchanting in their promise. Their differences unite and hold together
the man and the woman so that their bodily union is the solid nucleus of an immense fabric of interwoven strands reaching to the uttermost ends of the earth;
some lighter than the filmiest cobweb, or than the softest wave of music, iri-
descent with the colours, not only of the visible rainbow, but of all the invisible
glories of the wave-lengths of the soul."[38] Spiritual union held families together,
according to Stopes's explanation, while sexual union brought a mystical inter-
weaving of souls. Stopes combined romance and spirituality with the language
of science, allowing the realms to commingle in a single sentence. Talk of nuclei
and wavelengths, the scientific jargon of cutting-edge physics, became fused
with soft music, rainbows, and the glories of souls.

Stopes's first book, *Married Love*, came out in 1918 and became an instant best seller. *Married Love* went through seven editions by 1919; by 1925, it
had been reprinted thirty-nine times.[39] Clearly, she spoke to the moment, and
her focus on the achievement of sexual happiness through "modern" science
proved popular. The popularity of the book, even in midst of the war, suggests
the degree to which people responded to Stopes's style. Men, women, rich, poor,
young, and old turned to her books to make sense of themselves.[40] Historians
often rely on such measures to understand the impact of literature. However,
readers left a far more detailed record; thousands wrote letters in which they
spoke for themselves and explained their reactions to Stopes's work.

Reading Practices

In writing to Stopes, both men and women stressed their fundamental lack of
sexual knowledge and credited Stopes with giving them a vocabulary to talk
about sexuality. They noted her terms for bodies and its processes, and even
more, they valued her combination of romantic excess and scientific detail.
One man, for example, saw himself as "an average man" whose background
offered him few tools to discuss the issues. "Roughly I would say that the class
to which I belong either (1) never explicitly alludes to or discusses sex questions
at all: they are 'nice' people, with one sense of reticence; or (2) they frequently
talk about sex but always jocularly, coarsely and clumsily. Neither class can be
said to have any understanding of the matter, and of course, neither party has a
scientific basis."[41] For Stopes's readers, her combination of science, candor, and
clarity provided a welcome model for speaking about sexuality.

For some readers, however, just making sense of Stopes's terminology took effort. People's lack of knowledge about their bodies, reproduction, and sex play—emerging from late Victorian beliefs about the importance of raising children in a state of sexual innocence—could result in continuing problems.[42] Rather than accepting that lack of knowledge, though, individuals saw self-education as an appropriate response. Their reading practices were neither passive nor resigned; instead, they looked at reading as a tool to address their deficiencies, and they saw in Stopes a model for self-improvement. As one correspondent noted:

> I wonder whether I may ask for enlightenment on one point—you write a great deal about "orgasm" and its importance. After carefully reading each passage where you speak of it, I fear I still cannot understand what this is. It would be the greatest kindness if you would be kind enough to inform me.[43]

Both men and women read carefully and systematically to transform their understandings of sex. They used books to reconstruct their most intimate experiences. As one woman wrote, the book became a stand-in for experience. Despite her husband's background in biology from Cambridge, neither partner had any sexual experience from which to draw. They had no firm knowledge of how to achieve union: "However absurd it may sound, neither of us knew exactly where to find the vagina. We then consulted your book called Married Love, + eventually were successful, + he was able to make an entrance."[44]

Most writers saw their lack of knowledge as ignorance rather than innocence. They did not present their lack of knowledge as coy and appealing; instead, they talked about how the gaps in knowledge hampered their lives. They saw writing to Stopes as a way to overcome embarrassing limitations. Despite a discomfort with their limitations, Stopes's correspondents sought a sexual self-help program: "No doubt you will be surprised to receive this letter from me, as I myself feel ashamed at having to open up such correspondence with the opposite sex, but the complaint I am about to describe has made me so desperate that I just had to do something."[45] They wrote to Stopes fully aware that they made themselves open to ridicule and mockery:

> I am to be married very shortly and both my future wife and I are anxious about one or two points which we are not quite clear about from your books nor able to get . . . satisfactorily answered by a doctor. . . . On p. 49 "M.L." you say "meet face to face"[;] I am afraid you will think me ignorant or stupid, but does this mean standing?[46]

In writing to Stopes, they faced their own disquiet and embarrassment in order to transform their sexual relations. Writing cost them some dignity, perhaps, but they were willing to pay that price.

Letter writers could be quite resolute and focused. One writer, for example, wrote repeatedly for concrete sexual advice. This man saw his ignorance as limiting:

> We are both self-taught in the matter. To be candid for the first 4 months of our married life I did not know that it was necessary to move my body in any way. We only know of the one positions [*sic*] in which my wife is underneath + I am sure I nearly smother her sometimes.
>
> Now can you tell me of alternate positions + also is my wife supposed to move about?[47]

The writer's commitment to better sex encouraged him to ask for information absent from Stopes's work. Stopes replied that he should read *Wise Parenthood* and then offered a vague description of possibilities: "As regards positions, it is impossible for me to spend the necessary time writing detailed accounts, but I should suggest to you that extreme pliability, both on your part and that of your wife, should be practiced. Surely, unless you are stiff and rheumatic, there are a hundred positions in which you can intertwine." Rather than accept Stopes's generalities, the man asked again for information on positions. He persisted in his pursuit of information and remained committed to self-education.

Readers saw Stopes as an arbiter of appropriate behavior, and they wanted her to intervene and explain the right way to achieve marital bliss. For such writers, sensation alone did not legitimate sexual practices. Instead, most had an unspoken belief in the existence of a right way to experience intercourse. One couple with a very satisfying sex life worried that they could not achieve simultaneous orgasm if the husband did not caress his wife. This writer, like many, believed that mutual orgasms should come as a result of coitus alone. Any extra genital stimulation amounted to masturbation, a failure of sexual performance. The husband wanted to understand what failures in physiology or performance led to the need for extra stimulation: "During the past 3 years and more I have been continually wondering what it is that makes us, presumably, different from other married couples."[48]

Others believed that Stopes's authority on sexual matters would allow her to settle their marital and sexual disputes. For some letter writers, the desire to have sex "by the book" was stymied by the lack of mechanical explanation in the book. One man understood that his wife's self-stimulation brought her to orgasm, but he believed that the practice went against the natural order of things:

> As you know, at the mouth of the passage at which I enter, + perhaps slightly near the top when closed, there is a sensitive nerve, or small piece of flesh, which when touched by friction, give the feeling of desire, how if I am in, + my wife can press her finger in as well, + rub vigorously in this spot, she is sometimes able to come with me, I know then

how much she loves, + desires me, but the action is so unnatural + creates, such a tender place that it often makes her give way to Joy alone.[49]

The writer wanted Stopes to explain how his wife could orgasm the "natural" way with no digital stimulation. Stopes replied that the needs of the race justified a touch of unnatural stimulation: "Unfortunately civilized women are frequently so constructed that digital stimulation is necessary in addition to the normal friction of the sex act. . . . [T]ake it calmly and make the best of it and arrange and expect a certain amount of digital stimulation to achieve the orgasm."[50] According to Stopes, clitoral stimulation was a necessary by-product of civilized life.

Letter writers' deep engagement with the text and with Stopes's authority demonstrated that reading was not necessarily a simple and unilinear process in which Stopes taught and they learned. Instead, readers came to Stopes with ideas about sexuality, no matter how hazy and ill informed. In reading, they attempted to wrest from the text and from Stopes specific information, to apply that information if possible, and to use that information in negotiation with their sexual partners. Though many came to Stopes's work with a profound ignorance that they claimed handicapped their relations, they saw that ignorance as a testament to their upbringing rather than their abilities and therefore saw their sexual problems as surmountable. Their search for knowledge was an act of self-improvement in which the larger stakes of the relationship justified any discomfort from reading and writing about sexuality.

Writing Practices

Even though many of the writers had a particular reason for writing, individuals needed to present themselves to Stopes by explaining their interests and needs in recognizable terms. Individuals carefully crafted an idea of themselves in relationship to Stopes's book. Rather than launching into a full-blown explication of self, readers responded to the rhetoric set by Stopes and the narrative structures with which they were familiar. The letters emerged as a product of complicated negotiations.

Men, in particular, packaged their sexual problems in a language of scientific romance. One man illustrated the intercourse that followed his wife's desires in a chart that accompanied his letter. (See the chart, Exhibit A, in the gallery of illustrations.) He replicated Stopes's ideas of the rhythms of desire and reproduced sexual periodicity in his own life to follow Stopes's example. Such charts demonstrated the extent to which writers aligned their visions of sexuality within Stopes's language of scientific romance.

Another writer explained that he wanted to guarantee his wife's health through proper coitus but worried about the impact on her health. He saw sex as central to her vitality and their marital happiness. His language followed

Stopes's model of intermingling scientific information with a smattering of high passion.

> The practice of "coitus interruptus" has lowered my dear Wife's vitality. After our marriage we tasted the fullness+ beauty of Love,—we were intensely happy,—+ the sex-relation very rarely entered our thoughts, but by + by the desire for the sex embrace grew within us, + the dangers arose, of us becoming excessive in our sex relations,—so much so, that my dear little wife was suffering from a nervous breakdown for 11 months, during most of which time I was away from her, serving with the colours. At one time she was almost 10 months without a menstrual flow. . . . Yet, because my Darling has inherited a tendency towards consumption, + a minute frame, is she to be denied the sex embrace,? Or worse still, what wd hurt her more, is *her* Beloved to sacrifice, (even of his own free will,) the endearing + exalting Lovers embrace?[51]

The discussion of coitus interruptus and menstrual flows was counterbalanced with the description of the sexual act as a spiritually ennobling act of love. The man followed Stopes's model of writing a paean to love interspersed with sexual information and a medical history.

As marriage became a meeting of mind, body, and soul, the work that sex had to do in order to knit these realms together became more important. Couples responded to Stopes by stressing their desire to achieve—or more impressively—their successes at achieving marital unity. In the following description, a military officer asserted the couple's love, fidelity, and synchronicity as evidence of their marital success.

> We find one another intensely physically attractive + each feel a slight physical repugnance for other members of the opposite sex—I mean a repugnance for even slight physical intimacies—we each have numerous good *friends* of both sexes of course. It has always been a point of honor with me to give my wife physical pleasure + she has been as keen to please me. I have let my wife's instincts guide us to suitable occasions + we thoroughly respect one another in the sexual relation I have endeavored to be a gentleman as well as a lover.[52]

In his own eyes, this man achieved the model set by Stopes and fulfilled her injunction for physical and spiritual union. He and his wife were clearly the heroes of their own romance.

Others had a harder time balancing the spiritual, the physical, and the scientific. While they clearly modeled their writing on Stopes's, an inability to implement her program for transformative sex tipped them into strange narrative territory. In several cases, men wrote letters but refused to inhabit the first person or even the position of writer. In one, the officer created a pseudo medical report that allowed him to present himself as a case rather than a person:

CASE REFERRED TO

General Particulars of the parties
Married 20 Dec 1917. One child born March 1920. Present ages. Male
30. Female 26. Nature of work. Mental work (as farm accountant)
half-sedentary half in open air. both parties very healthy, live in
country and have good food and exercise. Both male and female are
University graduates.

Special Particulars Sex act frequently attempted in early married life
and occasionally now. Never completely performed. Male ejaculates
before, sometimes just a few seconds after, penis enters vagina and
never more than half-a-minute after doing so. No orgasm in the female has ever occurred. . . .

Results. Sleeplessness. Nervousness, Weeping at trivial matters in the
female exactly as described in 'Married Love'. General Unsatisfied-
ness.

Requirements To stop this premature ejaculation without at the same
time making erection impossible thus to enable the full sexual act
to occur.[53]

In this case study, the author referred to himself as "the male" so that he did not need to admit to his own failings or feelings. Instead of naming his wife, or even cementing her identity through their relationship, she became "the female." Even more illustrative was his inability to fix premature ejaculation to a particular person. Instead, it appeared to happen on its own. The author transformed his sexual problems into an abstract account that made the self into science.

Another man began with the first person but switched to the third person midway in his letter when he described his sexual problems. The use of the third person allowed the writer to distance himself from his own sexual history and communicated his discomfort with his own failings.

The writer has been very happily married for 12 years + has a lovely
child of 7 years; but greatly regrets he did not read your book years ago;
because he feels that, much as he loves his wife, he does not give her
any pleasure or satisfaction in the sex act + has never done so during
all these years. The reason being an almost instantaneous ejaculation
upon the part of the writer at the moment of uniting.[54]

The reference to Stopes's book in the midst of his case history interrupts the smooth flow of the story, much the same way that the writer believed that Stopes could interrupt his marriage's sexual unhappiness. However, his emotional and linguistic convolutions also complicate his ability to explain his sexual history or occupy a clear place in it.

Many writers saw themselves as patients in need of medical help. Women made use of the medical history model with great regularity—either because women's high rates of morbidity made the medical history a familiar model or because the role of patient offered them a limited agency. For women, pregnancies, childbearing, and child rearing exacerbated the effects of poverty. Women were shaped by their economic and social conditions; poverty made itself felt in "its embodiment in the figures of women, aged and diseased by hard work, numerous pregnancies, bad diet and insanitary conditions."[55] The Women's Health Inquiry in 1933 found that only 31 percent of working-class women felt "fit and well." Most suffered from anemia, headaches, constipation, rheumatism, gynecological problems, toothaches, varicose veins, ulcerated legs, and gastric and respiratory problems.[56]

Writers to Stopes showed themselves adept at medical history, a familiar system for organizing information that provided a well-known storyline, actors, and language. Narratives of illness allowed for a clear chronological organization. In one letter, the writer discussed her descent into illness after childbearing: "After weaning him I seemed to go weaker and weaker then pain came in my feet (which had always been good) and gradually got all over me. Now I am an awful wreck unable to walk or do anything."[57] Another woman wrote of the complications that childbearing brought: "After my youngest was born while in a weakened condition, I developed Tuberculosis."[58] In medical histories such as these, writers inhabited the first person and seemed to have no problem claiming ill health. Illness affected the self as subject in a clear-cut relationship, and these writers could say "I am ill" with few reservations. Such stories provided a well-established arc; for most writers, the stories had a natural end in the request for information.

By presenting themselves as medical patients, individuals had well-worn narrative tracks to follow. Though Stopes was not an M.D., individuals saw her as one and wrote their accounts accordingly. In some cases, she was just one in a series of medical consultations: "I have been to a number of medical-men, who tell me, that this deformity will not affect my sexual powers, nor lessen the chances of my having children if I marry."[59] In other accounts, patients saw Stopes as the leading authority on sexual medicine. One patient worried about the effects of treatment on her sex life: "A lady Dr. has advised me to enter Clapham Hosp. + have my womb treated with radium to end my courses. I am nearly 52 years of age + have a lot of back aches + nausea + she thinks it will help my general health to take the above step."[60] For this woman, Stopes's opinion trumped her physician's. Despite her lack of medical training, Stopes was happy to offer medical advice and warned the woman with "gravest urgency not to have radium treatment." Stopes further suggested that perhaps the doctors were hiding a diagnosis of cancer and that she should insist on clear communication and full disclosure.

Both Stopes and her correspondents saw the medical history as an appropriate narrative model. The medical history gave each a clear role to inhabit. Being a patient meant certain things; it implied a certain dignity in suffering, a certain frailty, and an ethical right to information. The medical model also offered a way to write that could be explicit without being prurient. Details of diseases, failing organs, symptoms, and treatments allowed individuals to embed their sex lives into comprehensible accounts while circumventing any accusation of eroticism.

However, medical histories mired individual accounts in illness, a stance that remained antithetical to the mutually satisfied, healthy couples that Stopes encouraged. Writers seemed to recognize this problem. Some responded by distancing themselves from their own bodies. Others stressed themselves as patients. Some writers tried to bridge the realms of science, spirit, and romance in their accounts. What often emerged was a hybrid: medical histories interrupted by romantic swoops and flourishes and scientific distance overlaid with declarations of love.

Stopes's model remained powerful, but few writers could fashion themselves with the same authority that she projected; perhaps the very awareness of sexual dissatisfaction made it harder for the writers to pull together the diverse realms of romance, spirit, and science and pin them to sexual union at a moment when that union for a variety of reasons had failed.

The Failures of Bodies

For many, the grand hopes for high romance were stymied by the all-too-human failures of bodies and minds. People wrote to Stopes because their failures demanded clarification and explanation. Despite the failures, it seemed easier to find fault with one's own body or that of a partner than dismiss the ideal. In responding to Stopes, writers made it clear that they embraced her model and instead found fault with their own circumstances.

In the following account, the woman found herself disappointed by her marriage. She made it clear that she saw herself as heroine of a great romance that her husband did little to support: "I realized from the beginning that I was the more idealistic + romantic of the two, + in some ways I was more impatient for our desired union—he was wisely, more cautious though willing to marry when we had a little more money." Though they married, it took a good bit of time for the couple to achieve sexual intercourse. Furthermore, she remained disappointed with the disharmony of spirit and body. Her letter hinted at her assessment of her husband's deficiencies:

> After some months I did have a few mild orgasms properly produced, + even about twice we achieved a mutual orgasm, the joy + spiritual well-being of this being so satisfying to me that it almost made up for the mildness of the sensation. The last time this happened, however,

was just two years ago. It began to seem almost impossible, although we talked and thought about it, + he tried to control himself + wait for me, it did not get any better. . . . I felt I was gradually becoming more + more disillusioned about all that I had once thought to be beautiful + magical in life. I had had dreams of *perfect* matehood; he, never, though of course he had hoped for a happy + full life together.[61]

Her account suggested that her husband's failures on the physical plane—he could induce only mild orgasms in her—matched the more serious problems of spiritual disillusionment. She had expected the alchemy of orgasm to wear away the boundaries between the two, but he remained uncommunicative and unsupportive of the project. Though the writer had not found the union she expected, she remained as committed to romance and idealism as ever.

Even more damaging to individuals' sexual relationships was the impact of the war and the ways that the war fit into this generation's sense of identity. Stopes's first work on sexuality came out in the midst of the Great War, and the war functioned as a backdrop for Stopes's success. Stopes herself experienced the impact of the war. Her husband, Humphrey Verdon Roe, had been a war hero in the RAF and had suffered a crash before their marriage. Stopes enjoyed the cachet of visiting with "a 'wounded' from France" and the prestige of having an officer as an escort.[62] Though he was gallant and handsome when they met and married, later in life old war wounds began to plague him, supposedly affecting their sex life.[63] Though Stopes enjoyed the glamour of the war, she showed little understanding of or sympathy for its potential consequences even in her own marriage.

For soldiers writing in the midst of the war, the particulars that affected soldiers on leave and returning from the front added to problems already endemic with sex. Premature ejaculation, common enough according to letters written to Stopes, became even more likely given a soldier's desperate circumstances. Such men often talked about the shortness of leaves and the inability to coordinate the rhythms of arousal with those of their wives. Marriages rushed to fit with the demands of service meant that slow courtships for physical learning became attenuated. Instead, wartime marriages heightened the reliance on a model of instant physical connection, one touted in modern romances as uniting the couple on an essential level. Marriage rates, as well as illegitimacy rates, spiked, hinting at an urgency for connection. Psychological trauma also affected sexuality. Men described suffering from the scenes of carnage and horror, from disabling anxiety, and from the high-impact shelling and nerve gas that contributed physical causes to psychological trauma.

Men and women recognized that the war also played a role in their sexual problems. Though Stopes did not mention the war, readers did, sometimes writing to Stopes from the trenches. Her prescriptions that men watch their wives closely and follow women's natural rhythm met with an emotional willingness but a practical inability given short leaves. Publication during the war made fixing sexual problems critical. While the war alone did not animate individuals to write to Stopes, it heightened the sexual tensions that drove people to find help, gave urgency to finding a quick resolution, and demanded a certain frankness.

One soldier, for example, had never consummated his marriage. He desired his wife but did not know how to control fertility. He feared that he would leave his wife pregnant and widowed and therefore resisted consummation. "I have been married for nearly a year, but owing to the fact that I have been serving as an infantry officer in France, + having therefore a somewhat uncertain tenure in this world, our marriage has yet to be consummated."[64] Whether the man would live long enough to find contraception and consummate his marriage added to the poignancy to his request for birth control. Life expectancy for officers on the Western Front averaged a single month—life was short and need was great.

The movement of soldiers back and forth between the war and home front made matters urgent. The shortness of leave and the desire to make homecomings meaningful animated individuals to write letters in response to Stopes's work. While many men tried to present themselves according to the model that Paul Fussell has characterized in *The Great War and Modern Memory* as "British phlegm," the problems of the war dissolved that protective coating. One officer stationed at the Italian front, for example, asked Stopes for a way to address sexual discord. The letter made it clear that marital consummation had gone poorly and that the problem of short leaves made the situation worse. The officer presented his problem as a matter of timing: premature ejaculation, his leave schedule, and his wife's rhythms. His request for a way to recalibrate their relations suggested that while he saw it as a simple problem, his wife saw it as a failure of "love."

> Stated briefly:—A woman on her honeymoon receives a physical shock owing to emissions in the first marital embrace taking place too soon— she feels it so much that she also feels she cannot really love the man, if she ever did.
>
> The husband then returns to the front + is away for some months and on his next return from leave, where she is in a weakened state after this + also just after menstruation the same thing occurs.
>
> Though she fights against it the thought that she does not love her husband preys on her mind until she is forced to tell him, and hints at a separation. The husband adores his wife. You will be doing the greatest kindness if you would inform me of anything which can be done.[65]

Though he used the third person and tried to distance himself from sexual failure, by the end, the writer fell to the more immediate first person to plead for information. His attempt to distance himself while expressing his emotional attachment—"the husband adores his wife"—fell short. Instead, the writing suggested that neither British phlegm nor the expression of emotional attachment captured the full range of wants, needs, pains, and hopes.

The war itself—not just its disruptions—could have emotional repercussions that affected sexual function. Individuals sought names and etiologies for the problems that war created, and in doing so, they tried to find an explanation for their bodies. One man who joined the army as a gunner and worked his way up to captain explained, "When I joined the army at the beginning of the war I became engaged to a girl. For some mysterious reason I now have what I believe is called sexual anaesthesia a complete absence of sexual feeling. As my fiancé is a healthy athletic girl and presumably normally sexed, I dread that this loss of sexual feeling on my part will lead to marital unhappiness." His explanation suggested that he could not be a hypochondriacal type of man, as evidenced by his progress to officer rank. In trying to return to life and pleasure, this man sought a way to capture normality. In Stopes's reply, she suggested that the problem was common: "I do not think it would be any good at all going to a doctor; I do not think there is anything the matter with you except what very many men are feeling, viz., the overstrain of the war. . . . [I]f you love her you should marry her explaining to her that you are overstrained and tired and that probably your sex activity will take a few months to recover."[66]

For those wounded or emotionally battered, the war became the history that they tried to escape. Most of them saw the war as critical to their personal histories, perhaps even the defining moment, but one that marked them in ways they needed to overcome. In some cases, the causes of tension were purely physical; in others, the overlapping of physical and emotional pain made the situation worse. One man tried to put his war service behind him, but despite his attempts, it intruded on his most intimate moments, since multiple wounds and shell shock limited his erectile function. His wife, according to his account, had developed a debilitating emotional fragility from the circumstances. Nonetheless, he attempted to put the war behind him and emphasize his recovery:

> I was wounded 3 times during the war, the last time in both legs + I had shell shock. I had a nervous breakdown in 1919 but recovered + worked very hard until + after I became engaged to my wife in 1923. In November 1924 I had another Nervous breakdown but thanks to proper treatment + my naturally optimistic nature I was sufficiently recovered, or at least so I imagined to get married in June 1925.

The man detailed his recovery but arrived at the point of concern: He could not consummate the marriage, though he and his wife tried repeatedly on their honeymoon. Eventually, they abandoned their attempts and returned home. The wife began to have hysterical attacks, some lasting for hours. Even more debilitating was her lack of desire.

> These attacks seemed to be at their worst during the few days when her desire for union should be greatest but she tells me now that not since before Easter has she had the slightest desire + I find it very difficult

indeed to rouse her ever so little even at the time when she is supposed
to desire union most. She explains that she thinks that a lot of this is
due to the fact that she is frightened for fear I shall fail in any further attempt at union but what worries her + me worst of all is that she doesn't
seem to have any natural desire for union at all now + when I caress +
fondle her she feels that this is a nuisance + she cannot be bothered
with it.[67]

The couple's relations shifted the location of nervous failure onto her so that he
attained stability while she broke down. The shift in location allowed him to
soothe her, though clearly he had his own fears. Though he does not describe
his wounds in any detail, the description implied that the war continued to affect his physical and emotional world. His longing for normalcy—for children,
sexual satisfaction, and love—seems stymied by both of their emotional reactions to events. From his accounts, as the physical realm became less critical,
the emotional reactions became more marked.

In the following case, the wife linked war wounds with emotional wounds.
Though the husband was seriously hurt, the wife ignored the emotional impact
on the husband, instead emphasizing how the husband's mutilation contributed to her own nervous condition.

He was so wounded, on the end of the Penis that a large piece of loose
skin had to be cut away. Would this numb his feeling during Coitus in
any way, the reason I ask is because sometimes it happens, that during
Coitus, he ejaculates the semen and is totally unaware of the fact. . . . I
want to say that very seldom indeed that I have any desire for Coitus,
and that I simply endure it, know that it is my duty to do so, I have a
loving and considerate husband who would not dream of forcing me
in any way whatever, yet when Coitus takes place it does not appeal to
me, although on average it only happens two or three times in a month,
when it does, after a short time I seem to lose all nerve and energy, and
often my husband does not complete the sex-act even on his part, and
on mine it may perhaps happen that I get the full benefit once in two
months perhaps not so often. It generally ends up with me having a
good cry, which sometimes leaves me upset for a couple of days afterwards. In fact I can truthfully say that it makes me ill.[68]

In this account, the husband's physical problems created the wife's nervous
troubles. According to her account, the lack of satisfaction contributed to her
illness. In this, she adapted a prominent theme of Stopes's writings to her own
circumstances. But the account also hinted at the ways in which the couple
framed their sexual relations according to the older conceptual model of a
wife's duty and a husband's consideration in not insisting too often and not using force. The mixing of conceptual models allowed the wife to explain her lack

of desire without ever acknowledging either the emotional impact of penile mutilation on her husband or the way that the mutilation affected her relation to his body. Furthermore, these strategies allowed the couple to avoid considering the full costs of the war and to place the burden for working through the emotional consequences on her.

The desire to escape the war and the inability to do so marred soldiers' emotional relations and affected the way that soldiers saw themselves in relation to others. To bridge intimacy, convalescing soldiers first needed to understand their own bodily capabilities, but they received little information. This problem—the dearth of sexual information, noted by civilians and soldiers alike—was worsened by the problems of physical isolation and the lingering pain, wounds, and disabilities. To find out how to be intimate, disabled soldiers needed to be able to confront their doctors on the issue—no easy matter. One soldier, writing from a convalescent hospital in 1921, was still recovering from his war wounds, which eventually warranted amputation. Though he planned to get married soon, he could get no clear medical advice on sexual function. As a result, he wrote directly to Stopes.

> It's rather funny that I should be in such a position after nearly three years in hospital: yet if I was to go to any of the M.O. s I have known and asked for advice, they would probably put me off by some incomprehensible jargon (you probably know how doctors are!) or else take a pitying attitude at my lack of knowledge. Doctor—I write to ask whether you have the time and sympathy to grant me permission to ask for advice + clear understanding from you.[69]

His account sees the pity and jargon as equally demoralizing. Years in convalescence resulted in concealment around altered bodies rather than an understanding of their functions.

Roughly 25 percent of veterans returned from the front with some sort of disability.[70] For many soldiers, the war did not go away, at least until the next one began. Although writers tended to make less direct connections with their experiences during the Great War as time passed, the war could still affect an individual's explanations of himself fully two decades later. One man suggested that his impotence might be a result of his wartime experiences even though the problem emerged in 1937. The strain of his experiences still affected his conception of himself.

> It is not necessary to tell you more than that I have been through many years of great mental strain + these years followed 2½ years as a prisoner of war in Germany of which 18 months were in solitary confinement.
>
> Whether my present condition is due to psychological reaction or to the period of my life through which I am passing and whether it

is permanent or transitory are questions which are causing me great concern.[71]

For this man, the last war continued to affect him, at the least by providing him with a viable explanation that linked psychology to physiology. Two decades after the war ended, he still pinpointed solitary confinement as something that marked him. On the eve of the next war, this man—writing from the Royal Citadel in 1939—still sought to put behind him the experiences of the last one.

The war became part of individuals' narratives through which they explained their lives. The war signaled fraught emotions, pent-up desires, failed attempts, and rushed chances. It made sexual matters worse, and in rejecting it, individuals tried to find a new version of marital harmony and sexual pleasure.

Making Sexual History

In some sense the Great War functioned as only the most drastic marker in a broader trajectory of an inauspicious past that the individuals believed they needed to overcome. Stopes and her readers conceptualized the past as "the bad old days" when marital sexual relations were a matter of misfortune and looked forward to a clean and modern future. In *Mother England* Stopes deliberately made history into a shorthand for all that had been wrong in the world. Her explanation for publishing this collection of letters articulated an idea that society's refusal to promote sexual health went beyond ignorance into willful disregard. In her preface, she claimed that the collection stood as "a True history of the common people." Her preface continued to conflate history with an appalling past and with the record of that past: "In the following pages will be found a chapter of contemporary English history, unique only in that it finds its way into print. It is a self-written record of the dumb class of working mothers of whose lives history has taken no cognizance."[72] In many ways, Stopes considered history as the record of Victorian sexual misery, that blank slate on which modernists redefined themselves.

The mothers in Stopes's volume illustrated a shifting emotional stance toward pregnancy. Most women in the volume explained themselves as caught by their circumstances. Rather than the supposed stoicism with which mothers in the past had faced innumerable pregnancies, these mothers wrote of "dread," "anxiety," and "fear." One woman wrote, "I have been married 20 years or practically so, and in that time I have had 12 children. I know that sounds disgusting but, as I did not know of any prevention or help, I just had to go through with it."[73] Mothers actively sought birth control. They lined up their past to create an arc of necessity. In allowing the poor "mothers of the race," as Stopes referred to them, to speak for themselves, she suggests that history could be recorded and overcome.

Similarly, individuals saw the past as if it signaled a symptom of some terrible misery. One writer, a naval telegraph operator in China, wrote Marie Stopes about reliable birth control. He was a married man who saw his wife only on leave, and he worried that he might saddle her with another child. His mother's life had been dominated by fifteen children and at least six miscarriages, and he wanted a different life for his wife.

> I love my wife dearly + I have no wish to see her suffer in the same way, yet our baby arrived when we had only been married 13 months, + I don't doubt there would already be another arrived or expected by now had I not been sent on foreign service when the one was 6 months old. . . . Perhaps you dont [*sic*] know it, but discussion of these matters is rather free among married naval men, more so I believe than with civilians, + it is remarkable how unanimous is the desire to possess this knowledge, for married sailors are as a rule not only husbands but lovers as well. If you gave me this information, hundreds of naval men would be eternally grateful to you, + as for my wife + myself, our gratitude would know no bounds.[74]

His description contrasted an idea of women's bodies wrecked by pregnancies against a newer model that stressed mutuality and love. He wanted to care for his wife rather than find only his own sexual pleasure in her, and he promised to share this knowledge among the fraternity of sailors. He saw birth control as a way to leave behind the past and enter a new age of marital relations.

In contrast to a morbid past, Stopes offered a radiant future, and readers responded. One woman rhapsodized about a future informed by Stopes's writings in which the world itself would be reconstructed though sexual happiness. "I did not want to write until I had finished 'Radiant Motherhood[.]' How I do so long now, my husband won't laugh at me, but will read, + agree with me in your lovely ideals; + oh what a world it could be! What a wonderful mind to conceive your 'lovely ideas,' 'high ideals of life' + oh happy happy, the [*illegible*] future brings, or woman designed such, by God means for years + years."[75] The lingering tension between husband and wife in this account diminished in the face of that happy, happy future. The new world promised to allow individuals to surmount the conditions they inherited and write an optimistic account of sex relations.

Stopes believed that she was bringing individuals into the age of pleasure and health, mutuality, and spiritual union. Her readers saw the modern future in an equally rosy light and characterized themselves as not only living but also embodying her best ideals. Their ideas of the modern marriage rejected degenerative modernism—what they saw as emblematic of dissolution and morbidity—and instead emphasized the embrace of health. "We are both normal, healthy people, and love each other very dearly, and are longing for the day when 'we twain shall be one flesh.' My fiancée is the best type of 'modern girl,' and though in no way lacking in sweet, maidenly modesty, is 'sensible,' and not afraid to discuss, in reverence & love, the most vital facts of our future life together."[76] The modern woman retained her wholesome, modest, healthy, normal, and forthright values and became a partner in a sensible and pleasurable relationship.

Thus, to Stopes's readers and to Stopes herself, *modern* had a very different connotation than it did among the elite. The literary elite's growing fascination with consciousness, experimentation, and sexual complexity did not fit with Stopes's model of modernity. For Stopes and her readers, *modern* signaled a rejection of Victorianism and prudery, an ability to surpass the poverty, stuffiness, and pinched circumstances of the nineteenth century. Modern meant healthy and forthright. "I am very anxious to find out the best modern books on purity in sex life for young men, books if possible simple + with plain honest medical reasons, no sentimentality. I have two sons 21 + 18 + I find my education in sex is too Victorian + vague to compete."[77] Modern meant clarity, science, and frankness.

For Stopes and her readers, *modern* did not imply *psychology*; indeed, *psychology* connoted an impediment to physical and sexual health. As Stopes wrote to a doctor from Bradford, "I am very much against the parade of unwholesome sex matters particularly by the psychoanalysts."[78] While some readers turned toward psychologists or psychoanalysts, Stopes's emphasis on biology promised to circumvent that need. Some of her readers followed her prescription: "I have followed the subject of Psychoanalysis for the past 12 years and five years ago was under treatment by analysis but not with the success I had hoped. I feel certain had I had the information contained in your books at that time things would have been different."[79] Proper sex information could stand in for years of counseling. According to Stopes's model, the future had no room for delicacy or neurosis. Freudianism was just another element of degenerative modernism that deserved rejection.[80]

Instead of being mired in sexual disorders fraught with family tensions and passed from generation to generation, the modern couple was a healthy couple whose sense of purpose united them. They learned together how to achieve union, guided by Stopes's book. It was because of this belief in the ideals of the modern couple, engaged in mutuality and health, that the simultaneous orgasm took on such power. Even more than children, the simultaneous orgasm marked out the perfection of the union. It became the moment of biological magic in which two became one—the couple.

> With patience the experiment was completely successful and at the cost of a slightly cramped position for one arm we were even able to regulate the process so as to achieve a simultaneous orgasm. It was a princely reward, for can a man's life hold any experience so sweet as the occasion when he first feels a woman—the beloved wife in his arms—shaken to the depths of her being in the ecstasy of physical union with him?[81]

The writer's extraordinary faith in and commitment to orgasm illustrated the ways that simultaneous ecstasy had become emblematic of the success of their relationship. It also demonstrated the ways that achieving shared sexual pleasure allowed him to become the kind of man he wanted to be. While his wife's pleasure clearly meant the world to him, shared orgasm also spoke of his sexual achievements and the ways that sexual success contributed to current definitions of masculine prowess.

Conversely, the failure to achieve full mutual orgasm meant something larger than a momentary breakdown of parts. If simultaneous orgasm became the celebration of marital union, the failure to achieve sexual bliss signaled a rupture of relations. It spoke to a larger and more ominous sort of failure than other forms of dysfunction. "I came from England to marry my husband 3 months ago in Colombo, since when we have not *once* experienced a *mutual* orgasm in our unions."[82] As the expectation for mutual pleasure grew, pressure to achieve made simple failures ever more charged:

> Last night my wife and I both felt we wished "Big Love" as we refer to the sex act, and after I petted her for some time and she felt eager for me we attempted Big Love, but after some moments—to me it seems a considerable time—my erection discontinued and of course, as although I was still inside, my wife could not really feel me, the whole thing was a failure, and my wife became terribly depressed and cried for some little time. This was very difficult for me to bear, and I made a vow to myself that it should never happen like that again.[83]

Big love had big consequences, in terms of both uniting the couple and fanning the fear of failure. Physical pleasure thus became more rewarding but more fraught. Orgasmic union came to stand for the sexual health of the couple, and success and failure could have ever greater consequences for the union. Orgasmic union became emblematic of the broader goals of health and fitness.

In these accounts, sexual health was a strand in the consuming life project of achieving health and fitness. The commitment toward health affected what people ate, wore, and experienced. The healthy life became a project that affected innumerable choices. As one man described, a thoroughly modern and healthy life controlled every aspect of his wife's existence: "You see, I have converted my wife to the no-corset method and also persuaded her to diet herself with plenty of milk and eggs, and she is a thorough fresh-air girl and performs her daily Swedish exercises."[84] People saw all aspects of the body and its care as ways to intervene in health. This commitment to health made sexual union into another form of health and fitness exercise.

In the pursuit of health and fitness, modern couples rejected the city and the enervation it brought. They sought the ideals of sunlight, fresh air, and healthy orgasms. As the following writer showed, the modern couple was made through its physicality. A devotion to health and physical fitness, including sexual fitness espoused by Stopes, resulted in mutual pleasures and long-term romantic love. According to this writer, the efficacy of health and sexual fitness proved itself in muscular orgasms.

> We read "Married Love" before we were married and have greatly benefitted by the knowledge you gave so ungrudgingly. Our marriage relations are based on said book + although we have been married three + a half years, I think we are just as much (if not more) in love with each other than as on our honeymoon. Romance has not died; and sexual intercourse is not only a most sacred, but also a most wonderful and novel experience to us both, in which we have a complete + intense muscular orgasm. I am 27 years old, weigh 140 lbs. height 5 feet 3" My husband is 6 feet 2" weighs 200 lbs and is 28 years old. We live on a farm between Johannesburg + Pretoria. But farm life in South Africa (where it is not an isolated farm miles + miles away from civilization) is very charming and sociable, and a progressive farmer in South Africa needs inteligence [sic] and education. Being on a farm a lot of our time is spent out of doors in plenty of sunshine + fresh air.[85]

Instead of old-fashioned farmers whose bodies were broken by hard physical labor, the modern farmer was an open-air sort who apparently walked the fields that others worked. Country life had been transformed into a health and fitness regime for the eugenically fit, and sex had become a muscular matter that glued together the sacred and the romantic.

The empire, in these accounts, supplemented the English countryside as a place to benefit from a return to nature in its fresh air, sunshine, and opportunities for wholesome physical fitness. These writers shared a sense of health and fitness despite writing from radically different locations and geographies across the British Empire. Writers from Australia, South Africa, New Zealand, Canada, and the United Kingdom shared a sense of what the wholesome, fit life might mean that emerged from an underlying idealization of country living. Across the "white dominions" in these accounts, one could benefit from all the qualities of modern life, such as access to books and charming sociability, without all the residua of industrial life. The culture of consumerism brought the best of modern life into the farthest recesses of the empire without all of its attendant problems. The empire, in these formulations, came without any sense of a racialized landscape. Almost unpeopled in such letters, farms and the countryside became a place of leisure for nature walks and physical communion.

The physical life became a good life, a wholesome and supposedly healthy antidote for those employed in intellectual work, both in England and across the empire. As one teacher explained herself, despite her occupation, she was not the bookish sort and could not understand her painful menstrual cycles: "I am very keen on open-air sport, and play golf and hockey, enjoy folk-dancing, and can walk longer distances with less fatigue than most of my companions.

In short, I am full of vigour, and am really 'alive' to all the joys and sorrows of life. I love music, and babies!"[86] Such testimonies suggest the degree to which individuals and couples began to see themselves according to the ideal of physical fitness. They saw themselves as deserving of pleasures and good health because they cared for their bodies in certain self-conscious ways, about which they were willing and eager to attest. Another woman wrote, "I have always been young for my age, being keen on sports, games, tramping, mountain climbing, etc + for more than 15 years was a strict vegetarian. I changed my diet 6 months before my baby was born on the advice of my (lady) Dr. I had always been strong very healthy + lived an active rational sort of life."[87] A third wrote, "We are both healthy and quiet-living middle class people—loving outdoor life and pure air. You will [be] pleased to know I have not worn corsets for 12 years. My husband is 40 and I am 32 yrs of age."[88] Exercise, careful eating, rational dressing, sunshine, and fresh air should have guaranteed these couples the kinds of modern and wholesome marriages that previous generations did not achieve.

This sense of British country life became the common culture that knit together elites across Britain and the empire. Writers shared with Stopes a model of the British race, as part of a leisured elite whose physical pastimes contributed to the good of the nation. Their idealization of country living stood in for qualities of race and class in its desire to leave behind the tightly packed, polluted cities and the workers who remained mired in them. Further, their idealization of country life refused to recognize the labor necessary to sustain country living across the empire. Just as Stopes saw "the British race" in cultural terms, writers prized a sense of the British race as a set of sensibilities and practices. Nonetheless, writers to Stopes rarely addressed the issue of race directly; nor did they see themselves as fitting into larger eugenicist ideals, though many, from their descriptions, embodied qualities that eugenicists valued.

Occasions when readers incorporated Stopes's sense of race into their letters were rare and noteworthy. One man, writing from Manchester in 1918, linked race to women's sexual pleasure in accordance with Stopes's ideals. He adopted Stopes's romantic language, her concerns about race, and her belief that women's sexual pleasure served the greater society.

> Of course, I have learned much from your book—but I am wondering if there is any way to release those female secretions . . . and produce that great experience so seldom felt by woman. There should be nothing one sided—for Woman is of more importance to the Race than the man. Those who realize this should treasure Woman, for the Race, as well as for her high personal qualities.[89]

This writer saw his wife as an embodiment of "the Race" and treasured her according to those eugenicist ideals. Sexual pleasure had a higher purpose in his account than mere pleasure. Here the reader's sense of Britishness as a set of class and racial characteristics overlapped with Stopes's sense of purpose. This writer saw his personal life as a microcosm of a broader sense of British mission.

Though supposedly written for the British race alone, *Married Love* spoke to members of other races. Readers ignored the eugenic and racial textual framing and wrote to Stopes seeking help with sexual lives. One man from Bhagalpur City, India, with weak vision and a hydrocele had been married before age twenty. His thrice-daily sexual relations resulted in impotence, according to his account. His story included elements that Stopes would consider clearly dysgenic, including poor eyesight, ill health, early marriage, and patterns of coitus that did not conform to women's monthly cycles. A native, a vegetarian, and a sensualist, this man nonetheless saw himself as deserving of Stopes's assistance. This writer misunderstood where he fit in Stopes's eugenicist mapping.

Other writers who would have been dysgenic disasters in Stopes's estimation saw the models of health and modern life as so compelling that they too sought to achieve them. Couples wrote of their relationships according to the ideals of health, mutuality, and pleasure, despite the ways that Stopes would characterize their unions. In *Wise Parenthood*, she had advocated sterilization for all cases of venereal disease (VD), epilepsy, mental illness, and alcoholism.[90] Despite her clear-cut condemnation of these unions, individuals with these conditions revised the script she handed them and wrote of mutuality and pleasure. One writer began her account with a description of her husband's service and wartime sacrifice. She documented their mutual commitment and love, despite her husband's diagnosis of VD and her accidental pregnancy. "We dream of the time when our love will be crowned by a new life but such an event at this stage can mean only sorrow to all concerned."[91] Such writers refused the language of disease and dysgenics. In another example, a woman explained that the couple became her sanctuary. Despite a history of seizures and ensuing fear of developing epilepsy, she chose to emphasize the happiness that her relationship brought:

> Then when we had known each other a year exactly, we had a glorious week's holiday together. We indulged in caresses which were intimate + wonderful, + we first said the magic words "I love you." and we meant it. After that we went a little too far + realizing the risk we were taking, exercised greater control, after a worrying time. Through it all, we were wonderfully happy in each other + all doubts left my mind, + I was joyful in the knowledge of his love for me + mine for him. This knowledge was like a sanctuary, where I found happiness no matter how topsy-turvy the rest of life was.[92]

Though these writers experienced debilitating illness, they saw themselves as moving toward a mutuality and completion defined by union. They wrote of themselves as embedded in a joint story, one that embraced emotional resonance and health. Individuals who embodied the dysgenic qualities that supposedly were leading to "race suicide" nonetheless attested to the vitality of the vision of the healthy modern couple.

Ignoring the ways that Stopes and others would characterize their unions, individuals remained deeply committed to finding health and happiness in each other's company. They wanted to live the ideals of the modern marriage and tried to see their relationships according to its lights.

> I write to you because I have such admiration of your pluck in writing your book "Married Love"—My wife + I are desperately in love—in a very real way—thank God for such a blessing—but I contracted syphilis in a mild form during the awful years of the War—+ have unceasingly had Private Treatment—but without complete success. My wife is devoted to kiddies + has always longed for a child of her own + to cut a long story short we have had an accident + she is expecting.[93]

Rather than seeing their relationship as broken by illness, the husband wrote of their hopes for health. They chose to ignore her injunctions about racial fitness and focus on ways to achieve sexual happiness. The unfit, whether ill, hurt, unhealthy, married to alcoholics or the mentally ill, or of questionable racial origins, wrote to Stopes about their sexual problems.

Others made no mention of whether they might be fit or not. Their letters about preejaculation or lack of sexual pleasure did not discuss the general state of their bodies and minds, and most never mentioned issues that eugenicists used as indicative of health, such as eyesight, lung capacity, skin condition, strength, or such stand-ins for race as skin color, ancestry, and national origin. Most instead used simple markers, such as "married woman" and "30 year old man," which spoke to how they conceptualized themselves—neither distinguished nor distinguishable, instead ordinary and deserving, defined by a sex, an age, and a marital status. These are the markers that they saw as most relevant, regardless of what Stopes suggested. Perhaps they saw Stopes's rhetoric of race as another sort of sermonizing or officiousness. Perhaps they saw it as ennobling and meaningful but too distinct from their lives to be adoptable. In most accounts, any echoes of Stopes's rhetoric of race fitness and identity was lost before more pressing problems of life.

Though Stopes saw the world in racial terms, most writers refused a broad sense of race in favor of a smaller sense of self. Instead of explaining their lives according to the rhetoric of eugenics, they emphasized the cozier construction of family. To writers, families might mean parents, sisters and brothers, relatives who lived and who died, and people they married or wanted to marry; family did not mean hereditary traits or ancestral trajectories. The specifics of each person might add up to a larger sense of race, but often, they remained as particulars. A wife meant a specific person, not a representative of something larger; a child meant an individual endearing or alarming in his or her

specificity. Writers talked about their histories in terms of their personal histories rather than of a trajectory of a people. Instead of seeing illness as an indicator of racial unfitness, they saw it as an impediment to daily life and a set
of painful circumstances that trapped them. Whereas Stopes wrote large about
parents reproducing fit offspring for the empire and the race, they wrote small.

In this divergence between the grand and ordinary, these letters reflected
the times in which they were written. For intellectuals and bureaucrats, the
pressing concerns of population, empire, and labor problems defined the age,
but for most people, those concerns refracted into smaller stories of an ill spouse
or a problem with preejaculation. As much as both sets of stories emerged from
the same context, these stories met only at the margins. For some writers, the
ability to achieve a modern life of fresh air and wholesome pleasures allowed
them to embody the best of the race, but for most, such concerns existed at the
periphery as a set of fine goals lost before the minutiae of daily life. Regardless
of whether they exhibited the best qualities of the race, writers to Stopes wanted
to break free from the problems that chained them and remake their world into
one of sexual success and pleasure. They wanted to see themselves at the center of a story told about sexual pleasure, health, and intimacy. The ability to
achieve the good life might have been a "racial" privilege, advocated by Stopes
and others, but for many writers the ideals of a healthy modern life proved so
resonant that they responded whether or not they fit within the boundaries of
such eugenic ideals. Excluded from such formulations in Stopes's prose, they
wrote themselves into the future. Racially fit or not, they sought to achieve the
sorts of orgasmic unions that married love promised.

Conclusion

Marie Stopes's correspondents demonstrate the ways that individuals used the
medium of the letter to make cases about themselves. Most saw themselves as
negotiating between the practical matters of logistics and the loftier goals of
transforming their lives. These individuals saw sexuality as a way to remake
themselves. From the simplest request for birth control to more complicated
queries about premature ejaculation, these writers saw sex as a place to intervene in who they were and how they existed in the world. Thus, they saw this
transformative process as charged with meaning. In these letters, sex mattered,
and any intervention into sexual performance realigned how individuals existed. Interventions into sexual behaviors allowed people to remake a problematic past, to forge a new future, to transform a union.

By transforming themselves, these writers tried to do the conceptual work
to leave their sense of history behind. History had become an archive of the
personal disorders and disabilities that afflicted the British, one characterized
by the broken bodies of men and women. Ill health, war wounds, pregnancies,
and disease had made bodies into a fragile building material that reminded
this generation of its links to the past. The memories of mothers haunted this

generation and galvanized their hopes for a healthy future. They thought of
the past and searched for birth control. They remembered their family histories and wanted more loving and less painful relations. The desire to leave the
past behind became an impetus to remake sexuality according to new models
of health, pleasure, mutuality, and fitness. For these writers, the success of the
couple was an issue of import, a matter worthy of embarrassment, exposure,
and explication. The success of the couple meant the world to these writers.

Nonetheless, most writers found themselves ill prepared to create successful unions. Few men could embody the easy sexual mastery exhibited in male
heroes from romance novels; nor could they shift easily between violence and
domesticity as men did in adventure stories and mysteries. The demands of
masculinity for authority, for bodily control, and for certainty weighed heavily on them. Though they wanted to be the sort of men that society and their
wives expected, few could master those cultural demands. The sexual act, so
deeply encumbered in the popular literature of the day as symbolic of love
and so powerfully sketched out as indicative of eugenic fitness, became a test
case for union. The sex act was supposed to strip people of artifice and allow
the commingling of essential selves. In the act, men would reveal the dominance of their masculine nature by understanding, guiding, and controlling
both partners' bodies, rhythms, and pleasures. In the act, women would reveal
their essential femininity through their trust and acceptance of their partner's
authority and skills. Despite the popularity of such models, men who wrote
to Stopes could not achieve mastery and fumbled with both ideas and bodies. They did not know if mutual caresses constituted masturbation, and they
could not maneuver their wives into the sort of responsive yielding that such
accounts said came naturally. In articulating how men could achieve mastery
when it did not come naturally, Stopes filled this gap. Her injunctions that men
needed to watch their wives for small signs of arousal and then woo women
with kisses and caresses meant that men had a program, no matter how intrusive and impossible to follow. Stopes's model created a checklist toward mastery, one impossible to fulfill but reassuring in its existence.

Although we cannot know what drove some people into writing to Stopes
while others refrained, writing a letter to Stopes demanded certain qualities
and skills. Letter writing insisted on a certain sort of courage, especially when
one was forced to write about problems that revealed the distance between
models of sexual fulfillment and failures of sexual experience. For both men
and women, the willingness to testify to one's own inadequacies and failures
demanded an emotional resilience. Writing demanded a vocabulary to describe
bodies, acts, beliefs, and models and a rhetoric to organize the account. Here,
Stopes's writing became central as respondents testified. She created a compelling vocabulary and rhetoric that many writers then adapted. Finally, writing
to Stopes took for granted a degree of cultural optimism, which at times seems
at odds with individual accounts. Broadly speaking, Stopes's model of sexuality saw room for individuals to remake their sexual lives, to improve their

marriages, and to achieve control over their bodies. In writing to Stopes, individuals looked for information and sought to implement Stopes's program in their lives. Their letters stand as testimony to their belief in a malleable future.

Stopes's readers, in developing stories of themselves, surpassed Stopes at articulating sexual subjectivity. Writing such letters encouraged individuals to create some sort of structure to their stories about themselves. Some writers could explain themselves as sexual subjects with coherent stories and a clear sense of who they were and how they wanted to be. Others could not find a comfortable place from which to speak. The strangeness in some of the accounts, such as when men wrote about themselves in the third person, illustrated the discomfort that people had in expressing themselves as sexual subjects. Stopes herself provided no model, thus hampering her respondents' ability to use her as a guide. Her account focused on universal claims about all women's bodies and souls, rather than narrating how she lived in her own body. Despite providing her readers with a vocabulary for acts and parts, she did not provide a model for how to write about lived experience as a sexual subject. Writers adapted what they could of her model and then went further in developing new sorts of stories. They used Stopes's vocabulary and metaphors and models of science and romance—which Stopes herself had derived from popular literature and sexology—to write stories of themselves.

Compare the stories they told about themselves with the stories told about them. Men read *Married Love* while serving on the Western Front. Given the poor odds of survival, one might think that mutuality would be their last concern. But, over and over again, these men showed that if they survived, they wanted a sense of union with their wives. And wives took on the emotional dislocation of their husbands, acting out a pain that disabled soldiers couldn't explicate for themselves. If mutilated and shell-shocked soldiers comforted their wives when their wives experienced hysterical attacks, perhaps it proved their masculinity. It certainly became a way to discuss the fragility of relations between the two and articulated the need for sexual completion.

This vision of veterans looks very different from the issue of soldiers and sex from *Lady Chatterley's Lover*. D. H. Lawrence's characterization of Connie's husband, wounded from the war, suggests that the war ruined the possibility of sexual warmth and tenderness: "How extraordinary he was, bent there over a book, queer and rapacious and civilized, with broad shoulders and no real legs! What a strange creature, with the sharp, cold, inflexible will of some bird, and no warmth, no warmth at all! One of the creatures of the afterwards, that have no soul, but an extra-alert will, cold will."[94] Soldiers on the front and those who returned from the front refused to be the "afterwards," and their wives refused to let them. Instead, they pinned together tattered bodies and tried to find some pleasures and solace in each other's company. The identities they wrote for themselves may have been far more naive and optimistic than those created by great writers, but they were also more pragmatic and forgiving than the characterizations that others wrote for them.

Certainly Marie Stopes did her part to proselytize the creed of marital union organized toward eugenics and race fitness. But of equal importance was the way that people rewrote themselves. These writers did not see their transformation as simply a top-down process; rather, the letters sent to Stopes demonstrate an engagement with the process of change. In countless letters, people talked of a desire to leave behind old patterns of mangled relations and unpleasurable bodies. They chased after the mutual orgasm that held such promise for their relationships. They embraced the model of British country living that united the race across the empire if it applied, but ignored racial injunctions with impunity if it denied them an orgasmic future. Their vision of modernism was much closer to the ideas of fringe organizations, such as those of body culture enthusiasts, nudists, and vegetarians, than to elite versions of the future. Mechanistic, naive, and ill informed, they nonetheless remade themselves as self-conscious creations. Their failures—of which there were many—did not nullify the purity of purpose. The stories they told about themselves show us the ways they tried to achieve the stars and heavens, as promised by Stopes— not for the race or for the state but for themselves as people who mattered.

3

Fashioning Fetishism from the Pages of *London Life*

Though largely forgotten by historians, a magazine called *London Life* flourished in interwar Britain. A glamour magazine replete with photos of movie stars and fashion advice, *London Life* looked like many others that dotted newsstands across Britain and the empire. Unlike other magazines, however, *London Life* became a medium for those "in the know" to communicate about sexuality and desires through its correspondence columns. Between 1923, when *London Life* established a regular correspondence feature, and 1941, when it ended, the magazine published tens of thousands of readers' letters.

In their letters, readers fashioned who they wanted to be and whom—or what—they loved. Letter writing allowed people to develop their own sexual subjectivities, unconstrained by the strictures of daily life. Regardless of the reality of their circumstances, individuals could remake themselves in the columns of *London Life* according to the dictates of their own desires. In the anonymous correspondence columns of the magazine, people could describe themselves as they wanted to be, plot their fantasies, and refine their stories of sexual desire. Readers actively shaped the stories they created as a social process that developed as part of consumer culture; by writing letters to the correspondence column, people scripted their sexual identities.

The range of stories told in the pages of *London Life* illustrates the varieties of desires that circulated in Great Britain and across the empire. Against calls for marital love and racial procreation that demanded sexual conformity, writers to *London Life* emphasized the nonprocreative impulse and celebrated the strange and unusual. The correspondence columns opened room for people to write their own narratives of desire, and the stories they wrote were resolutely queer. In great and compelling detail, people testified to their delight in corsets, stockings, lingerie, amputees, girl boxing, rubber, wetting, high heels, long hair, tattooing, piercing, cross-dressing, rings, and human ponies.

Readers recognized the ways that the magazine made room for people to write about a variety of pleasures that often went overlooked. In 1930, for example, one reader calling herself "Betty" wrote to the magazine's popular correspondence column about the diversity of thrills that could be found in its pages: "This interesting business of thrills—what queer ways people get them. Some by wearing super tight corsets, some by tying themselves up in all sorts of positions of discomfort, some by covering their legs in silk."[1] Another writer stated that he enjoyed the magazine because he had "a good all-round interest in queer and out-of-the-way subjects."[2] Letter writing allowed people to form a queer community. Whereas individuals wrote to Marie Stopes because she was an acknowledged authority to whom they could turn for advice, people used *London Life* to speak to each other. By reading and writing to *London Life*, individuals self-consciously transformed themselves into London Lifers, a queer community that allowed for a diversity of desires.

The letters, tucked between ads for rubber wear and art photos of nude models, let historians see how consumer culture and the broader historical context were refracted onto objects and stories of pleasure. As their letters attest, people's fixations happened in a cultural context that was changing, sometimes in painfully fast ways. Historical transformations created ruptures that played out in sexual and gender transformations. Sexual anxieties and desires emerged from the context of their times and spoke to the moments of their creation. Capturing the moment through a fetishistic practice allowed writers to engage with change in letter after letter. Letters to the correspondence columns allowed writers to repeatedly, sometimes compulsively, play and replay their reactions. However, these letters spoke to not only the specific time of their writing, between 1923 and 1941, but also the writers' sense of their place in history as they squeezed their memories for glimpses of corsets past, refracted trauma into a usable present, and envisioned an edgy future engaged with modern girls. Whether rendered through modernism, nostalgia, or memorials that screened the past and present, their sense of time created a context for their erotic desires.

Magazines and Consumer Culture

London Life, like any number of magazines that circulated in the interwar world, fed appetites for pleasures by offering consumers a look at the possibilities for fashion, glamour, and modern life.[3] Though it straddled the line between obscene publications and legal fare in the 1910s, by the time it gained its place as a queer magazine in 1923 and 1924, it had moved closer to the realm of a "slick paper" legal periodical that circulated with other sorts of newsstand magazines across the British Empire. Such publications were not entirely respectable given their place as lowbrow media for culture, but they stayed on the lawful side of the censorship divide by avoiding explicit depictions of genitals, sexual intercourse, and sexual desires.

Historian Edward Shorter mentions *London Life* in passing, but few scholars have delved into it in any great depth.[4] Art historian David Kunzle, in *Fashion and Fetishism*, uses the magazine to discuss fetishism during the 1920s and 1930s as part of a larger project on the history of corsets and body modification.[5] Valerie Steele, a fashion historian whose work derives largely from Kunzle's, also mentions the magazine, while Robert Bienvenu, a sociologist, examines it to consider the emergence of sadomasochism as a symbolic system.[6] The most painstaking work with the magazine comes from Peter Farrer, a reader who has meticulously transcribed many of its letters.[7] Though each of these scholars details a particular focus in *London Life*, more can be said about the way that the magazine provided a forum for a queer community and contributed to sexual identity formation. Though *London Life* did not discuss sexuality directly, a careful examination of its contents can tell us a great deal about sexuality, gender codes, and consumer desires in the interwar years.

Magazines and popular reading materials informed women about how to fashion themselves, both sartorially and emotionally. As Matt Houlbrook and Lucy Bland have noted, popular literature offered a language, a set of characters, and a series of narrative structures through which people could construct and make sense of their experiences.[8] According to Jennifer Scanlon's examination of *Ladies Home Journal*, early-twentieth-century magazines linked popular culture to consumer culture, both by providing stories of consumers and through advertising of products for consumer use. In Great Britain and the United States, recovery from the war necessitated a transition from industrial production to the consumer marketplace. Magazines lauded the world of goods and made consumerism a part of the landscape of daily life, facilitating the critical transition from wartime production to postwar consumption.[9]

Magazines, particularly movie and glamour magazines, allowed working-class women the cultural vocabulary to be stylish and modern.[10] From England to Australia, women wore the same standardized wardrobe of smart ready-made clothes for employment as salesclerks, typists, shop assistants, teachers, waitresses, and barmaids. Women completed the look with a bit of face powder and face cream that had been marketed through beauty parlors, department stores, and beautiful-girl competitions. Women saw such self-fashioning as an aspect of modern self-definition.[11] The image of the modern girl spoke of "the future, of modernity, and of the allure of popular culture."[12]

London Life emerged as one of the many glamour magazines that circulated in interwar Britain. The magazine's development out of a series of early unstable pulps into a stable paper magazine illustrates the larger process of the consolidation of consumer culture. *London Life* began as a one-penny eight-page serial, printed and published by Henry Pearce, 15 Harp Alley, Faringdon Street in 1879.[13] After disappearing for a number of years, it reemerged in the 1910s, sharing an address, editors, and advertisers with a number of comic papers, including

Photo Bits, established in 1911, which became *Photo Fun* in 1912 before being reborn as *New Fun* in the same year. By 1914, advertisements for *London Life* began to appear in *New Fun*, suggesting that a single publisher owned both groups of periodicals.[14] *New Fun* then became *Fun* in 1915. By this time, all of the magazines were printed and published at 13 Milford Lane, Strand. In 1917, the publication again changed its name from *Fun* to *Bits of Fun*. The editor gave the following reason: "The paper shortage and the calling up of members of our staff have between them caused this cheerful bundle of pictures and print to decide on 'joining up' with two of our joyous contemporaries (viz., 'Photo Bits' and 'Illustrated Bits'), who find themselves in a similar position, and the giddy triplets will appear in the future in a combined form."[15] However, the name change to *Bits of Fun* may have had less to do with paper and staffing shortages and more to do with the arrest of its editor. In 1917, Philip Henry-Hemyng, editor of both *Photo Bits* and *London Life*, was charged and found guilty for publishing obscene images at Bow Street Police Court.[16] After the arrest, trial, and subsequent fines, the new iteration of the paper appeared and *London Life* changed its name to *London Life and Modern Society* before resuming its original title a year later. In 1920, the publication group again ran into trouble with the law. Charles Arthur Lewiss, demobilized from the army, had taken over the editorship of four magazines, including *Bits of Fun* and presumably *London Life*. The courts fined Lewiss £30 and costs for sending obscene materials through the mail. Although *Bits of Fun* collapsed shortly after the prosecution, *London Life* continued publication, possibly with Lewiss at the helm.[17]

After *Bits of Fun* ceased publication, *London Life* adopted its practice of including correspondence. Short letters had appeared in the earlier publications, and by 1923, *London Life* picked up the practice of publishing correspondence; by 1924, the publication of letters became a central feature of the magazine. As well, the magazine began to incorporate glamour and fashion news and increased its number of photographs. During this period, *London Life* was printed on better quality paper and featured a color cover, important changes from the early comic papers. It advertised in *Willing's Press Guide* and *The Advertising Annual*. While it still featured many of the same ads as earlier versions of the paper, it upgraded its layouts and reset the typeface. Apparently, the new format gained it a measure of stability. At this point, *London Life* had made the transition to a "slick paper" periodical from its earlier pulp beginnings.[18] Like most "slick paper" magazines, it relied more heavily on advertising and visuals than text to fill content. By 1923, the magazine, after its earlier period of frequent editorial changes and legal troubles, achieved stability and an address on Fleet Street that lasted for the next eighteen years.

In the magazine's emblematic form, the covers of *London Life* featured the latest film stars as well as bathing girls and boxing beauties, while its contents included the latest MGM and Universal Studios publicity shots, gossip and fashion, columns, racy fiction, and expository essays. The layout of the magazine intermingled text with ads, drawings, film stills, "art house photos," and shots of chorus lines and revue girls. Similar to other magazines, the paper's inside cover combined short snippets of gossip and human interest. *London Life*'s "Talk of the Town" mixed the latest gossip about royalty with a summary of current events, canned histories about oddities and strange happenings, and snippets about nudism, the world's ugliest woman, and England's beauty queens. The body of the magazine included long-running columns about fashion, graphology, and astrology.

Stories emphasized bizarre incidents and thrilling tours. Its essays described strange and unusual happenings, such as "When Men Wore Silk," about the history of men's fashions, and "Thrilling Feats of One-Legged Aquatic Champion." The latter story combined cross-dressing and amputation in a single essay about "the marvelous exploits of the world's one-legged champion swimmer and diver, whose professional name is 'Dare Devil Peggy,' and who in private life is Mr. Frank C. Gadsby."[19] Early advertisements from 1924 for rug-making machines and electro-life belts gave way by the late 1920s to ads for products more tailored to the magazine's readers, such as high-heeled shoes (sent anywhere), corsets for men and women, surgical goods and birth control, restoratives, art photos, and racy books. The development of certain fetish interests in the magazine went noted by the readers. As G. Latimer explained, "Your paper has the advantage of being different. At the first perusal the reader feels that he has stumbled upon a new and amusing kind of magazine, but after a couple of months' regular reading it dawns upon them that you are catering for readers of a limited taste. Long hair, high heels and corsetting really only appeals to a few stalwarts who write to you in order to ride their pet hobby horse."[20] By the late 1920s, the magazine became the place to discuss such matters openly. By 1940, firms for fetish wear, such as Paul Lane, who made Macintosh clothing in "shiny black rubber" to order, openly advertised in its pages.[21]

Through newsstands and subscription, the magazine spread across the British world. Published on Fleet Street, the magazine was printed in London, sent via rail to surrounding cities and towns, and then shipped to news agents and subscribers across the globe. The placement of the magazine at nodes of cultural transmission at street corners and at train stations meant that its circulation went even farther. Bought at one train station, the magazine would travel to another; bought at a news agent in the city center, it could travel from the crossroads into the heart of the new suburban developments that defined interwar architecture. Bought on subscription, such magazines traveled the mails that linked the British Empire.[22] Readers purchased the magazine at newsstands across India and wrote back with their appreciation. "A. Signaller," in India, wrote to say that he was an "ardent admirer."[23] "Billy" and "George" wrote "An Appreciation from India" to say that the paper was, as they called it, "the goods."[24] Other readers reported its appearance in places even more remote. One reader stated that he had "never had trouble obtaining a copy [of *London Life*] in any place I have been, even in remote places like China."[25] A writer from Burma reported sending his runner to the coast to get the magazine.[26]

According to Anthony Quinn, regional distributors for magazines took the materials from the printers and sent them along to regional wholesalers.[27] These wholesalers "broke the bulk" of each title and sent sets of magazines bundled according to sales potential to news agents. *London Life*, for example, was distributed by Gordon and Gotch in Australia and the Central News Agency in South Africa, two of the main wholesalers of materials to newsstands in those regions, both of which had monopolies.[28] For subscriptions, copies would be sent in bulk to major urban centers and then broken down and mailed out second class to individual subscribers. Railways and steamships moved the magazines at an efficient pace so that printed publications would arrive at newsstands within a few days in Great Britain, though travels to distant parts of the empire would take much longer. Its publication rate as a weekly meant that it regularly pumped out gossip, news, fashions, photos, and letters that then circulated across these nodes, pushing forward a relentless pulse of newness and desire across the physical spaces of communication.

Materials spread like spider veins linking the surface of the empire, rather than merely connecting the main arteries. Letters in the magazine, such as "Stop This High Boot Horror!" from "An Australian Sheep Farmer," and "Proud of His Modern Sweetheart," by S.J.F. from Edmonton, Canada, suggest two things about *London Life*'s geographic range.[29] They show the direction that material culture traveled in the empire, marking places where the magazine, with its tall boots and silk knickers, made an impact. But such letters also demonstrated the ways that communication from the anglophone world spread back to the cosmopolitan center. Individuals received the latest communication from Fleet Street, but Fleet Street also received letters from the empire. The mails pulled together ideas across distances. As a result, readers influenced the direction of the magazine by becoming part of its record. Imperial readers registered their responses and complaints to the spread of culture, all the while keeping abreast of the latest fashions in London. Such readers also destabilized the center of cosmopolitan desires by reporting the pleasures that they enjoyed across the globe. From the latest rubber wear in France to tight kid gloves in South Africa, fashions could appear anywhere, waiting to be spotted by a well-schooled eye and described in loving detail.[30]

It was the letters that made *London Life* the premier fetish magazine in the United Kingdom. By 1939, the publisher knew that the correspondents made the magazine and proudly noted it as a selling point to news agents; according to the editor, "The novelty about 'London Life' is that it is very largely written by its readers."[31] The correspondence columns—called "What Our Readers Have to Say," "Letters from London Lifers," "Readers Views on This, That, and the Other," and "Correspondence"—provide a road map to the broad array of individuals' interests. Though few scholars have worked with the magazine, the assumption is that such letters were not written by readers. Edward Shorter suggests that the editors themselves wrote the letters, though he provides no evidence for his claim.[32] Valerie Steele argues that letters like those in *London*

Life and the *Englishwoman's Domestic Magazine,* an earlier publication, should be read not as readers' letters but as fantasies that reveal "the existence of sexual subcultures."[33] Whether a shadow figure—the editor, an unnamed and supposedly singular individual—wrote such letters or whether they were a product of a series of paid writers or unpaid readers seems central to understanding the publication.

This question of the truthfulness of the correspondence column goes back to the period itself. One reader argued that the correspondents were fakes and demanded that a letter be sent to a frequent writer to prove her existence. The editors tried to correct that misapprehension: "We never forward letters, not even to 'Sporty Wife,' but we can assure you that she is a delightful lady and not a 'fat male journalist.'"[34] In another letter, "'London Life' Brings Happiness," the writer also raised the issue of the veracity of the column before plunging into his pleasure at the publication. "This, our first letter, is the result of a dare on the part of my wife and niece. They say that all the letters in your correspondence columns are written in the Editor's office. So, to prove them wrong, I am hoping to see this letter in print, shortly."[35] The dare was a great gambit but does not prove the reality of the correspondents any more than the letters themselves.

Evidence does exist that individuals other than the editor had a hand in the publication. Some evidence comes from the editorial policies of the paper. Starting in 1927, the editor insisted on having a full name and address for correspondents, even if that name was not used in the column itself: "All letters to the Editor must be accompanied by the names and addresses of the writers, not necessarily for publication but as a guarantee of good faith."[36] This insistence on a good-faith declaration of identity suggests that the editor was as concerned with veracity as the readers. As well, the editor and the readers engaged in complicated negotiations. The magazine created a short editorial reply column to provide information, respond to queries, and counter claims made in the correspondence columns. For instance, in the May 12, 1928, issue, the editor attacked the practice of dressing children in embarrassing clothing. The editor then rejected the practice of corporal punishment in response to previous letters that endorsed it. Finally, it asked "Admirer of Wrestling Girls" from Twickenham for further information about where to "obtain photographs" about such girls.[37] Just as the editor reacted to readers, so too did letter writers react to the editor. Writers made specific requests: "Could we have a page of corduroy and velvet photos, Mr. Editor, for admirers and wearers of these delightful materials?"[38] They also hectored the editor. "Dear Sir,—It was with great interest that I read the letter by 'R.A.D.' in the September Double Number of 'London Life.' This ought to be pretty good evidence to you, Mr. Editor, that there would be a keen demand for a number containing special fare for your obviously large circle of one-legged girl readers."[39] Others wrote to thank the editor directly, as if printing the letter implied a personal favor: "I was awfully pleased to see my letter in your issue of Jan. 4th."[40] Letter writers alternated between demands, requests, queries, encouragement, and criticisms of the editor, and the back-and-forth between readers and editor suggests that the two groups viewed the direction of the magazine from different vantage points.

Evidence of the readers came from the photos they sent. Photos of men and women—booted, cross-dressed, dressed in high heels, with their hair down, on horseback, and amputated—accompanied correspondence. Certain aspects of the photographs such as amateurish lighting and masked anonymous subjects bolstered the claim that readers sent in the images. Furthermore, these images did not go unnoticed. Readers responded to letters and asked for further images and information. One writer, called "Inquisitive," wanted visual proof that women wore high heels. "I am a great admirer of girls who can wear high heels, but feel dubious that there are any who can walk in 4in. heels or higher. If there are any of your fascinating readers who are able to dispel my doubts I should be extremely glad to receive copies of photos or any letters from girls who are able to prove, but seeing is believing."[41] The editor even sent in tips on creating suitable photographs for publication. In response to a letter of February 15, 1936, from "Raymond" about the particulars of sending in a photograph, the editor suggested, "The photo should be as large as possible, but the size does not matter so long as the print is clear and detailed. Care should be taken to see that a suitable background is provided, to throw up the shoes. A white cloth is best."[42]

Advertisers responded to readers' interests and offered materials and services tailored to the community. Further, Laurence Lenton, a Fulham corset maker, who often advertised in the magazine, also sent in signed correspondence.[43] Companies such as the mail-order firm Charles and Company made long-term commitments to the magazine. The same ads for birth control, photos, and books ran week after week, year after year, changing only slowly with the incorporation of new visuals such as previews of racy photos. Other companies commissioned long-term ads in the magazine as well. Advertisements such as "Corsets and Belts of all Descriptions for LADIES AND GENTLEMEN. Tiny Waists our Specialty" and "High-Heeled Shoes and Boots All Sizes in Stock," extolling the availability of a private fitting room, also demonstrate a relationship between consumers and the magazine. This polyglot of services allowed individuals mail-order access to a set of services and to a stylistic vocabulary that may well not have been available in their local communities.

Though none of this evidence is conclusive, together it suggests that *London Life* was a product of an undeterminable number of individuals, rather than a single editor or a small set of associated professional writers. The editor's demand for a real name and address, the editorial reply column, letter writers' reactions to editorial decisions, the images that readers supplied, and advertisers' assessments of the readers suggest that individuals wrote to the correspondence columns, rather than these notes being in-house products created by the editor and paid writers. However, even if the letters were authentic in the sense that they were written by readers, they might still not represent the letter writer's reality in a straightforward way. Someone might have written a letter but be deluded or lying; a letter would be real but would not accurately illustrate something about lived experience. In this sense, *London Life* correspondence might be real but would not be tied to life experience in any robust way. Whether "Sporty Wife" or "Forward Minx," two frequent contributors, were actually sporty or forward or, for that matter, female, seems to be a preoccupation of readers then and now. A concern over authorial veracity spoke to anxieties generated by the culture of letters. The anonymity of print communication untethered one's sense of self from embedded social relations. On one hand, this anonymity liberated individuals from the community of origin, but on the other hand, that very liberation made room for uncertainty.

Concerns over veracity recognized the ways that the magazine allowed people to invent and reinvent a sense of gender and sexuality. "Sporty Wife" may or may not have been female. "Betty B." may not have ridden a human pony. More than just asking for proof that letters were not written by the editor, readers at the time wanted proof that their favorite writers existed as represented, and even more important that these writers existed as imagined. But here, proof broke down, not at the level of historical evidence, but at the correspondent's sense of emotional satisfaction. Proof fixed identity in permanent ways that could not match the pleasures of imagination. Frequent calls for photographs of contributors were most often ignored; when contributors complied with such requests, the photos proved counterproductive to the fantastical elements of their personas. For instance, calls for photos of "Sporty Wife" and her lingerie-clad curves had been frequent: "'Sporty Wife' must indeed have some beautiful undies, and she certainly must have a charming figure. Why not publish a photo of her?"[44] However, when she provided a photo, it showed the distance between fantasies of her person and the realities of her body. As one letter writer explained, "We are not the only ones sadly disillusioned by 'Sporty Wife's' photos. (She may as well retire.)"[45] The realities of bodies did not match the joys of fantasy. Though people often asked to have correspondents send pictures, anonymity in the magazine liberated people's imaginations.

Further, the anonymity of letters allowed writers to play with conceptions of race and gender. Letter writers toyed with racial codes constructed according to fantasies of empire, developed according to grammars of difference. Racial codes, particularly those organized around ideas of the modern girl, contributed to people's definitions of sexuality and gender. In a letter about voodoo, for instance, a reader describing herself as an "octoroon" played up the grammars of difference between modern dress and savage psychology. As the writer explains, "Although I am a modern girl, with all the modern love of high heels, daring frocks, etc., I am really as psychologically as savage as ever."[46] According to the letter, underneath the clothes of the modern girl lurked the mind and beliefs of a voodoo princess. Others, however, saw modern girls as problematic and extolled ideas about traditional women of color. A soldier stationed in India wrote a bitter letter about how women treated him. According to him, English girls were "stuck-up and proud," "too fond of freedom and cigarettes and cocktails and dances, whereas her place is at home, working and cleaning."[47] This man pitted English girls against traditional "black" or "Anglo-Indian" women whom he hoped to marry. Another man, writing from Burma, told of the pleasures of seeing white girls in *London Life* after years in the tropics: "I found the pictures quite thrilling, not having seen a white girl—save about six with tropical figures and complexions—for nearly ten years."[48] Across these accounts, people understood race as a set of comparisons, and they mapped that understanding of a racial order onto their understandings of the world.

Other writers, though they did not discuss race explicitly, still created detailed descriptions of desire that rested on codes of color. "Mounted Mannequin," "Candidus," and "Sporty Wife," all frequent contributors to the magazine, described themselves as modern, stylish, well-dressed women. Their style of comportment, their relationship with their surroundings, and their interactions with men marked them as cosmopolitan Englishwomen who enjoyed the new sorts of cultural codes available only to white women in London.

Though these ideas about race and the exotic contributed to pernicious sexual stereotyping, the anonymity of the correspondence columns destabilized the race codes that existed across Britain and the empire; though the contents built on grammars of difference, the lack of veracity between writers and purported narrators undercut them. Writers, regardless of who they might be, could enjoy writing themselves as Haitian or British, male or female. They could envision themselves as men fighting their way through the jungle telling tales of exotic women or decrying the immorality of Englishwomen in favor of smiling black and Anglo-Indian women, whether or not they were men in life and whether or not such opportunities ever arose. The anonymity of the columns meant that writers could try on identities in letters for themselves even if they could not do so in real life. There was no guarantee that "Mounted Mannequin" ever mounted her favorite pony; she might have been a poor man who dreamed of dressage. In writing these accounts, letters both exploited ideas of race and obfuscated its pernicious effects, making difference into markers of erotic appeal.

The ability to leave behind the limitations of real-world constraints allowed people to perform sexuality and gender in ways that they could not in other realms. Anonymity released people from the restrictions they faced in their daily lives. The problems so minutely explicated in letters to Marie Stopes, such as failing bodies, pregnancy, and ill health, could disappear in these accounts, leaving the limitless opportunities of people's imaginations. In letters to *London Life*, people could become someone else, someone desired and desirable, someone with a special understanding of sexual currents that the rest of the population overlooked.

Liberated through the medium of anonymity and expanded by the associations of empire, writers' letters were then shaped by the demands of the state. As the magazine became stabilized in the 1920s, letters maintained certain standards of decency. Censorship policies insisted that the letters remain nongenital and that they limit sexual descriptions. Thus, censorship shaped imaginary erotic practices in people's letters to the magazines. Censorship made sexuality into an energy in which desire always beckoned because writers could explicate the origin of desire but could never describe an orgasmic conclusion. Censorship codes decentered desire away from human interactions, making items and articles more fraught because they stood for other markers. The policy also forced writers into describing sexuality as located in the mind rather than in the body, even as they resolutely described bodies in ever greater detail.

The focus on nongenital desire and on nonorgasmic interchanges encouraged writers to see erotic potential in all sorts of interactions. Thus, rubber could be erotic but one could not kiss, caress, or have intercourse with that rubber-garbed person, as in the following letter by someone calling himself "The Mac Kid," a writer with well-articled homoerotic desires for a man dressed in rubber.

> His ski-ing suit was in one piece—trousers and vest. It had no sleeves, leaving his bronzed arms bare from shoulders to finger-tips. Round his amazingly slim waist was a white rubber belt pulled as tight as possible, and his ski-ing suit—mark this, lads!—was made of the shiniest, strongest, smooth black rubber waterproof.
>
> To see this godlike figure, with his laughing face, clad in this sheath of rubber all glistening in the sun, was an experience not soon to be forgotten.[49]

The encasement of the man's body in rubber came to suggest all sorts of erotic potentials for the Mac Kid. The language of rubber caressed the body, in part because the Mac Kid could not describe caressing a body in more direct ways. The result of such censorship programs was to push the place of erotic desire into a nongenital consumer realm in which pleasure happens in relation to certain presentations, rather than triangulated between people and their objects.

The censorship patterns of the British state created a particular sort of marketplace for erotic ideas by constraining erotic publications. In many ways, the effects of censorship illustrate Foucault's position that constraint did not repress, it incited. In the world of erotic publications, the state's outlawing of certain sorts of publications about sexuality incited the black market on one hand and incited desires that skirted the edge of legality on the other. In both ways, conscription created desires. The same legal code that pushed obscenity off the British Isles and created the continental system of obscene publications simultaneously insisted that legal publications display only certain forms of sexuality. In the case of popular magazines, publishers needed to take care to constrain sexuality so that eroticism did not describe sexual unions. Censorship codes inadvertently pushed legal publications further into the realm of kink, rather than building human sexual connections. The vagaries of censorship laws let relationships formed with consumer culture stand in for relationships between the self and other. Representations illustrating sexual caresses were illegal, but publications that showed corsets were not. *London Life* could say a lot about the erotics of rubber as long as no one kissed; it could detail fetters and piercing at great length as long as no one orgasmed. Erotic pleasure became spread across the body in ways that electrified it. Rather than eliminate desire, such legal codes extended it across a range of acts and displays. To avoid descriptions of individuals as the site of erotic pleasure, such publications masked the individual in consumer plenty and made the plenty the location of erotic fantasy, a perfectly legal way of expressing desire. Thus, looking at men's genitals would be illegal, but admiring another man "kitted" out in tight rubber wear was not. One could eroticize rubber wear as an expression of longing for the male body encased within it. Censorship laws did not intend to ratchet up kink, but the specific ways of maintaining the legal boundaries imposed by censorship laws made the display of kink legal while making the explicit display or discussion of orgasmic union illegal.

This point does not suggest that censorship created kink or that kink stood in for other sorts of longings; nor does it imply that erotic desires have an underlying stability that were forced into certain expressions. Instead, it posits that censorship affected erotic imaginings in particular ways. The intersection of censorship policies, of consumer culture, and of popular publishing during the 1920s and 1930s created opportunities for specific erotic potentials. The intersection of these factors allowed for kink as a story of sexual identity. Letters in these magazines demonstrate that constraint and discipline fit into the construction of stories of self in ever more detailed ways.

Fetishism in Sexology

In many ways the letters in the correspondence section were predicated on the proliferation of consumer goods in the interwar years. In a straightforward way, *London Life* signaled economic recovery and a return to normal life after the disruptions caused by the Great War. Its advertisements relied on the sale of consumer products, and its fashion columns rested on the revival of the fashion calendar. In another sense, the proliferation of desires detailed in the magazine demonstrated a commitment to consumer goods such as lingerie and rubber wear that seem anything but straightforward.

These desires were linked in the sexological literature under the broad rubric of fetishism. The term *fetishism* emerged in the sexological literature, adapted from the fields of sociology and religion toward the end of the nineteenth century. Indeed, before that time, *fetishism* referred, rather pejoratively, to systems of religious worship. In the fourth edition to his foundation text, *Psychopathia Sexualis*, Richard von Krafft-Ebing developed the concept of fetishism, building from ideas of Alfred Binet and Cesare Lombroso.[50] According to Harry Oosterhuis, fetishism formed one of Krafft-Ebing's four major forms of perversion.[51] Other continental writers noted fetishism but without a systematic causal explanation or etiology. Charles Samson Féré, a contemporary of Krafft-Ebing and author of *L'Instinct Sexuel* (translated to English during the 1920s as *The Sexual Urge: How It Waxes and Wanes*) suggested that sexual fetishism was a variety of touch-mania. Ivan Bloch, in *A History of English Sexual Morals*, mentioned hair and clothing fetishism but did little with them.[52]

Sigmund Freud developed the most detailed model for fetishism. His explanation treated it as a category of behavior and a practice that had distinct origins in psychic trauma. According to Freud, fetishism emerged as a way to disavow the mother's castration. In avoiding the site of the mother's castrated genitalia and the awareness of the vulnerability of castration to one's self, individuals focused on a stand-in for the doubly painful moment of awareness. Fetishism, in the model, both screened and memorialized.[53] Freud's explanation can have fascinating consequences in terms of interpretation, as discussed below, but this area of his work had a limited impact on English writers.

English writers did little with fetishism as a distinct set of practices or approaches to sexuality. Havelock Ellis, for example, did not follow the continental school of seeing fetishism as a distinct pathology.[54] His description of erotic symbolism thus placed foot fetishism (as he spelled it) within the realm of natural human behavior. As he explained, such manifestations "may perhaps become more intelligible to us when we realize that in earlier parts of civilization, and even today in some parts of the world, the foot is generally recognized as a focus of sexual attraction, so that some degree of foot-fetichism becomes a normal phenomenon."[55] Ellis thus normalized the practice and put it in a continuum of human variability.

Kenneth Walker discussed fetishism under the rubric of "sexual deviations." His explanation, derived from Ellis's, noted how certain erotic symbols such as clothes or shoes gained the place of primary importance rather than serving as an area of passing interest on the way toward the more central focus on intercourse.[56] Eustace Chesser provided one of the more interesting discussions of fetishism. Chesser treated common fetishes such as stockings and tattoos as part and parcel of a prostitute's "desire-stimulating techniques."[57] The fetish, in his estimation, provided women with tricks to increase their desirability—a tattoo here, a bit of silk there—that might help ameliorate sexual problems rather than create them.

The proliferation of fetishism in the pages of *London Life* in interwar Britain happened against this backdrop. Rather than a pervasive discourse that had sunk into all of the nooks and crannies of the British psyche, sexological ideas about fetishism appeared only in curtailed and limited form. Thus, the practice of storytelling about fetishism in *London Life* did not just keep apace; in fact, it appears to have pulled ahead of the sexological literature. Rather than people picking up on sexology and reconfiguring pertinent messages and ideas to suit their own ideas of self, in these cases, individuals outpaced science.

Though the fixations in *London Life*'s correspondence letters appear random, seeming to support the psychological contention that objects functioned as a means of disavowal around erotic anxiety, these anxieties emerged quite clearly from the cultural context, even if some of these fixations were intensely nostalgic. The following discussion examines girl boxing/wrestling, corsets, and amputees to explore distinct orientations toward bodies and sexuality in reference to the interwar world's own sense of time and space. An examination of these topics does not imply that they are more popular or important than others. Instead, these interests mark out individuals' relationships toward modernity in ways that may be of interest to historians.

Boxing, Wrestling, and Modernity

The long-term repercussions of the Great War included a stagnating industrial economy, a discomfort with the swelling obligations of a welfare state, and long-term problems accommodating a traumatized population. These issues became critical to gender relations, particularly during the 1920s, during the brief and incomplete economic recovery. As the older, industrial economy limped along, the newer consumer economy gained momentum. Most industrial workers had been men and as these jobs dried up, so did men's employment. Compounding this misery was the inability or unwillingness of the state to fund long-term pensions and benefits for veterans, who could not necessarily resume full employment even if they could find jobs. Further, coal mines that had employed communities for generations began to play out, leaving whole towns without work. Though these broad economic problems had little to do with modern girls, the press and the population blamed girls for problems, particularly because women gained full suffrage in 1928 and the growth of women's consumer culture made it appear that women gained at men's expense.[58]

Men's falling fortunes were seen as tied to women's rising ones. Questions over women's dress, manners, morals, and place in society preoccupied writers in a variety of publications.[59] The image of the modern girl made up and dressed like an actress contrasted with the image of the slouch-capped unemployed man of the interwar years, according to Sally Alexander and Lucy Bland. The man spoke to the tragedy of the past, while the image of the girl spoke of "the future, of modernity, and of the allure of popular culture."[60] Girls and modernity went together, according to both critics and their admirers.

Against this backdrop, it should come as no surprise that the figure of the modern girl gained a remarkable salience in *London Life*. The charges against the modern girl had been made so often that they tripped off readers' pens with great ease. One writer saw the modern girl as a particular social problem of the moment: "May I suggest that the problem of the modern girl is one which could usefully be discussed by your readers? Many students of life are stating today that lack of parental control (partly due to war conditions) is in large measure responsible for the butterfly outlook and pleasure-madness of many modern girls."[61] The examination of modern girls as a social problem did not arise from readers' letters alone but also came from stories and essays in the magazine and materials in the broader culture.

The focus on the modern girl made issues of gender paramount. The magazine took as given that the gender roles had changed. However, writers still worried about the psychological and physical consequences of that transformation. The corporal embodiment of the modern girl allowed *London Life* to literalize the larger society's metaphoric questions about girls within its pages. Through figure training and boxing, *London Life* provided twinned answers to the same set of concerns over women's growing strength. Whereas figure training illustrated one set of strategies to approach girls' bodies, boxing provided the antithesis. Sitting next to each other in the magazine, these approaches both saw women's bodies as a way to work through the problems of modernity.

The question of women's metaphoric strength became literal in *London Life*'s frequent references to boxing and wrestling. From its inception, the correspondence columns featured letters from female boxers and wrestlers that pitted these amazons against young men. As early as 1923, right at the inception of these columns, "Marie and Doris Ilkley" wrote of wrestling against Marie's brother: "I soon had him on his back, though, through a favorite throw of mine, and pressed his shoulders firmly to the mat, and then sat on his chest a few minutes. My girl chum Doris (a pretty flapper of 15) also had a bout with him, and was not long before she too, threw him, and was soon pressing his shoulders close to the mat and keeping him there some time."[62] The figures of these girls, plump, strong, tall, and well developed, became punitive and erotic at the same time.

Female writers reveled in the strength of their bodies and found in the pages of *London Life* a place where they could brag of their prowess without sanction. Writers took pride in the ability to muscle men into a position of submission. The ability to force men into a supposedly feminine helplessness had its own erotic appeal, as a "Muscular Miss" made clear. "I find that, thanks to my extraordinary strength, I am easily more than a match for the average man, and there is nothing I like more than to feel one of the so-called stronger sex struggling helplessly when I get a good grip on him!"[63] The writer understood the gender codes of female weakness and male strength but delighted at their inversion.

In another such letter, a writer says that she never had the luck to see a girl boxer or wrestler but that she did see a young woman chastise a man. "Freda" then recounts the comeuppance of a male manager who tormented his female workers in a munitions factory during the war. "Tiny," a strong woman who stood five feet, eleven inches, according to the writer, clocked the manager when he called her an "ugly-sounding name." She then "got hold of him by the back of the neck and forced him across a bench. After a sharp struggle she had him prepared for his punishment. He was actually spanked by her with a heavy hand."[64] The backdrop of war work muted the gender politics, since the manager interfered with the girls' ability to do their bit for the war effort. Instead of undercutting all men, "Tiny," in this story, emasculated only those puny and cowardly men on the home front who interfered with female war workers.

As opposed to girlie shows that promised titillation, female wrestling allowed viewers a wider range of reactions from amazement to disgust, titillation to revulsion. A photograph of female wrestlers made women's strength subject to erotic display. The photograph of a nightclub featured men, dressed in evening wear, seated at tables alongside the mat where two women, dressed only in brassieres, camisoles, tights, and ballet shoes, wrestled. The caption reads, "The beginning of a half-Nelson between two girl wrestlers who were photographed wrestling vigorously on the mat before spectators at the famous Bal Tabarin Cabaret, Paris, where wrestling bouts between women occur nightly."[65] The lure of the female wrestler came from the image of half-naked women grappling. The delights of such vistas could be multifold; these displays showed off the wrestler's erotic curves, promised a display of female dominance and submission, and raised the possibility of sartorial misadventure and accidental nudity.

The magazine also allowed the confession of male weakness and subjugation to female strength. Another letter, "Wrestling Girl Defeats Soldier," made the links between men's weakness, female freaks, and erotic subjugation quite explicit. The letter described a soldier's experience in Cairo in 1916 when he saw female wrestlers associated with a circus. According to his account, a "Greek Amazon" challenged him. "I prepared to meet my fate, which was soon upon me. What happened I don't quite know, for I was speedily in such a position that I was totally incapable of movement. I was lying flat on my chest, head firmly wedged between her thighs, which were exerting great pressure, while my arms were drawn up tightly behind my back." A second bout took place, and she again pinned him. "She next proceeded to secure my arms at the wrists, and inconveniently bent them across her own outstretched legs. I was thus in a somewhat humiliating position, for my opponent was sitting her full weight on my face; and being breathless and helpless, I speedily acknowledged her as my conqueror."[66] According to the description, she sat on his face to force him into submission. The letter played with ideas between humiliation and eroticism that other venues could not.

The physicality of these sports tested new models of corporeality for women in ways that writers found strange and compelling.[67] According to one writer, "reading the letters on 'The Dominance of Woman' in your very original paper" encouraged him to write. According to his account, his girlfriend always bested him at wrestling. "My fiancée is a very well-built, powerful girl, and although I am no weakling, I have to admit that she is my superior in physical strength. Many are the wrestling bouts indulged in, and invariably I finish up on the floor with my fair adversary sat upon me." He seemed undeterred by his frequent losses and hoped only that one day he would "prove the victor" and "get his own back."[68] His girlfriend's strength came across as compelling, and even the nod to female dominance left the writer undisturbed. Modern girls, in such letters, proved a fascinating spectacle worth watching and grappling with in all their muscled strength.

The essays and letters in *London Life* occasionally recognized the incipient violence in these descriptions. In 1929, a story titled "Nottingham Amazons Feint and Faint" described a boxing match between two girls for a £20 purse. Both boxers became furies, according to the article, throwing serious punches and pummeling each other. They hit each other repeatedly in the face, causing nosebleeds and black eyes.[69] The fight lasted a full ten rounds, and one of the mothers had to be removed because of hysteria. The story played up the violence of the fight such that girl boxing went beyond clean shows of strength into the violent and bloody realm of a real contest. That the subjects of the story were young and scantily clad women must have added to the erotic frisson of blood sports—long noted and denounced in the areas of men's prizefighting and animal fights. These stories recognized the brutal pleasure in blood sports and allowed readers to enjoy the spectacle rather than denounce the idea, as many venues required.

Boxing and wrestling allowed readers opportunities to consider the new place of women in society. In some sense, these pages saw the strong young woman take on all comers and win. Certainly, these pages gave writers a place to flaunt girls' new sporty strength. The anonymity of the correspondence column meant that individuals writing as girls could forgo a renunciation of female physical strength and could instead indulge in bragging rights. However, these stories also had an appeal that went beyond that of health and fitness. One pleasure of wrestling came from forcing bodies into submission. Girl wrestling necessitated a measure of dominance and submission that many recognized. Readers could watch girls get pummeled and pinned and could watch girls punch and control. As these letters and photos made clear, wrestling exposed bodies to examination by placing bodies in unnatural and revealing positions. Finally, these documents also illustrated the consumer pleasures of sporty culture. Cabaret shows, freak shows, and sports exhibitions promised amazement and disgust, arousal, and dismay. For a small fee, watchers could marvel at exhibitions of female strength.

The motif of the boxing girl allowed writers to actualize a discomfort with new gender roles. These stories made room for submissive men and dominant women. They allowed readers multiple ways to come to terms with the modern girl, who supposedly changed society in strange and uncomfortable ways. They could watch her punch her sister, eroticize her as she lay pinned to the mat, envision her sitting on the face of other men, or visualize her beaten and bloody in the ring. What could better signify the possibilities of the modern age than to watch the sporty girl wrestle with all its possibilities?

Corsets and Nostalgia

If girl wrestling and boxing came to speak to the modern age, then the corset became a nostalgic marker of the past. Many writers in *London Life*'s correspondence columns longed for a day when girls had discipline and figures were trained. In many ways, the figure itself became the raw matter that let individuals work out the volatile relationships of gender, sexuality, and history.

Figure training in the letters to *London Life* came to be linked with repression. Though Michel Foucault's *History of Sexuality* has upended the idea of the repressiveness of the Victorian era, readers who wrote to *London Life* not only believed in that repression but also eroticized it. In many ways, they provide evidence for Foucault's claims that the endless discourse around repression and control incited desires. Writers saw the corset as the marker of that repression and, in longing to return to the corset, they hoped to reinstantiate the erotic tensions of renunciation, repression, and control. Although nostalgia rarely fits into discussions of sexuality, the focus on the corset suggests that it has a more central function to sexual processes than generally recognized.

Though corsets changed throughout the nineteenth century in style, shape, and even function, they nonetheless continued to mark out femininity, particularly for middle-class society. The corset, according to Leigh Summers, shaped female curves at the same time that it prevented any unsightly wobbling.[70] By the end of the nineteenth century, images of the corset had become overtly sexual; both pornography and advertisements featured corseted women set in an intimate space, reaching over their heads in a gesture that lifted the breasts.[71] Even that sort of overt sexualization did not end the reign of the corset; affluence played itself out in the S-curve and the ability to swath oneself in layers of fabrics, lace, and ornamentation. As Cheryl Buckley and Hillary Fawcett suggest, Edwardian fashionability displayed itself in excess. The corset shaped and held the body so that fashion could ornament it.

Between the end of the nineteenth century and the beginning of the twentieth, a number of converging factors contributed to the slow demise of the corset. Rational-dress reform, feminist agitation, and new models of health that emphasized exercise and fitness routines ended the mandate for corsets, though it took the exigencies of the war to make it clear that the demise of the corset would be more than temporary. Light corsets early in the war gave way to more informal modes of dress as practicality took precedence over rituals of dressing. By the end of the war, the Edwardian matronly silhouette that relied on the corset had been replaced by a new waiflike form.

The fashionable women of the interwar years, with cropped hair, short skirts, and sheer silk stockings, were the "shock troops" of industrial restructuring and modernity.[72] The rejection of older styles of fashioning the female body did not mean that women ignored underclothes or body sculpting in favor of a natural look, as the innumerable letters about lingerie, tattooing, and other forms of ornamentation make clear. Instead, new cami-knicker combinations, brassieres, and garters ornamented a body enjoined to be both strong and wobbly. Against this new model of the body—dressed in slouchy clothes, frilled in lingerie, dangling pillion on her boyfriend's motorcycle—the older model of the corseted body had continued relevance as a point of comparison and nostalgia.

London Life fed an interest in corsets through the correspondence columns and from articles and features in the magazine. The regular fashion column even suggested that corsets were coming back into fashion as late as 1928.[73] Hollywood contributed to the imagery with frequent photos of Mae West and the endless delights provided by the corset scene in *Gone with the Wind*. Bolstering the content, however, was the backlog of underwear scenes from historic venues. In corset wearing, the reinvented past and the recirculation of the past merged seamlessly together. Articles such as "Figure Training throughout the Ages," for example, suggested a Neolithic version of the corset in which bark and animal skin molded women's waists and hips.[74] According to the article, "Once women discovered the assistance and comfort of the corset that even the crudest form of the corset gave to the figure, she never let it go." Women throughout the ages made use of the corset from the Greek girdle to the Egyptian sash.

Testimonials provided evidence to corset wearing in the past. Aficionados of corset memories honed their recollections of their youth. One writer, for example, relived the memory of "Mademoiselle Polaire, a French eccentric actress" whom the writer had seen in 1909. The actress had a thirteen-and-a-half-inch waist. A later writer to that week's column mentions the tight-lacing habits of both Catherine de Medici and Mary, Queen of Scots. The writer then quoted a publication from the 1890s to speak to historic tight-lacing practices.[75] Another writer spoke of her induction into "the wasp-waist cult," as she called it, more than twenty-five years before.[76]

The nostalgia for corset wearing had sexual inflections that the letters and fiction codified. The eight-column story titled "Wasp Waists on the Continent: What a Globe Trotter Has Seen," inset with two photographs, provided a recollection of unspecified "earlier times" when continental girls went corseted. The apparently prewar photos of women bore the captions "I adore being laced" and "surveying herself with pleasure." Particularly effective at establishing an erotic energy was the dialogue that transposed the catchphrases of sex onto the language of corset wearing. According to the story, the narrator had the pleasure of meeting Fraulein Z., who introduced him to two young wasp-waisted girls.

> "You are going to have the privilege," said Fraulein Z., "of lacing in these young ladies as tightly as ever you can. They love being turned into the veriest wasps!" she said.
>
> "It's just lovely!" exclaimed Olga, the elder girl, while the other contented herself with nodding and pretending to be shy.
>
> It was Olga who presented herself first. I took hold of her laces and pulled steadily upon them, while the girl moved her hips like a Nautch dancer, as though to assist in the lacing. All went well. It seemed incredible that this plump girl could so apparently easily endure the lacing I was inflicting on her. Her waist grew steadily tinier and more slender, and except that she turned her head back to smile at me when her waist

was laced to within an inch of the corset's closing, she said, "Lace me—
don't stop!" . . .

It was now Zita's turn. . . . [S]oon she, too, was being clasped by the
mauve corset she wore as in a vice [*sic*]. She was more emotional and
freer in her exclamations than Olga. As the lace slipped through, and
her tiny waist became more wasp-like, she murmured, "Pull, oh pull,
lace me in two! I am swooning with ecstasy. Oh, don't loose or let the
lace slip! I can scarcely breathe, but I am thrilled. Lace me! Pull yet
harder!"[77]

The girls called out at the critical moment "of ecstasy," according to the story, al-
ternating between the pleas not to stop and demands to do it harder. The writer
provided a model of female desire in which women found pleasure through
constriction and pain. The story took the brothel tale, familiar to generations
brought up on "white slave trade" exposés—and reinvented it for tight-lacing.

Curiously, in these descriptions, though men insisted on tight-lacing,
women experienced it as ecstasy and men merely served their desires. Most
writers interested in the corset saw the sadistic implications of the garment.
However, the transformative process of corset wearing acted on women and
men equally though the relationship of tight-lacing to dominance and submission. Through submitting, according to the embedded theory, one could
dominate. Indeed, in this model, the greater one's submission, the stronger
the ability to bring the other sex to its knees. A serialized article titled "Dora,
the Dominant: Early Adventures," about a young dominatrix's relationship to
corsetry, played with the ideas of dominance and submission quite openly:

For, as I can clearly see now, even at that tender age my thoughts were
turning more and more to the possibilities of dominating the opposite
sex. All that I heard at home about the vaunted superiority of man, and
all that I saw of my father's tyranny and my mother's meek submission
to his will at times, only served to anger me and to inflame my gradually
forming determination to be dominant. I knew, of course, little or nothing about sex-appeal (it is a word, by the way, which we did not use in
those days!), but I certainly did realize that to attract the opposite sex by
one's face, one's figure, and one's clothes—to say nothing of personality—
was one step on the road to dominating them; and this, I think, nay, I
know—was the real reason which lay below my desire to appear in public—and particularly at school—in, so to speak, full warpaint.[78]

Here, men's tyranny and women's weakness became internalized. Dora turned
to corsets because of her parents' example, and in becoming better at submitting
to discipline than her mother, she manipulated masculine appreciation. Only
by adhering to figure training and confinement did Dora become dominant.
Tight-laced stays enslaved men with desire even as they constricted women

with pain. Women became dominant by causing themselves pain, while men became weak with the sight of women's transformed bodies.

The tight-laced girl was the antithesis of the girl wrestler in that she could barely walk, bend, or stand, let alone pin a man to the ground. Nonetheless, corsets and wrestling made similar physical and emotional demands, according to letter writers. Reforming the female figure—at great cost to the girl— was seen as an act of courage and training. The process of renunciation took the same sort of courage as stepping into the ring. Rather than shying away from the pain caused by corsets, writers enjoyed it and stressed that through the ability to take pain, women became dominant: "Feet were crushed into tiny high laced boots; calves strained on stilt heels and cased in taut hose. Corsets of relentless strength were literally screwed about the body, while the longest and most closely fitting gloves imprisoned the arms. To have walked at all, let alone gracefully, must have been difficult. However she may have felt about it at the time, the fact remains that Diana is still one of the most attractive women I have ever met. Her high spirits remain unimpaired. She is certainly of the 'dominant' type, as her daughter, my cousin Monica, has reason to know."[79] Figure training in these accounts constituted a form of physical punishment as demanding as the blows that female boxers faced. The ability to suffer united both female forms. As well, both corseting girl and girl boxer were seen as dominant. Both triumphed over their bodies, pain, and men.

Women also wrote of the exhilaration that came from attending to the body. Indeed, the strictures that controlled their forms seemed to liberate their pleasures at its existence. "Only those who have overcome the first strangeness can realize the intense exhilaration and joie-de-vivre that is the accompaniment of extreme tight lacing. The whole body feels light and buoyant, and there is a sense of poise and alertness that nothing else can give."[80] The body in these descriptions becomes intensely aware and blithe, a sealed and buoyant version of its sexual self. "It may be possibly immoral or sensuous, or both, but most girls feel a certain ecstasy when clothed in silk. Some may feel it in velvet, others in fur; but there is certainly some subtle connection between dress and a feeling of well-being and sex consciousness! If you dress dowdily, you feel dowdy; alluringly, you feel an allure emanating from you. . . . Brushing the hair, lacing the corset snugly and closely, easing-in the feet into high-heeled shoes, fastening the skirt or dress at the waist—all these call forth a tingling of the fingers, which is pleasurable and harmless, surely."[81]

Another level of the appeal came from the helplessness that figure training produced. The corset, and the accompanying high heels and tight gloves that served as accessories to quell and control the female figure, caused a heightened sense of bodily awareness and a recognition of physical helplessness. Writers hyped a sort of controlled descent into a stylized invalidism. One writer, who wore a steel band around the waist, praised it for the numbness and helplessness it produced. The letter, titled "The Appeal of Complete Weakness," valued such physical and psychological states: "And it has the additional merit of causing a delightful numbness below the waist, which Clara Elwell also mentions. All this, if one wears very high heels, produces an extraordinary feeling of helplessness which is quite different from that which is enjoyed in actual bondage."[82] The writer relished weakness and incapacity.

The descent into helplessness demanded a willing devotee. Indeed, the necessity of attendants became part of the pleasure. "I have a pair of black patent boots which lace up to my knees, so high that I cannot bend more than is necessary to sit down. These have 5 in. spike heels, and are strengthened with steels each side for 7 in. or 8 in. to support my ankles, and I shall always remember the first time I wore them. I had to get a friend to lace them up, because I was already dressed, and my corsets prevented me from bending down enough."[83] The female body formed the raw matter to be disciplined but within a set of social relations that invested time and care in her physique.

Though many women wrote about other women, especially mothers and aunts, inducing them into figure training, they also suggested that masculine pleasure and devotion became the reward for feminine pain. Male writers seemed to agree and took a pleasure in the role allotted them. As K.P. made clear, the lure of the corseted body tied him to his wife. "Later on in life the lady who honoured me by becoming my wife, and who had from girlhood cultivated, at her father's wish, the curved and rounded figure then considered attractive, soon found my liking for the article, its method of application and the result it brought about, and, like a sensible wife, played up to me by loitering over this portion of the daily morning or evening act." The corset demanded a stylized dressing and undressing that both wife and husband enjoyed. The wife made sure that her partner attended to her primping, and the husband gave every indication of enjoying the tightening and loosening of the stays. The husband suggested that at his wife's urging, he too took up the corset. He finished his letter with a rather cryptic query worth thinking about: "All I can add is, which you, Mr. Editor, will doubtless endorse, 'If this is pleasure, what is pain?'"[84]

Many of these accounts had a nostalgic longing, as if they lived right after the end of the age of the corset. That may not have been surprising in 1924, when adults in their thirties and forties may have remembered the rituals of an older generation dressing in the natal home. It became a bit more of a stretch in 1939, when most people came to adulthood after the age of corsets had ended. Nonetheless, the sense of nostalgia continued. Members of the London Life League, a group formed in the 1980s and 1990s dedicated to the corset and to the memory of the magazine, described themselves as "outside of their time."[85] In 1984, league members mourned the age of the corset that "vanished from the scene so suddenly and so totally more than 25 years ago."[86] Their estimate would put the demise of the corset in 1959. Each generation saw the corset disappearing from view and mourned what looked like its recent death. This insistent longing for a golden age just passed suggests that by the interwar years, corsets suffered from a movement into memory. Individuals memorialized a past constricted with corsets. If boxing girls spoke to the modern, then corsets spoke to a generation just passed into manufactured memory in which gender misalignment could be served up in a haze of erotic longing.

Amputees and the Interwar World

The focus on amputees also let the figure work as the matter with which to consider social change. If boxing girls spoke to ways that context informed desire and corsets to the ways that nostalgia sweetened it, then the focus on amputees brought the issues of memory and displacements into the consideration of such longings. All three fixations spoke to the plasticity of the human figure and the ways that readers ramified desire through the human form. However, more than other sorts of desires detailed in the pages of *London Life*, amputee fetishism raises questions about gender displacement and the erotics of trauma.

A remarkable series of letters and stories that celebrated amputation as an erotic interest in *London Life* deserve a careful focus. Early expository essays and fiction in *London Life* set the stage for this extended interest. After a slow beginning in the early 1920s, there was a small spike in 1928 and then a sustained interest during the 1930s, reaching a peak in 1940 against the growing violence of the next war, when the letters, and this analysis, end. All told, there are at least 322 letters and 32 short stories about amputees during this period.[87] The graph in the gallery of illustrations demonstrates the incidence of amputee stories and letters in the magazine.

Early letters and essays displayed little of the sexual charge that later letters displayed. Nor did they hint at the sexual anxieties and disavowals that appeared in other mediums. Instead, these early accounts described amputation as part of a panoply of oddities, engaging but not necessarily fraught. For example, a 1924 essay titled "Marvellous Feats of One-Legged Dancers" recounted a number of men and women worldwide who laid claim to fame through their dance routines. Like many such stories embedded in the body of the magazine, this story combed the past for strange and distinctive figures and came up with "Donato," a one-legged dancer who performed in England and the continent during the 1850s. The column then mentioned a series of disabled men including Jack Joyce, who lost his leg in the war, and the Bistrews, two former French soldiers who performed publicly, before turning to the American stage and German freak shows including an erotic performance by a one-legged woman in the scantiest of clothes.[88]

A letter to the correspondence column that followed a few months later asked for swimming tips.[89] The writer wanted information to help his sister who sorely missed swimming after she lost her leg. The responses were informational, and a back-and-forth of letters about girls' amputations began. *London Life* became a place to openly discuss disability in ways that more reputable venues did not allow. However, largely in response to fiction written by Wallace Stortt, a strain of erotic energy emerged. In numerous venues and over a period of more than a dozen years, Stortt contributed to an erotic energy around girl amputees.

His first explanation of his desire for amputee girls happened in the short story "The Scarlet Slipper," an amputee version of Cinderella.[90] The main character, Jack Durrant, had previously loved an unnamed young woman, who experienced a terrible and unspecified accident. He eventually traced her, only to find that she had died and he could not make amends (whether for the accident or his treatment of her remains unclear). Years later Durrant saw a beautiful woman who was speeding away in a two-seater lose a charming scarlet slipper. Durrant arranged to return it at a club. At first, he could not find her; then he realized that she was a performer in the club rather than a patron. She was really "the One-legged Venus." Appalled by the revelation, he eventually realized that her disability would allow him to make up for his previous failure. His reaction to the realization is worth quoting at length: "Dazed by the shock of seeing her revealed in all of her maimed beauty, he had read his emotions wrong. He realized that, subconsciously, he had been thinking of the effect of her condition upon others—his friends, his men acquaintances. He himself only needed the strength to ignore the opinions and prejudices of such people and that strength had come to him. He knew now that he loved Pauline unreservedly, despite everything, and that, at last, he could try to make amends for his ghastly failure of long ago."[91] According to the short story, his love for "the One-legged Venus" served a compensatory function, and his relationship with her healed his "shattered self-respect and help[ed] him back to happiness." His remorse over a previous trauma resulted in an erotic attachment to another amputee.

Later explanations by Stortt turned to the work of sexologists to understand his fascination with amputees. As Stortt explained, "We enter the field of what is technically known as 'Fetishism.' In simple and non-technical language, 'Fetishism' may be defined as a sort of overmastering obsession, on the part of the lover, for some particular quality, or object, possessed by the beloved. It is a condition that has long been recognized by psychologists and psychotherapists, and a great deal of space has been devoted to it in the work of Havelock Ellis, Kraft-Ebbeing [sic] and other famous authorities of this kind."[92] Clearly Stortt had read widely on the topic.

Though Stortt was aware of sexology, his descriptions focused on the erotic appeal of girl amputees rather than the problems of obsession. His stories focused on the round and well-formed stump ("it put on flesh quickly until it had become quite plump and round"), a single leg beneath a dress ("a chic little one legged figure swinging neatly along"), one-legged dancing and hopping, and the dressing of the stump in silk and jewelry.[93] Key phrases were repeated across his fiction and became tags of desire. "The display of the single leg below a short skirt, the magnetic appeal here always was in the contemplation of a perfectly fitting silk stocking and with the added appeal of the small, neat, only foot in a dainty, high heeled slipper, the various fascinating incidentals such as the expert use of neat slender crutches or the even more expert accomplishment of being able to dispense with crutches altogether and hop blithely and smoothly on a single foot—all were very important facets of the inextricable attraction onelegged [*sic*] girls had for me."[94] His happily disabled beauties inhabited an edgy interwar world, dominated by speed and pleasures. For Stortt, the modern nightclub, the automobile, and the laughing new dances became the very setting to explore the happily disabled beauty. As he described her character, "her fads of to-day became the fashions of tomorrow."[95] His disabled beauties were as much a reflection of the edgy dangers of modernism as the cocktail, the transatlantic flight, and the craze for the Charleston.

Most important to his model of desire was the idea of the lively and consenting girl. Girls must not only have a disability but also perceive an erotic appeal in that disability. In another piece by Stortt, the narrator described his attraction to one-legged beauties. The narrator compared his experiences with women who understood the erotics of amputation and a girl who regretted the loss of her leg: "The girl's unremitting sadness, the obvious thing, almost of horror, with which she regarded her loss, took away practically all of the pleasure I should normally have extracted from our friendship."[96] Stortt was so committed to the idea of consenting women that his fiction skirted the edge of cosmetic amputation. As one of his characters explained in "Dr. Nicholas," perhaps his most famous short story, she consented to having all her limbs removed by a "queer" master of plastic surgery: "And, in my way, I'm quite as blameworthy as the doctor. But we are all queer in some way, Sonia—you, I, Tina, everybody. None of us is quite the same. It's a weird and wonderful world."[97] Stortt, for all of his self-consciousness about the meanings of fetishism, remained entirely committed to seeing a love for amputees as part of a reciprocating relationship that suited both the whole man and amputee woman equally. According to his model, if men had a kink for female amputees, then perhaps women had the reciprocating desire to be amputated. "If the affection of certain men is for women in some way deficient, isn't it at least a very great possibility that certain women may wish to satisfy that preference?"[98]

At the same time that Stortt laid out erotic projections of amputation through his fiction, disabled girls wrote into the column to discuss both the real and fantastical realms. Numerous constituencies made use of the pages. Some writers made use of the same cues and projected themselves as girls with the same modern, eroticized sensibilities as Stortt's characters. In 1925, a woman wrote to the correspondence column advocating "pretty clothes and dainty footwear" to gain admiration from the opposite sex. That writer, calling herself "One-Legged but High-Heeled," suggested that her sleeveless silk dress worn with skintight knickers, a silk stocking, and a four-inch open-toed, high-heeled sandal accounted for her popularity with men. Clearly, this writer found an erotic appeal in some of the same visual cues as did Stortt. Indeed, the early date of this letter suggests that her description may have influenced Stortt's later stories.[99] In 1928, the writer who called herself "Only a One-Legged Girl" mentioned Stortt's fiction and referred to letters by other women who wrote about their attire. She had been tracking the topic in the magazine for years. Her descriptions about the appeal of amputation seem taken directly from the pages of Stortt's fiction: "There is a subtle fascination that appeals to something bizarre in one's nature, in beautiful girls, perfect in form and figure, who possess only one shapely leg and, possibly, the neatest stump."[100] Another writer discussed vulnerability in ways similar to characters in Stortt's fiction. "My own utter helplessness somehow thrills me. It sounds crazy, I know, I think it is this acceptance of our utter dependence on others that keeps we legless folk interested in life."[101]

Instead of seeing it as a place to exchange erotic thrills, others saw the correspondence columns as a clearinghouse for information. They treated the paper as a guide to disability and as a resource that might tell them how to model themselves. "One and a Half," for example, had an underdeveloped leg. Though she dressed smartly and attracted attention, she wanted advice on how to mark out her emotional reaction to the world: "I wonder if they were formed as I am if they would still be proud?"[102] One writer requested advice about silk stump stockings, pretty crutches, and garters.[103] Another woman, L.N., asked about artificial limbs.[104] When no one answered her first query, she wrote again.[105] The use of the column to exchange information was by far its minority purpose; in some sense L.N. did not realize the extent to which the magazine dealt in fantasies of limblessness rather than its practicalities. Her naive reading of the magazine suggests the ways that even deeply engaged readers could overlook the sexual implications of the paper.[106] When readers asked for direct advice, correspondents stayed silent. Instead, the magazine offered its own set of almost unattainable physical and emotional ideals: grace, beauty, optimism, sex appeal, high heels, and fashionable clothes.

Furthermore, some correspondents protested amputee fetishism. "Forward Minx," a frequent contributor to the correspondence columns, explicitly linked the trauma of veterans' disabilities with the fiction of Wallace Stortt, whom she reviled. "A crippled person should evoke nothing but sympathy. They are so dependent upon others, and miss so much life has to offer. (I talk from experience, as my brother lost one of his legs on the Somme.) I think therefore that to try to thrust sex appeal upon women whose bodies lack limbs is positively disgusting. It is unnatural and horrible, and I condemn it as the worst possible taste."[107] Four years later, the issue of eroticizing disability surfaced again. "Crippled Girl" leveled criticism at women's letters that described their attire and high heels. She disliked the erotic modeling of disability. She hated the markers that Stortt and letter writers liked to dwell on, such as the "short skirts slit up the sides, and long silk hose, and high heels" that women described "in order to add to allure to their one-leggedness." Instead of creating narratives of their own erotic potential, "Crippled Girl" suggested that women should disregard their infirmities and not draw attention to them. She suggested that "this unhealthy cult of short-skirted defiance by monopedes and cripples will only add to the great burdens we must already carry." In short, according to her account, the disabled should present themselves as dainty, graceful, and unassuming, rather than practice a "perverse parading of our ills in the world."[108]

Readers rejected these critiques of amputee eroticism. One of the more interesting replies came from another writer who stressed the compensatory pleasures of being eroticized. "Helen Fivetoes" responded to her by asking for psychological room: "Be fair, 'Forward Minx,' and let we who are short a limb or who are attracted by the deficiency, have what little pleasure we can from reading about the subject."[109] Another reader, "Monopede Admirer," suggested that even if it "is a perversion, it is certainly a very innocent one."[110] Another writer, this time "Husband of Single-Heel," suggested that "Crippled Girl" was merely bitter in her "criticisms of her fellows" and that she should allow them to display their disabilities as they chose.[111] She received little more than a "cheer up" from other correspondents.[112]

Clearly, more than one group of people made use of the magazine, and each group had its own distinct vision for how amputees should present themselves to the world. The issue of how amputees should model themselves physically and emotionally carried a good bit of emotional freight for these writers.[113] For some who experienced amputation, the idea of eroticizing a hardship only opened them up to further ridicule in an already hard world. For others, this psychological space for projections hurt no one and formed a harmless pleasure.

Despite the split between the two camps, a number of questions arise that neither group was willing to acknowledge, let alone address. Why girls? Why voluntary amputation? And why focus on otherwise healthy, nubile bodies? Since most amputees lost limbs unwillingly, why develop fantasies of volition? Since most amputees in interwar Britain were men, why focus on women? Since the war and industrial accidents that caused the loss of limbs left profound physical and emotional trauma, why focus on curvy girls who willingly cut off their own extremities? The consideration of these differences illustrates the strangeness of *London Life*'s formulation of disability, which featured a particular sort of healthy modern girl who desired amputation.

London Life discussed a particular sort of disability and very carefully reconstructed the social and cultural context of disability that deflected social conditions into a funhouse alternative. The idea of bodies, especially the disabled woman's body, became reconstructed in these pages into ones that recognized trauma but did not engage it. *London Life*'s formulation of amputees resolutely ignored the conditions of bodies and disability in the interwar world, creating a way to accommodate a sexuality that might otherwise have been elided. This disavowal became particularly resonant in the context of the interwar years. As Seth Koven makes clear in his work on disability, a great deal of cultural work happened around disability to deal with the issues that such bodies raised. According to Koven, "The British state and society constructed institutions and discourses that allowed them to simultaneously remember and forget. . . . The deformed children of late nineteenth and early twentieth-century Britain and the tens of thousands of men who returned from the battlefronts of World War I permanently disabled, many lacking arms and legs, were dismembered persons in a literal sense but also in a social, economic, political, and sexual sense."[114] The extent of the damage to soldiers during the war makes it sound as if nary a full-bodied man remained. According to Joanna Bourke, 41,000 British soldiers lost limbs during the war, 272,000 suffered injuries to the limbs, more than 65,000 suffered head wounds, and 89,000 suffered other damages.[115] Disability marked the interwar years. A 1920 census claimed that the war was responsible for crippling ten million people who joined the roughly one million who had been crippled in peacetime.[116] In 1923, according to the Ministry of Labour, roughly 900,000 wounded veterans received pensions. Even at the beginning of World War II, 220,000 officers and 419,000 servicemen still received disability pensions for their service during the Great War.

Artists used the motif of physical amputation to express a psychological sense of powerlessness. The distorted canvases of the German expressionists were replete with losses. In these paintings, the wounded soldier—unable to paint, walk, or copulate—confronted civilian society with reminders of a trauma that would not dissipate.[117] In Britain, however, painters did not confront amputation. According to Suzannah Biernoff, "There was no British Otto Dix, Max Beckmann or George Grosz: The mutilated body of the war veteran was not explored as a site of shame and revulsion the way it was in Weimar Germany."[118] Instead, interwar literature made use of the idea of the wounded soldier to mediate between a problematic masculinity, a failed sexuality, and a society that could not come to terms with its past. Though often overlooked in discussions of Lawrence's fiction, the husband in *Lady Chatterley's Lover* was a war veteran reduced to hysteria and childishness through his disability. According to Modris Eksteins's examination of the impact of World War I, a period of disavowal after the war gave way to a rise of reworking the trauma into usable narratives in the late 1920s. The publication of *All Quiet on the Western Front* in 1929 was followed by a "war boom" made up of novels, memoirs, plays, paintings, and films that encouraged a psychological return to the front and the horrors that it entailed. Eksteins points out that the "'real war' ceased to exist in 1918. Thereafter it was swallowed by imagination in the guise of memory."[119]

The wounded soldier may well have been rewritten in the pages of *London Life* into a psychological fascination with amputee girls. As one writer explained in the magazine, his own war wounds resulted in his interest in female amputees. In 1931, the male correspondent wrote that he enjoyed the letters from one-legged lady readers. He had married a one-legged woman whom he encouraged to wear four-to-five-inch heels. What makes this writer particularly interesting was that he lost his leg during the war.[120] Another writer mentioned veterans as well and suggested that there might be a relationship between disabled men and the love of amputee girls. "Gladys," as she called herself, said that her husband, Jim, "lost his leg during the war." According to her, Jim had "the kink" for amputee girls to a remarkable degree. She noted that the "affinity caused by his own disability may be the reason for this."[121] Gladys further noted her own compulsion toward amputation, first having her left little toe removed for the thrill alone. Though she wanted to remove her foot, it was only after a motoring accident that she inveigled a doctor to amputate, though the procedure was not strictly necessary.

In the interwar context, disability could not be avoided, and the broader society needed to come to terms with it. The numbers of disabled adults and children meant that individuals confronted disabled bodies with alarming regularity. According to the novelist and playwright John Galsworthy, "in every street, on every road and village-green—we meet them, crippled, half-crippled, or showing little outward trace, though none the less secretly deprived of health."[122] The emotional impact of such meetings might have had enormous consequences. Such meetings could result in a fascination with disability and psychosexual attempts to come to terms with it. Certainly, one writer to *London Life* saw the process in those terms: "During the many years which I spent as an inmate of hospitals and crippled children's homes, I found that many people were inclined to cherish or profess a morbid love for what they most hated or feared, and I think that if Wallace Stort [*sic*] and others confessed frankly that it was an inborn horror of being one-legged themselves that had inverted itself and emerged as an admiration for one of the opposite sex who happened to be so afflicted, they would really be telling the truth for once!"[123] According to her model, men's disgust transmuted itself into fascination; a fear for the integrity of their own bodies encouraged men's focus on girls' disabilities.

In this context, Freud's assessment of fetishism begins to make an eerie sort of sense. Freud suggested that fetishism was a response to the trauma caused by seeing the mutilated female genitals. Boys, realizing the deficiency—the castration of the mother—fixated on an object as a way of disavowing their own vulnerability and their mother's incompleteness. Freud suggested that a "horror of the mutilated creature" resulted in a fixation as a means of disavowal.[124] Disavowal did not mean rejection; instead, it became a way to refuse to acknowledge what one knew. According to Henry Kripps's reading of Freud, the fetish functioned as a memorial to the realization of "maternal lack." It safeguarded what could not be remembered directly.[125] Perhaps women's amputation screened other forms of disability.

Interwar amputee fetishism suggests a way to work through the trauma around disability that could not be expressed in other ways. The desire to surround the amputation with a stump circlet, to wrap it in silk, and to dress the body in high heels that played up the missing limb suggested one way of memorializing amputation. In a society rife with disability, amputee fetishism allowed an overt fascination with body modification and plasticity. It allowed an erotic reworking of pain into an idea of mutuality. The emotional conditioning of pain into the cheerful acceptance of disability—and even a will to amputation in some of the accounts—became a way of negotiating vulnerability and mitigating a horror of bodily dissolution.

These erotic rewritings of amputation had deeply gendered expectations and implications. Women acted as the agents in amputee fantasies. Through reading and writing those fantasies, men could explore the pleasures of passivity and dependence, rather than mastery and mutuality. By inhabiting the space of the female character, men might be able to enjoy passivity and helplessness, a rare opportunity for men whose gender roles demanded authority. Writers labeled themselves as women or men (or more often as girls or admirers) but whether the pseudonyms matched the biological sex cannot be known. In some ways, these fantasies could be liberatory in that they could encourage individuals to shuck off those restrictions of personal desire they often faced. In another way, however, these renderings were not merely conservative but painfully so, because the mapping of qualities onto gender continued quite relentlessly. In these fantasies, men carried their amputee girlfriends, they picked up their wives' crutches, and they admired women's cheerful courage in the face of disability. There was no reciprocity. Amputee men did not get to dance to the cheers of an admiring audience. No women or men swooped in to care for their stumps, and no one followed them admiringly down the streets. The few disabled men who wrote to *London Life*, including one man who asked whether lady readers "would feel a one-legged husband an utter impossibility, or whether my condition would excite their pity and admiration," received little in the way of advice or even shared fantasies.[126] No one could find room to imagine masculine helplessness as erotic or disabled masculinity as masterful. If men wanted to make use of the figure of the eroticized amputee, they needed to fit themselves into a feminized figure.

The development of shared sets of fantasies did not come without costs: Some voices, such as Wallace Stortt's, received support and admiration and set the tone for others to imitate. Others, such as women who wanted practical advice on negotiating disability with dignity, received little support. Not all voices received equal recognition; indeed, the injunction against bitterness stifled conversations. The policing of emotional registers left little room for fantasies that deviated from a preferred form. The modern amputee girl—optimistic, curvy, and willing—became the only sort of disability that readers of *London Life* would engage.

This fictional figure became the poster girl to inject eroticism into the idea of disability and allowed the broader society a motif for the disavowal of trauma. In some sense, what readers did to the fantasy of girls differed little from what modernists did to the physical form of women in other venues. How far off is Pablo Picasso's vision of women's distortion in *Three Dancers* from Wallace Stortt's fantasies of dismemberment? How different are René Magritte's amputations of female form in *The Rape* and *Dangerous Liaisons* than the versions put forth in these letters? The insistence that girls bear the burden of modernity allowed disability to escape from the older models based on the crippled child and wounded soldier. Instead of pity and remorse, the figure of the amputee girl could excite a fascinated and horrified pleasure. As one letter writer resolutely explained about men's investment in disabled girls, "He is not exactly in love, but is purely fascinated."[127] This fascination in one way mediated between traumas that could be neither forgotten nor remembered; in another sense, however, this mediation edged out other sorts of conversations in the clamor for fantasy. The fantasy of disabled girls may have helped negotiate trauma, but the insistence on a particular form of that fantasy guaranteed that girls who wanted space in the correspondence columns were disregarded in favor of more appealing voices. Even in fantasy space, there was not enough room for everyone.

Reading Correspondence and Making Community

The question of how to read *London Life* preoccupied individuals to no end. They not only read the magazine but also wrote at great length about the process of reading it. Reading in such portrayals became a deeply invested act that allowed correspondents access to a community and its practices that might have been physically out of reach. Through the processes of reading and writing, correspondents created a mediated collectivity.[128] Reading became a physical act that allowed people to declare a community of allegiance.

In one such letter, "'London Life' Brings Happiness," the writer provided a context, a ritual, and a process to reading. His account created a reading practice that organized his family's leisure time with joint pleasures and individual fixations. Indeed, his account inserted *London Life* into the Sunday ritual. As his letter stressed, explaining his reading process mattered as much the reading itself: "I must tell you that the event of the week is 'L.L.' which is read to us Sunday evening by my wife, she having locked it away until then. We, with the majority of your readers, find most pleasure in the letters, which, after being read, we discuss together. I wonder if your readers do the same as us? We each have a cuttings book, into which we paste our own pet items, my wife taking all the items of Fashion, Fads and Fancies (she being the one to make all our undies, mine included), my niece the high heels and corsets, myself the letters, etc."[129] In his account, the latent suggestiveness of the magazine was divided into rational interests. The improbability of the account should not interfere with the weight given to process. The idea of a controlled and ritualized reading suggested the ways in which the letter writer saw reading as an activity. The writer interrupted his narrative to invite others into his process by asking, perhaps rhetorically, how others read: "I wonder if your readers do the same as us?" Reading became a way to process the magazine and its interests and suggested a desire to fit those interests within a larger community of readers.

Another writer calling himself "Experienced" made his reading practices central to his letter writing. In "Filing Your Cuttings," this writer meticulously detailed his devotion to the magazine. From roughly 1929 until 1939, he had created a cutting file from the correspondence columns. The reader pasted the cuttings into small, loose-leaf books bought from Woolworth's for six pence apiece. Each book contained fifty pages. On the right side of the page, he pasted the correspondence columns, and on the left side of the page, he pasted illustrations. Every three months, he would go through thirteen back issues of the paper and carefully cut and paste items of interest. As he explained the process, "Thus I am keeping three pictures of Dorothy Lamour in chains and fetters to illustrate 'Tit for Tat's' letter about her adventures in tying Joyce's hands behind her back, as that appears to have been the only letter about bondage in the thirteen issues I have just gone through. Similarly, any illustrations of high heels are kept to face letters on that subject, and so on." The writer explained that although he knew the contents of his collection, he liked to refresh his memory of the magazine by rereading his collection from time to time. His collection focused on "high heels, corsets, domestic discipline, make-up, bondage, dressing up, [and] party games, together with a few [cuttings] on rubber wear." All told, his collection comprised "more than 8,500 inches of column space."[130] Clearly, "Experienced" invested the reading of *London Life* with an emotional weight. His process standardized the act of reading and found a creative opportunity for processing the written text and illustrations. Once bound, the books became a reminder of pleasures past.

Another writer saw the process of reading as distinctly intimate, as a way to forge a relationship between himself and his favorite correspondent. The writer, calling himself "He-Man," expressed a deep admiration for "Mounted Mannequin." According to his letter, he kept her letters in an album, and he would reread them whenever he felt "blue." He finished his letter by wishing he were a horse so he could be ridden by her.[131] His description treated the correspondence columns in *London Life* in the way that one might keep the letters of a lover. Indeed, these published letters became personalized in his treatment of them. Through the cutting and pasting, he remade them into more meaningful objects that spoke to desires for physical contact. Reading *London Life* was not a passive act. Instead, writers tried to transform the magazine into their own personal property. They not only kept clipping files but also wrote about them. They wanted to read about their own process of reading and transform a private act into a public declaration of devotion.

Formulating the persona of the magazine seemed to be an important preoccupation of the writers. Shaping the content of specials, ranking the pleasures provided by various contributors, and suggesting the sorts of illustrations that might best be featured proved a favorite pastime. Correspondents commented on the quality of contributions in great detail. Two writers, "Olive" and "Doreen," for example, collaborated to rank their preferences. "Doreen" listed her preferences as follows:

(1) the correspondence.
(2) Candidus's letters and Frances George on the Fashion page.
(3) The photographs—especially the occasional Continental ones, deliciously audacious!

   (4) Miss Stanton's illustrations (her girls' legs are the finest I have ever
       seen).

Her collaborator had her own list of likes:

   (1) the correspondence—especially "Sporty Wife," "Modern Woman,"
       and "Sun Girl," not forgetting "Bas de Soie."
   (2) H. B.'s drawings, the female figure in excelsis!
   (3) Hettie, Candidus, and the Sporty Girls' Club.[132]

This sort of detailed list making became a popular activity among correspondents. It encouraged readers to explain how they read the magazine. By reading and then making lists, readers articulated their pleasures in the reading
process. List making also allowed individuals to articulate coded desires. One
did not have to express a lingerie fixation; one could instead say that one liked
"Sporty Wife."

Furthermore, the collaborative process allowed the formation of a fictive
community. Another writer detailed a survey taken at her workplace. The article, titled "What We Think of 'London Life,'" suggested the importance of a
community:

> Dear Sir,—I work in a large store, and in my department are twelve girls
> and eight men. We are all regular readers of "London Life," and a more
> enthusiastic band of supporters would be difficult to find. I have been
> delegated to write and tell you what we think of our favorite paper, so,
> while on holiday, here goes.
>   We place the main features in the following order of popularity.
>   1. Correspondence.
>   2. Reader's photographs.
>   3. Miss Stanton's drawings. [*The list skips number 4.*]
>   5. Fashions, Fads, and Fancies.
>   6. Sporty Girls' Club.
>   7. Full-Page Photographs.
>   8. Talk of the Town.
>   9. Nights Abroad
>   10. Shining Stars of the Screen.[133]

Regardless of whether the workplace discussion actually happened, the writing
about it created a fictive community. People envisioned themselves in such a
workplace bound by common interests in racy photographs and sporty girls.
Further, these lists of preferences almost invariably put the correspondence
columns up front. People wanted to read of others' desires. While essays, illustrations, and fiction received favorable reviews, the correspondence columns
always received mention. In some sense the ever-popular correspondence

columns allowed readers to become so-called London Lifers, a community bound together by their reading habits.

This community had its own splits and fissures. Letter writers often showed little sympathy for interests other than their own. Readers not only expected the editor to mediate but sometimes felt the need to humiliate other correspondents in the process: "For some weeks I, and probably other readers, have been bored with long epistles from lunatics who still think a 16 in waist with a huge bust overshadowing it is beautiful. The same people have the courage to send photos of themselves which have been absolutely ridiculous to look at."[134] For many readers, it was not enough to have a place to express desire. Instead, they wanted to force others to see desire the same way.

Some writers understood that though fixations changed from reader to reader, something deeper united the people who inhabited these pages. A few even pleaded for tolerance and understanding. "I should like to see a little more tolerance on the part of some of your correspondents with other people's kinks; for while not understanding the pleasures others get from riding, macs, boxing and wrestling by girls, we appreciate the fact that they do in the same way we do."[135] Another writer, quoted at the beginning of this chapter, commented, "This interesting business of thrills—what queer ways people get them. Some by wearing super tight corsets, some by tying themselves up in all sorts of positions of discomfort, some by covering their legs in silk."[136]

Wallace Stortt saw the magazine as a community but one composed of subsections who had little understanding of each other's fetishes. "Each little 'kink' has its group of enthusiastic adherents, and I have no doubt that each group considers the 'kinks' of other groups quite silly and uninteresting."[137] For Stortt, the ability of the magazine to cater to a group of fetishists provided a modern revelation. In his fiction, he often used the idea of the "club" as a way for like-minded fetishists to meet and revel in their attractions. These clubs served as projections for how he saw the magazine. One such club, featured in "The Strange Quest of Anthony Drew," allowed for bejeweled women, corseted beauties, amputee girls, and cross-dressed men to dance with cross-dressed women. He characterized this fictional creation as "a temple of strange gods."[138]

At moments when writers saw themselves as united in their kinks, they had the capacity to challenge the sexological community that saw sexuality in terms of binaries such as dominance versus submission, heterosexual versus inverted. United, London Lifers had the capacity to be queer in the most expansive sense of the term and in ways that can undercut any clear sense of center and margins. As one columnist suggested, "If kinks were a definite sign of insanity, then a surprising number of people would have to be classed as insane. For almost everyone has a kink of some kind, although few will readily admit or talk about it."[139] London Lifers had a capacity for cherishing inchoate desires that merged from one to another, and they saw satisfaction in something other than genital moments. Stortt's vision of a temple of strange gods is worth savoring because it provided an image so at odds with contemporary versions of appropriate sexual and gender roles.

Stortt and other writers created a place for the expression of desires in the pages of *London Life*. Correspondents clearly cherished that world; one writer wanted to create the club in real time. The "League of London Lifers," as he proposed to call it, could meet and have a social evening with "songs, games, dances, and perhaps, boxers and wrestling."[140] Such a club materialized more than sixty years later with the formation of the London Life League (L3). Even then, however, desires remained fragmented by inclination, and L3 devoted itself to corsets alone. Nonetheless, L3 paid homage to the magazine where readers and writers created a place for themselves through the articulation of their desires.

Conclusion: Readers Views on This, That, and the Other

London Life allowed individuals to read about a wide range of sexual desires that were barely acknowledged in the sexological literature of the day. The magazine's weekly circulation ran to tens of thousands of copies, and it reached from Asia to Europe and across the Americas, allowing it to feed fantasies and articulate identities across a wide swath of the world. The comparison of publication numbers of the works of Freud and Ellis (printed in the thousands) with such ephemera (printed in the tens of thousands and published weekly for years on end) meant that sexology might have had a narrower impact than ephemera in articulating sexuality. Furthermore, *London Life* provided not only a numerically more significant pattern but also a model of pleasure, something rarely addressed in sexology at all. Sexology provided an incomplete and in some sense dismaying school of understanding, while materials in such magazines provided an alternative in which people found pleasure.

The popularity of the correspondence columns illustrates that the narration of identity mattered a great deal to individuals. People wrote to these columns not only to get information but also to declare their place in the world. "Constatia," in 1939, wrote, "Once again I take up my pen to express thanks to all who make 'London Life' what it is today—a real bumper. My favorite section is the correspondence section. Until quite recently I thought—and so have many of my friends—that I was one of the queerest and the only one of my kind in the world."[141] Letters like those written to *London Life* allowed individuals to plant their flags; in writing such letters, individuals marked that they existed. The choice to write these letters in such quantities and the desire to read the letters of declaration, week after week, suggests the need to see the sexual self as a presence in the world. These letters suggest that it was not enough to like gloves or corsets or amputees but that individuals needed to see their stories in print. The fetish letter in *London Life* illustrates a need for narration. The tens of thousands of letters demonstrate a need for a story of self in which one's impulses are made recognizable to the world.

The existence of these letters played an important part in the articulation of sexual identities. Writers crafted stories that illuminated who they thought they were. They tried to understand the meaning of their desires in time and space, and they sought—however problematically—an understanding of desire as part of individual and social processes. Furthermore, they actively shaped the stories they created. These stories did not come fully articulated from the center of self but emerged slowly as part of a consumer process that developed as part of an emerging ephemeral article. Lovers of amputees responded to Stortt's fictions and developed their sense of the amputee girl against the pleasures of reading such stories. Letter writers responded to what compelled them and stonewalled what they could not face. The building of such stories was a social process. Individuals wrangled over the emergence of fetishistic codes and attacked each other about the appeal of boots, corsets, and lingerie. Writers tried to humiliate each other into reworking their interests and tried to undermine each other before the all-powerful editor, who was seen as arbitrating something important to letter writers. Narratives did not spring unbidden from the hearts of isolated individuals but came as a social process that responded to previous writers, reverberated off the editor, rearticulated fiction and essays, reflected the broader social moment, and detailed the minutiae that made up daily life.

The ability to see oneself in the pages of the magazine reassured individuals about their sexual desires and the manifestations of their sexual identities. The ability to find a community, even a virtual one, meant that the individual had a place in the world, one shared and recognized by others. The reassurance that recognition provided was valued in and of itself. Recognition became a way to negotiate an anonymous existence. *London Life* thrived on recognition and anonymity, the twinned states of modernity.

Such recognition linked individuals to a broader community. If that community was a fiction, it was a powerful fiction that allowed individuals to see themselves as "strange gods." However, it was not entirely fictitious in that it had its paraphernalia of existence. Fetish wear, such as boots, corsets, and rubber clothes, became a consumer presence in the magazine, and vendors used its pages to build a mail-order existence.

These sexual desires did not just spring, unchanging, on the world; they emerged from the context of their times and spoke to the moments of their creation. Sexual anxiety and sexual desire spoke through the material and social realities of the interwar world. Despite the psychological community's insistence that interests conform only to personal history, letters to *London Life* suggest that they are instantiated in the historic moment. The specific interests responded to the historical context and the meanings of bodies at the moment. Although the recirculation of the ideas and images may dissociate them from a specific context, that process does not make them ahistorical. Instead, changes seem to build on a sort of counterhistorical movement as nostalgia and memory become influential in the making of sexual desire. Corsets had meaning in relation to nostalgia; boxing girls spoke to the modern; the relationship of society to its history affected desire. Rather than illustrating a central internal story of some sort of universal origin, the pages of *London Life* suggest that sexual stories emerged in context and that these stories reflected the hopes and fears of the moment.

Finally, the pages of *London Life* testified to a diversity of desires against any relentless call for sexual conformity. Readers to the magazine articulated desires for a bewildering range of ideas—each of which had its own devotees and each of which developed its own set of literary characteristics. The ever-growing list of sexually inflected objects, actions, and decorations allowed a wide range of emotional reactions to sexuality. If the exposé demanded outrage, and the popular romance asked for cloying sentimentality, *London Life* allowed for nostalgia, love, fascination, anxiety, thrills, chills, arousals, ecstasies, and horrors. Readers could enjoy all of these reactions to a dizzying array of fetishes and, for a mere six pence a week, have a community with which they could identify.

Magazines provided a wide range of sexual ideas to the masses. While sexological works by Havelock Ellis circulated in the hundreds of copies, the weekly circulation for magazines could reach the thousands or even the tens of thousands. Note the open display of girlie and nudist magazines at the newsstand in this image from Customs, the agency charged with keeping foreign obscenity off British soil. *(Courtesy of the National Archives, Public Records Office, CUST 49/1638.)*

LONDON LIFE

Right: At first glance, *London Life* seemed like any other glamour magazine, but the magazine also catered to a fetishist community. This February 3, 1934, cover illustrates the enduring theme of boxing girls.

HEALTH ⑥ᵖ
& EFFICIENCY

February

THE NATIONAL SUN BATHING AND HEALTH MAGAZINE

ONE FOR HIS NOB. The magnificent new bathing pool at Hastings is not being wasted during the winter months. Provision has been made for practically every kind of sport, and here you see one of the prettiest residents of Hastings dealing with Commander Drinkwater, the manager of the pool.

NELL
in
BRIDEWELL

FROM THE GERMAN OF
W. REINHARD

Above left: Health and Efficiency was a long-running magazine devoted to the promotion of nudism and sunbathing. However, the number of magazines in circulation outstripped the number of nudists in Great Britain. Such magazines could be used for multiple purposes, including providing information, titillation, and masturbation. Shown here is the cover of the February 1936 issue.

Left: Original and subsequent editions of books sometimes circulated for generations. *Nell in Bridewell*, for example, was a nineteenth-century exposé that was originally published in Germany. Translated, repacked, and published by Charles Carrington, one of the premier pornographers of the early twentieth century, the book was then advertised as a flagellant classic. The cover shows a warden whipping a naked and chained female prisoner.

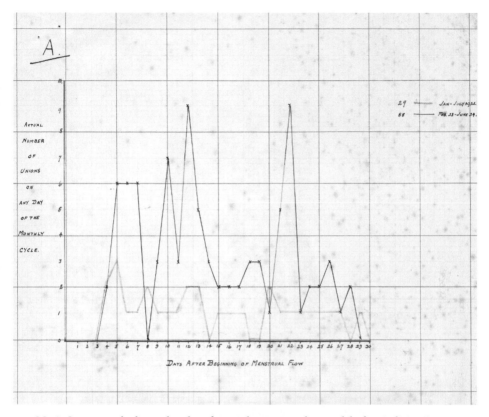

Marie Stopes graphed sexual cycles of arousal to support her model of periodicity. In response to her call for evidence, readers graphed their own incidence of arousal and sexual activity. This image, which its creator labeled Exhibit A, illustrates how one couple viewed their sexual relations after they read Stopes's book *Married Love*. *(Courtesy of the Wellcome Library, London, Marie Carmichael Stopes Papers, PP/ MCS/A.127.)*

gowns our club members had, but last week we all went to our president's house, where his wife and daughter (Joyce) entertained us to tea, when we all wore our favourite summer nightgowns.

Our footwear was either mules or a dainty pair of bedroom slippers.

The tea was for we girls only, but we enjoyed it very much, and especially the parade (each girl had to be a mannequin in her own nightgown in front of the others). They were all beautiful, and all were delightfully airy and cool.

Yours truly,
FRANCES GEORGE.

CORSETTING EXPERIENCES.

Dear Sir,—In your recent Correspondence Supplement you publish a most interesting letter from A. T. Morris, in which your correspondent displays a most intimate knowledge of corsets. Unfortunately, there is a hint of sadness in his letter; for whilst he has undoubtedly a strong passion for the tightly-corsetted figure, he does not appear to favour the restriction of being tightly laced.

I would bid your correspondent to still have hope, for great mountains of opposition can be moved by gentle persuasion. For instance, I have not yet been converted to the wearing of a nose-ring, which I believe would be my husband's final passion. But that is not to say that I shall not one of these days be writing to you and describing the sensations of having a ring put through my nose.

But to return to Mr. Morris's letter, I would point out that I have never habitually tight laced, and in consequence I have not developed a really small waist. I have written to you about being laced into 16in. corsets, but it must be remembered that I only indulged in this extreme lacing occasionally, and for ordinary wear I had my waist laced to 20in.

In regard to the depth of a corset, it is always a matter of some difficulty. In order to get the best results as regards appearance, it is almost essential for the corset to come well down on the hips; but in order to allow the wearer to sit, it cannot be stiffly boned for its full depth.

In my own case, I had corsets in which I was not intended to sit down, and these afforded me the most pleasure. I had to remain standing, or with assistance I could recline on a settee. I quite agree that the front of the corset must be cut away if the wearer is to be allowed to sit as otherwise, as your writer explains, the effect will be a mass of unsightly wrinkles.

At the top the back should be carried higher than the front, where, in my opinion, the corset should be just high enough to support the bust. One of the most important features about a corset is that the busks be absolutely unyielding. I usually had 12½in.

busks in my small-waisted corsets, and these kept me perfectly straight in front. The back was curved in, and the waist-line sloped steeply from back to front.

I am aware that it is perhaps not

This lady is wearing a black kid corset and high-heeled knee-length black kid boots. Notice that her shoulder-length black kid gloves are lined with white. Mr. Laurence Lenton, the maker of this corset, made it specially to the order of a well-known Continental beauty.

possible to reduce quite so much in a corset of this type as in the pattern with the usual horizontal waist-line and more or less flexible busks, but the effect for appearance was simply exquisite.

I was interested to see reference

made to the use of kid for a corset, and some years ago my husband made enquiries if it would be possible to make a small-waisted and well-boned corset in black kid. We were informed, however, that the kid would not with-

stand the intensity of lacing, and the idea was abandoned.

I should imagine, however, that to be laced into a tightly fitting kid corset would be a wonderful experience, one would get a beautiful smooth effect, and there would be also that

exquisite heavy natural odour that one gets from new kid gloves.

Before I close I should like to ask "Corsetted Beauty" how her grey corduroy skirt is finished at the waist. I have never been able to quite decide how a skirt should be finished to give the best effect to a small waist.

The alternatives seem to be either a high-waisted corselet, in which the top of the skirt tightly moulds the figure and is carried high enough to display the curves of the waist, or the skirt can finish exactly on the waist-line, in which case it may be a plain top without a belt, as in what were recently and, to my mind, quite wrongly called corselet skirts. Or finally a belt can be worn which, of course, draws definite attention to the waist-line. I have tried all three methods, but cannot decide which is the smartest when tightly laced.

I trust that "Corsetted Beauty" and your other corset enthusiasts will continue to write and let us have their views and further experiences.

Yours truly,
NORAH WEST.

(Thanks to the courtesy of Mr. Laurence Lenton, we are able to publish a photograph of a lady clad in a unique kid corset made specially to her measurements by Mr. Lenton.—Editor.)

VELVET CLOTHES AND PINAFORES.

Dear Sir,—"Velvet Lover," whose letters always interest me, enquires as to how my stepson reacts to his velvet clothes and pinafores, and whether I have much difficulty in getting him to wear them.

In the first place, the boy hates his indoor attire, and has frequently begged of me to let him go in ordinary boy's clothes. In regard to any difficulties, these are out of the question, as he is compelled to wear what he is told.

"Velvet Lover" will realise that a boy of thirteen clad in velvet shorts, a white silk blouse, girl's high-heeled patent shoes, socks, and a white fancy pinafore, stands very little chance of getting his own way in anything when he is continually under the sole dominance of his younger sister, his stepmother, and her lady friend.

We want to hear more from "Velvet Lover" and whether she has adopted the pinafore system for her velvet-clothed son, which will improve his behaviour to her and also to his sisters, beyond all doubt.

Yours truly,
MILLICENT.

(In the Editor's opinion, manliness in boys is preferable to nice manners, although there is no reason why there should not be a combination of both attributes.)

ANOTHER TIGHT-LACER.

Dear Sir,—When are we going to have some stories about tight-lacing? Everyone seems to have forsaken the topic now. Some time ago my husband asked me if I would start tight-lacing. At first I said it was silly, and that nobody did it now. But after reading about it in your delightful paper I agreed to try it. Now I can wear 19in. corsets but I want to get

This image from the July 29, 1933, issue of *London Life* features a woman posed with a whip and dressed in thigh-high, skintight, high-heeled leather boots; shoulder-length gloves; and a lace-up corset. Surrounding the picture are the letters that, according to its readers' own assessment, made the magazine so popular.

High heels were an enduring fixation. This advertisement from the January 27, 1934, issue of *London Life* featured heel heights up to 8 inches (or even higher for special orders), a wide range of sizes (particularly important for male cross-dressers), and worldwide, anonymous shipping.

SWEDISH FASHIONS IN HIGH HEELS.

Dear Sir,—To my mind, your correspondents as regards high-heeled footwear and high boots have been

No. 2.
Lacing knee boots of brown kid.

of late both few and rare. I venture, therefore, to stimulate such interests by enclosing a few new photos of rather exclusive footwear that you may find some space for in your delightful columns.

First a pair of boots of rather historical interest and not very much up to date, the heels being only 2½in. They reach, however, quite up to the knee, having not less than twenty straps to button.

Number 2 is a pair of lacing boots made of black kid with 6in. heels. Number 3 is a pair of afternoon shoes of glace kid with golden cross straps. They have a button fastening and golden edging round the instep and are very smart.

I may tell you that I have visited lately a niece living in Copenhagen. I have brought some rather interesting photos of her. She is always high-heeled and high-booted. Her interest in exclusive footwear is quite a craze. I may add that she has a lovely slim figure and the shapeliest legs I have ever seen.

She possesses the most wonderful boots in Stockholm. They are as charming as Trixie herself. She has a pair of the most lovely soft kid boots reaching 8in. above the knees, the heels being 5½in. Also another pair of boots lacing well up above the knees, these being made of a very soft kind of calf, dark brown and giving a wonderful fit the whole leg up from the ankle to the thigh. The heels of these boots are quite 6in. high.

Trixie tells me she is having another quite wonderful pair of boots made, and perhaps I shall have a chance to give you photos of these boots if you think, Mr. Editor, that you will get an opportunity to publish them.

Speaking of photographs, why has not your correspondent "S. H. C." in your issue of April 29, 1933, enclosed the photos she is mentioning in her letter? Or have you, Mr. Editor, not found them suitable for reproduction? I also refer to the letter signed "Beatrice" in your issue of June 10. Why could "Beatrice" not let us have some photos showing her over-knee lacing boots, her tiny waist, and her

twenty-button gloves? She must be marvellous in her complete costume as described in her most interesting letter.

Trusting many of your readers will contribute to a special heel and boot number of exceptional completeness.

Yours truly,
MADAME HIGHBOOT.

Stockholm.

Motto: More actual photos from high-heeled and high-booted ladies!

CORSETS FOR BATHERS.

Dear Sir,—Having only an academic interest in the corset question, and wearing only the fashionable corset myself, I have been rather sceptical regarding the statement about corset wearing by men. I have been aware, of course, that many men wear a belt as distinct from a corset, but scarcely credited the statement that a shaped and laced corset was habitually worn.

However, during my last holiday I spent much time at the bathing pool, and on the second day of my stay I was coming from my cubicle to the pool when a young man of 25 or so came out of his cubicle on the opposite side and proceeded me by a step or two down the gangway. He was wearing a backless bathing suit and, being so close to him, I could not avoid noticing the tell-tale criss-cross marking of corset laces on his back.

My interest being aroused, I managed a closer look, and then saw also the mark of the steels—three on each side of the lacing, and also a trace of the corset top. Judging from the evidence thus supplied, I was forced to the conclusion that he was wearing a quite high corset and that furthermore it must be fairly tight all the way up to cause the marks to show.

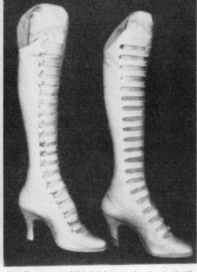

No 1— These boots are of historical interest and are knee-length with twenty straps to button. Sent by Madame Highboot.

I did not make his acquaintance, but after that I kept my eyes open, and during the fortnight I spent on holiday I counted four cases similar where a corset must have been worn.

I became quite friendly with a lady who had a tent each day on the sands, and who, while she allowed her two daughters of about 15 and 17 to run about in the briefest of bathing suits, insisted on them each, when dressing, lacing the other into a trim and very businesslike pair of corsets, and the dressing was not proceeded further till the lady was satisfied that both girls' corsets were properly laced. The girls made no protest, seemingly accepting the lacing-in as a matter of course.

Yours truly,
VERA HOLLINGS.

THE LURE OF FRILLY UNDIES.

Dear Sir,—I have only lately become a reader of your most unusual paper. The letters are of absorbing interest, and my only regret is that you do not devote more space to them. May I also suggest that lovers of long hair and tight-lacing have more than their share of interest?

I am one of those who feel that there is nothing more thrilling in the feminine make-up than frilly under-clothes. I have no use for the coloured variety. Pure, fresh whiteness is essential.

Recently, when in Paris, I found that the famous Can-can dancers at the Bal Tabarin had taken to wear ing black knickers under their frothy petticoats. It was quite a shock when they lifted their skirts, and I at once lost interest in a performance which had previously fascinated me. I am glad to say they have gone back to white again and that their knickers are not over-elaborate.

When they have many rows of frills they are so obviously part of a stage dress, but when quite simple and adorned with a lace edge and a single threading of ribbon through the insertion they are much more suggestive of normal femininity.

It is a misfortune that the drab

No. 3—Black patent-leather shoes with golden cross straps. See Madame Highboot's letter.

fashion of silk bloomers has infected the stage. Chorus girls in charming frocks spoil the effect with their bare legs and plain "trunks." Do not theatrical managers know the stimulating charm of long black silk stockings and short frilly knickers?

It is quite the exception and a treat to see glimpses of knicker frills afforded by Miss Beatrice Lillie at the Savoy Theatre in the scene where she is dressed as a French schoolgirl.

I am glad to say my wife shares my opinion on this question, and always wears white cotton or cambric knickers with wide legs and real frills—not just a straight edging of lace. A well-stockinged leg encircled by a dainty frill some seven or eight inches above the knee is, to my mind, a delicious sight.

When our daughter, aged 14½, comes home for the school holidays, her uniform tunic and bloomers are immediately exchanged for proper girlish garments, which include white knickers with goffered frills of Swiss embroidery. Though the knickers do not ordinarily show below her frocks there are many occasions when they are revealed, and I am amused to see how visiting friends of her brother's (who in these degenerate days are not accustomed to such pretty displays) are not averse, on some pretext or other, from watching for another glimpse.

As for Joan herself, she delights in pretty undies, though she was rather naughty the other day when we had a rather elderly, spinsterish cousin staying with us. Joan came down to breakfast last, and before she was down she said, "Do look at the sweet little knicks mummy has given me," thereupon raising her skirt just enough to show two shapely legs, the glint of suspender clips and four or five inches of snowy white knicker frills. Jim (her 16-year-old brother) and I made matters worse by expressing our evident satisfaction.

In a French paper recently there was a letter from three young girls who had revolted against the artificial silk bloomer fashion. It was so lightheartedly written but, best of ill, was accompanied by a snapshot showing to what good purpose they had revolted. Will not some of the wearers and admirers of frillies among your readers favour us with some snapshots?

Yours truly,
LOVER OF FRILLS.

See letter from "Liveried Man."

Images of tattooed women and of the acts of tattooing and piercing—such as this photograph from the July 29, 1933, issue—periodically illustrated the pages of *London Life*.

Facing page: Correspondence column readers sent *London Life* their own amateur shots. This poorly lit photograph from the April 8, 1939, issue showed off this masked reader's rubber cape. The editor offered instructions on taking such photographs and suggested that the print should be clear and detailed and that the background should be white.

This image from the September 19, 1936, issue of *London Life*, featuring a kilted woman dressed in skintight lace-up boots and posed with a riding crop, combines the appeal of fashion photography with fetish wear.

Readers sent in pictures illustrating a wide variety of interests and desires. This image, which appeared in the December 25, 1937, issue of *London Life*, features a female amputee. Limbless beauties were celebrated in the stories of Wallace Stortt. *(Courtesy of the Kinsey Institute for Research in Sex, Gender, and Reproduction.)*

See letter from "Rex".

This graph illustrates the growing popularity of letters and stories about amputees in *London Life* between 1924 and 1941.

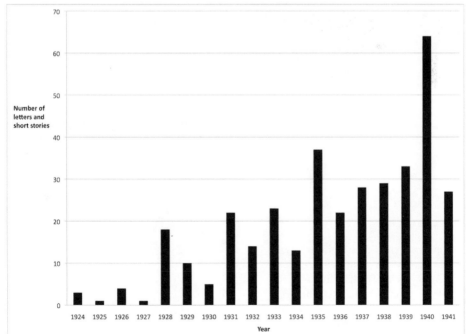

This photograph of a man dressed as half bride and half groom was featured in the February 8, 1930, issue of *London Life*. *(Courtesy of the Kinsey Institute for Research in Sex, Gender, and Reproduction.)*

Images of cross-dressing—such as this postcard with a caption that reads, "Are you a little dickie bird?"—were always good for a cheap laugh. The term "little dickie" referred to a cross-dressed man, here situated in the tree.

ARE YOU A LITTLE DICKIE BIRD.?

VANITY, THY NAME IS—NOT ALWAYS WOMAN!

Wife—WELL, I'M JIGGERED! NO WONDER I COULDN'T FIND MY NEW CORSETS AND BOOTS!!

The popular press circulated a broad range of ideas about cross-dressing, often referred to in these publications as "the kink." In this cartoon from the May 14, 1910, issue of *Photo Bits*, at first glance the man's masculine attire seems to counterbalance his wife's voluptuous curves. But a second look reveals the husband's corseted figure and high-heeled shoes. The caption conveys the wife's response: "Well, I'm jiggered! No wonder I couldn't find my new corsets and boots!!" *(Courtesy of the Kinsey Institute for Research in Sex, Gender, and Reproduction.)*

No matter how loaded, political symbols and paraphernalia—such as this image from the September 18, 1937, issue of *London Life*—were recycled in letters to the magazine. The "heel-Hitler," which transformed the swastika into a high-heeled and corseted coat of arms, revealed a vacuity to consumer pleasures that became increasingly problematic with the changed political landscape of the late 1930s. *(Courtesy of the Kinsey Institute for Research in Sex, Gender, and Reproduction.)*

4

Mr. Hyde and the Cross-Dressing Kink

This is the story of Mr. Hyde.

Mr. Hyde was like any number of individuals trying to make his way in the world. He grew up in India, but the death of his father when he was still a child helped sever his ties to the colonies. As a result, he came to London looking for an occupation or adventure. He hoped to work as an imperial police officer and return to the colonies in a position of authority, but he failed his exams.

When the Great War began, he greeted it with enthusiasm. Like any number of men, he thought the war provided him with a chance to prove himself, and he enlisted. Young, tall, and healthy, he made a fine officer. After training, he was sent to the Western Front as part of the British Expeditionary Force (BEF). And as was true for many such men, the war broke his nerve.

After the war, he had neither a permanent job nor a permanent home. He had no trade, no avocation, no family, no pension, and apparently no lover. Like countless others, he stayed alone in the anonymity of a single room in the great metropolis of London. But Mr. Hyde had a secret: Mr. Hyde cross-dressed. According to his own letters, Mervyn Hyde was "ardently enthusiastic" about "high heels, tight-lacing, discipline, Heel drill, etc. etc. including Female impersonation."[1]

When searching his rooms because of his involvement in the obscene book trade, the police found "a quantity of female costumes and boxes of face powder together with two obscene articles called dilldoes and a cane with leather thong." Hundreds of pages were entered into the police record that documented what Hyde read, wrote, wore, and owned and whom Hyde met and knew. The police noted the books that Hyde had in his possession, including his pornography collection, and they documented his search for old magazines, including *Photo Bits* and *Modern Society*. Although he might have been marginal, the records in his case file are not; few individuals leave behind records with this depth of detail.[2]

The assortment of documents in Hyde's case offers a rare opportunity to compare the stories about male cross-dressing with the practices of a cross-dresser who read them. Building on the anonymous letters from popular correspondence columns detailed in Chapter 3, this chapter ties the circulation of such materials to an identifiable person and his community. Mr. Hyde lived the narratives that appeared in popular magazines. By using the police files about Mr. Hyde, by considering the books he read, the people he knew, and the trade with which he became associated, this chapter illustrates the links between the circulation of ideas and the formation of people's sexual stories.

Through the examination of the cross-dressing community in print and person, this chapter demonstrates that narratives of cross-dressing responded to ideas of gender and sexuality much like other stories circulating in *London Life*. While Chapter 3 focused on the ways that the British refracted anxieties and desires off the modern girl in her myriad iterations, this chapter explores the ways that male cross-dressing engaged the gender changes and sexual anxieties that emerged in the wake of the Great War.

Finally, this chapter suggests that people had a keen sense of who they were and what cross-dressing meant on the basis of ideas of cross-dressing that circulated in the popular press. These ideas were rich, variable, well articulated, and well understood in the interwar years. Sexology, which did not produce significant works about cross-dressing until relatively late, had only a small impact during the interwar years. When it began to make an impact after World War II, sexologically defined identities for cross-dressing lost this richness in the process of shoehorning people into atomized identities. By considering Mr. Hyde, his community, and the array of reading and writings about the practice of cross-dressing, this chapter connects ideas to practices, gender to men, and popular culture to sexual storytelling in the interwar years.

Mr. Hyde, Cross-Dressing, and the War

Mervyn James Conville Hyde was born in 1892 in the Indian frontier of the British Empire. His father, Edward James Clarendon Hyde, Assistant Superintendent of the Indian Government Telegraphs, maintained telegraph communication between field offices and the government headquarters. In 1895, Hyde's father was wounded and died in service. In 1912, Hyde came to England to make a place for himself. He tried to join the Indian police but failed his examinations.

Despite the suggestion in popular writings that white men ruled the colonies with the force of their implacable will, the work necessary to create a colonizer remained quite elaborate, based on extensive cultural codes, class-based systems of education, and connections to race—attributes best achieved in Britain.[3] The ranks of the police came from the local population, while Europeans manned the senior post.[4] Entering into colonial service required success at the competitive exams that stressed proficiency, merit, and character, attributes that an Oxbridge background would cultivate for a future in colonial administration.[5] To be able to succeed and achieve a First Class degree meant that one had the "pluck" that prepared one to be an English gentleman and rule.[6] If examinations served as "tests of character," then Hyde failed that test. He could make no place for himself in colonial service.

When the war broke out, Hyde volunteered. The Great War introduced all sorts of questions about men and masculinity. In many ways, the war offered new opportunities for men to prove their bravery, honor, and valor. Men saw the war as a place to test their physical fitness and their willingness to fight. A "turn to hardness" in both the high and low press had emblazoned soldiers with a fit, tough, and sculpted masculinity.[7] After a generation of men had been inundated with rhetoric about social Darwinism, the opportunity to prove oneself was welcomed. For men like Mervyn Hyde, the war offered a way to make a mark in the world.

In 1914, Hyde stood 5'9" and weighed 144 pounds with good teeth, good hearing, and adequate vision—an A-1 specimen overall, according to army records.[8] He had brown hair, a fresh complexion, and hazel eyes. He had been vaccinated as an infant, and his only distinguishing features were several small moles on his neck, chin, and lower back. Though short by today's standards, in 1914 he was considered strong and tall. In that, he was in the minority. Physical examinations for enlistments during the Boer war demonstrated that 40 to 60 percent of volunteers were unfit for service.[9] During World War I, the Glasgow Medical Commissioner's Report detailed the poor health of the population, which was largely because of malnourishment and environmental conditions. According to that report, professional men averaged 5'7" and weighed 149 pounds, shopkeepers averaged 5'6" and weighed 141 pounds, engineers averaged 5'5" and weighed 127 pounds, factory workers averaged 5'4" and weighed 123 pounds, and laborers averaged 5'2" and weighed 124 pounds. By these standards of an ill and stunted population, Mr. Hyde was tall and fit.

Hyde received a commission as a second lieutenant in the Royal Fusiliers. His place in the Royal Fusiliers came during the rapid expansion of British divisions. Losses among the professional soldiers of the BEF called for the replacement and then expansion of the new army. The Royal Fusiliers, known as the City of London Regiment, provided forty-seven battalions and was one of the larger regiments. In 1915, Hyde went to France to fight in the BEF. By then, the Western Front had settled into its emblematic form of trenches, bunkers, and battles across no-man's-land for no discernible gains. The Second Battle of Ypres (called *Wipers* by the English) brought the use of poison gas but did not significantly shift control of the field; nor did the use of tanks or flamethrowers.[10] The Western Front had become a stalemate.

According to his records, Hyde served honorably until July 1916, when he resigned his commission and returned to England. His commanding officer, Lieutenant Colonel Lord Crofton, stated that he was useless under fire and a danger to his platoon, though circumstances around those charges were deeply confused. Crofton himself was sent back to England within two days of making the report. Brigadier General E. H. Wilkinson recommended that Hyde work the communications line, but Wilkinson, too, was relieved of his command within the week. The general officer commanding the 21st Division was also deprived of his command within a fortnight of the report. Consequently, according to Hyde, those military authorities remaining had no real acquaintance with the case. Hyde, who believed he was "perfectly all right" before leaving for France, was diagnosed with neurosis and cashiered from the army without a pension.

Though the diagnosis of "neurosis" became common during the war, the meaning of the affliction remained inexact and suspect. Neurosis as a medical diagnosis could designate any number of problems and was used interchangeably with shell shock and neurasthenia to suggest tics, mutism, hysteria, paralysis, contractions, and anesthesia, among other symptoms.[11] Medical evaluations of returning veterans found a high proportion of mental irregularities; perhaps eighty thousand cases of neuroses were diagnosed in British war hospitals.[12] The inability to differentiate between emotional trauma and the physical trauma to the brain and nervous system made the diagnosis of neurosis suspect and left those diagnosed open to charges of malingering. Indeed, the possibility of malingering lay at the heart of the government's minimal apportioning of pensions for neurosis.[13] The exact meaning of neurosis in Hyde's case remains unclear.

What we do know is that when Hyde was later arrested, he was interested in sexual acts made illegal by the British state. In 1923, when the police raided his room because he was suspected of trading in obscene materials, Hyde's possessions included a great quantity of cross-dressing materials, a few items related to sadomasochism, and photos of himself dressed as a woman. Perhaps Hyde began to explore this panoply of sexual choices during the war, and the diagnosis of "neurosis" reflected some sort of sexual nonconformity. Whether the government's refusal to grant him a pension for neurosis indicated some sort of sexual or gender irregularity or whether it suggested some sort of malingering remains unclear, not only in Hyde's case but also in the broader case of neurosis.

Even if Hyde's diagnosis of neurosis was based on sexual irregularities, those irregularities were rarely used in diagnosis, despite reports of soldiers experiencing sexual symptoms such as nocturnal emissions, sexual excitement, and the longing to commit sodomy. Veterans' descriptions of the desires linked terrors, anxieties, visions of mutilations, blood, dismemberments, and entombment with sexual desire.[14] Doctors in Britain tended to reject the discussion of sexuality and instead suggested that the conflict between "fear" and "duty" caused neurotic disorders.[15] Though Ernest Jones, Freud's disciple, linked sexuality and war trauma and believed that battle returned the violent impulses that civilization had dampened, most doctors did not.[16] The question of the relationship between sexuality and psychological trauma fractured the psychoanalytic community, limiting the acceptance of Freudian theory in England.[17]

Despite the refusal of most doctors to address sex and gender, the war encouraged a range of gender and sexual ambiguities.[18] Men clung to ideals of domestic life and the care and nurture that women provided. As the letters to Marie Stopes demonstrate, men longed to resume relations with their wives and looked to balance the masculine realm of the front with a focus on femininity. On the front, the language of maternal care became one socially sanctioned way for men to work through a loss of femininity; the joining of corsets and khaki became another. The disruptions of the war provided a social context in which men could dance together, shower together, and engage in casual physical affection in public. Tight physical conditions and emotionally fraught circumstances created new sorts of bonds between men.[19] The demands of the front also brought gender ambiguity as public female impersonation emerged to make up for an absence of women. Entertainment such as singing, dancing, and theater allowed men to recuperate from the physical and emotional demands of the war.

In letters sent to popular magazines, writers testified to the pleasures of appearing as women in these productions. According to these accounts, a need for a feminine presence at the front overcame the distrust of female impersonation and made room for men with cross-dressing desires to move through the public realm in ways that civilian life would not allow. For some, the socially approved opportunity to cross-dress supposedly revealed a heretofore hidden pleasure: "I was, when I joined the Army, I suppose, one of many who looked down on female impersonation as something to be despised." After serving on the line, "Queenie" became a staff member of the Divisional Concert. When one of the "girls" was ill, he played the part. "After the first few nights I began to like the frilly clothes and high heels, corsets, etc., and used to look forward to the evening when I had to dress up. This went on until the push in 1918, when I was once more put into a line battalion, was wounded, and subsequently discharged."[20]

Rather than desexualized displays in which men stepped into women's clothes without registering the erotic potentials of gender bending, letters to magazines suggested that entertainment reviews offered opportunities for erotic pleasures. Some men saw these reviews as opportunities for public disclosure of a secret self. One man for example, always had "the kink of effeminacy" but "the war has given me opportunities of publically displaying my hitherto secret garments." This sergeant in the Mechanical Transport impersonated women so well that he was transferred to a military review. As he explained, "For the past 18 months I have shown almost every night and all over Macedonia and that part of Serbia which then remained in Allies' hands, dressed up in women's clothes, and wearing the tightest of corsets . . . high heeled boots and shoes . . . long, tight-fitting black or white kid gloves, silk stockings, ladies' undies, a wig, and above all, long heavy earrings, for which I had my ears pierced."[21] Entertainment reviews during the war allowed men to enter into new forms of self-display.[22] The fantasy of such public cross-dressing suggests that the front served as a theater of desires as well as a theater of combat.

Other writers in these magazines tried to integrate cross-dressing and combat. Rather than focusing on entertainment reviews as a way to incorporate feminine clothes into military service, these writers sought ways to link the masculine values of bravery, honor, and camaraderie with displays of femininity. One writer, calling himself "Sapper"—a colloquial term for a trench digger—testified to his willingness to fight that went with his longing to wear women's clothes. He ended his letters with a rousing cheer: "Tight lacing and high heels for ever! I trust they will never die."[23] Other writers responded in solidarity. One soldier, in a letter titled "A Bit Kinky," stated that Sapper was "not the only one in khaki who is a lover of corsets and high-heeled footwear." If he lived long enough, the soldier vowed to "obtain a pair of really small stays" and a "pair of high-heeled lace boots."[24] A color sergeant on leave from France stated that he had had a pair of corsets made: "I do not claim that tight lacing has made me more manly, but I can say that I have never had a day's illness, that I have won many prizes for athletics, especially distance running (and I hope to win many more), and that I have roughed it in France since August, 1914, and am going back to rough it as long as may be necessary."[25]

Much like other remembered pleasures, memories of cross-dressing sustained some men at the front. For one soldier, memories of his favorite outfit helped him deal with the demoralizing effects of hospitalization: "A favorite dress of mine used to be silk combies, with plenty of embroidery at the neck and knees, black silk stockings, a long pair of corsets, which I had made for me especially in Paris. I think the thoughts of being able to wear all these things helped me when I was very bad (wounded in hospital) and did not stand much chance of getting about again."[26] Reliving the pleasure of dressing in the outfit sustained him, and the need for privacy to return to cross-dressing hastened his recovery.

Writers used the context of the Great War to think about fitting masculinity and femininity together through the motif of cross-dressing. In some versions, the absence of femininity at the front made room for men to adopt it. In others, cross-dressing compensated for heroism and virility. Though the war contributed to "neurotic" breakdowns and widespread shell shock, it also created a space to consider what that breakdown could mean in terms of gender and sexuality. The extremes of the war dislocated people and enlarged the sphere of the possible. As a result, people worked out a wide variety of ways to envisage fitting cross-dressing into daily life. Certainly, some individuals read accounts of cross-dressing in the midst of the war. Magazines, including ones that featured cross-dressing materials, appeared on the Western Front. One sergeant indicated that soldiers read *Fun* on the front lines as it was "sold extensively in France, and is very popular with all the bhoys," a colloquial term for lads.[27]

Further, some men cross-dressed at the front and appeared in public reviews in women's clothing. Finally, the variety of letters written about corsets and khaki suggests that the canvas of the war allowed people to experiment with gender roles, using the technologies of communication that they had in place.

Cross-Dressing and Contextual Meanings

The motif of cross-dressing continued to circulate after the war and into the 1920s and 1930s in the popular press. The sheer variety of meanings for cross-dressing has implications for how we understand the impact of sexology. The relatively late publication of key sexological books on the topic combined with the continuation of older motifs about the practice in popular literature under-cuts the idea that people absorbed ideas from sexology and began to develop identities as a result. Instead, it looks as if older popular ideas of cross-dressing continued to circulate, affecting how people saw and wrote about themselves. Other scholars have noted this point as well. Alison Oram, for example, ex-plains that she expected to find that sexological ideas helped construct new identities when she began her research on cross-dressing women. Instead, she found an array of stories in the popular press that documented women's brave and mysterious adventures dressed as men. Her study of cross-dressing women demonstrates that such figures remained popular rather than pathological well into the twentieth century.[28]

Gender and sexual flexibility have been found in broader society as well during this period. George Chauncey demonstrates in *Gay New York* that sexual identities did not come in a binary configuration of heterosexual and homosexual in the critical period before the 1930s; instead, an overlapping array of queer articulations allowed for individuals to style themselves in a variety of ways, including cross-dressed, in the metropolis of the city.[29] Laura Doan suggests that in the decade after World War I, British society did not have a unitary way of reading masculine clothing on women. Instead, British society allowed for sexual and gender fluidity. Only with the trial of Radclyffe Hall in 1928 did a masculinist fashionability become tied with sapphism in the popular mind.[30] Matt Houlbrook sees interwar London as central to understanding the range of queer identities. Houlbrook believes that "forms of understanding that we of-ten assume to be timeless—the male sexual practices and identities around the binary oppositions between 'homo- and heterosexual'—solidified only in the two decades after the Second World War."[31] All of these scholars see the inter-war world as central to queer culture. The continued popularity of older mod-els and meanings of cross-dressing confirms their accounts of queer culture.

British society afforded surprising latitude for cross-dressing into the 1920s, though the practice often had unsavory connotations.[32] The theater, for example, had a tradition of cross-dressing woven into its history. Tales of star-crossed lovers and mistaken identities made cross-dressed characters central to Shakespeare's plays. Further, cross-dressing was well established in the theatrical tradition; theatrical productions had historically used male actors to play female characters well into the seventeenth century and female actors for parts of young men in the nineteenth century. According to Marjorie Garber, more than fifty professional actresses played Hamlet in the nineteenth century without the reviews even bothering to note that gender crossing.[33] If the formal world of theater featured cross-dressing in plot lines and casting, the informal theatrical world made room for a diversity of mores, such as men wearing makeup in public and women having sex outside marriage with women as well men. Cross-dressing signaled another latitude given to "theatrical types."

Popular culture assigned a wide range of meanings to the variety of cross-dressed styles. On the stage and in popular culture, cross-dressing was played for comedy and burlesque. In cheap ephemera, the sight of a man dressed as a woman was always guaranteed to get a laugh. Seaside postcards of men in women's dress and women in men's costume were comical and racy, as befitting the pleasures of a seaside holiday. Stories about cross-dressers circulated in such true crime accounts as *Bad Companions* and *Venus Castina* and in newspaper reports that detailed the trials of Radclyffe Hall and "Colonel Barker."[34] Fashion allowed new ways to pattern oneself as ambiguous; fashions for women emphasized the boyish form during the 1920s with the Eton crop, the monocle, and cigarette-stained fingers while men's fashion reformers emphasized the health benefits from sunshine and looser clothing.[35]

Cross-dressing also edged into other forms of social masquerade. Mummers dressed in women's regalia, and social protesters in Enclosure and Luddite riots cross-dressed.[36] Women dressed as men to garner new economic and social opportunities, as cases of women dressing as soldiers and sailors attested.[37] The ability to "pass," whether as a worker for "social detectives" like Arthur Munby, Jack London, and Beatrice Webb or as a "native" for T. E. Lawrence and Richard Burton, had provided a staple form of gathering knowledge in exposés and fiction.[38] Such masquerades had allowed individuals, both respectable and less so, to don disguises and descend downward into the underworld. Even more ominously, some adopted disguises to move upward into the world of their betters. Con artists like Princess Sophie de Bourbon, a cross-dressing man who entered into elite French society in order to steal, kept the perception of cross-dressing at the edge of danger. Such masquerades suggested that public personas concealed deeper truths about people's private selves.

Cross-dressing appeared in both obscene goods and the popular press. Letters and columns about cross-dressing had appeared in the magazines *Modern Society* and *Photo Bits*. *Photo Bits*, after being renamed *New Photo Fun* and then *Photo Fun* before being shorted to *Fun* and then again renamed *Bits of Fun*, resumed publication and printed cross-dressing letters until 1920, when it again failed. In 1923, *London Life* picked up the practice of publishing correspondence including a strain of cross-dressing letters that augmented articles about the practice. More than a thousand letters about cross-dressing as well as several dozen short stories, articles, and exposés were published in these venues.[39] Most of these letters detailed men's personal histories, their current concerns, and preoccupations. These letters described men's investments in cross-dressing in rich detail. Occasionally individuals wrote about stories they read or heard (including urban rumors that took on a life of their own), but usually people discussed their own cross-dressing practices. Stories and correspondence rarely considered female cross-dressers, except in the case of gender swapping.[40] Certainly women cross-dressed, but the pleasures of the cross-dressing letter apparently eluded them.[41]

In these popular magazines, letter writers created their own definitions and meanings for the practice. In popular parlance, cross-dressing was "the kink," implying something involuntary and morally blameless. According to these writers, they did not choose the kink. As one writer explained it, "I consider my 'kink' a most innocent one, and I live a most blameless life with no thought of evil."[42] The use of the term "kink" became a way of assessing one's variance from the rest of society. The language of kink suggested that those with the kink were just like the rest of society, not really backward or regressive, not perverted, or inverted; instead just a bit bent. The nebulousness of the term *kink* allowed people to use it to describe a wide variety of practices. The term allowed people to describe themselves in a language different from the one used by sexologists or by the larger community. "I, like many of your readers have this kink, and love girls clothes."[43]

Writers relied on slang terms and developed their own explanations for cross-dressing. They discarded the idea of hereditary degeneration. Instead of a path downward, writers posited cross-dressing as a sort of higher or more refined inclination. As one writer stated, "I am neither an idiot nor a degenerate, but I think the love of dainty feminine clothes must have been born in me."[44] This story of innate desire for feminine goods provided a compelling model. Writers believed that good taste was refined taste; in essence, a certain sophistication in taste created an appreciation of feminine garb. As one man, invalided out of the army, explained, "The main principle of male effeminacy is that it is a psychological emotion intuitively engendered by an aesthetic nature, and being aided by refined training."[45] In essence, aesthetic superiority made men vulnerable to the seductive influence of femininity and its regalia.

The model of good taste emphasized gender divisions and furthered gender scripting. Girls, in this model, loved frillies, while men enjoyed the rough-and-tumble aesthetic. Male cross-dressers savored femininity in garb and behavior instead of enjoying a male aesthetic with all that grubby physicality. As one writer explained, "I am supposed to be a man, have to wear coat and trousers, and answer to the name of Dick. And yet I am most womanly in all my tastes and inclinations, and simply loathe and abominate sports and pastimes. Anything rough and boisterous jars and upsets me, while I am passionately fond of all kinds of fancy work, music, singing and painting."[46] Womanly tastes meant hyperrefined tastes that spoke to upper-middle-class modes of comportment. Contemporaneous models of femininity—riding pillion on a motorbike, engaging in sport, and eschewing fancy work—saw men and women meeting on a more neutral ground of gender ambiguity. In contrast, writers to *London Life* wanted to revel in a sense of difference, not similarity. They saw gender distinction as emotionally satisfying.

Writers found cross-dressing a compulsion; once one became bent, it was hard if not impossible to straighten out. One writer calling himself "Badly Kinked" described himself as becoming a cross-dresser as a result of his mother's punishment. After he dirtied his clothes, his mother dressed him as a girl.[47] Another writer saw his kink as innate: "I suppose this kink, if so one can call it, is born with us, and some incident, little or otherwise, calls it to life—at any rate it was so in my case, of which I may say more on a future occasion."[48] Another man explained how a fellow soldier with the "kink" maneuvered him into girls' clothes. While on leave, his friend stole his clothes, leaving in their place a "full rig-out of female attire." The soldier was forced to dress as a girl; according to his account, "The silk underwear felt lovely after wearing khaki so long." Ultimately, he "spent all my leave as a girl, and wore evening dress at dinner, and I had a splendid time, and I now possess the 'kink,' and I suppose I will now my whole life."[49] Whether learned or innate, once men got the kink, they could not conceive of abandoning female dress. For many men, the desire to wear women's clothes became a craving too strong to resist. "I have tried my best to give it up, and on many occasions have destroyed my stock of clothes, but the craving has been too strong, and I have again bought more."[50] Another man had worked up only enough nerve to wear a corset, but he wanted a complete set of women's undergarments: "I crave for a complete set of girls' things."[51] The language of longing made cross-dressing more powerful than mere desire. These writers suggested that the craving to cross-dress took on an urgency often reserved for drink and sex. Once the kink got a hold of men, it kept them in its grip.

The kink did not merely stand in for sexual orientation in letter writers' accounts. It could imply effeminacy in men, but it might not. One writer, for example, suggested that his cross-dressing emerged from a deep form of effeminacy: "For some years I have been prone to forget my sex, in as much as I have always delighted in donning female attire."[52] Others distinguished their desires to cross-dress from any effeminate tendencies. One man liked to wear "dainty, lace-trimmed underwear" and a tight corset but still asserted that he had no feminine hobbies, nothing "namby-pamby in that."[53] Another reviled any sign of effeminacy. "I positively hate the slightest trace of effeminacy in men, and loath the fancy cloth boots which some wear; but tight lacing does not come under that category." Despite his rhetoric, however, he showed himself as willing to think about men and women in sexual terms. He hoped that someday he might join with "other tight lacers of both sexes, when we could indulge in veritable orgies of compression and bondage of the corset in the sympathetic presence of ladies and men who have the gift of enjoying our common 'kink.'"[54] Letter writers to the popular press illustrate the variety of ways people conceptualized cross-dressing, showing how a broad range of individuals scripted their identities and desires. Cross-dressing in the early twentieth century did not merely signal sexual orientation; instead it spoke to aesthetics, to compulsions, and to ambiguity. Indeed, cross-dressing for men continued to have associations of humor, danger, and aesthetic superiority well until the 1930s, when sexological conceptions began to take root.

Sexology theorized cross-dressing relatively late. Rather than emerging in the late nineteenth century as Foucauldian genealogies suggest, key ideas about cross-dressing began to develop in the sexological literature in the 1910s and 1920s. This delayed development gave the popular press latitude to circulate older ideas about cross-dressing in the early twentieth century. As a result, popular ideas about cross-dressing like those in magazines trumped sexological taxonomies well into the 1930s. Magnus Hirschfeld published *Transvestites* in 1910, but the volume was not translated from German into English until the 1990s, thus limiting its circulation in Great Britain.[55] Only in 1928 did Havelock Ellis publish *Eonism*, a supplement to his earlier work on sexual inversion.[56] Despite Ellis's familiarity with Hirschfeld's use of the term *transvestitism*, he built his model from the story of the Chevalier d'Eon de Beaumont, an eighteenth-century nobleman, who midway through his life crossed over into living the life of a woman. Ellis identified five chief classes of eonism:

1. The Heterosexual variety.
2. The Bisexual variety, with an attraction to virile men and feminine women.
3. The Homosexual variety.
4. The Narcissistic variety (regarded as common) in which the feminine components of the subject's nature give satisfaction to his masculine components.
5. The Asexual variety, often impotent and finding full satisfaction in some feminine occupations, as that of a domestic servant.[57]

This taxonomy suggested a wide range of possible identities and desires. According to this rubric, male eonists wore women's clothes and loved women, wore women's clothes and loved both men and women, wore women's clothing and loved men, wore women's clothing and loved the self, and wore women's clothing because they wanted to assume a women's occupation or identity. The single marker for eonism in Ellis's formulation remained sartorial.

Concomitant with Ellis's publication was Radclyffe Hall's *The Well of Loneliness*. Hall explicitly and implicitly used sexological models in the creation of *The Well of Loneliness*. She justified the writing of the book as a case study of inversion: "Being myself a congenital invert, I understood the subject from the inside as well as from medical and psychological text-books."[58] Havelock Ellis wrote the introduction to her original edition and she referred to the works of Richard von Krafft-Ebing and Karl Ulrichs in the body of her book. Hall's story of a masculine woman who dressed as a man and loved women created a direct link between sexological theory and identity. In the body of the novel, the main character's beloved father had a library filled with sexological theory that she read upon his death. In reading the books and the marginalia, she understood herself.[59] Hall thus articulated a way that sexological literature could illuminate the self. However, Heike Bauer points out that rather than just incorporating such sexological notions of inversion, Hall actually reformulated them. Having read German sexology during the year she spent in Dresden, Hall adapted theories of inversion to her literary creations by applying models of male inversion to masculine women. As Bauer notes, Hall's model "derived from the translation of her own life experience into a more accessible fictionalized form, which enabled her to push the boundaries of existing fictional representations of life between women in English while also exceeding the limits of auto/biographical observation that bind the sexological case study."[60] At the point where sexological theory ended and lived experience faltered, Hall created a fictional identity. Laura Doan concurs that Radclyffe Hall made use of sexological ideas of inversion but refashioned it to create the sorts of masculine identity that she wanted. According to Doan, "Hall's novel . . . is not a literary realization of either Ellis or Carpenter but a fusion of sexologies, myths, utopian evolutionary theory, and religion."[61]

Jay Prosser offers an oppositional reading of Hall's work by suggesting that it was not a lesbian text, as it is most often considered, but one that made room for the categories of transgender and transsexual, areas that also received sexological consideration in the 1920s and 1930s.[62] According to Prosser, the text allowed for the emergence of new identities based on gender reassignment. These new identities were augmented by the willingness of medicine to transform the body through surgeries and new hormonal therapies. From Vienna came reports of research done on rats and guinea pigs while transplantation surgery tried to "fix" sexual aberrations during the 1910s. By the 1920s, the Institute for Sexual Science under the leadership of Magnus Hirschfeld began to facilitate surgeries for sexual reassignment. Surgical reassignment of sex became possible during the 1920s and 1930s and quickly made it into public notice.[63] Dorchen Richter began to modify her sex through a series of surgeries including castration in 1922 and vaginal construction in 1931. She stayed at Hirschfeld's institute as a demonstration model until the Nazis shut down the institute in 1933. Sex changes, though problematic given the state of plastic surgery, nonetheless became a possibility by the 1930s. The choice of sex change made the links between biological sex and gender roles more tenuous and allowed the differentiation of transsexual from transvestite.

This period in the late 1920s was critical in the formulation of the ideas of inversion, lesbianism, transvestitism, and transsexualism, but these ideas came late in comparison with the ideas circulating in the popular press. As a result of this delay, sexological conceptions had only limited impact on the circulation of ideas in popular magazines until after the late 1930s. Few writers in popular magazines mentioned theories about cross-dressing, and among those who did, one stressed the need to read German, for example, while another thought that Hirschfeld's theories on impersonation as a form of escapism might be true.[64] These two mentions of Hirschfeld were surrounded by dozens of letters that detailed the delights of the corset for men. Even when psychotherapy promised to illuminate sexuality, popular ideas about the kink remained paramount.[65] Instead of standing as the final word, a psychology columnist remained junior partner to the long-running column on graphology (handwriting analysis) and wedged between such letters as "The Peacock Propensity," "A Lover of Tights," "We're the Tops," and "Oh Boy!"

Thus, popular conceptions of cross-dressing—rather than sexologically de-rived ones—continued to circulate well into the 1930s. The circulation of these ideas in popular magazines did not mean people lived such scenarios, however. While people may have enjoyed reading about cross-dressing in such maga-zines as *Photo Bits* and *London Life*, they may not have incorporated ideas from popular mediums into their own sexual stories or into their sexual practices. Further, censorship patterns meant that any erotic scripting in such magazines needed to curtail the overt discussion of sexual behaviors in order to be sold legally in Britain. As a result, such materials demonstrated the ways that ideas of cross-dressing circulated in the ephemeral press, but they did not explain people's erotic attachment to the practice or detail how people experienced cross-dressing as a set of sexual desires. To consider how readers understood cross-dressing as a set of practices linked to erotic desires, this chapter ad-dresses the market in erotic materials in order to return to Mr. Hyde.

Mr. Hyde and the Erotics of Cross-Dressing

The marketplace in materials about sexuality had been split at the end of the nineteenth century into one that sold obscene goods from the continent and another that sold legal materials published in England. Through a series of laws passed in the nineteenth century, the state forced publishers and vendors of ex-plicit materials out of Great Britain by the 1890s. Rather than ending the sale of explicit materials, however, the restrictions on obscene materials bifurcated the market. Restrictions on erotic content created the mail order market in which continental vendors sold obscene materials to a population in England. Even as the restrictions on the sale of obscenity created the marketplace for materials through mail order, it also created a particular sort of legal market. A series of legal, though disreputable, magazines began to spread in the early twentieth century. These materials discussed the practices and emotional connections but did not discuss intercourse, genitals, caresses, kisses, or even sexual desire more broadly. The censorship practices of the British state created two distinct markets.

Mr. Hyde described himself as a regular reader of *Photo Bits* during the last few years of its publication and said that he mourned its demise in 1912. However, he must have been reading back issues of the publication because he mentioned the years 1898–1902, when he would have been only a child. He also mentions *Society* from the years 1900–1901. Though he had never read it, he had heard a lot about it and remained committed to finding copies in the used-magazine trade. Such references suggest that the circulation of ephemera could last for decades, and ideas published during one's youth could still affect an adult's desires. Hyde was looking for old magazines because they provided information still relevant to his desires. According to his own account, "The correspondents of *Photo Bits* generally discussed High Heels, tight-lacing, discipline, Heel drill, etc. etc. including female impersonation, and I would very much like to know if these are the subjects dealt with and if so, to purchase them."[66]

By 1923, Mr. Hyde was staying at the Mandeville Hotel in London. He described himself as a clerk. He apparently had a few investments that offered him a bit of ready cash. He also seemed to have augmented his formal income with some sort of trade and possibly a bit of blackmail. At least he seemed to have a large number of acquaintances with people, such as G. Conway Williams and Jules Cohen, who, according to Hyde's own account, would not respond well to the mention of his name.

Hyde wrote to Cyril Benbow in response to an advertisement in *The Bazaar*. Benbow was considerably older and billed himself as an antiques dealer, according to his business card.[67] He was born in 1872 and operated out of Exeter.[68] Benbow had been acting as agent for Ricardo Gennert, a pornography dealer operating from Barcelona who sent obscene goods to customers across Europe. Cyril Benbow found clients in Britain and took orders for obscene books and photographs. He sent along the orders to Gennert. For his assistance, Gennert paid him a third of the total purchase price. Benbow was not a major player; he made perhaps £40 off the trade in all.[69] Harry Cocks suggests that Benbow worked out of the poorly regulated personal columns to garner customers. By vehemently denying any knowledge of erotica in such advertisements, Benbow guaranteed his customer base.[70] Benbow was suspicious of Hyde's return address at a hotel, but Hyde convinced him that it was his permanent residence: "I live here and shall continue to live here." Hyde was looking for either companions or a dealer in goods. As he explained:

> You see I am ardently enthusiastic about the subjects I mentioned in the first letter, not only in theory but also in practice and would be much obliged if you would give me the full particulars of the books and pictures on these subjects not forgetting to mention their respective prices. Please tell me, are you a professional buyer and seller or is it you are an enthusiastic amateur?

Benbow as it turned out was not "enthusiastic." While sorry not to have met a companion, Hyde decided that "all that matters is that you have books and pictures, photographs, etc: on those subjects." In fact, Hyde replied with an offer that suggests he was not unfamiliar with the trade; rather than paying outright for the price list (£1 as a deposit), Hyde suggested instead that he buy a catalog at a reduced price. He showed himself a canny—or cautious—negotiator, holding out his association with a "number of other enthusiasts of both sexes" as part of an exchange.[71] Roughly a week later, he made a more explicit proposal. Hyde offered to barter with Benbow: "I will give you the names and addresses of all my friends and acquaintances who would be most likely to buy the goods you offer for sale." If Benbow did not want to swap names—though what Hyde planned to do with Benbow's list of names remains unclear—he was willing to sell or barter the names of his acquaintances: "Please let me know how much you want for 20 or 50 names bearing in mind that I shant be making money out of these people (men and women) but you certainly stand a chance of making something."[72] Apparently, Benbow cut a deal with Hyde because Hyde promised to send along a list of his contacts: "I shall get out my address book tonight when secure in my room and send you all the names and addresses of friends and acquantances [sic] to whom it will be quite safe for you to get in touch with."[73] Hyde may have had a dodgy relationship with many of these acquaintances, as he explicitly stated and then reiterated that Benbow should not use his name in many cases and that some knew him only by his accommodation or by a pseudonym.

Hyde worked as an intermediary between continental dealers in obscenity and British consumers for obscene goods, but in a small way since he did not count himself "in the trade" as much as an enthusiast about the trade and its paraphernalia. However, he supplied Benbow with the names and addresses of alternative dealers when Benbow's price list proved a disappointment. One of the dealers that Hyde recommended, a G. Karoly, operated out of Barcelona and may have been an alias for Gennert. Hyde recommended him as "a Good seller of very nice photos, etc., very cheap who might be useful to you. Mention my name." The other dealer, R. Bourzac, 15 Rue Collette, worked from Paris. The difference in prices was made more clear when Hyde compared costs for the same batch of photos, Lot E, No. 65. It cost 32 shillings 4 pence for twenty-two photos on Benbow's price list, whereas Hyde bought them in two different sizes for less than twenty francs or slightly more from Spain. This point of comparison also illustrates the ways that images circulated across Europe and would appear and reappear in numerous countries. (Prints would be made from the negatives and from new sets of negatives made by rephotographing another's stock.) Hyde knew agents in England as well and mentioned a Charing Cross book dealer by the name of Davis. He also proffered the name of a photographer, one James Johnson Esquire, from Clapham Junction, with the note that "he could help you I think among his own customers[.] [S]uggest it to him."

Hyde provided Benbow with exactly twenty-five contacts as promised. Most lived in London, though Hyde also mentions individuals in Birmingham, South Wales, Bristol, and New York. Hyde inscribed a note alongside the names that suggested whether Benbow should mention his name, mention a pseudonym (such as George H. Barker), or not mention his name at all. For instance, Benbow should not mention Hyde's name to either H. A. Jager Esq. from London or Capt. T. P. Pugh, Royal Automobile Club, Pall Mall. Hyde thought it might help to have his name mentioned to Major C. A. Hope of Wilts and Jack

Biden Esq. of Charing Cross Road. Two of the names had substantive notations suggesting the sorts of contacts these might be. According to Hyde, Madame Corti, who lived in the top flat of Majestic Mansions, Tottenham Court Road, would "do also for your friend who likes corporal punishment, get him to write her."[74] K. (Kitty) Rowade of New York, according to Hyde, was a "very useful person who buys lots of little waist photographs, write to him & tell him I gave you his address."[75] Hyde's descriptions of Corti and Rowade suggest that they were the "enthusiasts of both sexes" that he mentioned in the previous letter. The fact that he wanted his name kept from more than half of the contacts raises questions about the nature of these relationships. He may have been dealing in obscenity, as the notation about Rowade implied; he might have been blackmailing them, a frequent occurrence for sexual irregularities, according to Angus McLaren's brilliant study of the practice; or he may have worked hard to maintain his anonymity.[76]

In his statement to the police, Hyde admitted his relationship with Benbow, including his part in supplying names and addresses. In fact, according to the testimony, he was willing to "admit everything." Hyde's police testimony noted the seriousness and his regrets: "I wish I had broken away from those people. I did not realize until now the seriousness of what I was doing."[77] The police took possession of Hyde's trunk in which he locked all of his indecent matter and cross-dressing paraphernalia. According to the police list, it contained the following:

3 hair fringes
1 lady's navy blue costume.
1 lady's pink silk nightdress.
1 pair lady's red garter's.
1 pair lady's pink stockings.
3 pair dark stockings.
5 arm bangles.
1 set black beads
2 hair combs.
3 boxes face powder.
1 tube lip salve.
1 blue skirt.
1 black silk skirt.
1 pink silk petticoat.
7 pairs high heeled shoes.
1 pair high heeled boots.
1 cream skirt.
1 white neck fur.
1 pink lace petticoat.
1 pink jumper.
1 white wool jumper.

2 pairs corsets.
1 skirt (blue and red stripe)
2 white nightdresses.
1 pair lady's white kid gloves.
1 pink underskirt, trimmed black.
1 white jumper.
1 white undervest (lady's)
1 cane with leather thong.
2 rectum extenders.
1 lady's wig.
1 set lady's suspenders.

Five Books as follows:—
1. Phoebe Kissagen
2. In wallpaper cover, containing indecent photographs.
3. Le Musee Secret de Naples.
4. Red Book containing indecent photographs.
5. Typed book on figure training.

Hyde's collection also contained two photographs of Hyde in female attire, one packet of indecent photographs, and one file of indecent sketches.[78]

Hyde's wardrobe made the most of the revival of consumer culture. If the standard women's uniform consisted of white silk stockings, a skirt, simple white blouse, and cardigan or overcoat, with gloves and a hat for the street, then Mr. Hyde had surpassed the standard and had fashioned himself at the flirty edge of style.[79] He had invested in the latest colors and showed himself committed to full sets of lingerie. His pink stockings, petticoat, and underskirt matched a pink lace petticoat and jumper. While he showed a marked preference for clothes to be worn in private, his outerwear did not skimp. A black silk skirt, a white neck fur, and white kid gloves suggest his financial commitment to display. The materials demonstrate a willingness to make the most of the sumptuous market of the interwar fashion scene.

Hyde may well have been trying to pass as a woman; however, the seized possessions were heavy on lingerie. The number and assortment of nightdresses, petticoats, stockings, garters, and suspenders suggest that Hyde wore these articles as erotic gear in private. Hyde also made quite an investment in high-heeled boots and shoes, an area of considerable erotic focus and one that mail order made easy to arrange. Both Mr. Oliver of Chancery Lane and Mr. Johnson of Bristol made very high heels, according to Hyde's address book.[80] Eight pairs total would be no small financial investment and would rival the number worn by female aficionados of high heels. Hyde also noted Dr. C. H. Willi for Aesthetic Surgery; appointments with Gertrude Hope, of Portman Square, for Hair Destroyer; and Helen Ray 15 Hanover Street for Hair Killer.[81] The photographs of Hyde cross-dressed attest to the fact that he wanted not only to cross-dress but also to see himself cross-dressed, that part of the pleasure emerged from the scopic value rather than from physical sensation of silks on skin.

Because the popular press curtailed the discussion of sexual intercourse, excised simple sexual acts such as kisses, and eliminated discussions of sexual desire, the ability to insert sexual longings into a discussion of cross-dressing proves eminently valuable. Mr. Hyde's possessions demonstrate that cross-dressing spoke to not only masculinity and femininity but also sexual desire. Hyde's books, photos, sketches, and possessions connect sexuality with cross-dressing. Hyde's possession of a cane suggests flagellant desires, the books of indecent photographs suggest a desire to envision nudity and various forms of copulation, and the rectum extenders may have been dildos. His appointment book noted "dildoes" next to Miss Ivy N. Bornford of Slough, Bucks, while a catalog of Benbow's included both male and female dildoes.[82] Together these articles suggest sexual desires that extended beyond mere presentation into some form of sexual activity.

The police also found a box, sealed and tied with a string, that contained a number of books. The list included the following:

1. The Horn Book.
2. The History of the Rod.

3. Love's Encyclopedia.
4. Gynecocracy.
5. Susan Aked.
6. My Married Life.
7. Lustful Turk, 2 volumes.
8. Nemesis Hunt, 3 volumes.
9. Venus and Adonis.
10. Spirit of Flagellation.
11. Figure Training.[83]

Together, these volumes represented old standards of pornographic fare rather than a particularly specialized set of books. *The Lustful Turk* (1828), a nineteenth-century classic written as a series of epistles, described harem life. *The Horn Book*, alternatively titled *Modern Studies in the Science of Stroking*, first appeared in French as a calligraphic manuscript that had been published as lithographic reproduction titled *Instruction Libertine*. It was translated into English in the 1890s and then republished, reprinted, and advertised throughout the 1900s, 1910s, and 1920s. A new reprint in 1923 had just been struck from the 1899 plates. An early advertisement stated that "this is one of the most shocking books ever printed. It is perfectly obscene; in fact, a Storehouse of obscenity; a Mass of filth pure and simple. The author whoever he was, has sought out the very lowest, filthiest, and most obscene words to be found in the English language in order to describe scenes that would make a Gorilla blush for shame." A later ad suggests it represented "Good Value for Money." *The Horn Book* included dialogues on masturbation, sodomy, and tribadism, ways of varying pleasure, and postures without "introduction of the virile member."[84] *Susan Aked* was also a nineteenth-century publication, though usually printed under the title of *The Simple Tale of Susan Aked*. Hyde's copy may have been some sort of expurgation or altered text, a common practice in the trade. Similarly, *My Married Life*, a work first published in 1900, seemed to be a translation of a 1893 French volume and may have been a fragment of a larger volume. *The History of the Rod* and *The Spirit of Flagellation*, both whipping stories, were also standard pornographic texts in the British market. *The Spirit of Flagellation* was first published in London in 1827 and saw frequent reprints throughout the nineteenth and twentieth century. *The History of the Rod* was first published in 1870 under the title *Flagellation and the Flagellants*.[85]

Gynecocracy (1893) featured "petticoat discipline," a more specialized niche in the market that focused on cross-dressing as a putative act. Peter Mendes traces the volume through the *Enfer* catalogue, where it was suggested that 'un avocat Londinen, M. St. nisl. s. de Rh. d. s." wrote the book, who may have been Stanislaus Matthew de Rhodes, who was a barrister at the Inner Temple during the period of its initial publication.[86] The novel was written as a fictional memoir of Julian Robinson, Viscount Ladywood. Its structure as a memoir creates a nostalgic quality, even when originally published in the 1890s. This narrative structure dwells on a childhood long past. By the 1920s, when Hyde's copy was seized by the police, this past was at least two generations removed.

According to *Gynecocracy*, petticoats generated a powerful pull, and corsets left fantasies in their wakes. Emblematic of the separate and mysterious world of women, the petticoat—layered, ruffled, frilly, smelling of the "strange intoxicating perfume" of female bodies—disciplined men through sexual longing.[87] Women's petticoats became the wrappers of their sexual bodies, and the petticoat functioned as the portal into feminine sexuality.[88] The desire to crawl under a woman's petticoat could trap a man and make him into mere lapdog to women's needs. Once men were trapped by petticoats, they would be subject to what was called "petticoat discipline." First, they would be dressed as women, according to *Gynecocracy*. The layers of female clothing—the stockings, garters, belts, corsets, drawers, petticoats, dresses, and high heels—trained individuals into compliance and submission irrespective of biological sex. Rather than femininity emanating from the soul onto the body, this book suggested that femininity emerged from the body and then spilled onto the soul. In a second iteration of petticoat discipline, by spanking, whipping, and birching boys and men, women returned them to the nursery, where they become suspended in a state of childish longing and terror. The reminder of an earlier weakness deflated any sense of masculine superiority and revisited a moment of female authority.

These forms of petticoat discipline mutually reinforced each other in *Gynecocracy*. The story becomes a bondage/domination, sadomasochist (BD/SM) fantasy. Julian is birched, beaten, half drowned, forced to drink urine, tickled along his palate and throat, circumcised, sodomized, pierced, tied up, and hanged. His longing to crawl under a woman's skirts inevitably led to other forms of petticoat discipline in which he was dressed as a woman and then beaten into submission. At an even broader level, the story presented petticoat revenge as a fantastical nightmare of powerlessness in which adult women tortured adolescents for sexual pleasure. The brutality of the account, articulated through crushed testicles, bleeding foreskins, bloody backs, and other bodily markers carried its own evocative register that spoke to male vulnerability and female physical strength. The digs and twists, casual cruelties, and calculated violence in these elaborate scenarios of sex and torture suggested that another femininity lay underneath a formal and prettified surface. And who's to say that such a femininity did not exist? Perhaps this fantasy recouped the damages done, or perhaps it rehearsed pleasures experienced long ago. The question of male submission to female dominance rested on memories of childhood and nostalgia about inequalities.

Similarly to the ways that *Gynecocracy* memorialized a relationship between pain and femininity, writers to correspondence columns used memories of childhood to dwell on the patterns of earlier pain and submission. In eroticizing inequalities, these letters often focused on memories from childhood and detailed the forcible cross-dressing of boys. They entreated mothers to dress boys as girls and encouraged men to recount their own histories.[89] "I was exceedingly interested in the pinnies for boys letters. These were to me, of real interest, having once been dressed in petticoats and lacey knickers etc., myself as a boy."[90] These letters detailed an inequality of adult-child relations that played out in clothing. The ability to make boys submit to female authority heightened their humiliation and eroticized the abuse. Rather than suggesting that gender did not matter, these letters created elaborate rationales and justifications for cross-dressing that played up the distinctions of gender. One writer, for example, detailed his adoption and enforced conversion to female garb in great detail. "My parents died when I was about twelve years old, and I was adopted by a wealthy relative who had no children. This lady was a widow of about 25, who had been abominably treated by the husband, and in consequence, hated the male sex. She determined that I was to be brought up as a girl, and this plan was immediately put into execution."[91] Forced gender conversion highlighted the differences of the sexes and articulated gender as a BD/SM system, for both the female relative and the boy. For these writers, gender trapped everyone and cross-dressing became a way to consider the confines.[92]

The recurrent theme that women punished boys by dressing them as girls saw gender as a form of discipline and sexual humiliation that could curb male excess. "Now he regularly wears pinafores and girl's shoes in the house and strap shoes for outside. He is quite reformed, and now that he has grown used to them I think he likes his pinnies and stockings and little shoes."[93] Though women often initiated male cross-dressing, they did so to make boys compliant. "She has told him that if this does not mend his ways, she would put him into frocks and frilled petticoats. There is no need to make the boy suck the baby's dummy [pacifier]. The fact that it is there humiliates him."[94] In these elaborate scenarios, women humiliated boys through gender reversal and by dressing boys as young girls.

In letters that focused on gender reversal, gender functioned as a completed relationship, a closed economy of roles. In this closed system, changes to one side brought changes to the other. However, these letters attested to more than a simple reverse sexism. Instead, writers used cross-dressing to discuss the differences between sex and gender at a moment when the vocabulary was incapable of making that distinction. Because of a dearth of terms, writers adapted ideas already in circulation to new purposes. One writer, for example, described a gender economy in which men would have to assume the petticoat since women had abandoned it. For some, the changes in women's fashion created an imbalance in roles and relations. A letter called "When Girls All Wear Breeches" described the double inversion of girls in trousers and men in skirts.[95] If women wore pants, according to this logic, men would have to wear dresses.

Gender, according to this logic, insisted on complementarity whether between equals or between dominant and submissive. As one writer explains, "A complete metamorphosis is taking place. This is to say, that ehe [sic] female sex will, within a comparatively short time, become the dominant sex and the power in the land. In contra-distinction to this man must, and by all laws of consequences, become subservient to woman." Clothes functioned as the symbol of that superiority; whoever dominated should wear the pants, according to the writer: "The trousers have always been a sign of superiority. Also, I would add, the petticoat has ever been a symbol of weakness. When, therefore, man becomes definitely under the heel of woman, he will be forced to step into the petticoat which woman has discarded."[96] In this model, clothes meant more than adornment or artifice. Instead, they tied gender roles to power dynamics in the relationship. If women dominated, men would be forced to submit. Another writer labeled the submissive energy as specifically female. According to "Submissive Husband," "Certain men, so science tells us, have a strong feminine streak in them, and feel no regret, but rather pleasure, in submitting to a woman of dominating personality."[97]

This idea that femininity in men called for a masculine woman reached an apogee in a letter titled "Wanted: A Masculine Soul-Mate" in which "Hopeful" sought a masterful wife. "Hopeful" had been reading London Life for years and found special pleasure in letters by "Effeminate Man" and "Masculine Woman." His letter urged "Effeminate Man" to wait until a "girl who is thoroughly able to control him come[s] along—as she surely will some day—and then he will be dominated by her to his heart's content." The letter writer was himself holding out for the right type of woman. His ideal partner would be not only masculine, "tall and strong . . . impervious and compelling" but also dominant. "She will quell me with a glance, and a gesture will bring me quaking to my feet. Not only would she take me for herself and marry me, but she would compel me to take her name, and vow to love, honour and obey her. To such a woman I could not only love, but adore and worship, for I am of very pronounced feminine character."[98] For this writer, masculinity alone was not enough in a woman; instead, his future wife needed to sweep him away with all the charm of a suave and debonair Hollywood Lothario. These letters stressed a gender polarization, rather than a gender ambiguity. While these fantasies offered room to envision gender apart from biological sex, they played off stereotypes about masculinity and femininity by magnifying them.

In these accounts, mastery and servility stood counterpoised. Female masculinity—with all the paraphernalia of authority—spoke to a desire to humiliate and dominate the biological man, now feminized into hypersexualized servility. As one letter explained a scenario of these relations:

> The wife will don an evening suit with starched shirt front, and the husband a "dinner gown" reaching to his knees, made of "Cellophane" material to show his undies and his tattoo or identification mark. After the evening's entertainment, home to bed.

In all things the husband will be made to obey the wife implicitly, and be completely subject to her dominance. A wife will parade an erring husband before her friends with a collar round his neck and on a thin silver or gold chain, like a dog, to show who is master. Or she will make him kneel before her for hours, and use him as a human footstool. In extreme cases of insubordination or disobedience, he will be severely whipped after being tied to a whipping post.[99]

When they exchanged clothes, men and women role-played gender as differences in power. Tattoos, dog chains, and whipping became markers of dominance and submission. Rather than undoing gender, cross-dressing saw in gender codes all sorts of fraught potentialities and exploited them.

In both obscene books and legal magazines, the ideas of cross-dressing allowed writers to consider gender apart from biological sex. To stay on the right side of the law, legal magazines eschewed all sorts of sexual caresses. As a result, letters in these magazines highlighted the physical and emotional realms but minimized their sexual implications. Nonetheless, these letters hinted at the erotic appeal to such scenarios. Illegal publications, such as *Gynecocracy,* complemented such letters by adding sexual organs, sexual intercourse, sexual pleasure, and sexual pain. While letters to the correspondence columns mapped the continued appeal of such scenarios, the circulation of obscene texts mapped the erotic implications of the letters. The two fit hand in glove.

Queer Desires and Queer Networks

Hyde's possession of obscene books illustrates the ways that older publications and ideas continued to circulate in Britain and across Europe. New books rarely entered the stream of obscene publications, and older texts remained around for generations, no doubt affecting people's sexual consciousness. These books shipped from abroad—sometimes even struck off older plates—still garnered strong prices. The state limited sexual knowledge about pleasure—rather than knowledge about pathologies or illness—so that illegal and antiquated pornography formed a repository of ideas about pleasure.

Hyde's ownership of these volumes also suggests that he had a passing interest in penile/vaginal intercourse, orientalist eroticism, sodomy, flagellation, older women, tribadism, and cross-dressing. His ownership of *Gynecocracy,* his cross-dressing, and his flagellant paraphernalia indicate that Hyde incorporated some of these motifs into his sense of self. Unfortunately, they do not indicate whether he liked men or women. Few books in the marketplace featured male-male sexual relations. *Teleny* and *The Sins of the Cities of the Plain or Recollections of a Mary-Ann* were among the exceptions. Even if Hyde enjoyed such works—and it is not at all clear that he would have—their relative rarity made them hard to find.

Benbow's other clients had interests that differed from Hyde's. Thompson Cockcroft, for instance, a clerk from Salford, Manchester, ordered *Forbidden Fruit*—a book about pedophilia—but that book was out of stock, so Benbow offered him *My Beautiful Mother* instead.[100] Ronald Matheson, a commission agent for a coed preparatory school, ordered *Flossie—A Venus of Fifteen*.[101] Matheson was also interested in cinema films, but these were hard to come by and quite expensive. Benbow offered to find one if given a £5 deposit. He had sold a 520-foot film for roughly £8 and had already shipped it to Florida.[102] John Stewart desired photographs including "licking and sucking, pissing scenes, young ladies pregnant, corpulent ladies, big and clear sexual organs, big-breasted women, women being licked by dogs, white backsides, standing cocks, he-goat and peasant woman, sexual parts, woman fucked from behind, and her first fuck." Stewart also ordered a fairly standard list of books, though the only ones that overlapped with Hyde's were *Love's Encyclopedia* and *The Horn Book*.[103] Children, film, pregnancy, and bestiality seem absent from Hyde's list. In comparison to Benbow's wider clientele, Hyde's choices were antiquated in terms of themes, publication dates, and delivery styles. His tastes ran to flagellation rather than children, and nostalgia rather than the latest technology.

Scrupulously transcribed into the court notes, Hyde's address book gives further hints about his life. His address book illustrates a network of relationships that tied together cross-dressing, flagellation, male-male sexual relations, high heels, and corsets. Hyde littered people's names, addresses, and interests throughout his calendar, and his address book became a way to keep track of contacts: John Cooper of Sussex ("Female Impersonating"), John Dawson of Wolverhampton ("Flagellation, Discipline"), H. G. Day ("Photo Seller"), F. Servin ("Anything"), and Dr. A. V. Fiddian ("Men and Men").[104] In October, Hyde met additional contacts including Edgar Humphrey, R.H.T. Ives, and T. Prince, who liked "all kinds of stuff." So did W. E. Johnson, though Hyde notes additional damning information "(a parson, all kinds of stuff, lots of it.)." F. R. Stevens liked flagellation; W. H. Thravis was interested in "men and men." Granville Pickup, an automobile engineer, liked high heels and answered Hyde's ad for "re: 2 pairs for sale" that had been placed in "Exchange and Mart." J. W. Fitzwilliam was interested in high heels and corsets.[105] Hyde maintained a list of addresses throughout the United Kingdom, though his network linked individuals as far away as South Africa and New York.

Hyde's contacts demonstrate a great deal about queer culture, including its geographic spread, the range of queer practices, and its class associations. His list of contacts connected London to a range of places from provincial towns to large cosmopolitan centers. The shorthand notations of addresses showed that each contact was something to be noted and treasured. Just as the list linked regions across Britain, so the list of predictions created a network of desires. Hyde's list linked female impersonators, flagellators, "men and men," and discipline. His list also forged relations between classes, as the placement of a parson and a mechanic (automobile engineer) on his list attest. Queer relations pulled together people, rather than dividing them into separate communities. Heterosex and homosex did not divvy up into neat frames. Hyde's case demonstrates the ways that desires overlapped, pulling together queer desires wherever the mails would reach.

Hyde paid close attention to a wide range of newspapers and read the advertising columns carefully, and he used them for gathering information. The *Daily Mail*, the *Morning Post*, and the *Times*, all highly respected venues for news, became paths for the transfer of illicit knowledge. In the *Daily Mail* he found "Wasp waists, etc wanted articles, books, correspondence." In the *Times* he found any number of intriguing ads, including these: "Very high heeled footwear as new. What offers?"[106] and "A Lady of good social position would like to correspond with others interested in tight lacing."[107] He also found this: "Will any lady or corsetiere interested in the super-corseted figure give experience or advice."[108] All of these ads gave post office boxes for replies. In the *Morning Post*, someone published a "books-wanted" ad for the *Englishwoman's Domestic Magazine* (1866–1872), a well-known but legal flagellant periodical; *Family Doctor* (1885–1892); Coleman's *Rodiad*, another whipping work; *Earl Lavender*, known as a spanking classic, a flagellant romp by John Davidson; and *Order of St. Bridget*, a whipping story.[109] Hyde took note of a letter by Jean Wallace titled "Health and High Heels" that was published in the *Daily Mirror* on March 3, 1922.[110] Hyde found coded information in the respectable press that spoke to illicit longings that many individuals might have overlooked. Rather than hidden away in illegal publications, flagellants and cross-dressers corresponded through the toniest of venues.

Hyde showed an interest in women through cryptic notations written with a sense of grand desires: "At last I have found her!" Miss. E. Madge Burgess's name followed the note, but he copied it in only to cross it out. (The police transcription followed the practice of copying and crossing out the name.)[111] Two years later, another woman captured his interest. "The Bomb has been dropped and is fusing. it will burst I know it will. How shall I miss her. Will she come back into my life???"[112] Later in the month, he noted someone at Piccadilly Circus who caught his interest: "black patent leather lace shoes, pointed toes, very high heels, looked very smart, short & pretty."[113] Clearly, Hyde had passionate feelings for women and carefully noted women's garb. On another occasion, he took note of an evening of dancing at the Ritz Hotel. "Black beaded frock, Spanish comb, Red (high) heeled black satin pointed toed shoes with brilliant buckles (large) inserted with red. Very nice."[114] Hyde was queer in his desires, and who or what he desired remains ambiguous.

In 1923, Mervyn Hyde was convicted of "conspiring with other persons to corrupt public morals, to publish obscene libels and to send indecent articles through the post; inciting persons to sell and publish obscene books; and aiding persons to publish obscene libels and to send indecent articles through the post." He pleaded guilty and was sentenced to serve nine months without hard labor while Cyril Benbow received eighteen months.[115]

After prison, Hyde traveled extensively.[116] By 1935 he was a manufacturer's representative and crossed the ocean again, this time traveling from Sydney to San Francisco.[117] He left the States only to return again in 1939, when he traveled to New York as an export manager, with someone listed as Mr. George Long.[118] In 1960, he retired to England, and in 1967, Mervyn Hyde died in New York of unknown causes.[119]

Conclusion

The case of Mervyn Hyde illustrates the ways that sexual opportunities and middle-class identity were hard to acquire. Hyde grew up in the colonies and sought to make a life for himself in the metropolis. Though the colonial world supposedly provided a pressure valve for young men's aspirations, and colonial emigration was lauded as a manly alterative to urban life, Hyde could not find a place for himself on the frontier and could not replicate his father's example of entering into colonial service. As a result, he, like millions of other men, saw war as the answer. In good health he enlisted and received a commission. By 1916, however, the Western Front made a hash of his aspirations. His own analysis that the war contributed to his neurosis may well be true. Serving on the Western Front may have snapped his nerves, resulting in a life on the margins. Alternatively, his sexual predilections may have shown themselves during the war and contributed to the loss of his commission.

In any event, he returned from the war to the great metropolis, where he lived at the margins of respectability. Though he called himself a clerk, there is no evidence of continuous employment. Instead, investments in various industrial enterprises offered small dividends of ready cash. Hyde traded along the edge of a sexualized consumer culture, answering ads for erotica and posting ads for cross-dressing paraphernalia. His diary indicated an attention to building relations with men and women involved in sexual nonconformity. He not only met a wide array of people; he also recommended them to one another. He took note of male-male desires, cross-dressing, and flagellation. Hyde may have used these contacts for pecuniary purposes, but he may also have seen himself as creating social and sexual networks between outcasts.

Hyde's life on the margins shows us how individuals exchanged information about illicit sexuality. People passed along the location of stores, photographers, and mail-order premises through notes sent to anonymous P.O. boxes, through ads placed in newspapers and magazines, and through the back pages of personal columns. These methods of transmission supplied Hyde with what he wanted—face powder, women's shoes, dildos, and canes. They also connected him with services—such as photography, cosmetic surgery, and hair removal—that let him see himself as he envisioned. A lively trade in back issues of magazines and erotica that circulated and recirculated provided a background for people's own constructions of desire. For Hyde, the trade in books and magazines provided him with a set of ideas about "the kink."

Hyde's life illustrates that readers' letters to magazines such as *Bits of Fun* and *London Life* spoke to practices as well as fantasies. The desire to live sexual stories as well as articulate them in print culture encouraged some individuals to act out their fantasies in daily life. Letter writers talked about dressing men in the frilliest of women's clothes. Hyde had the clothes to match the fantasies. Writers explored the idea of men wearing women's clothes in a variety of public venues; Hyde's photographs of himself cross-dressed showed that he appeared in at least some public areas dressed as a woman. Letter writers desired to meet each other and engage in "orgies" with others who enjoyed a "common 'kink.'"[120] Hyde had the contacts to prove that he did. Letter writers suggested that the practice proved a respite from hypermasculinity in a time of war. Certainly, Hyde—and those around him—saw the war as a moment that ruptured his emotional framework, resulting in neurosis. Letter writers linked "the kink" with ideas of BD/SM, and Hyde had the cane. Letter writers suggested erotic energies around the practice, and Hyde had the pornography that articulated how cross-dressing could have orgasmic potential. In short, Hyde's material existence correlates with the mental world that a variety of letter writers articulated.

Published correspondence in the ephemeral press certainly demonstrates how people chose to conceptualize themselves. However, the question of veracity has haunted these letters. Hyde's existence begins to answer questions of the truthfulness of these accounts. Though some letter writers may have offered entirely fictitious projections (and may never have been dressed as a woman in public, for example), Mr. Hyde lived what others described. His case links practices with projections. This point does not suggest that cross-dressing letters merely reported facts. Instead, it suggests that "the kink" described more than just the fantasy of a few editors. Certainly, Hyde existed in ways that letter writers described, and his interests correlated with the stories they told. His existence suggests that the narratives of cross-dressing may have had real relevance in people's lives and that such fantasies could contribute to the making of a sexual self.

Further, his case extends the realm of queer scholarship by showing that cross-dressing practices, beliefs, and identities overlapped in the interwar years, before the broad acceptance of sexological taxonomies. Despite the tendency for cross-dressing to become a derivative of inversion in the sexological literature, in ephemeral literature cross-dressing appealed to men who saw it as a relief from masculinity, sadomasochists who saw it as a humiliation, and adults who remembered erotic moments of childhood. Cross-dressing meant many different things simultaneously, and the consideration of the practice extends the realm of queer. By rejecting androgyny, cross-dressing in these accounts built on a gender economy that eroticized difference and that valued extreme examples of masculinity and femininity. Femininity needed masculinity even if those traits were not tied to biological sex. This point suggests that perhaps people in the early twentieth century had a stronger concept of gender apart from biological sex than most accounts of the past suggest. Certainly, cross-dressers and those who wrote letters about cross-dressing saw masculinity and femininity applying equally well to men and women. They understood gender as separate from sex and pointed out the ways that sex and gender fit together. For many, the point of cross-dressing was to savor gender as antithetical qualities. Men who dressed as women delighted in embodying an excessive notion of femininity, and women who explored a masculine self did so at the most butch margins.

Furthermore, cross-dressing had an erotic component that would be easy to overlook if not for the examination of obscene sources. The addition of pornography to cross-dressing letters returns the erotic element that has been leeched out of legal publications. The case of Hyde shows us that there is a highly sexual subtext—illustrated in *Gynecocracy*—that underlay legal letters in *Bits of Fun* and *London Life*. While the letter writers detailed how they dressed and how they felt, they rarely mentioned genitals or sexual acts. In Hyde's case, the circulation of obscene stories fills in the missing pieces. In obscene and outlawed literature, men renounced the burdens of masculine satisfaction to be beaten like children. Such publications expressed genital arousal in punishment and mixed orgasmic delights with cruelty. Dressing as women was but one of the many arousing humiliations that could be visited on men. It may have been easier to reason through cross-dressing without sadomasochism, dildos, and obscenity, but that would offer a desexualized and incomplete understanding.

Finally, the case of Mervyn Hyde illustrates a moment in the articulation of the sexual self before sexology separated cross-dressing into distinct taxonomies. Cross-dressers played with anxieties about masculinity and explored the tensions between gender and sexuality. In their iterations, cross-dressing suggested the overlapping need for aesthetic superiority, humiliation, masochism, pleasure, pain, relief, return, and cosseting. Sexologically defined ideas lost this richness in the process of squeezing people into atomized identities after World War II. Mr. Hyde demonstrates that lives in the interwar years did not correspond to clean divisions. Though a marginal figure, he nonetheless connected ideas to practices, individuals to communities, and a range of desires to the cross-dressing kink.

5

Whipping Stories in the Pages of the PRO

Frederick Holeman, a man diagnosed by the medical officer of Brixton Prison as having a "weak character" and "childish demeanor," wrote more than three dozen poison-pen letters to the mothers of Croydon, Wimbledon, and the surrounding area between 1930 and 1938.[1] In each of the letters, Holeman told the mother that her daughter was a lewd and vulgar hussy who needed physical chastisement. If the mother beat her daughter and placed an advertisement in the local newspaper testifying to that punishment, Holeman promised to take no further action and to consider the matter finished. Although his own daughter had been corrupted and he would allow no future associations between the girls, he would not make the indiscretions public. He finished the letters by stating that he was acting only as a concerned *mother* interested in "old fashioned" and "common sense" morality.

This chapter begins with the sad story of an obscure individual who personified the chaotic and often contradictory assumptions about sex and corporal punishment of the interwar years. Although clearly at odds with his society, he was still responding to the well-established beliefs that circulated at both official and subversive levels. Although historians have considered the fixation on whipping to be a result of elite public school discipline, the whip ranged beyond a single institution, affected more than the elite, lasted longer than commonly acknowledged, and—most important for this chapter—became a sexual sign across society.

At the same time that Frederick Holeman wrote innumerable documents about sex and whipping, so did the British state. During the critical years of Holeman's letter-writing campaign, various officials in the Home Office and Colonial Office tabulated, assessed, and examined the state's practice of whipping prisoners, largely for sex crimes. Concurrently, reformers denounced whipping as a sort of state-sanctioned perversion. Their campaign convinced members of the British government that whipping inspired a range of perversions including sadism, masochism, and sexual inversion for all involved. In essence, reformers convinced members of the British state of the preexisting perversion of its own policies. As a result, the British government changed long-established policies. By considering Frederick Holeman's letters in the context of the wider culture's fixation on sex and whipping, this chapter demonstrates that Holeman was not so out of tune with his society as it may first appear and that sex and whipping remained joined in British society.

Frederick Holeman

When arrested on April 6, 1937, Frederick Holeman was sitting in St. Michael's Church writing a letter to Mr. and Mrs. Young. In his pocket were a rent book, twelve press clippings, and a list of four girls' names. He had been writing such letters for at least seven years. Recipients had handed thirty-eight of these letters to the police since 1930; Holeman admitted to writing forty-seven letters, but he may well have written and sent others that were not brought to the police's attention and entered as evidence.

The letter to Mr. and Mrs. Young stated that their daughter, Ethel, was "vulgar" and "immoral" and that Ethel and Vera—Holeman's ficticious daughter—were "a pair of deep. sly. untruthful dishonest hussies." (All misspellings, punctuation and emphases appear in Holeman's case file.) The letter recommended to the parents, "Make your girl hold out her hands & *bend* over. *give her about* 18. *hard sting*ing cuts *across* her palms & as many *or* more *across* her legs. *etc.* over her *thin* stockings, knickers. *etc.*"[2] This letter was not completed. In completed letters, Holeman was more specific about the immorality of the girls and more extensive in his explanation of the need for punishment.

Girls' supposed transgressions included "making rude noises. lifting their dress to the waist. pinching & poking front & slapping—when bending & various rude actions with fingers. etc."[3] These alleged transgressions linked innocent girlish behavior to wild sexual excess. In these letters, smoking cigarettes led to fellatio and drinking alcohol became modeling for pornography. He accused one girl of "boast[ing] of the good time she has been having with boys of the cigarettes. gin, port. champagne . . . that she can always get a few shillings from the boys by allowing them to do as they like with her which she enjoys & boasts intimacy with several. which give & leaves her with strange & lovely *internal* sensations. & of having a double event a few days ago with Peter leaving him weak & limp & she strong. after sucking & drawing the hot cream out of him how she trembled & wriggled with the movements of his comforter up her inside tickling and itching . . . we have found some several pages. *marked* pictures & verses, sexual tabs. dope. *nude* photos of herself & of boys showing all their trimmings. stiff and dripping & sex accessories & pills for preventing pregnancy."[4] The accusations of sexual immorality repeated across letters and over the years.

He accused the girls of allowing boys to take liberties and of taking such liberties themselves, including putting their hands into "boys trousers pockets" and playing with their "comforters." He made accusations that fit somewhere between incoherence and pornography: "Sexual & private & *nude* photos. girls & boys *marked* certain places. sexual pages about babies. dope. pills. etc. also a letter she gave our girl last week. saying she intends to let men play with her & have a good time that she has been told that all film stars & actresses do if they want to be popular and get a lot of money & presants & she talks of long stiff comforters. rubbing. skin back. swelling & hot cream."[5] These sorts of accusations were no accident; he hit on every overwrought accusation made of the modern flapper: hard alcohol and drug use, cigarette smoking, promiscuous sex, prostitution, and predatory behavior. However, Holeman—in comparison to most writers who denounced such behaviors—could not separate prurience from denunciation.

He recommended that the parents punish their girls in excessive ways that focused on the eroticized zones of the body. He urged that parents thrash their daughters on the palms, the stockings, and the knickers. He suggested that parents cane the girls on the hand, but then he shifted his descriptions to more erotic regions: "so I hope you will see fit to get a cane & use it frequently & sometimes severely accross her hands (palms) & legs over her thin knickers and stockings waist to ankles."[6] In his letters, he cited his treatment of his fictitious daughter, "Vera," as an example of how to beat a girl on the thighs and buttocks, by particularly focusing on her stockings. "We thrashed her *severely* last week [while she] was wearing a pair of those *fine expensive real* silk knickers and stockings."[7] By detailing the whipping he gave "Vera," he provided a model of the canings that other mothers were to administer. He suggested to one mother, "make your 19 year old daughter Barbara *hold out* her hands & *bend* over. give her *about* 20 *hard stinging* cuts *accross* her palms & as many *or* more accross her legs. etc. over her *thin* stockings. knickers. etc. make her *squeal*. sob *dance* & *rub* for a time."[8] The emphasis on cuts across "*thin* stockings" seemed to be a sort of sexual trigger; he used that phrase in almost every letter, often multiple times. The phrase was emphasized, repeated, and underlined. He also accused girls of hiding objects in their stockings and knickers, making those garments more fraught than usual. "X'examine search her & her belongings *including* round *down* the tops of her stockings. etc. x. bottom of knickers where she *conceals* stolen & *forbidden* small items."[9] His insistence that girls hid forbidden objects in their stockings and knickers justified his intrusions and punishments; clearly these regions were highly charged.

As well, his prescriptions that mothers should beat their daughters until they "squeal" and "rub" clearly had sexual implications. In one letter, he wrote that such a caning made his daughter "*squeal*. dance. *sob* & *rub* for a time *as our girl is doing* now."[10] The sexual implications of the beating did not end with the entirely fictitious event; instead, girls lived in the stocking-clad state of post-beating arousal for days. According to Holeman, "his daughter" "wore an *extra* pair of stockings (common) & for several days to *conceal the cane* marks on her *calves*. showing through her transparent ones she rubbed and twitched for days."[11] His "cure" appeared as fraught as his accusations.

Holeman insisted that parents post a note in the local paper after they beat their girls. According to one set of instructions, the mother should "*insert* in per-so*nal column*. Croydon times. (*Lily post news. Irene*)."[12] His desire to read about the beatings in the paper finished off the girls' public humiliations. If the parents posted such a note, Holeman promised that he would keep the matter of the girl's indiscretions quiet; otherwise, as a "concerned mother" he would be forced to tell other parents about the immoral behavior. The coded language created a secret link between the parents and him, and Holeman could experience a voyeuristic delight in knowing that the girls had been beaten. Apparently, he savored such exchanges, because he clipped such notices and carried them with him.

He relied on the press not only to communicate a shared secret about whipping but also for an understanding of the world around him. He read the local papers for reports of girls' activities, and he plucked girls' names from local stories. He also searched for stories of interest from the "News of the World" and looked for notices about corporal punishment. Lucky for him, the years between 1930 and 1938 featured many such articles on the topic of penal reform as well as innumerable letters, articles, essays, and books about corporal punishment and disciplining girls. *London Life*, for example, occasionally featured stories that could have come from Holeman's pen. One such story from 1930 featured a concerned mother forced to discipline her children: "May I say that as a mother of four, I think it is a mother's duty to correct her children? From my own experience, I can certainly recommend the chastisement of the Victorian days. I punish my children (and with very good effect) as I was punished when I was a child."[13] Another "mother" in that magazine detailed the many offenses committed by her daughter and requested suggestions about appropriate punishments: "I have a very wilful and troublesome daughter, 17 years of age, who has lately become an inveterate cigarette smoker, is picture-house mad, and idles about the house reading all day. She refuses to do any little household jobs to assist me, and I am becoming dreadfully afraid she will become absolutely useless if not disciplined somehow."[14] These sorts of articles appeared in the popular press; the police reported that they confiscated and entered into the evidence against Holeman "a bag containing Press cuttings dealing with spanking, caning, etc." His ideas show the influence of others. His faith in the magic of mutual orgasm (to be discussed later) sounds straight out of Marie Stopes. Even more, Frederick Holeman seemed to play out the sorts of cross-dressing fantasies detailed in Chapter 4. Like Mervyn Hyde, Holeman made use of the sorts of fictitious identities described in *Bits of Fun* and *London Life*.

The medical officer of Brixton Prison believed that Holeman "obtained a certain amount of sexual satisfaction by writing the letters, and from the phantasy associated with this conduct" but did not consider him insane.[15] The doctor believed that Holeman's "present conduct" was the result of "repression."[16] The police did not believe that Holeman was a social danger, however, and did not intervene in his household arrangements. Thus, the police report noted briefly that by 1937 his adopted "step-daughter," Ethel Boakes, lived with him, but it went no further in its assessment of that arrangement. The year before, a girl named Ethel Boakes had been employed by Dorothy Hunt as a servant. A letter from Holeman accused Mrs. Hunt's daughter Sylvia and her servant Ethel of immorality and suggested that Mrs. Hunt separate her daughter from the servant. Mrs. Hunt spoke with Ethel about the matter and then fired her. Sometime between 1936 and 1937, Ethel went from Mrs. Hunt's household to Mr. Holeman's.[17] The police did not respond to this problematic situation. Ethel Boakes's life went unremarked and unnoticed. The Society for the Prevention of Cruelty to Children was not alerted to her presence, and the police did not call her to testify at Holeman's trial.

Frederick George Holeman of 9 Kenmore Road pleaded guilty to six cases of publishing defamatory libels. Holeman was found guilty, but the court handed down a remarkably light sentence: Holeman was bound over in the sum of £20 for three years by the Central Criminal Court when it let him out on bail on the promise to refrain from further letter writing.[18]

Despite his promises, by 1938 he resumed writing obscene letters. On June 6, 1938, Miss Barbara Treasure, newly affianced, received an obscene letter signed with the name of someone who purported to be an old friend, Evelyn May Shore.[19] This letter was even more lurid than previous ones and featured a new element—a relationship with "Sid," Shore's fictitious husband. According to the new batch of letters, the couple had a mutually satisfying sex life. In one letter, Holeman stated that he and Sid had spied Mr. and Mrs. Lawrence beating their three beautiful daughters. According to the letter, they saw the parents "lower their knickers & smack them severely. Connie the eldest also held out her hands. to her Father who gave her 6 hard cuts across her palms with a cane & a few across her legs over her stockings as she stood in short school tunic sobbing & rubbing & nursing & shaking her hands." That night, according to Holeman, he and Sid had profound sexual relations: "that night our sexual relations. enjoyable & easy the unity was secure. we both came at the same moment. the fluid cells from him seemed to meet & mix with those of mine into my womb. waking the next morning. with lovely deep internal sensations & strange feelings I told Sid I was sure I had conceived & it would be a girl."[20] According to Holeman, they conceived a daughter named Grace. They also adopted a girl, Connie, but from the explanation, it is not clear whether Connie was the daughter they had seen beaten or another girl by the same name. Instead of writing as one parent to another, his new *modus operandi* was to write as one woman to another about the nature of passion. Two women took these letters directly to the police.

By this time, Holeman was doing casual work for a baker. In his free time, he would loiter at a girls' school as the students left the premises and write letters in the public library. The police knew that Holeman was once again disturbing the populace but could find no reason to arrest him. To make a case, they followed him. When Holeman picked up the basket of groceries left behind by a boy struggling with his dog, the police arrested him and charged him with theft. The Divisional Detective Inspector used this as an opportunity to check Holeman's property both on his person and at his home. While the state was intrusive in other ways, their actions remained tentative despite Holeman's previous convictions and the new complaints made by neighbors. During questioning, Holeman admitted to writing three letters and even to going to London to mail them. At the trial, the police argued that it "was quite clear that Holeman ha[d] broken his recognizance entered into the Central Criminal Court," but he received the lightest of punishments, a mere warning.[21] Here we lose sight of him. There are no further references to him available in the criminal record, no further police reports that explain his doings, and no further letters written by him. Frederick G. Holeman died at age seventy-four in 1956.[22]

Poison-pen cases are usually little more than a passing annoyance, but Holeman's case raises all sorts of questions central to the history of identity and to the nature of historical sources. Unlike previous chapters, which made use of correspondence but could not pinpoint the authors, this chapter uses documents whose authorship was well known. Police work tied Holeman to the obscene letters and caught him with pen in hand. Holeman existed. His arrest and the impressive numbers of letters entered into the evidence means that we can correlate the letter writer's external identity with his internal or "interior" identity. But even though we know the author of the letters, questions remain. When we talk about Holeman's identity, should we refer to him as a woman or a man? His case raises questions about interiority that generally emerge only during explorations of fiction. His imagined position in the psychodrama remains open to question. Did he take pleasure as the whipped girl, as a man thinking about the girl's whipping, or as the mother administering the whipping? Did he see himself as the boy (with whom the girl cavorted), as the girl (who was whipped), as the mother (who whipped), or as a voyeur (who watched the whipping from afar)? This riddle points to an uncomfortable problem. Holeman's case feels like a fragment of a story that does not conform to easily identifiable genre expectations; is it a true-life exposé, a mystery, or a psychological profile? Even if we may want to privilege his sense of himself as a woman, Holeman himself argued against believing in others' claims. Indeed, that was the basis for his letter-writing campaign. His claims about degenerate girls rested on the assumption that mothers were incapable of reading their own daughters. According to this set of beliefs, mothers could not know the inexplicable hearts of girls, and the older generation should never believe the corrupt and dissembling youth. Even in its own age, it would not be clear how to read it, since the case developed in tandem with the arrival of psychology as a field. He might be a victim of his age, a victimizer, or a voyeur—or perhaps all three.

We can say that something about adolescent girlhood motivated Holeman. Out of a world of possibilities, he wrote letters about only adolescent girls—focusing intently, page after page, on describing their bodies, their relationships, their pleasures. When women left their teens, they no longer seemed to interest him. Furthermore, he mentions boys only as the girls' sexual partners, rather than as sexual actors in their own rights. Holeman wanted to conserve the Victorian notion of female sexual purity, and he was willing to condemn deviant girls to guarantee it. We can also deduce that the descriptions of these girls contained fictitious elements, since the central motif of his letters is clearly fictionalized. Since he had no daughter, we have to assume his daughter's escapades are fictitious. And since there is no Vera, there is no daughter being beaten. What, then, can we make of the descriptions of beatings, of the imagined common and fine stockings, of the murmurs of pain days later, of the squeals, the rubbing, and the twitching? We can deduce that Holeman received something—some satisfaction, pleasures, or confirmation—about punishment and the ways that punishment played on the body. We can also say that there is a degree of compulsion to Holeman's letter writing. He admitted to writing almost four dozen letters over eight years of writing; this was no incidental lark. Indeed, he knew that the letter writing would get him into trouble, but he could not stop himself.

To make sense of this case, we must look to the broader culture and place his predilections in context. We cannot reconstruct a psychological profile from the evidence; the total description of his mental state was that he had "repressed his sexual desires," according to the medical officer of Brixton Prison.[23] However, we can see the ways that his sexual triggers worked in the broader culture. Adolescent girls, stockings and knickers, and caning and corporal punishment bore enormous weight in his psychological makeup, but Holeman was not alone in these fixations.

Girls, Stockings, and the Whip

Frederick Holeman seemed to have a problem with adolescent girls and young women. For Holeman, they functioned as both the locus of pleasure and the place to obviate modern sexual identities and practices. His hopes rested on girls' perversions, and his desires fixated on returning them to their proper states. In focusing on them so tightly, however, he magnified their cultural importance, much like the rest of British society. As fashion historians Cheryl Buckley and Hillary Fawcett explain, anxieties about gender often focused on clothes as markers of sexuality: "Fashion in the interwar years did not clothe a neutral body, it brought it into discourse, and the dominant discourses which related to women were constituted around sex, the sex wars, sexual freedom, sexual promiscuity and the anxieties which this provoked."[24] When Holeman made claims about independent girls who resisted authority, who imitated cinema idols, and who drank champagne and smoked cigarettes, he merely repeated the claims made about the generation coming of age after the war.

That Holeman dressed these imaginary young women in elaborate fantasies about stockings and knickers could be anticipated by the sexual cachet of those articles in interwar Britain.[25] Stockings spoke to the most intimate and hidden areas of the woman's body that fashions had recently revealed. While flapper fashions moved the hemlines upward, such fashions revealed more of the stocking-clad leg, rather making the garter and stocking obsolete. The baring of the stocking-clad leg only made such areas more visible, more thought-provoking, and more erotic. By the 1920s, the relationship of stockings to flesh had become more pronounced. Before World War I, most stockings were black. More than 95 percent of the stockings produced in the United Kingdom were dyed black, not out of a sense of propriety or a funereal fantasy but to hide the ubiquitous soot and dirt of the city.[26] The rise of sunbathing and the body-culture movement led to stockings that emphasized the color of skin rather than hid it. Nude, sunburn, and beige stockings became the rage. These flesh-colored stockings remained in fashion in the interwar period, and the sense that they emphasized the skin only intensified during the 1930s, when shiny stockings went out of vogue. Silk stockings and artificial silk stockings (rayon) became more popular as a sign of affluence and emancipation.[27]

It would be no accident that Anthony Berkeley's psychologically motivated murder mystery from the period featured a "homicidal maniac of the sexual type" who used women's stockings to strangle them. *Silk Stocking Murders* (1928) set into motion the stereotypes of young women from the age.[28] The plucky minister's daughter investigated the mysterious deaths of a racy showgirl and a rich and stylish heiress. Set squarely against these stereotypes of femininity were men's counterparts, including the Jewish financier, the amateur detective, and the bluff aristocrat. Stockings in this novel became just one of a series of markers for the dissolution of women and the (smart and likable but violently insane) Jewish financier who used women's stockings to strangle them. Silk stockings whetted desires. In the second Tarzan and Jane movie released in 1934, *When Hearts Beat like Native Drums*, silk stockings stood as one of the benefits of civilization that might tempt Jane to return from the jungle. After dressing in full evening kit, Jane allowed Tarzan to explore her stockinged leg. "These are stockings. Like them?" Tarzan touches her leg and replies, "Like them."[29]

A subcategory of shoddy American magazines catered to the taste for silk stockings in venues such as *Handies Silk Stocking Revue*, *Sheer Folly*, and the longer-running *Silk Stockings*. All of these magazines had been judicially condemned for obscenity, though not officially "banned," as the Home Office made quite clear to the police when circulating the list to the chief constables. The Home Office suggested that the police should warn news agents and suggested that they might be liable for confiscation.[30] However, the police were to be careful not to suggest that such magazines were censored because, according to the Home Office, "neither the Secretary of State nor the Police have any power to prohibit the circulation of any publication."[31]

Other magazines not mentioned by officials catered to the same tastes, such as *High Heel Magazine*, a Silk Stocking publication from 1938.[32] In the magazine's numerous photo spreads, the camera lingered on the line between stocking and flesh. In spread after spread, women showed the tops of their stockings. Garters demarcated the thighs while hemlines were pulled up and stockings rolled back. This carefully marked-out swath of flesh gave the magazine its currency—between high-heeled shoes and the bottom of the hemline lived the stocking-encased sexualized leg. In one such example, backstage of the revue, two girls chatted while one pulled on her stockings and the maid straightened the wardrobe. The transformation from wholesome ingenues to chorus girls was complete when the two girls appeared in their lingerie. Strangely, the photo spread featured different women and implied that they were undressing rather than dressing: "Some very intimate glimpses of just what goes on back stage— or should we say goes off? Here's where the chorus girl who has to make up and live, lives and makes up."[33] No matter; the stockings, the glimpses of lingerie, and the bonhomie of public smoking galvanized the image. In spread after spread, girls knowingly showed off their stockings and acknowledged the sexual gaze aimed at them. While Holeman's desire to whip girls around the silk stockings and thighs might be an individual predilection, the appeal of silk stockings went much further; silk stockings marked the body as sexualized.

Like stockings, whipping and caning had a sexual cachet, one that was an open secret in British society. The idea of whipping as a sexual pleasure had a long history in British pornography, one that followed the trajectory of erotic publications more broadly. Writers during the Renaissance saw flagellation as central to sexuality, and early imports gave way to an English-centered tradition by the late eighteenth century. Whipping became central to English erotic publications. In *Memoirs of a Woman of Pleasure* (1748–1749), *Venus School Mistress* (1808–1810), and *The Pearl* (1879), whipping as a sexual "painful pleasure" reverberated in British fictional portrayals of sex. The poet Algernon Swinburne wrote secretive odes in which he celebrated the boy and the birch, while H. S. Ashbee's bibliographies of erotica maintained a separate subjective heading about flagellation.[34] Even William Gladstone himself contained his yearnings for illicit sex with a bit of the whip.[35] A good whipping had an erotic appeal that the British obscene and ephemeral trades long recognized. Just a hint of the lash promised future sales.[36]

The Home Office banned a class of magazines and certain sets of papers because of their focus on whipping, including "Painful Punishment," nos. 1–7; "Recollections of Count Rodini," nos. 1–2; "Ruled by the Rod," nos. 1–8; "Strict Discipline," nos. 1–4, "Tales of the Birch"; "The Domineering Duchess"; "The Island of Anguish," nos. 1–10; "The Whip throughout the World," nos. 1–4; "Under the Lash," nos. 1–6; and "Whip at Boarding Schools," nos. 1–4. Most of these series came from France or America, although some misrepresented themselves as coming from abroad only to throw off the police. One petty dealer of obscenity supplemented his £4 a week wages as a wine salesman at the Terrace Winestores Ltd. by hawking whipping stories. These stories, including titles like "Swish," "Wow," "Disobedient Girls," and "Unruly Flappers," retailed at 2 shillings 6 pence per envelope. He had been earning about 15 shillings a week by selling them on his lunch hour. He "thought they were harmless as he had seen them on sale in many book shops in the West End of London." When arrested, he had fourteen photographs of flagellation scenes, a projector bought from British Cinespect Slough Bucks, and a film that showed "two women romping about in the open air."[37] The idea of whipping naughty young flappers generated its own erotic fiction. *Two Flappers in Paris*, for example, featured two delightful young beauties, Nora and Evelyn, who were seduced by watching obscene films, tied up "with the result that the lovely girl's thighs were forced wide apart," whipped with a birch, and masturbated with a cat-o'-nine-tails.[38]

Correspondents in magazines like *London Life* made use of the same motifs that Hyde did, and the two sorts of letters looked remarkably similar. The beating of girls received a good bit of press in *London Life*. In a letter titled "A Mother on Daughters," one writer commented that letters about mothers disciplining their children were the most interesting in the paper: "Discipline for girls is the best topic now, and it is what they want." The writer contributed to the popularity of the topic by advocating discipline for both boys and girls: "If every mother corrected her children there would be a lot less girls going astray."[39] Another writer, lamenting the impact of too much freedom on girls, suggested a return to a heavy hand. "Would it not be better that they [young girls] should be controlled by a 'benevolent despotism,' even (in the case of some temperaments) by the fear of humiliation and pain of punishment, which have no permanent effects, than that they should risk either ruin or at least the probability of making much less useful wives and mothers than their grandmothers?"[40] Another correspondent calling herself "Docteur Ruba" commented on a letter by "Elsie." "Elsie" wanted more novels "bearing illustrated covers which depict the figure of the female who has been subjected to brutal violence or cruel restraint." "Docteur Ruba" suggested that this desire, along with the "impulse to inflict a form of violent restraint on members of their own sex[,] is just another form of sexual perversion which is rife among a certain class of emotional individuals today."[41] Another letter commented about girls "paddling" each other in American colleges. "A photograph published in your excellent paper some time ago, showing a girl apparently about to be smacked with a paddle having some initials carved on it, made me more inclined to accept the stories I had heard."[42]

The beating of girls merged into the administration of such beatings by girls and women. The motif of women administering discipline received its share of letters, such as one by a writer who described the punishments he received as a child. He had, he recalled, "a very strict governess to teach me at home until I was thirteen, and she believed implicitly in Victorian methods, maintaining that to spare the rod meant spoiling the child."[43] Another reader argued that in interest of fairness, girls as well as boys deserved a good birching. "When a boy is naughty, his master, very properly, gives him a taste of the birch. Why shouldn't his sturdy rebellious sister receive identical treatment from her schoolmistress."[44] The relationship between discipline and clothes was also noted by correspondents. One writer, stating that she had been tightly laced since she turned ten, linked her attire to her husband's control and discipline of her person. "All the year round I have to wear the same attire, which is a pair of woolen combinations with long sleeve, a woolen vest, a pair of woolen stockings, a pair of flannel knickers, a serge dress with high collar and ankle length, and, of course, my stays, which are always laced to the absolute limit. I can assure you that dressed like this, it is anything but comfortable, and my husband would not hear of me removing any of my clothes or loosening my stays at all."[45]

Many writers in the popular press commented on the erotic potential of silk stockings. One correspondent wrote that the "the shimmer of long silk stockings, is the most compelling of all!"[46] Another writer emphasized the allure of silk stockings. "Silk stockings, of course, thrill one even as one draws them on over the leg each morning."[47] Stockings and girls, sometimes together and sometimes alone—were well established in the popular press. Reconciling girls and stockings as erotic took little effort, but coming to terms with the erotics of whipping presented certain problems. The British state recognized the overlap between sex and the lash when it banned flagellant magazines, but it had a harder time coming to terms with the erotics of flagellation because of its use in the judicial system.

Sexual Pleasure and Corporal Punishment

The state had begun relinquishing the use of corporal punishment for criminal offenses throughout the nineteenth and twentieth centuries because of humanitarian agitation but continued to use the whip in the case of certain sex crimes. However, the continued application of corporal punishment by the state for sex crimes became increasingly problematic during the interwar years with the advent of psychological theory. During the 1930s, the British state began to recognize the erotic implications of whipping in its own practices. Ultimately, the state had to abolish the lash because of the psychological implications of its use.

Some scholars, such as Ian Gibson, tied the phenomenon of sexual flagellation to public school discipline; others, such as Colette Colligan, saw it as linking the world of slavery with the world of sexuality.[48] While both of these theories may well stand, the overlap between whipping and sexuality had broader implications for British society. The two flogged bodies—the sexual body and the punished body, the two moments of flogging—the intimate and the punitive—shared a basic terminology, apparatus, and impetus.[49] Prisoners were whipped as well as students. The poor were whipped as well as elites, and the process of whipping worked equally well in Kenya and Borstal, the town whose name became synonymous with reform schools. While colonial and postcolonial scholars see the application of flogging as racist, coercive, and hierarchical—and surely it was all those things—flogging also happened equally in the metropole as in the colonies, on the self as well as the other.[50] Flogging connected pain, shame, and excitement across all these realms.

The continuation of flogging went against the sea change in the logic of corporeality that had begun with the Enlightenment. Critiques of brutality changed personal sensibilities, shifted people's approach to violence, and transformed state policy.[51] The end of the slave trade in 1807 and then the abolition of slavery proper throughout the British colonies in 1833 created a right to self-ownership and bolstered the integrity of the body. The government abandoned the "Bloody Code" that mandated capital punishment for more than two hundred crimes in the nineteenth century.[52] As early as 1820 the state abolished the right to whip women prisoners.[53] The British army abandoned flogging over the course of the nineteenth century, first by reducing the number of strokes from the surely fatal 1,500 to the grotesquely bloody 1,000 strokes downward until it rested at 25 during peacetime in 1879 and then disappeared altogether in 1908.[54] Even the navy abandoned flogging, though it did not abolish it. The navy retained the right to flog sailors in case of emergency and kept the practice of flogging on the books for cadet training.[55] Although the state curtailed the practice of whipping grown men over the course of the nineteenth and early twentieth century, it retained whipping as a way to humble and discipline young men in naval academies, state schools, and reformatories, and the practice continued in public schools.[56] Girls were rarely caned and then most often on the hand.

However, crime sprees (and more important, the panics that they inspired) repeatedly brought the whip back. The great "garroting" panic of the 1860s brought back whipping even though the government had just abolished whipping for adults in 1861. The Maiden Tribute of Modern Babylon scandal also returned the whip. The 1885 Criminal Law Amendment Act, best known for raising the age of female consent and outlawing male-male relations, applied whipping to boys under sixteen for carnal knowledge of girls under the age of thirteen. In 1898, the government passed an extension of the Vagrancy Act making men liable to the cat-o'-nine-tails for living on a prostitute's earnings, even though the 1824 Vagrancy Act made being an incorrigible rogue a whipping offense. (Living off a prostitute's earnings would qualify a man for that title.) Hence, one faced double jeopardy under the lash. Finally, the white slave trade panic in 1912 found another cause for applying the whip.[57]

During the interwar years, sexual crimes warranted whippings; sex and the lash overlapped in Britain. According to the secretary of state, the law allowed men to be whipped for a wide variety of property and personal offenses including robbery with violence, garroting, unlicensed slaughtering of horses and cattle, and being an incorrigible rogue, among a few others. While property crimes could be punished by whipping, whipping was the punishment of choice in certain types of crimes that revolved around sexuality, particularly public sexuality. For example, forty-two men were whipped for indecent exposure, another nine for exposing their persons, sixteen for living on prostitutes' earnings, eleven for soliciting, one for soliciting men, and one for showing obscene pictures.[58] The only other types of offenses that could be summarily punished with whipping were crimes of poverty and begging.

In the colonies, a wider range of offenses could result in whipping, including placing wood on railways and witchcraft. Across the colonies, however, a cluster of offenses again begin to stand out. Out of forty-three whipping crimes aggregated from across the empire, eighteen related to sex. These offenses included rape and attempted rape, procuring, living on immoral earnings, unlawful carnal knowledge of a young girl, unlawful carnal knowledge of imbeciles or idiots, unlawful carnal knowledge of a young girl by a guardian, unlawful carnal knowledge by fraud or false pretenses, permitting a girl to be on the premises for immoral purposes, indecent assault, procuring white women for intercourse with natives, natives attempting indecent assault, Buggery and Sodomy (in capitals), gross indecency with a male, assault to commit sodomy, indecent assault on a male, indecency with a boy, male importuning, and indecent exposure.[59]

In practice, most adults were whipped for sex crimes in the colonies, while juveniles were whipped for a variety of offenses. For example, in Kenya, out of twenty-eight adult men sentenced to caning between January and June 1933, only three committed nonsexual crimes (abuse of opiates, theft, and store-breaking by night), while the remaining twenty-five committed a variety of sexual crimes, such as attempted rape, indecent assault, and unnatural offenses. In contrast, far more juveniles received canings—116 juveniles in all—but sex crimes remained fairly incidental.[60] In 1936, out of sixty-nine adult men sentenced to canings, thirty-six had committed sex crimes, while thirty-three committed other types of violent or property crimes. In comparison, only six out of 219 juveniles caned for illegal acts had committed sex crimes. This speaks to two related issues: (1) The state used caning as punishment in a far wider range of cases for young men than for adults, and (2) the state used whipping as punishment for adult sex crimes.[61]

Efforts to abolish whipping on humanitarian grounds continued during the interwar years, and reformers made inroads into state policy; however, ambivalence toward corporal punishment continued as well. Just when it looked like corporal punishment might be repealed for children, proponents brought it back.[62] In 1932, the government repealed judicial birching from the Children and Young Person's Act, but during the reading of the repeal, the House of Lords returned the section "word for word." The House of Commons rejected the amendment, but then the Lords mustered even greater support for its retention.[63] As a result, birching children remained a legal punishment. Ambivalence created legal stasis. The government considered reform but could not implement it. Critics attacked whipping but could not advance policy against it.

Only with the recognition that whipping had something to do with sexuality could reformers begin to affect state policy. In effect, as sexuality became conceptualized as a central drive—noted and discussed in psychoanalytical theory—members of the state began to mark out the ways that whipping related to sexuality and recoiled at their own practices. When the secretary of state analyzed evidence about the efficacy of corporal punishment, that office took note of the fact that whipping was the punishment of choice in certain types of crimes that revolved around sexuality, particularly public sexuality. As the Howard League for Penal Reform pointed out, "The retention of the lash in the English penal code is due partly to the belief that it is a deterrent of special efficacy, and partly to the revulsion felt against obnoxious forms of crime, especially of a sexual nature."[64]

Officials testified about corporal punishment in ways that illustrated their recognition that whipping's continuation had little to do with its efficacy and a great deal to do with its symbolic power. A member of the Colonial Office wrote in his official memorandum that "our successors in 50 years['] time will regard us in this matter as the barbarians which we regard our predecessors of 100 years ago. My own view is that there is a great deal too much flogging in the Colonies."[65] An editorial from the *Justice of the Peace and Local Government Review* savaged the idea of whipping: "Colonel Blimp and other he's [*sic*] who ascribe their present perfection to being beaten when young, believe in corporal punishment. So does the secret sadist, who often, with crocodile pathos, assures his victim that the executioner feels far more pain in his mind than the sufferer does in his body."[66] Even members of the Home Office recorded ambivalence toward the practice: "The Home Office is quite unable to produce any body of facts or figures showing conclusively the advantages or disadvantages of corporal punishment."[67]

Despite—or perhaps because of—the debates about corporal punishment and the near abandonment of it as policy, the Home Office and Colonial Office attempted to systematize it. These offices tried to create a bureaucratic system for corporal punishment that would make it look bloodless and dispassionate. They began to survey the number of whippings and canings. The Colonial Office and Home Office regularly reported the number of prisoners whipped and the methods used for those whippings. These reports were then tabulated into reports called "returns of punishments for whipping and flogging." These "whipping returns" allowed the state to review its own practices. As well, the secretary of state made sure that all administrators in boys' industrial schools used exactly the same cane. That office sent packages composed of four canes to each school with a message that stated: "No cane must be bound or dressed in any way, and if any of the prescribed canes becomes split a new one will be sent to you on application to the Chief Inspector."[68] One had to be careful with the rods and make sure they were handled correctly since they were doled out one at a time despite the half gross that had been back-ordered to replace them as they broke. Birch rods also became uniform in size and weight. To help save money in their production, the British state used prison labor to manufacture them.[69] Birches came in a number of sizes and weights depending on the age of the person to be punished. Birches were soaked before used, but, despite the persistent rumors, they were soaked in water, not brine. The cat-o'-nine-tails also came in a standardized model.[70] Thus, the old practice of making birches from branches or using a horsewhip on prisoners was abandoned; a new policy of industrial efficiency allowed everyone to use the same equipment across Britain and the empire.

These attempts to standardize whipping occasionally backfired, as in one case in which colonial officials misunderstood the proper method for punishment. The Colonial Office had been advocating canings rather than use of the cat-o'-nine-tails across the British colonies: "We thought the cane should be substituted for the chikoti (or zikoti), and the Governor sent us an indent for such canes."[71] If colonial officials insisted on using the whip, they would need to use the standard model. Accordingly, the Colonial Office sent a circular asking whether the standard cat-o'-nine-tails (unknotted) was being employed. Rather than eliminating the cat and the chicotte—a type of whip made infamous for its use in the Belgian Congo—in favor of the cane, Northern Rhodesian officials misunderstood the directives and began to rely on the cat.[72] A flurry of concerned memos followed, and corporal punishment became regularized according to Colonial Office standards.

Finally, the state began a full review of whipping and caning. The review described the canings and whippings as a process. In England, when the courts sentenced boys to a birching, the local police administered the punishment:

> The birch is applied across the buttocks, on the bare flesh. The method commonly adopted is to bend the boy over a low bench or table. His hands, and sometimes his feet also, are held by police officers. . . . In some Police Forces one constable takes the boy on his back, drawing the boy's hands down over his shoulders; another constable holds the boys feet, drawing his legs round the sides of the first constable, and the birch is applied by a third. We have also heard that in one Police Force the custom is for the constable to bend the boy over and hold his head between his knees, while a second officer administers the birch. And in one district the boy is strapped to an apparatus similar to the triangle used for corporal punishment in prisons.[73]

The review found not only a great deal of variation in the way the police administered such punishments but also a good bit of erotic tension in the practice. Despite the attempt to render whipping and birching as dispassionate and bloodless, the relationship between whipping and sex remained. The descriptions of birching boys followed models for "horsing" young men and women in pornography.[74] The whipping of adults had an erotic subtext as well:

The prisoner who is to undergo corporal punishment is strapped to an apparatus, known as a triangle, which is best described as a heavier and more solid form of the easel used to carry the blackboard in a school-room. His feet are strapped to the base of the front legs of the triangle. If the cat is to be administered his hands are raised above his head and strapped to the upper part of the triangle. If he is to be birched, he is bent over a pad placed between the front legs of the triangle and his hands secured by straps attached to the back legs of the triangle. In both cases he is screened, by canvas sheeting, so that he cannot see the officer who is administering the punishment. The birch is administered across the buttocks, on the bare flesh. The cat is administered across the back, also on the bare flesh, so that the ends of the tails fall on the right shoulder-blade. When the cat is to be administered, a leather belt is to be placed around the prisoner's loins and a leather collar around his neck.[75]

These procedures remained highly suggestive of BD/SM role-playing that had been well described in pornography. No doubt, such fantasies developed their codes from punitive measures, rather than the reverse, but by the interwar years, such procedures were tinged by associations with erotica. The symbols—leather belts, straps, canvas sheeting—all heightened the sexualized overtones in bureaucratic whipping. Instead of appearing mechanical, whipping and birching remained about blood and passion, sex and violence.

Recognition of this erotic subtext came in the unanimously approved and widely circulated report developed by the Home Office, Departmental Committee on Corporal Punishment. Hermann Mannheim reviewed the report in the *Modern Law Review* and found it an "outstanding piece of work, equally distinguished by the clarity of its expositions as by the soundness of its recommendations."[76] The Home Office kept track of press opinion and noted the responses in fifty newspapers.[77] This document came close to labeling the birching of boys as a form of sexual sadism.

This element of sadism, which is present in all punishment *qua* punishment, is accentuated when the punishment takes the form of inflicting physical pain: for corporal punishment is not only an expression of the hate impulse, but it is also a direct or indirect expression of the sexual impulse. Conscious sadism is recognised as a form of sexual perversion, and a system of judicial corporal punishment may pander to unconscious impulses which in essence are sadistic and sexual.[78]

According to this report, the state, in inflicting corporal punishment, acted out of hatred and sexual longing. In doing so, it pandered to the basest of all community sentiments and might very well "satisfy" sexual impulses toward sadism and masochism among some members of the community. In ordering corporal punishment, then, the state was implicated in a perverse system of sexual exchange.

Others saw these sexual connotations of corporal punishment as well. In a note dictated from the Authors' Club and sent to the Home Office, Lieutenant Colonel Arthur Osburn, author of *Must England Lose India?* (1930) and *Unwilling Passenger* (1936), delineated twenty-three points against corporal punishment.[79] Almost all of his points associated flogging with sexual perversions; in particular he saw flagellation as causing voyeurism, sadism, masochism, and sexual inversion. He argued that "when the police raid disorderly houses, whips are frequently found." He suggested that the lash or birch caused a rush of blood to the sexual organs, bringing an involuntary sexual excitement. He stated that spectators would watch the prisoner's arousal, creating a voyeuristic impulse. The administrator of the flogging, as well as the spectators, would become aroused. Osborn suggested that people convicted of sexual offenses stated that their interest in sodomy emerged from watching boys and young men being birched and beaten. Osborn believed that "the Masochistic or effeminising effects of being 'passive' to 'punishment' inflicted on the buttocks could contribute to homosexual passivity." By point number twenty-three, corporal punishment had led to all sorts of inappropriate sexual responses and inappropriate sexual arrangements including sexual humiliation, voyeurism, sadism, masochism, and inversion, according to Osborn's account. The conclusion that flogging caused perversions seemed unavoidable.

Even the Home Office began to accept that whipping could contribute to these types of sexual irregularities. In responding to the question about punishing boys for homosexual relations with whipping, the Home Office stated that the "Home Office view would be that, whatever may be the arguments for or against corporal punishment in general, this form of punishment is peculiarly unsuitable for sexual offenses. As you know, flagellation is associated with sexual vice and perversion, and there is medical evidence that in some individuals (perhaps exceptionally constituted persons) the application of physical pain by beating increases sexual feeling."[80] This statement associated corporal punishment with perversion; clearly the age of psychological theory had arrived. A sea change had happened, but few took note.

This shift in attitude toward flogging, from casual acceptance to ambivalence to recognition of perversion, responded in part to a campaign promulgated by the Howard League for Penal Reform. According to the league's latest papers, corporal punishment affected the unconscious just as the unconscious affected the state's application of corporal punishment. According to this perspective, flogging could cause perversions, as in the preceding Home Office statement, but flagellation also resulted from perversions. For the Howard League, using corporal punishment for sex crimes was itself a sort of sex crime but one perpetrated by the state. According to their pamphlets, "the psychological truth, by which alone penal policies should be measured, is that punishment by flogging repeats the crime." In this assessment, the individuals who ordered and administered flagellation took part in perversion. This happened at an overt conscious level and at an unconscious level. According to the Howard League, "It may be sufficient to say, however, that in dream life flogging instruments are very definite sexual symbols (i.e., the equivalent of the phallus) and that in the dreams of those individuals whose sexual development has tended to remain fixed at an early (homosexual) phase, the 'cat' or cane or whip figures prominently."[81] Thus, the Howard League suggested that officials who ordered floggings were caught at an early, homosexual stage of development.

The pamphlet paraphrased Freud's paper "A Child Is Being Beaten" to show how penal punishment contributed to flagellant fantasies. According to their reading of that paper, when people heard about corporal punishment, the idea would be lodged in the unconscious mind to reappear as daydreams. "Some of the most persistent of these day-dreams are vague in content; 'someone' is simply 'being beaten,' perhaps 'a child.' In other instances the individual is in phantasy the onlooker at the scene, or takes an active (or passive) part, i.e. beats or is beaten."[82] The doubly passive nature of the scene in which someone "is being" beaten made it clear that perverse desires would work without will, without morality, without choice on the subconscious mind. Any "rational application" of corporal punishment that happened later might well be a later iteration of the first fantasy that someone is being beaten. The consequence of this theory was that any rationale for corporal punishment could instead substitute for unconscious desires. No one could know whether the explanation for corporal punishment hid a deeper longing. Did flagellation cure crime, or did that explanation merely cover up a sexual desire to beat or witness a beating? It remained impossible to separate the two. Thus, the longing to beat and be beaten tied the state to the pervert, whether or not the state—and the respectable members of society who supported the state—recognized that relationship.

As a result of the findings in the "Report of the Departmental Committee on Corporal Punishment," published in 1938, the Home Office planned to abolish corporal punishment in all cases except prison discipline.[83] The state saw its own policies as contributing to perversion and planned to end a practice that had infused violence with eroticism for generations. Humanitarian concerns and psychological theory joined together to justify this change in policy.[84] However, the war interrupted and the changes were postponed for a decade. Between 1938—when the report was approved and widely lauded by the press, by the public, and the government—and 1948 when its recommendations were finally implemented, more than three thousand juveniles and three hundred men were flogged in England and Wales, while many more were beaten across the British Empire. Thus, while the state flirted with abandoning flagellation, it could not bear to give up its painful relationship to flogging for over a decade.

Whipping and Consciousness

According to Colleen Lamos, James Joyce used flagellation—in *Ulysses*, *Dubliners*, *A Portrait of an Artist as a Young Man*, and his personal letters—as a theme to consider the multiple ways that desire worked.[85] In the heart of *Ulysses*, Joyce descends into Leopold Bloom's hidden fears and fantasies; as a result, the novel becomes increasingly fragmented. Mrs. Bellingham, a nightmarish figure testifying against Bloom, charged that "he addressed me in several handwritings with fulsome compliments as a Venus in furs and alleged profound pity for my frostbitten coachman Balmer while in the same breath he expressed himself envious of his earflaps and fleecy sheepskins and of his fortunate proximity to my person." Joyce's reference to "Venus in furs" pointed to Sacher-Masoch's classic text of flagellant desires by the same title in which Wanda beat Severin until he became man enough to seize back the whip. To compliment one as such a Venus implied homage to masochist desires. Mrs. Bellingham continued her list of Bloom's perversions: "He lauded almost extravagantly my nether extremities, my swelling calves in silk hose drawn up to the limit, and eulogized glowingly my other hidden treasures in priceless lace which, he said, he conjured up." Bloom, like Holeman, fixated on and imagined the secrets of women, hidden in lace and silk finery. However, where Holeman reacted with fury, for Bloom these articles brought a longing for submission: "He implored me to soil his letter in an unspeakable manner, to chastize him as he richly deserves, to bestride and ride him, to give him a most vicious horsewhipping."[86] After a chorus call for stripes over Bloom's various flirtations, Bloom offered his reply: "All these people. I meant only the spanking idea. A warm tingling glow without effusion. Refined birching to stimulate the circulation."[87] The fragments of each phrase force the reader to connect the ideas. "All these people" works almost as a sigh of regret. Then comes an apologetic explanation that does not relate at all to the previous phrase. His phrase "I meant only" blunts Mrs. Bellingham's call to chastise, rise, and bestride. His grammatical breakdown expresses the faltering of desire in the face of the furies he has aroused. Sexual desire, retributive desires, and the subjection of desire became articulated through the rise and fall of language.

Joyce's strengths at representing the convolutions of consciousness around sexuality were recognized at the time. In particular, Judge John Woolsey saw these elements as critical for allowing the legal importation of *Ulysses* into the United States. As he explains, "Joyce has attempted—it seems to me, with astonishing success—to show how the screen of consciousness with its ever-shifting kaleidoscope impressions carries, as it were on a plastic palimpsest, not only what is in the focus of each man's observation of the actual things about him, but also in a penumbral zone residua of past impressions, some recent and some drawn up by association from the domain of the subconscious."[88] For Woolsey, since the subconscious concerned itself with matters of sexuality, Joyce must then address sexuality to achieve an accurate representation of the workings of the mind: "For his attempt sincerely and honestly to realize his objective has required him incidentally to use certain words which are generally considered dirty words and has led at times to what many think is a too poignant preoccupation with sex in the thoughts of his characters."[89] The truthfulness of his representation lifted Joyce's work from obscenity to art. British responses followed from Woolsey's assessments. According to a Home Office assessment, while opinion on the book might be divided, if the book were to be prosecuted the defense would argue that it is an "admirable literary description of the gradual transition from complete consciousness to a state of dreams, showing the gradual loss of control over the mind, and that the second [obscene passage] similarly portrays the 'stream of consciousness.' It will be argued that it is Freud in novel form."[90] Even the British government could not avoid acknowledging Freud's conception of the mind. Thus, the fragmented portrayal of consciousness justified *Ulysses*'s entrance into Britain.

While Holeman's prose cannot compare with Joyce's in terms of technical skills, bodies of knowledge, or imaginations, the two writers shared a sense of sexual abjection, and both worked around a fragmented nature of consciousness—though Joyce illustrated what Holeman lived. In some sense, the inchoate became the meaning. Thus, Holeman's letters illuminated the sexual sensibilities of the period not only for content but also for form. Like other writers from the period, his writing demonstrated the impossibility of forcing language to fit within the parameters of consciousness and, in particular, the problems of fitting the sentiments of sexuality into proper explanations of causes, desires, and consequences. He was both eloquent in his lack of grammar and cutting-edge in his inability to complete a thought without merging into another. In a strange way, his inabilities mirrored Joyce's abilities around the convoluted nature of consciousness, emotion, memory, and culture through the fragmentation of narrative form.

Holeman's prose broke down in the face of his sexual compulsions. In essence, grammar attempts to control communication, but that control rapidly deteriorated as Holeman began to list his sexual triggers. Each fragment in Holeman's prose became a complete action: The words "*squeal. dance. sob & rub*" worked without subjects, objects, or actors. Instead, each phrase explained a desire in its totality. Dependent clauses stood alone, creating a nonreferential and unrestrained sense of sexual actions: "after sucking & drawing the hot cream out of him how she trembled & wriggled with the movements of his comforter up her inside tickling and itching."[91] The descriptions indiscriminately piled up triggers. The more sexual the description, the more his control over form deteriorated. His writing was not skilled or planned, but he arrived at a similar inchoate description of consciousness as did more skilled modernists.

Strangely, an earlier case of poison-pen letters exhibited a similar use of language. In the earlier obscene postcard case that was much discussed in the press, two feuding neighbors expressed their hatred through a series of anonymous postcards sent between 1921 and 1923. As a result, first one neighbor and then the other was arrested and sentenced to prison. Obscene language became the way to force the state to intervene over the paltry questions of whose family was worse and why did the backyard smell. One such missive read like a modernist poem gone wrong. "You bloody fucking flaming piss country whores go and fuck your cunt. Its your drain that stinks not our fish box. Yo fucking dirty sods. You are as bad as your whore neybor" (orthography as in original).[92] The meanness of the list, the degeneracy of language, and the sparseness of punctuation made it appear as if sex and fury can erupt, geyserlike, at any moment. So deeply melded, so resolutely pressurized, the sex could not be separated from the hatred.

This missive, among the series of other obscene scraps of fury and sex, came to be entered into a court case as evidence. The state, forced to intervene as the neighbors used the mechanics of law and order to continue their feud, found itself trying to deal with irrational hatred through rational means. An investigation commenced. The police interviewed the suspects and the suspects' employers. Cards were collected. Stories began to accumulate. Statements were taken. Judgments were handed out, first against one neighbor, and then as the missives continued, the first neighbor gained her release from prison and the second was arrested. Despite the confusion and hatred, the state tried to work its way—or at least present itself as working its way—slowly and with care: "The facts were most carefully sifted and marshaled to the jury by the Judge, who put to the jury the case for the defense with every suggestion which a reasonable mind could make upon it. It was after that very careful summing up that the jury made their verdict."[93] The state modeled itself as slow, disinterested, and outside passions. Rather than the state forcing itself onto the populace, the neighbors used language and social relations to frame each other's weaknesses before the state.[94] Allegations of child neglect, insurance swindling, bastardy, and loose morals brought before the police and the National Society for the Prevention of Cruelty to Children (NSPCC) amounted to little, despite the severity of the claims and the apparent impropriety of people's lives. The state found no reason to intrude in the village drama.[95] Instead of intervening over such acts as bastardy and cruelty, the state intervened over language—the passage of obscene notes. In doing so, the state found itself on the cusp of a dilemma over the nature of modernism—what is the relationship of language to consciousness—in a way that it seemed hardly prepared to deal with. How could the state decide who wrote what despite the distinct style of writing and the distinctly irrational character of the obscenity? How could the state make sense of such obscene and vicious ramblings?

Across these cases, sexuality brought little pleasure—instead, the language of sex became the way to transmit pain. Obscene letter writers used sexual terminology—the language of "whores" and "fucking"—to transmit hatreds and antagonisms. Sex and anger were bound together. This melding of sex and fury were not out of sync with the age. Ultimately, the police, the judge, and the jury could decide only who passed the notes (and even there may well have reached the wrong conclusion), not what was behind the notes. Bureaucracy could not make sense of passion; it certainly could not do anything about the mingling of viciousness and sexuality.

Conclusion

Frederick Holeman, a concerned mother who wanted to whip girls bloody for their profligacy, embodied all the contradictions around whipping and sex of the 1930s. While he benefited from popular conceptions of sexual variation, he firmly rejected sexual variation in others. While he performed gender, it is not clear that he chose his role in the performance; furthermore, he certainly did not allow new gender performances for others. His sense of himself as an old-fashioned mother left no room for modern girls to enjoy their new freedom. If he had been the proper nineteenth-century matron that he purported to be, he would be of the most reactionary ilk, notable for his inability to adapt to the modern realm. His sexual and gender performances do not absolve him of these tendencies. If anything, they demonstrate the unevenness of the incorporation of modern identities into society. The "truth" of his gender and sexual identity remains hidden, but they nonetheless affected the world. As a result of his letters, the broad condemnation of flappers in society affected specific girls in Croydon and the surrounding area in the years between 1930 and 1938. Whether these girls were whipped by their parents, fired from their positions, or defended by their families, their names were entered into the court records and the secret spaces in their stockings and underwear became fictitious repositories of contraband.

In his basic sexual desires, Holeman seems to be responding to ideas that circulated broadly in society, whether those ideas revolved around degenerate girls, stockings and knickers, or the pleasures of corporal punishment. However, where other writers explored their fantasies in the correspondence columns of the ephemeral press, Holeman could not contain his fantasies to such venues. In trying them out on the world, he disregarded the difference between the readers of correspondence pages and the parents of young girls in his community, a tactical mistake of extreme importance. There was room to explore these fantasies in the ephemeral press but not in the region of Croydon. Not all stories are meant for all audiences.

John Kucich and Ian Gibson argued that sadomasochism functioned as a middle- and upper-class preoccupation during the nineteenth century.[96] As such, it became a popular and culturally important way of disciplining masculinity among elites. Most popular accounts of corporal punishment repeat these claims, and few scholars have examined corporal punishment into the twentieth century to assess the value of those claims in the modern world.[97] However, corporal punishment was used in reformatory schools and the Borstal system as well as public school. Authorities applied the cat-o'-nine-tails to sailors, soldiers, convicts, and perverts. The same type of corporal punishment was applied in England, Wales, Ireland, Jamaica, India, and Africa. Workers were whipped; elites were whipped; black and white were whipped. The whip itself functioned as a unifying signifier of authority, and particularly bodily authority, until World War II. It ranged beyond a single institution and became a sexual sign across society. While elites may be remembered for their odes to birch and boy, everyday people also dreamed of the lash.

However, flagellation increasingly became tinted with associations of sexual perversion. The growing belief in the perversity of corporal punishment created untenable associations for the supposedly rational application of discipline. No matter how hard the state tried, the whip did not speak to bureaucratic control. As a result, the state finally abandoned corporal punishment shortly after World War II. This, then, is the story, not of growing perversity, but of the growing belief in the perversion of preexisting practices. In some sense, this shift finished a process started generations earlier, in which Enlightenment humanitarian reform created a pornography of pain. That pornography made use of the same symbols as the punitive state.[98] As the overlapping symbols became more apparent, the state had to distance itself from its own disordered creations including the whip, the birch, and Frederick Holeman.

Conclusion

Narratives and History

I n 1937, a *London Life* reader sent a drawing to the magazine. She had been thinking about the design for a while but had lacked the skills to create it. Then, one of her many boyfriends drew it according to her specifications. She called the design, which featured a high-heeled swastika with a corset "coat of arms," the "heel-Hitler."[1] (See the gallery of illustrations.) At a moment when Hitler's regime was tightening its control across Germany through the coordination of major institutions, through the extension of the party organization, through the administration of propaganda and culture, and through the passage of such legislation as the Nuremberg Laws, this writer used the power of the Nazi insignia to represent fetish wear. Rather than lambasting the insignia of the Nazi state and what it represented, this writer introduced it to the fetishist community as a way to identify common fetishist interests in public. "Since a very long time, I thought it would be interesting to have an insignia by wrich [*sic*] high-heeled shoe and corset fans would recognize themselves all over the world. Could not this design be reproduced in the size of a post stamp, in order to be turned into medals, tiepins, etc?"

Either not recognizing the political associations of the swastika or—more likely—recognizing them but rechanneling their associations for erotic pleasure, this writer took one of the most politically loaded symbols of the twentieth century and remade it into fetish design. In this desire to reformulate the world's symbols into sexual pleasure, the writer demonstrated a callow and inadequate reading of the circumstances. The unconcern for anything but fetish pleasures illustrated a sense of sexuality formed in the consumer pleasures of the interwar world that became increasingly out of place. Though *London Life* had three of its most productive years ahead of it, the "heel-Hitler" foretold an end to consumer identities in the changed context of the forthcoming war.

Three years later, in 1940, Wallace Stortt wrote his final short story for *London Life*, called "Confessions of a Lover of the Limbless." This story, like his first, combined an interest in beautiful, modern girls with a focus on the spectacle of amputees. In it, as in others, Stortt adopted the voice of an international traveler who toured the world in search of amputees. He ended his tale with a description of a former dancer who had been rendered limbless.

Stortt's weaknesses as a storyteller—his lack of character development and absence of plot—nonetheless made him a good writer for *London Life*. Because of his singular interest in the bodies of limbless beauties, he could muster any number of ways to describe them. Stortt also made good use of the telling detail, such as when he described the woman as smoking innumerable "cigarettes placed in her lips and lighted by her husband." In that single detail, the full dependence of the limbless woman was made clear. Stortt's story linked the existence of a photograph, published in an illustrated weekly much like *London Life*, to the erotics of looking at limbless beauties. Stortt ended his story with the description of the photograph:

> Only one photograph ever appeared in the Paris papers smuggled out, it was said, from a large collection in the husband's possession through the agency of a maid. It appeared before it could be suppressed, in one of the illustrated weeklies specialising in photographs, and showed her reclining in the cushioned corner of a beautiful period couch. She was clad only in a diaphanous, skin-tight, black silk "maillot" revealing her as a slim but voluptuously curved torso.
>
> Well, there was the legend. The story the general public believed was that the unfortunate girl had developed a progressive necrosis of some kind that forced her to leave the stage and eventually resulted in the successive amputation of all her limbs. And that her elderly admirer had gallantly stuck by her and married her in spite of her completely maimed condition.
>
> That, of course, may have been the truth. But, on the other hand, there were many odd and bizarre aspects of the case which were significant only to a crowd like ours at the Two Pigeons.[2]

For those in the know—as opposed to the general public—the story hinted at voluntary amputation, an enduring fixation in Stortt's fiction. His fiction emphasized "knowingness" and a shared understanding that set readers apart. These qualities solidified the readers of *London Life* into the self-defined community of London Lifers. Stortt described his story as a rendering of his youth in Paris. True or not, such descriptions fixed the story in time and place that would soon be lost to memory. Published just a few months before the fall of

France, such remembrances grew more distant given world events as tales of nostalgia took on new and unintended inflections.

These two examples, the "heel-Hitler" and Wallace Stortt's story, point toward the inadequacies of *London Life* as a way to negotiate the changing world. The relentless focus on personal pleasures and the compulsive detailing began to appear more vacuous during the late 1930s and early 1940s, especially when set against competing narratives of world events. As the political world became increasingly fraught, the pleasures of consumer culture began to look less persuasive. The attempt to reconsider and reconfigure the paraphernalia of consumer pleasures seemed increasingly out of place. Older narrative models did not disappear, but their cutting edge had dulled. As a result, the foundations of the magazine began to give way. Within a year, the magazine—at least in its emblematic form—had collapsed, helped along by world events.

Nonetheless, these examples illustrate the importance of ephemeral publications and the opportunities they offered readers. In considering the many stories by Stortt, the hundreds of letters that swirled around Stortt's fiction, the thousands of letters detailing other sorts of desires, and the millions of readers of magazines and popular books, this book suggests that these publications had an impact on people's formulation of themselves as sexual subjects. Instead of psychology or sexology creating discourse that people adopted, this book suggests that popular culture allowed people to develop their own stories of sexuality. Popular culture gave people a wide access to such stories and created a method through which individuals could recirculate them.

Though sexology produced important volumes with widespread influence, their circulation remained limited. Small print runs, high prices, and limits to distribution guaranteed that only a small group of people could access these works. As a result, the refraction of ideas often mattered more than their original publication. Marie Stopes's incorporation of Ellis's idea of periodicity had a larger impact than Ellis's original explanation of sexual cycles for the simple reason that more people could afford to read Stopes's work, more copies were published, and more copies circulated. The derivative had more impact than the original.

Magazines incorporated ideas from sexology but then circulated these ideas and variants in far greater numbers. While both Wallace Stortt and Marie Stopes simplified the ideas they read and adapted them to their own goals, they also popularized sexological terms and made them more widely available. They rewrote narratives to suit their own purposes.

Stopes and Stortt, as well as others, served as conduits for a broader access to ideas, which in turn allowed the masses to remake those ideas. Neither sexology nor popular culture alone created sexual identities, despite the often overlooked impact of popular culture that this book demonstrates. In some cases, it may appear that sexology contributed to self-conceptions in a straightforward way, such as when letter writers modeled their language after Marie Stopes. However, even in that case, the relationships between sexology, popular culture, and self-conceptions were muddled. People modeled their letters after Marie Stopes. But Marie Stopes modeled her ideas off the works in the Cupboard collection of the British Library. That collection included ephemeral pornography and the works of serious sexologists. Instead of slow diffusion downward from the elite to the masses, the dissemination of ideas looks like a more dynamic process with popular culture interacting with sexology and people choosing bits and pieces of these versions at will. The narratives changed with each permutation. Sexologists published and republished, popular writers used and revised, and the broader society read and rewrote. Individual writers worked with the sexological, ephemeral, and popular literatures that they read—adapting, adopting, and rejecting ideas, languages, and explanations.

Consumerism itself marked these accounts, in their delivery as part of both the book trades and the ephemeral press but also in the ways that consumer goods shaped desires. Letters were wedged between ads for corsets and birth control in *London Life*. People made their living through the sale and resale of books, magazines, obscenity, and fetish wear. People's imaginations were lit by products they saw in shop windows and on the streets. Even for those who could not afford the lingerie that glamour mags touted, consumer culture circulated those magazines so that images could become a reservoir for wants and needs. An extensive popular culture allowed people to communicate those desires and work through sexual and gender relationships in new ways. Rather than seeing sexual scripting emerging from some deep internal center of self—formed through pain and pleasures—consumerism created an alternate route to form desire. It provided a method for the circulation of ideas that models of trauma and edification do not recognize.

Further, people actively sought ideas and forged their conceptions of gender and sexuality from what they found, as the chapter on Mr. Hyde demonstrates. In magazines that circulated at that moment and in the pornography he had in his collection, ideas of cross-dressing used notions about feminine men and masculine women to discuss the performance of gender. However, we should be careful to keep track of individual agency before we suggest that popular culture affected individuals in some sort of causal model. Individuals actively traded in materials that illuminated their desires. Hyde and others searched for older ephemeral literature to meet their desires for fashions gone out of vogue, and then they played with ideas of high heels and tight corsets to drill the physical form into pleasured compliance. People sought out materials that allowed them to refashion themselves in ways they found compelling. Ephemera did not make them do it in any simplistic way.

Reading was a willful act, and people selected what they wanted from the materials they found. People read intensively, pointedly, compulsively, jointly, and selectively. People looked for particular books such as *Married Love* despite the embarrassment of seeking them out. People gave Marie Stopes page numbers and quoted her verbatim when asking for clarification. They ignored materials that they did not like and focused on materials they found compelling. They clipped articles and letters from *London Life* and combined images and letters to make new meanings. They commented on which writer they liked and who should retire. They built their own meanings out of their readings, and then they treasured what they thought they had learned. If we look at only the circulation of books, then we presuppose that individuals were all strong readers who read all materials with an even-handed interest. However, that was clearly not the case. People came with different skills and longings, and then they read willfully and selectively.

Instead of seeing sexology or popular culture as somehow causal, this project sees meaning made through the relationship between individuals and the groups they formed. Individuals wrote letter after letter attesting to these desires, and in the process they scripted themselves. They settled on certain ideas that then became emblems of sexual desire. Descriptions of high heels, drill, and corsets began to sound more and more alike and became a tight script of compression, renunciation, and adulation. Once scripted, the ideas circulated, some in the local community (such as the amputee beauty who hopped crutchless) and others in the broader press and society, where they influenced standards of beauty (such as tight, high-heeled leather boots). The circulation of ideas charged the period with an energy that moved in multiple directions. Not only did the circulation of ideas demonstrate a certain complexity; people also used ideas in ways that added to a chaotic dynamism.

The period between the wars opened a window for experimentation. The limitation of family size, begun in the late nineteenth century among the middle class and extending across classes soon thereafter, let sexuality mean things other than another mouth to feed or another child to raise. Widespread literacy allowed people to rely on reading as a way to learn about the world and writing as a way to speak to it. The mad emphasis on pleasure in the interwar years stood as testimony to the fierce desire to rewrite old narratives and the willingness to face psychological compulsions. The relative affluence made consumer culture widely available. This combination of factors allowed for a dynamic articulation of sexuality during a relatively brief time period.

That dynamism was swept aside by the next war. The relative wealth of the population that allowed it to engage in consumer pleasures came under stress, and material standards declined during wartime. As early as 1940, the German patrols of the Atlantic limited importations to Great Britain. The blockade curtailed consumer goods and necessitated rationing. This dearth of consumer goods transformed the meaning of stories about consumer pleasures, especially those emphasizing the quantity and quality of material. To individuals scrabbling with dearth, endless lists of gloves, frillies, rubber wear, and perfume that had in the past offered a fantastical retreat from reality now offered a rebuke for impoverishment and a lack of plenty. Once the war began, corsets and pink satin gloves became less compelling as rationing and bombing began.

By 1941, *London Life*, as a magazine based on correspondence, had ceased circulation. The London office of the magazine was leveled by the blitz, marking a decidedly changed world.[3] International events intruded on narrative circulation; the enormous potential of the interwar years came to an end. Not only did *London Life* cease to be published in its emblematic form; other sorts of interwar experimentation sputtered as well. Paper rationing cut back on ephemeral publications once the war began. Pornographic publications from the continent slowed and almost ceased. The war also meant that ephemera no longer circulated so easily across the empire and dominions.[4]

Letters to Marie Stopes slowed down, though some still trickled in. The ones that arrived could demonstrate a torturous slowness for sexual change. A flying officer with the Royal Air Force (RAF), for example, wrote to Stopes because he saw premature ejaculation as ruining his own and his wife's health and mental stability. The officer believed that such problems could make him vulnerable. "If this continues I am afraid of becoming morbid and permanently introspective—which does not make for longevity in my present job!"[5] The poignancy of his concerns, given the death rates of RAF flyers, remains reminiscent of other soldiers' letters during the Great War. A new generation faced the same sexual problems. Concerns over contraception continued, and many noted the problem of getting quality rubber. As Stopes wrote to one man who noted the poor performance of condoms, "the truth is, everybody concerned with contraceptives is driven nearly mad by the inferior quality of the rubber permitted by the Government, the rationing of the amount they get, the interference with the usual chemicals they use, and everything."[6] The new war, much like the last one, heightened the urgency of dealing with sexual problems even while it limited people's access to resources.

The war itself further separated the interwar world from later conceptions of sexuality. Historians have yet to come to terms with the sexual changes wrought by the war in most areas of the world, including Great Britain, because the enormity of the war as a political and diplomatic watershed. Few historians comment on the war's impact on people's sexuality or gender construction, despite the recognition of brutality during the war and despite an awareness of sex crimes including mass rape and state-sponsored prostitution during the war. Before the war, police worried about sexual deviance. After the war, the police worried about violence and indecent assaults. In Leicester, the number of indecent assaults rose to seventy-eight for the years between 1946 and 1948. In Sheffield the number peaked at one hundred in 1946 alone. The Leeds police also noticed the trend and commented that the "most disturbing feature in addition to the increase in numbers, is the fact that the degree of brutality used in the majority of cases of this nature has also increased, particularly during the past year."[7] The war ended a particular moment in sexual history and started a new one.

However, sexual ephemera recirculated after the war, creating new contexts for meaning. Clipping files continued to circulate, but they did so in a different context with altered connotations. The edginess of interwar possibilities thus became rewritten into a new political framework. A memory of the potential of the interwar world began to coalesce. The formation of the London Life League (L3) was dedicated to the spirit of the correspondence columns in the original paper. L3 organized itself after an idea of that magazine.

Members of the group wanted to hang on to the idea of corset wearing, which had circulated in the magazine. According to the group, the interwar magazine allowed iterations of corset wearing in an absence of a broad understanding of sexological and psychological theory. As the editor of the newsletter explained, the development and adoption of sexual theory had innumerable consequences for corset wearers: "Regrettably the noun 'fetish' and its common derivatives 'fetishist' and 'fetishism' have in the past decade, like the word 'gay', been purloined from the realm of respectable use and are now commonly and pejoratively used in the more liberated climate of discussion of matters sexual. As a consequence the words are generally understood by the general public to be associated with sexual deviation or kinky sex."[8] L3 clearly rejected psychological notions of corset wearing as a fetish. The Foucauldian sense of identity construction, in which individuals recognized themselves in the impersonal descriptions of sexology and adopted them, was thoroughly rejected by L3. Instead, L3 sought to return to presexological notions of corset wearing. The editor wanted to hang on to older methods of defining the self based on popular culture, description, and shared stories. He sought to save corset wearing from the recognition that sexual liberation gave "gays."

As part of that process of creating a sense of shared identity, members of L3 projected their desires about corset wearing onto the past. The club dedicated itself to a vision of the magazine, but that vision should not be confused with the original.[9] L3 focused on corset wearing, while *London Life* made room for any number of desires: a longing for amputees, a fixation on tight kid gloves, or a fetish for piercings, jewelry, wetting, human ponies, and so on. Nostalgia rewrote what the magazine had been into one devoted to corsets, perhaps accompanied by high heels and drill. In doing so, club members chose to exclude a diversity of desires. Further, the nostalgic vision blinkered itself to the frequent references to kink and queer that appeared in the pages of *London Life*. In the original magazine, people used the language of kink and queer to speak to the erotics of difference in the interwar years, but L3 saw the language of kink and queer as a new way of typologizing corset wearing. As well, L3 ignored the ways that *London Life* contributors flirted with psychological theory including the theory of fetishism. In constructing a nostalgic vision of the past, L3 drained the original of certain acknowledgments of desire. Instead, they saw the interwar years as a moment when corset wearing could skate below the surface of recognition, providing erotic pleasure as part of daily life.

In some sense, L3 merely followed a precedent established in *London Life* by reiterating the nostalgic vision circulating in the magazine. During the interwar years, writers to the original magazine wrote longingly of a time just before their coming of age in which corset wearing was admired, erotic, and part of the everyday process of dressing. Corset enthusiasts, both male and female, celebrated an antiquated version of dressing, gender, and body modification. Rather than liberating sexuality, these writers played the structures of constraint. Their stories did not consider sexuality and gender apart from the factors that took such a deep psychological toll on individuals; instead, they offered mediation with some of the most fraught, painful, and compelling aspects of their world. But even during the interwar years, that model of corset wearing grew historically more distant. Someone coming of age in 1935 would not have seen streets full of corseted women and men. But people believed that they would have. To each generation, corset wearing remained just beyond their grasp. This nostalgia carved out a distinct vision of the past. The need for an engagement with history has not ended. Today's corset wearers post older copies of L3 newsletters and the original *London Life* online.

It is not merely that the historical context affected constructions of sexuality but that people triangulated themselves and desires according to an idea of historical time. People created a vision of sex that was bound up between notions about the past and the future. Historians need to consider the ethical implications of this use of history. Though these projections onto a past are largely harmless, a problem in the conception of self and other remains. Amartya Sen suggests in *Identity and Violence* that a cost for identity construction can be the miniaturization of the human being. According to Sen, we become singular creatures defined by solitary qualities, pitted against each other in a variety of ways.[10] The materials used in this book suggest that Sen could well be right. In *Bits of Fun, London Life*, letters to Marie Stopes, and obscene letters housed in the National Archives Public Records Office, people tried to legitimate themselves, sometimes at the expense of others, often using a sense of history to do so. In birth control advocates' use of eugenicist conceptions of race and sex, in amputee fetishists' refusal to listen to amputees, and in the misogyny and misanthropy exhibited in flagellant desires, people pitted their own desires against the material and cultural well-being of others, sometimes even those whom they purported to love. Instead of inoculating individuals against social cruelties, the process of narrating the self could inure people to others' miseries. The costs of defining the self deserve consideration. And the costs of defining the self on the basis of nostalgic visions of history deserve historians' consideration. Though sexual identity has been hard fought, it remains—like other forms of identity formation—a historical process based on a historical consciousness. Historians need to account for these costs rather than allow others to settle into stories about the past that do a disservice to history.

At the same time, though, there is something admirable in these accounts. People responded to a pressurized society with ingenuity and verve and did creative work with the cultural materials at hand. Rather than merely accepting what was offered, they transformed the possibilities into compelling alternatives. Their creations spoke to their abilities to imbue their world with meanings. Furthermore, some people forged ways to see beyond self-interest and the process of self-definition to call for mutuality and kindness. This call for tolerance came from a variety of people who—when exposed to a sexuality different from their own—nonetheless found a recognition of sameness and asked that sympathy be given to others. That insistence on tolerance and mutual decency continues to speak.

Notes

INTRODUCTION

1. "King Edward's Farewell 'My Choice Alone,' a Broadcast from Windsor," *The Times*, no. 47556, December 12, 1936, p. 14, col. D.

2. "Abdication of King Edward VIII Final Appeal by the Cabinet Rejected, Prime Minister's Story of the Crisis, 'Let Us Rally behind the New King,'" *The Times*, no. 47555, December 11, 1936, p. 7, col. A.

3. Diana Souhami, *The Trials of Radclyffe Hall* (New York: Doubleday, 1999), 186.

4. Quentin Crisp, *The Naked Civil Servant* (New York: Holt, Rinehart and Winston, 1977), 21.

5. E. P. Thompson, *The Making of the English Working Class* (New York: Pantheon Books, 1964).

6. See, for example, Eugen Weber, *Peasants into Frenchmen: The Modernization of Rural France* (Palo Alto, CA: Stanford University Press, 1976); and Benedict Anderson, *Imagined Communities* (London: Verso, 1991).

7. Rita Felski, "Introduction," in *Sexology in Culture: Labeling Bodies and Desires*, edited by Lucy Bland and Laura Doan (Chicago: University of Chicago Press, 1998), 1; Michel Foucault, *The History of Sexuality*, vol. 1, *An Introduction* (New York: Vintage Books, 1990).

8. See, for example, Alysa Levene, Samantha Williams, and Thomas Nutt, eds., *Illegitimacy in Britain, 1700–1920* (New York: Palgrave Macmillan, 2005); Phillip Howell, *Geographies of Regulation* (Cambridge: Cambridge University Press, 2009); Paula Bartley, *Prostitution: Prevention and Reform* (London: Routledge, 1999); Judith R. Walkowitz, *Prostitution and Victorian Society* (Cambridge: Cambridge University Press, 1982); Seth Koven, *Slumming* (Princeton, NJ: Princeton University Press, 2006); Thomas Laqueur, *Solitary Sex: A Cultural History of Masturbation* (New York: Zone Books, 2003); Peter Logan, *Nerves and Narratives: A Cultural History of Hysteria in 19th-Century British Prose* (Berkeley: University of California Press, 1997); Louise A. Jackson, *Child Sexual*

Abuse in Victorian England (New York: Routledge, 2000); and Lisa Z. Sigel, *Governing Pleasures: Pornography and Social Change in England, 1815–1914* (New Brunswick, NJ: Rutgers University Press, 2002).

9. Foucault, *History of Sexuality*, 51–73.

10. Harry Oosterhuis has aptly demonstrated how psychiatrist Richard von Krafft-Ebing used the stories from patients and other informants to develop sexual types. Harry Oosterhuis, *Stepchildren of Nature: Krafft-Ebing, Psychiatry, and the Making of Sexual Identity* (Chicago: University of Chicago Press, 2000). For further explorations of sexology, see Lucy Bland and Laura Doan, eds., *Sexology in Culture: Labeling Bodies and Desires* (Chicago: University of Chicago Press, 1998).

11. Felski, "Introduction," 2.

12. Compare Havelock Ellis, "Sexual Periodicity," in *Studies in the Psychology of Sex*, vol. 1 (New York: Random House, 1942), 86–159, with Marie Stopes, *Married Love* (1918; reprint, Oxford: Oxford University Press, 2004), chap. 4.

13. John K. Noyes, *The Mastery of Submission* (Ithaca, NY: Cornell University Press, 1997), 5–6; A. Maxwell, "Confidential," April 8, 1938, National Archives (TNA), Public Records Office (PRO), Customs (CUST) 492/2334. The British state found four classes of magazines particularly suspicious and liable to seizure: French illustrated magazines, cheap American magazines, miscellaneous, and whipping stories.

14. See, for example, Richard von Krafft-Ebing, *Psychopathia Sexualis* (New York: Putnam, 1965), 434; and Frank Mort, *Capital Affair: London and the Making of the Permissive Society* (New Haven, CT: Yale University Press, 2010), 248.

15. Routine cross-dressing in music hall performances provides another model of popular culture's impact. See, for example, Katie Hindmarch-Watson, "Lois Schwich, The Female Errand Boy," *GLQ: A Journal of Lesbian and Gay Studies* 14, no. 1 (2008): 69–98; Angus McLaren, "Smoke and Mirrors: Willy Clarkson and the Role of Disguises in Interwar England," *Journal of Social History* 40, no. 3 (2007): 597–618; and Marjorie Garber, *Vested Interests: Cross Dressing and Cultural Anxiety* (New York: Routledge, 1992).

16. Alison Oram, *Her Husband Was a Woman! Women's Gender-Crossing in Modern British Culture* (London: Routledge, 2007), 155.

17. This engagement with books stood at the center of Edith Thompson's notorious 1922 trial for the murder of her husband. Part of the reason for Thompson's presumed guilt was her love of cheap literature, especially romantic novels. Lucy Bland, "Trials and Tribulations of Edith Thompson: The Capital Crime of Sexual Incitement in 1920s England," *Journal of British Studies* 47, no. 3 (2008): 635.

18. Regina Kunzel, "Pulp Fiction and Problem Girls: Reading and Rewriting Single Pregnancy in Postwar United States," *American Historical Review* 100, no. 5 (1995): 1486.

19. Kunzel, "Pulp Fiction and Problem Girls," 1470.

20. Q. D. Leavis, *Fiction and the Reading Public* (1932; reprint, London: Pimlico, 2000), 3.

21. Ibid., 4.

22. Laura Doan, *Fashioning Sapphism: The Origins of Modern English Lesbian Culture* (New York: Columbia University Press, 2001), 133.

23. Jonathan Rose, *The Intellectual Life of the British Working Classes* (New Haven, CT: Yale University Press, 2001).

24. Clarissa Smith, *One for the Girls! The Pleasures and Practices of Reading Women's Porn* (Bristol, UK: Intellect Books, 2007).

25. Oliver Sacks, *The Man Who Mistook His Wife for a Hat and Other Clinical Tales* (New York: Touchstone Books, 1998), 111.

26. Marya Schechtman, *The Constitution of Selves* (Ithaca, NY: Cornell University Press, 1996).

27. Galen Strawson, "Against Narrativity," *Ratio* 17, no. 4 (2004): 447.

28. H. G. Cocks, *Nameless Offences: Homosexual Desire in the Nineteenth Century* (London: Tauris, 2003); Matt Cook, *London and the Culture of Homosexuality, 1885–1914* (Cambridge: Cambridge University Press, 2003); Matt Houlbrook, *Queer London: Perils and Pleasures in the Sexual Metropolis, 1918–1957* (Chicago: University of Chicago Press, 2006); Doan, *Fashioning Sapphism*.

29. David M. Halperin, *How to Do the History of Homosexuality* (Chicago: University of Chicago Press, 2002), 3.

30. Chris Waters explains the choice: "Do we look for what was emergent (and subsequently emerged), or do we focus on the logic of those 'hundred different experiences' and their meaning for those who had them at the time?" Chris Waters, "Distance and Desire in the New British Queer History," *GLQ: A Journal of Lesbian and Gay Studies* 14, no. 1 (2008): 147.

31. Vern and Bonnie Bullough, Roy Porter, and Angus McLaren, for example, have investigated the histories of sexual behaviors since the 1970s. Each of these scholars has been prolific. See, for example, Roy Porter and G. S. Rousseau, *Sexual Underworlds of the Enlightenment* (Chapel Hill: University of North Carolina Press, 1988); Vern Bullough and Bonnie Bullough, *Sexual Variance in Society and History* (New York: Wiley, 1976); Vern Bullough and Bonnie Bullough, *Cross Dressing, Sex, and Gender* (Philadelphia: University of Pennsylvania Press, 1993); Angus McLaren, *Birth Control in Nineteenth-Century England* (New York: Holmes and Meier, 1978); Angus McLaren, *Sexual Blackmail: A Modern History* (Cambridge, MA: Harvard University Press, 2002); and Angus McLaren, *The Trials of Masculinity: Policing Sexual Boundaries, 1870–1930* (Chicago: University of Chicago Press, 1997).

32. To scholars outside these fields, the differences between them may appear slight since all of these areas of scholarship consider sexuality in the past; however, between the fields, the differences have been magnified by different models of scholarship, political goals, and generational differences. See, for example, Waters, "Distance and Desire." See also Jeffrey Weeks, "Queer(y)ing the 'Modern Homosexual,'" paper presented at the British Queer History Conference, Montreal, McGill University, October 14, 2010. Both Waters and Weeks consider the difference between gay and lesbian history and queer studies.

33. Matt Houlbrook, "Sexing the History of Sexuality," *History Workshop Journal* 60 (2005): 217.

34. Regina Kunzel made the point that the sophistication of work on gay and lesbian history has meant that we know more about how gay men and lesbians constructed identities than about how others constructed their sexual selves in 1995. This assessment still holds true. See Kunzel, "Pulp Fiction and Problem Girls," 1468n13.

35. Peter Farrer has republished the correspondence from *Bits of Fun, London Life*, and other sources concerned with cross-dressing and sexual discipline. In *Confidential Correspondence on Cross-Dressing, 1911–1915*, he transcribes 202 letters; in *Confidential Correspondence on Cross-Dressing, Part II: 1916–1920*, he adds another 286; in *Cross Dressing between the Wars: Selections from London Life, 1923–1933*, he transcribes another 255 letters; and in *Cross Dressing between the Wars: Selections from London Life, 1934–1941*, he transcribes 318 letters. I have also consulted the collections at the Kinsey Institute for Research in Sex, Gender, and Reproduction, a clipping file from California State University–Northridge from the Harris/Wheeler collection, my own copies of the

magazine, photocopies made by Farrer, and the copies of *Bits of Fun, Fun, Illustrated Bits, London Life, London Life and Modern Society, New Fun, New Photo Fun,* and *Photo Fun* at the British Library. While I cannot say that I have a comprehensive knowledge of all such letters, I can say that I have read and thought about a group of letters that numbers in the tens of thousands. See Peter Farrer, ed., *Confidential Correspondence on Cross-Dressing, 1911–1915* (Liverpool, UK: Karn, 1997); Peter Farrer, *Confidential Correspondence on Cross-Dressing, Part II: 1916–1920* (Liverpool, UK: Karn, 1998); Peter Farrer, *Cross Dressing between the Wars: Selections from London Life, 1923–1933* (Liverpool, UK: Karn, 2000); and Peter Farrer, *Cross Dressing between the Wars: Selections from London Life, 1934–1941* (Liverpool, UK: Karn, 2006).

36. Tiffany Joseph, "'Non-combatant's Shell-Shock': Trauma and Gender in F. Scott Fitzgerald's 'Tender Is the Night,'" *NWSA* 15, no. 3 (2003): 66.

37. Joanna Bourke, *Dismembering the Male: Men's Bodies, Britain, and the Great War* (Chicago: University of Chicago Press, 1996), 21–22; Jay Winter, *Sites of Memory, Sites of Mourning: The Great War in European Cultural History* (Cambridge: Cambridge University Press, 1995), 2.

38. Bourke, *Dismembering the Male*, 15.

39. Robert Holland, "The British Empire and the Great War," in *The Oxford History of the British Empire: The Twentieth Century* (Oxford: Oxford University Press, 1999), 116.

40. See, for example, Magnus Hirschfeld, *Sexual History of the World War* (New York: Cadillac, 1941), chap. 12.

41. See, for example, John M. Mackenzie, "The Imperial Pioneer and Hunter and the Masculine Stereotypes in Late Victorian and Edwardian Times," and Allen Warren, "Popular Manliness: Baden Powell, Scouting and the Development of Manly Character," both in *Manliness and Morality*, edited by J. A. Mangan and James Walvin (Manchester, UK: University of Manchester Press, 1987); Graham Dawson, *Soldier Heroes: British Adventure, Empire and the Imagining of Masculinities* (London: Routledge, 1994); and Paul R. Deslandes, *Oxbridge Men: British Masculinity and the Undergraduate Experience, 1850–1920* (Bloomington: University of Indiana Press, 2005).

42. Michael Roper, "Between Manliness and Masculinity: The 'War Generation' and the Psychology of Fear in Britain, 1914–1950," *Journal of British Studies* 44, no. 2 (2005): 342–362.

43. McLaren, *The Trials of Masculinity*, 233–234.

44. Bourke, *Dismembering the Male*, 168–169; Martin Francis, "The Domestication of the Male? Recent Research on Nineteenth- and Twentieth-Century British Masculinity," *Historical Journal* 45, no. 3 (2002): 641.

45. Gabriel Koureas, *Memory, Masculinity and National Identity in British Visual Culture, 1914–1930* (Aldershot, UK: Ashgate, 2007), 6. Campaigns to shame cowards and force enlistments contributed to the fraught sense of masculinity and bitter gender divisions. See Nicoletta F. Gullace, "White Feathers and Wounded Men: Female Patriotism and the Memory of the Great War," *Journal of British Studies* 36 (1997): 178–206.

46. Mrs. Florence C., Lancashire, February 23, 1926, Papers of Marie Carmichael Stopes (PP/MCS)/A.57, Wellcome Library, London.

47. See, for example, Mary Louise Roberts, *Civilization without Sexes* (Princeton, NJ: Princeton University Press, 1994); Sandra Gilbert and Susan Gubar, *No Man's Land* (New Haven, CT: Yale University Press, 2002); and Susan Kingsley Kent, *Making Peace: The Reconstruction of Gender in Interwar Britain* (Princeton, NJ: Princeton University Press, 1993).

48. Billie Melman, *Women and the Popular Imagination in the Twenties: Flappers and Nymphs* (New York: Palgrave Macmillan, 1988), 19–20.

49. Jay Winter, *The Great War and the British People* (Cambridge, MA: Harvard University Press, 1986).

50. The classic study of women's wages remains Louise Tilly and Joan Scott, *Women, Work, and Family* (New York: Routledge, 1987). See also Susan Kingsley Kent, *Gender and Power in Britain, 1640–1990* (London: Routledge, 1999), 285, 286, 292–293.

51. Penny Tinkler, "Women and Popular Literature," in *Women's History: Britain, 1850–1945*, edited by June Purvis (New York: St. Martin's Press, 1995), 141–142.

52. Cheryl Buckley and Hillary Fawcett, *Fashioning the Feminine: Representation and Women's Fashion from the Fin de Siècle to the Present* (London: Tauris, 2002), 115.

53. Seth Koven, "Remembering and Dismemberment: Crippled Children, Wounded Soldiers, and the Great War in Great Britain," *American Historical Review* 99, no. 4 (1994): 1167–1202.

54. Koureas, *Memory, Masculinity and National Identity*, 126.

55. Winter, *Sites of Memory, Sites of Mourning*, 2.

56. Modris Eksteins, *Rites of Spring: The Great War and the Birth of the Modern Age* (New York: Anchor Books, 1989), 290–291.

57. Winter provides a summary of the discussion of the impact of the war on traditional versus modern motifs in art history. Winter, *Sites of Memory, Sites of Mourning*, 2–5.

58. Paul Fussell, *The Great War and Modern Memory* (Oxford: Oxford University Press, 1975); Eksteins, *Rites of Spring*. The question of the relationship between modernism and the war has developed such a life of its own that it generates its own historiographical essays and volumes, a considerable achievement in the current publishing climate. Stephen Heathorn, "The Mnemonic Turn in the Cultural Historiography of Britain's Great War," *Historical Journal* 48, no. 4 (2005): 1103–1124.

59. Bland, "Trials and Tribulations of Edith Thompson," 625.

60. See, for example, E. W. Shanahan, "Overpopulation, Emigration, Empire Development," *Economica*, no. 9 (1923): 215–223; Harold Cox, "The Peopling of the British Empire," *Foreign Affairs* 2, no. 1 (1923): 117–129; and W. A. Carrothers, *Emigration from the British Isles* (London: King, 1929).

61. The number of works on the British Empire is staggering. To understand the historiography, a place to begin would be S. E. Stockwell, ed., *The British Empire: Themes and Perspectives* (Malden, MA: Blackwell, 2008), which includes a series of excellent essays documenting recent research and approaches to the field; for introductions to each region and age of empire, see William Roger Louis, ed., *The Oxford History of the British Empire* (Oxford: Oxford University Press, 2001); for general overviews of the empire, see, for example, Bernard Porter, *The Lion's Share: A Short History of British Imperialism, 1850–2004* (London: Longman, 2004); Ronald Hyam, *Britain's Imperial Century, 1815–1914: A Study of Empire and Expansion* (New York: Palgrave Macmillan, 2002); and Ronald Hyam, *Britain's Declining Empire: The Road to Decolonization, 1918–1968* (Cambridge: Cambridge University Press, 2007). John Mackenzie's series published through Manchester University Press remains central to understanding the culture of imperialism in the United Kingdom.

62. Canadians, for example, at least nominally remained British subjects and British citizens throughout the interwar period. In fact, only after World War II did Canada introduce a Citizenship Act through which Canadians remained British subjects by extension of their citizenship to Canada. See Randall Hansen, *Citizenship and Immigration*

in Post-war Britain: The Institutional Origins of a Multicultural Nation (Oxford: Oxford University Press, 2000), 40–41. For West Indians, the emphasis on respectability and Christianity took precedence over issues of race and color. They fashioned Britishness as an imperial identity that united elites globally. Anne Spry Rush, *Bonds of Empire: West Indians and Britishness from Victoria to Decolonization* (Oxford: Oxford University Press, 2011).

63. See Catherine Hall, "Culture and Identity in Imperial Britain," in *The British Empire: Themes and Perspectives*, edited by S. E. Stockwell (Malden, MA: Blackwell, 2008), 204.

64. John M. Mackenzie, *Propaganda and Empire: The Manipulation of British Public Opinion 1880–1960* (Manchester, UK: Manchester University Press, 1984).

65. Laurence Lenton, "Interesting Experiences of a Corset Maker," *London Life*, January 5, 1929, 26.

66. See Lisa Z. Sigel, "Filth in the Wrong People's Hands: Postcards and the Expansion of Pornography in Britain and the Atlantic World," *Journal of Social History* 33, no. 4 (2000): 859–885; Philippa Levine, "States of Undress: Nakedness and the Colonial Imagination," *Victorian Studies* 50, no. 2 (2008): 189–219; and Richard Price, "One Big Thing: Britain, Its Empire, and Their Imperial Culture," *Journal of British Studies* 45, no. 3 (2006): 604.

67. Hazel H., Victoria Australia, February 23, 1921, PP/MCS/A.114.

68. Mrs. D.J.E.E., n.d., Transvaal, South Africa, PP/MCS/A.82; Daisy E. H., Wallasey, Cheshire, February 7, 1930, PP/MCS/A.118; Lillian A. Plymouth, August 18, 1928, PP/MCS/A.3; Dorothy E., Melbourne, Australia, December 20, 1932, PP/MCS/A.76.

69. My thinking on these matters has been enriched by Deana Heath, *Purifying Empire: Obscenity and the Politics of Moral Regulation in Britain, India and Australia* (Cambridge: Cambridge University Press, 2010).

70. Ina Zweiniger-Bargielowska, "Building a British Superman: Physical Culture in Interwar Britain," *Journal of Contemporary History* 41, no. 4 (2006): 599–601. See also Elizabeth Toon and Janet Golden, "'Live Clean, Think Clean, and Don't Go to Burlesque Shows': Charles Atlas as Health Advisor," *Journal of the History of Medicine and Allied Sciences* 57, no. 1 (January 2002): 39–60. As Vike Martina Plock demonstrates, the form of Eugen Sandow and the physical fitness movement provided the counterpoint to Leopold Bloom's sense of self in Joyce's "Ithaca" scene. Sandow's book decorated Bloom's bookshelf, and Bloom's fantasies of physical potential and self-improvement derived from the fantasies of perfection advertised in Sandow's publication and person. Vike Martina Plock, "A Feat of Strength in 'Ithaca': Eugen Sandow and Physical Culture in 'Joyce's Ulysses,'" *Journal of Modern Literature* 30, no. 1 (2006): 129, 130.

CHAPTER 1

1. Mrs. M.E.A., Somerset, November 30, 1929, Papers of Marie Carmichael Stopes (PP/MCS)/A.10, Wellcome Library, London.

2. Miss E.M.A., Dorset, n.d, PP/MCS/A.6.

3. V.G.A., Plumstead, September 26, 1939, PP/MCS/A.8.

4. Lucy Bland, "Trials and Tribulations of Edith Thompson: The Capital Crime of Sexual Incitement in 1920s England," *Journal of British Studies* 47, no. 3 (2008): 635.

5. One correspondent with Marie Stopes used an old book to frighten himself out of masturbating. "We have an old book of grandmother's, and I often sneaked readings from that. It maximises the practice, and promises disease, insanity, etc., and saying in effect;

'May God help you, nobody else can.' I was literally driven mad, whilst dreading madness, but I was still mastered by it." V.F.T., Adelaide, Australia, March 24, 1937, PP/MCS/A.229.

6. Mass-Observation, "The Press and Its Readers" (London: Art and Technology, 1949), 11. Illiteracy, meaning the inability to sign one's name, had dropped to 1 percent of the population by 1914. Clive Bloom, *Bestsellers: Popular Fiction since 1900* (Basingstoke, UK: Palgrave Macmillan, 2009), 29.

7. Roy Porter and Lesley Hall, *The Facts of Life: The Creation of Sexual Knowledge in Britain, 1650–1950* (New Haven, CT: Yale University Press, 1995), 251–253.

8. See, for example, Heike Bauer, *English Literary Sexology: Translations of Inversion, 1860–1930* (Basingstoke, UK: Palgrave Macmillan, 2009); Katherine Mullin, *James Joyce, Sexuality, and Social Purity* (Cambridge: Cambridge University Press, 2003); Adam Parkes, *Modernism and the Theater of Censorship* (Oxford: Oxford University Press, 1996); Celia Marshik, *British Modernism and Censorship* (Cambridge: Cambridge University Press, 2006); Elisabeth Ladenson, *Dirt for Art's Sake: Books on Trial from Madame Bovary to Lolita* (Ithaca, NY: Cornell University Press, 2007); Allison Wee, "Trials and Eros: The British Home Office v. Indecent Publications, 1857–1932" (Ph.D. diss., University of Minnesota, 2003); and Christopher Pollnitz, "The Censorship and the Transmission of D. H. Lawrence's *Pansies*: The Home Office and the 'Foul-Mouthed Fellow,'" *Journal of Modern Literature* 28, no. 3 (2005): 44–71.

9. Hera Cook, *The Long Sexual Revolution: English Women, Sex, and Contraception, 1800–1975* (Oxford: Oxford University Press, 2005), 167–178.

10. Kate Fisher, *Birth Control, Sex, and Marriage in Britain, 1918–1960* (Oxford: Oxford University Press, 2006), 41.

11. Cook, *The Long Sexual Revolution*, 180–181.

12. Fisher, *Birth Control, Sex, and Marriage in Britain*, 6.

13. Ross McKibbin, *Classes and Cultures: England, 1918–1951* (Oxford: Oxford University Press, 2000), 477. Materials and ideas were highly stratified by wealth, location, sophistication, and social class, often collapsed by commentators onto the ever-popular brow index of culture. The brow became a way for intellectuals (highbrow) to discuss the tastes and discriminations of everyone else (middlebrow and lowbrow). See Q. D. Leavis, *Fiction and the Reading Public* (1932; reprint, London: Pimlico, 2000), 35; and Virginia Woolf, "Middlebrow," in *The Death of the Moth and Other Essays* (San Diego: Harcourt Brace, 1970), 178.

14. Victor Gollancz, "Banning: A Publisher's View on Censorship," *Time and Tide*, March 22, 1929, p. 323, National Archives (TNA), Public Records Office (PRO), Home Office (HO) 45/15139. "List Showing States of Issue, Number, Etc., of Magazines, Books, and Photographs Seized at No. 23, Newport Court, Charing Cross Road," May 10, 1937, TNA, PRO, Metropolitan Police Department (MEPO) 3/938 Central Office, New Scotland Yard.

15. For example, one Canadian reader stated that she and her husband had read *Married Love, Wise Parenthood*, and *The Theory, History and Practice of Contraception*, though the reader might have meant by the last title *Contraception: Its Theory, History and Practice*. Muriel H., Regina, Saskatchewan, Canada, June 22, 1930, PP/MCS/A.115. Another reader from Quebec stated he had read Stopes's book on birth control. A.A.J., Quebec, Canada, September 19, 1930, PP/MCS/A.145. Stopes suggested that western Canada was a good region for women to find men and satisfy their sexual instincts in her reply to Miss K. M., Breamore, nr. Salisbury, August 10, 1919; Stopes reply, August 19, 1919, PP/MCS/A.169; Jonathan Rose, *The Intellectual Life of the British Working Classes* (New Haven, CT: Yale University Press, 2001), 218.

16. The "Report of the Departmental Committee on Sexual Offenses against Young Persons" believed that the lack of education contributed to children's sexual vulnerability. The report suggested that greater education might lower the number of rapes, assaults, cases of indecent exposure against children. See "Report of the Departmental Committee on Sexual Offenses against Young Persons" (London: HMSO, 1925), 83, TNA, PRO, HO45/25433.

17. TNA, PRO, Ministry of Health (MH) 102/1081. The entire file discusses sex education in council schools in 1935. From a survey sent to parents, it seems as if most would support sex education in schools, as would most educators; in that file, see A. H. Gem, Miss Grant L. Clark, Organisers of Physical Education, "Some Notes on Sex Instruction for Residential School," p. 2, and Dr. Shrubsall, "Some Notes on Questions Involved in Sex Education," p. 4.

18. As one man explained in his letter to Marie Stopes, "Your books have shown me the importance of correct performance of the sexual functions, and I have read very widely on the subject since then." A.B., South Africa, December 6, 1926, PP/MCS/A.29.

19. See, for example, the Louise Lawrence Collection at the Kinsey Institute. Lawrence informed Kinsey about the transvestite and transsexual community in California. In her collection are newspaper clippings, letters, and scrapbooks about cross-dressing and sadomasochism from the 1890s and 1900s. She also copied materials from her own collection and from her colleagues and friends about those topics for Kinsey, including magazines such as *Illustrated Bits*, *London Life*, and *New Fun* and books such as *Gynecocracy*. The materials accumulated by George Ives also stand as evidence to this claim. See "George Cecil Ives: An Inventory of His Papers" at the Harry Ransom Humanities Research Center, University of Texas, Austin. Yale University Library owns Ives's scrapbooks of clippings on topics such as murders, punishments, freaks, crime and punishment, cross-dressing, homosexuality, cricket scores, and letters he wrote to newspapers. See Paul Sieveking, *Man Bites Man* (London: Landesman, 1981).

20. See Chapter 4 for further discussion of this issue.

21. Bloom, *Bestsellers*, 37.

22. Leavis, *Fiction and the Reading Public*, 10.

23. For the discussion of censorship in libraries, see Anthony Hugh Thompson, *Censorship in Public Libraries in the United Kingdom during the Twentieth Century* (Epping, UK: Bowker, 1975).

24. The British Museum demanded proof of scholarly credentials and then made readers sit in the Rare Books room at a table that allowed easy surveillance.

25. Judy Mabro, *I Ban Everything: Free Speech and Censorship at Oxford* (Oxford: Ruskin College Library, 1985).

26. The Home Office met with the secretary of the Associated Booksellers of Great Britain and Ireland, who sought a list of censored works. He said that "his members dislike dealing in objectionable books" and that he sought the list of censored books that would help them avoid the selling of such works. He brought with him the American version of such a list and offered the Home Office a chance to copy it. Memo Regarding M.W.J. Magenis, n.d., TNA, PRO, HO45/15139. For a fuller discussion of voluntary censorship, see also Lisa Z. Sigel, "Censorship in Inter-war Britain: Denial, Publicity, and the Extension of the Liberal State," *Journal of Social History* 45, no. 1 (2011): 65–83.

27. For overviews of the censorship of obscenity, see Lisa Z. Sigel, *Governing Pleasures: Pornography and Social Change in England, 1815–1914* (New Brunswick, NJ: Rutgers University Press, 2002); Walter Kendrick, *The Secret Museum: Pornography in Modern Culture* (New York: Viking Press, 1987); and Wee, "Trials and Eros."

28. Norman St. John-Stevas, *Obscenity and the Law* (London: Seeker and Warburg, 1956), 70.

29. "The Stoppage of Letters to or from Dealers in Obscene Matter," 1898, TNA, PRO, HO45/9752/A59329.

30. Deana Heath, *Purifying Empire: Obscenity and the Politics of Moral Regulation in Britain, India and Australia* (Cambridge: Cambridge University Press, 2010), 171.

31. Emma Larkin, "The Self-Conscious Censor: Censorship in Burma under the British, 1900–1939," *Journal of Burma Studies* 8 (2003): 65.

32. Resident Commissioner's Office, July 15, 1911, TNA, PRO, DO119/865. Office of the Minister of Justice, Cape Town, February 6, 1912, TNA, PRO, DO119/865. The file in its entirety documents the changes in law and punishments.

33. "League of Nations: Accession of His Britannic Majesty for Certain British Dependencies to the International Convention for the Suppression of the Circulation of and Traffic in Obscene Publications, Geneva, September 12, 1923," November 18, 1926, TNA, PRO, Colonial Office (CO) 323/960/7.

34. The conception of obscenity within the commitment to a free press carried over to British colonies until almost the end of the nineteenth century, when more serious legislation allowed nationalist protests to edge into sedition. Robert Darnton, "Literary Surveillance in the British Raj: The Contradictions of Liberal Imperialism," *Book History* 2 (2001): 148–150, 156.

35. Sir William Joynson-Hicks, Home Secretary, stated that if the state censored, then there would have to be a certificate indicating that the "book was fit to be sold" and that all books would need to be read by the censor to get that certificate. "Indecent Books," *The Times*, March 6, 1929, TNA, PRO, HO45/15139. See also letters from the Secretary of the Cabinet to the Imperial Secretary, August 12, 1924, February 14, 1924, and May 13, 1925, TNA, PRO, HO267/225; "Obscene Publications," March 5, 1929, TNA, PRO, HO45/15139; report on obscenity, January 9, 1939, TNA, PRO, HO45/24761.

36. For discussion of censorship in cinema, see James C. Robertson, *The British Board of Film Censors: Film Censorship in Britain, 1896–1950* (London: Taylor and Francis, 1985); Neville March Hunnings, *Film Censors and the Law* (London: Allen and Unwin, 1967); and Caroline Levine, "Propaganda for Democracy: The Curious Case of *Love on the Dole*," *Journal of British Studies* 45 (October 2006): 846–874. For discussion of censorship in the theater, see Nicholas de Jongh, *Politics, Prudery, and Perversions: The Censorship of the English Stage, 1901–1968* (London: Methuen, 2001).

37. Memo Regarding M.W.J. Magenis, n.d., TNA, PRO, HO45/15139; London Public Morality Council Minutes, June 28, 1930, TNA, PRO, HO144/14042; letter from C. P. Hill to A. E. Howell, April 11, 1938, TNA, PRO, Customs (CUST) 49/2334.

38. "Confidential Report on the Stoppage of Letters—A Brief History, 1898," TNA, PRO, HO144/9752/A59329; "Importation of Indecent or Obscene Publications," March 19, 1934, TNA, PRO, CUST49/1683.

39. Heath, *Purifying Empire*, 93.

40. Ibid., 116.

41. For consideration of the London Public Morality Council's relationship with the British state, see "Indecent Books," *The Times*, March 6, 1929, TNA, PRO, HO45/15139; Bishop of London, Minutes, March 24, 1930, PRO, HO144/14042.

42. The entire structure of film censorship in Britain rested on the principle of self-censorship by reputable filmmakers and distributors. Films that showed people having sex did not try to get approval from the film board; instead, such films sold privately through pornography vendors and were hard to find. See letter from C. Benbow to

R. E. Matheson, March 6, 1923, TNA, PRO, Central Criminal Court (CRIM) 1/234, Exhibit 17. The British Board of Film Censors (BBFC), though supposedly formed to keep state control out of film, "frequently—and covertly—consulted the Home and Foreign Offices," according to Caroline Levine. Levine, "Propaganda for Democracy," 848. The BBFC banned some films, including Sergei Eisenstein's *Battleship Potemkin*, on political grounds, and Tom Ricketts's *Damaged Goods*, a film about the effects of venereal disease, on moral grounds. Marie Stopes's *Married Love* was heavily cut, was renamed *Massie's Marriage*, and had Stopes's name removed from the credits. In the colonies and dominions, the government took on a larger role in censoring films, though the agency responsible varied according to local needs and available manpower. In some areas, a central board—appointed and answerable to the governor—decided the fate of films; in others, village and township boards previewed the films, and in still others, censorship devolved onto the local police department. In all regions, however, the state remained central to censorship; most imperial agents hoped for even greater state involvement through the establishment of a principal censorship bureau or board in London. See Hunnings, *Film Censors and the Law*; Jeffrey Richards, "Controlling the Screen: The British Cinema in the 1930s," *History Today* 33 (1983): 12; "Undesirable and Harmful Films: Plea for Stricter Censorship," *Birmingham Post*, May 8, 1931, TNA, PRO, HO45/14276; "The Home Secretary Replies to Our Open Letter," *Methodist Times*, August 20, 1931, TNA, PRO, HO45/14277; "Copy of Note Prepared in 1922 as to Film Censorship in the Dominions," TNA, PRO, HO45/22906; and "Report of the Colonial Films Committee" (London: HMSO, 1930), TNA, PRO, HO45/14272.

43. See Lisa Z. Sigel, "Filth in the Wrong People's Hands: Postcards and the Expansion of Pornography in Britain and the Atlantic World," *Journal of Social History* 33, no. 4 (2000): 859–885; Philippa Levine, "States of Undress: Nakedness and the Colonial Imagination," *Victorian Studies* 50, no. 2 (2008): 189–219.

44. Celia Marshik, "History's 'Abrupt Revenges': Censoring War's Perversions in *The Well of Loneliness* and *Sleeveless Errand*," *Journal of Modern Literature* 26, no. 2 (2002–2003): 148.

45. A. Maxwell, "Confidential," April 8, 1938, TNA, PRO, CUST49/2334. For example, while the government said that certain magazines were not banned, they were held to be "obscene and ordered to be destroyed." In particular, four classes of magazines were particularly suspicious: French illustrated magazines, cheap American magazines, miscellaneous, and whipping stories.

46. For example, Mr. Bonnaire, a wholesaler of books and postcards, was found guilty of obscenity and charged ten guineas costs for the trial. Bonnaire foresaw bankruptcy as a result of the trial and the court costs. "Copy of Minutes on H.O. Papers, No. 567500/417," 1931, TNA, PRO, MEPO3/935. The 1935/1936 summary of cases reported to the League of Nations mentioned that legal proceedings occurred for sixty cases and resulted in the imposition of sentences ranging from five-shilling fines to three months' imprisonment and two months' hard labor for obscenity. League of Nations, Advisory Committee on Social Questions, "Summary of Annual Reports for 1935/36, prepared by the Secretariat" (Geneva, February 28, 1937) Official No.: C. 138M.87, 18–19, TNA, PRO, CO323/1432/1.

47. Jesse W. Keech, Chief Inspector, report, Metropolitan Police, Criminal Investigations Department (CID), New Scotland Yard, June 1935, TNA, PRO, MEPO3/2459.

48. Lieut. Leonard S. London, March 8, 1919, PP/MCS/A.216.

49. "List Showing States of Issue, Number, Etc., of Magazines, Books, and Photographs Seized at Cambridge Bookshop, Charing Cross Road," Central Office, New Scotland Yard, May 10, 1937, TNA, PRO MEPO3/938.

50. "List Showing States of Issue, Number, Etc., of Magazines, Books, and Photographs Seized at No. 21, Newport Court, Charing Cross Road," Central Office, New Scotland Yard, May 10, 1937, TNA, PRO MEPO3/938.

51. "List Showing States of Issue, Number, Etc., of Magazines, Books, and Photographs Seized at No. 23, Newport Court, Charing Cross Road," Central Office, New Scotland Yard, May 10, 1937, TNA, PRO MEPO3/938.

52. H. G. Cocks, "Saucy Stories: Pornography, Sexology and the Marketing of Sexual Knowledge in Britain, c. 1918–70," *Social History* 29, no. 4 (November 2004): 465–484.

53. Chart of Warrant Issues, 1898, TNA, PRO, HO45/9752/A59329; letter from Charles Carrington to Rt. Hon. R. McKenna, M.P., December 7, 1911, TNA, PRO, HO45/1051C. For the most accurate biographical details of Charles Carrington, see Peter Mendes, *Clandestine Erotic Fiction in English 1800–1930: A Bibliographical Study* (Aldershot, UK: Scolar Press, 1993); and the website of Sheryl Straight, The Erotica Bibliophile, which has an extensive and well-documented section on Carrington, at http://www.eroticabibliophile.com/index.php. See also Patrick Kearney, *The Private Case* (London: Landesman, 1981) for the catalog of materials in the Private Case collection at the British Library, including many of the erotic publications by Carrington.

54. Report, Metropolitan Police, St. Ann's Road Station, "n" Divn., December 7, 1950, TNA, PRO, MEPO3/2459; Jesse W. Keech, Chief Inspector, report, Metropolitan Police, CID, New Scotland Yard, June 1935, TNA, PRO, MEPO3/2459; Report, Metropolitan Police, CID, December 29, 1936, TNA, PRO, MEPO3/12459.

55. *Charles and Co. Circular,* [London], n.d., TNA, PRO, MEPO3/2459.

56. See H. S. Ashbee, *Index Librorum Prohibitorum* (1877; reprint, New York: Documentary Books, 1962), 238–256; and Simon Eliot, "Hotten: Rotten: Forgotten? An Apologia for a General Publisher," *Book History* 3 (2000): 70.

57. League of Nations, Advisory Committee on Social Questions, "Summary of Annual Reports for 1935/36, Prepared by the Secretariat," Geneva, February 28, 1937, Official No.: C. 138M.87, 18–19, TNA, PRO, CO323/1432/1; League of Nations, Advisory Committee on Social Questions, "Summary of Annual Reports for 1937/38, Prepared by the Secretariat," Geneva, February 28, 1939, Official No.: C. 69.M 31, 2–3, TNA, PRO, CO323/1656/5.

58. E. A. Sowter and Reverend Neville Hudson received twelve months' imprisonment and three years' penal servitude for making indecent films and photographs of young boys. "Report on Obscenity," January 9, 1939, TNA, PRO, HO45/24761.

59. The seizure of works was set into policy. Both Customs and the Postal Office would send copies to repositories of record including the British Museum, Bodleian Library, University Library Cambridge, National Library Scotland, and Trinity College Dublin as well as the City of London Police, the Director of Public Prosecutions, and the Home Office so that these departments would have copies for future reference. To forestall the "possibilities of temptation," especially in cases where the police had confiscated "large quantities of something for which it would be easy to get high prices in certain markets," confiscated books that could be shoved in a furnace were immolated, while larger runs were destroyed by means of "guillotine machinery." Letter from Bicknell to Howgrave-Graham, December 4, 1929, TNA, PRO, MEPO3/383; reply from Bicknell to Howgrave-Graham, n.d., TNA, PRO, MEPO3/383.

60. In some sense, obscenity responded sluggishly to change and formed a reservoir of antiquated ideas about sex. Joseph Slade has suggested that regressive tendencies may illustrate an ambivalence to the sex trades. Joseph Slade, "Eroticism and Technological Regression: The Stag Film," *History and Technology* 22, no. 1 (March 2006): 32.

61. Leavis, *Fiction and the Reading Public*, 10.

62. Chris Baggs, "How Well Read Was My Valley? Reading, Popular Fiction, and the Miners of South Wales, 1875–1939," *Book History* 4 (2001): 285.

63. George Orwell, "Boys Weeklies," in *The Collected Essays, Journalism and Letters of George Orwell*, vol. 1, *An Age Like This* (New York: Harcourt Brace, 1968), 460.

64. Robert Graves and Alan Hodge, *The Long Week-End: A Social History of Great Britain* (1940; reprint, New York: Norton, 1994), 1.

65. Orwell, "Boys Weeklies," 461.

66. Anthony Quinn, e-mail communication, November 17, 2011. Anthony Quinn answered my query about the distribution of magazines on the basis of his research, his experiences as an editor, and his discussion with people in the trade. He is currently working on two books, one on British magazine design for the Victoria and Albert Museum and one for the *Cambridge History of the Book*, vol. 7. These books are scheduled to be published in 2012 and 2013. Details of the Gordon and Gotch company come from the company history, "Our History," Gordon and Gotch, 2009, available at http://www.gordongotch.com.au/ggweb/Aboutus/OurHistory/tabid/105/Default.aspx (accessed November 20, 2011).

67. London Metropolitan Archives, Public Morality Council Papers, A/PMC/207/1-121, contains copies of such magazines.

68. *High Heels* (magazine) 1, no. 10 (January 1938), London Metropolitan Archives.

69. E. B. Mann, "Gun Glory," *Ranch Romances: Love Stories of the Real West* (January 1929): 329.

70. See, for example, the cover of *Health and Strength*, London, May 23, 1936.

71. Brian Hoffman, "'A Certain Amount of Prudishness': Nudist Magazines and the Liberalisation of American Obscenity Law, 1947–58," *Gender and History* 22, no. 3 (2010): 709.

72. Thomas Waugh, *Hard to Imagine: Gay Male Eroticism in Photography and Film from Their Beginnings to Stonewall* (New York: Columbia University Press, 1996).

73. G. Walsh, "Simple Exercises to Build a Powerful Neck," *Health and Strength*, May 36, 1936, p. 607.

74. See Karl Toepfer, *Empire of Ecstasy: Nudity and Movement in German Body Culture, 1910–1935* (Berkeley: University of California Press, 1997); Waugh, *Hard to Imagine*, 191–205; Michael Hau, *The Cult of Health and Beauty in Germany: A Social History 1890–1930* (Chicago: University of Chicago Press, 2003); and Chad Ross, *Naked Germany: Health, Race and the Nation* (Oxford: Oxford University Press, 2005).

75. For example, see Frances Merrill and Mason Merrill, "Nachtkultur Assails Us," in *Among the Nudists* (New York: Knopf, 1931), 3–11, in which the authors describe being shown a photo album by a German nudist. According to their description, Herr Koenig saw the images as wholesome, but they secretly believed that he was a sexual exhibitionist.

76. David Kunzle, *Fashion and Fetishism: Corsets, Tight-Lacing, and Other Forms of Body-Sculpture* (Stroud, UK: Sutton, 2004), 212; see also Robert Bienvenu, "The Development of Sadomasochism as a Cultural Style in the Twentieth-Century United States" (Ph.D. diss., Indiana University, 1998).

77. Martin Pugh, *We Danced All Night: A Social History of Britain between the Wars* (London: Vintage Books, 2009), 328.

78. Bloom, *Bestsellers*, 134.

79. Ibid., 134.

80. Leavis, *Fiction and the Reading Public*, 35.

81. Bloom, *Bestsellers*, 13.

82. Agatha Christie, "Death on the Nile," in *Poirot in the Orient* (1937; reprint, Berkley Books, 2005); Agatha Christie, "Murder in Mesopotamia," in *Poirot in the Orient* (1936; reprint, Berkley Books, 2001).

83. William Le Queux, *The Doctor of Pimlico* (London: Cassell, 1919), 15.

84. Margaret Pedler, *The Barbarian Lover* (New York: Grosset and Dunlap, 1923), 277.

85. Ibid., 147.

86. Edgar Wallace, *The Girl from Scotland Yard* (New York: Doubleday, 1926), 26.

87. Le Queux, *The Doctor of Pimlico*, 15–16.

88. Anthony Berkeley, *Silk Stocking Murders* (London: Penguin, 1941), 29.

89. Consider the description of Nurse Leatheran in Agatha Christie, "Murder in Mesopotamia," 8, and the characterization of Anne Manners in Berkeley, *Silk Stocking Murders*, 192.

90. Olive Wadsley, *Possession* (London: Cassell, 1924), 306.

91. Le Queux, *The Doctor of Pimlico*, 305.

92. May Christie, *Love's Miracle* (New York: Grosset and Dunlap, 1930), 268.

93. Berkeley, *Silk Stocking Murders*, 40, 47.

94. Wallace, *The Girl from Scotland Yard*, 5.

95. Graves and Hodge, *The Long Week-End*, 93.

96. Jonathan Rose, *The Intellectual Life of the British Working Classes*, 139.

97. For a fascinating discussion of the working classes relationship to modernism, see ibid., 393–438.

98. Graves and Hodge, *The Long Week-End*, 93.

99. Lawrence expected the state to censor *Lady Chatterley's Lover* and tried to publish both an expurgated and unexpurgated version of the work. The unexpurgated version, printed in Florence, was to be sold by subscription only, a method through which legally marginal books like Burton's translation of the *Kama Sutra* had circulated in the past. However, the ruse of private circulation did not work, and *Lady Chatterley* was subject to suppression. Rather than trying to deflect attention, Lawrence—ill and suffering from abroad—complained about his affairs in innumerable letters, wrote inflammatory essays about the nature of censorship, and sent paintings, poems, essays, and novels to England, despite the knowledge that they would enrage state bureaucrats, according to Christopher Pollnitz's fascinating account. Pollnitz, "The Censorship and the Transmission of D. H. Lawrence's *Pansies*," 44–71. Furthermore, once subject to censorship, the volume was open to piracy because the state would not protect its copyright. See Parkes, *Modernism and the Theater of Censorship*, 108. The original file for the suppression of *Lady Chatterley's Lover* appears to be missing from the National Archives, Public Records Office files. More information about the circulation and censorship of the work would be in that file.

100. See, for example, Leavis, *Fiction and the Reading Public*, 274n4.

101. D. H. Lawrence, *Lady Chatterley's Lover* (1928; reprint, London: Penguin, 2006), 136.

102. Ibid., 196.

103. Ibid., 202.

104. Ibid., 203.

105. D. H. Lawrence, "A Propos of *Lady Chatterley's Lover*," in *Sex, Literature and Censorship* (New York: Viking Press, 1959), 104.

106. Steven Kellman, "James Joyce for Ordinary Blokes?" *Chronicle of Higher Education*, September 21, 2009, available at http://chronicle.com/article/James-Joyce-for-Ordinary/48427/.

107. Ladenson, *Dirt for Art's Sake*, 80.

108. Quoted in ibid.

109. Laura Doan, *Fashioning Sapphism: The Origins of Modern English Lesbian Culture* (New York: Columbia University Press, 2001), 10.

110. Radclyffe Hall, *The Well of Loneliness* (1928; reprint, New York: Anchor Books, 1990), 313.

111. Part B: The Mechanics of Sex, Chapter 2: The Facts of Life, circa 1948, microfilm, Adam Matthew Publications, Part 12: Topic Collections, Sexual Behavior, Box 15, Reel 217, Mass-Observation Archive, University of Sussex.

112. Part B: The Mechanics of Sex, Chapter 2: The Facts of Life, draft copy, pp. 4–5, 1949, Mass-Observation Archive.

113. Most people received no formal instruction about sexuality, and many did not know the origin of their own sexual beliefs. The first results of the Mass-Observation study of sexuality found that one in four said they "just picked it up." Others said the knowledge just came to them; they learned from other children or from a parent. Part B: The Mechanics of Sex, Chapter 2: The Facts of Life, circa 1948, Mass-Observation Archive. Sex education seemed to be making an impact. Fully 16 percent of the 2,052 respondents had received sex instruction, and that percentage was on the rise. A third of those under twenty-five (in 1949) received formal sex instruction, while only a twelfth of those over forty-five had done so. One in twelve learned facts about sexuality from reading. "First Results of Mass-Observation's Survey of Sexual Morality," circa 1948, Mass-Observation Archive.

114. Ralcy Husted Bell, *Some Aspects of Adultery* (New York: Critic and Guide, 1921), foreword.

115. Marie Stopes, *Married Love* (1918; reprint, Oxford: Oxford University Press, 2004), 11.

116. June Rose, *Marie Stopes and the Sexual Revolution* (New York: Faber and Faber, 1992), 78–79.

117. Lesley Hall, "Review of *Marie Stopes and the Sexual Revolution,*" *Medical History* 37, no. 2 (1993): 219. Two main streams of materials went into the Cupboard collection: the works of sexologists and ephemeral works of erotica. Stopes acknowledged the works of sexologists; however, certain theories that she propounds, such as the benefit of male semen for women's health, seem custom-built from the erotica. This suggests that she may have read those works as well.

118. Ross McKibbin, "Introduction," in Marie Stopes, *Married Love* (1918; reprint, Oxford: Oxford University Press, 2004), xxxvi.

119. Porter and Hall, *Facts of Life*, 209.

120. Given the extraordinary number of editions of these works, there is some variation in the pagination. See Claire Davey, "Birth Control in Britain during the Interwar Years: Evidence from the Stopes Correspondence," *Journal of Family History* 13, no. 3 (1988): 335–336.

121. Alexander C. T. Geppert, "Divine Sex, Happy Marriage, Regenerated Nation: Marie Stopes's Marital Manual *Married Love* and the Making of a Best-Seller, 1918–1955," *Journal of the History of Sexuality* 8, no. 3 (1998): 397.

122. Stopes, *Married Love*, 10.

123. Lesley Hall has written an excellent entry on Chesser in the *Dictionary of National Biography*.

124. Eustace Chesser, *Love without Fear* (New York: Signet Books, 1947). Chesser references sexologists throughout his book; see pp. 23, 61, 85, 107, 112, and 116.

125. See, for example, Kenneth Walker, *Diseases of the Male Organs of Generation* (London: Oxford Medical Publications, 1923).

126. "Male Sexual Disorders," review, *British Medical Journal* 1, no. 3622 (June 7, 1930): 1054; see, for example, Kenneth Walker, *Physiology of Sex* (New York: Penguin, 1945), chap. 2.

127. Angus McLaren, *Twentieth-Century Sexuality* (Oxford: Blackwell, 1999), 52.

128. See, for example, T. H. Van de Velde, "Position and Action during Coitus," in *Ideal Marriage* (New York: Random House, 1930), 211–243.

129. Laura Cameron and John Forrester, "'A Nice Type of the English Scientist': Tansley and Freud," *History Workshop Journal*, no. 48 (Autumn 1999): 64–100.

130. A. G. Tansley, *The New Psychology and Its Relation to Life* (London: Dodd, Mead, 1922), 12.

131. Graves and Hodge, *The Long Week-End*, 90; Donald A., Second Lieut., Cairo, December 2, 1918, PP/MCS/Box 2/A.15. Ellis also published shorter volumes such as *Man and Woman* (Boston: Houghton Mifflin, 1929), though most references at the time referred to his masterwork.

132. Ivan Crozier, "Taking Prisoners; Havelock Ellis, Sigmund Freud, and the Construction of Homosexuality, 1897–1951," *Social History of Medicine* 13 (2000): 449–450.

133. Lesley Hall, "The English Have Hot Water Bottles," in *Sexual Knowledge, Sexual Science*, edited by Roy Porter and Mikulas Teich (Cambridge: Cambridge University Press, 1994), 357.

134. Morris Ernst, "Foreword," in *Studies in the Psychology of Sex*, by Havelock Ellis (New York: Random House, 1936), vii.

135. L. Hall, "The English Have Hot Water Bottles," 357.

136. Ivan Crozier, "Becoming a Sexologist: Norman Haire, the 1929 London World League for Sex Reform Congress, and Organizing Medical Knowledge about Sex in Interwar England," *Science History*, 39 (2001): 302.

137. This observation comes from Ivan Crozier's study of the sociological of knowledge between Freud and Ellis. Crozier, "Taking Prisoners," 449–450.

138. McLaren, *Twentieth-Century Sexuality*, 49; Porter and Hall, *The Facts of Life*, 167.

139. Havelock Ellis, "Sexual Inversion," in *Studies in the Psychology of Sex*, vol. 1 (New York: Random House, 1942), 341. For further discussion of Ellis and homosexuality, see Joseph Bristow, "Symonds's History, Ellis's Heredity: Sexual Inversion," in *Sexology in Culture: Labeling Bodies and Desires*, edited by Lucy Bland and Laura Doan (Chicago: University of Chicago Press, 1998), 79–99; Chris Waters, "Havelock Ellis, Sigmund Freud and the State: Discourses of Homosexual Identity in Interwar Britain," in *Sexology in Culture: Labeling Bodies and Desires*, edited by Lucy Bland and Laura Doan (Chicago: University of Chicago Press, 1998), 165–179; Crozier, "Taking Prisoners," 449–450.

140. Compare Havelock Ellis, "Love and Pain," in *Studies in the Psychology of Sex*, vol. 1 (New York: Random House, 1942), with Freud's "A Child Is Being Beaten," in *On Freud's "A Child Is Being Beaten,"* edited by Ethel Spector Person (New Haven, CT: Yale University Press, 1997).

141. Porter and Hall, *The Facts of Life*, 166.

142. Jill Fields, "'Fighting the Corsetless Evil': Shaping Corsets and Culture, 1900–1930," *Journal of Social History* 33, no. 2 (1999): 358.

143. This framework developed concomitant to Freud's ideas within a mutually supportive relationship. The two men even lived for a time within a few miles of each other

but never met. Although they borrowed ideas from each other, their models of sexuality were so divergent that they remained irreconcilable. Ellis even wrote an account of Freud's contribution to understanding sexuality in the *American Journal of Sociology* for the November 1939 edition, published shortly after Freud's death. Havelock Ellis, "Freud's Influence on the Changed Attitude toward Sex," *American Journal of Sociology* 45, no. 3 (November 1939): 309–317.

144. Porter and Hall, *Facts of Life*, 183.

145. Renate Hauser, "Krafft-Ebing's Psychological Understanding of Sexual Behavior," in Roy Porter and Mikulas Teich, *Sexual Science, Sexual Knowledge* (Cambridge: Cambridge University Press, 1994), 210–211.

146. Oosterhuis, *Stepchildren of Nature: Krafft-Ebing, Psychiatry, and the Making of Sexual Identity* (Chicago: University of Chicago Press, 2000).

147. Bauer, *English Literary Sexology*, 33.

148. Ibid., 35.

149. McLaren, *Twentieth-Century Sexuality*, 111; see also Sigmund Freud, *Three Essays on the Theory of Sexuality* (New York: Basic Books, 1975).

150. Dean Rapp, "The Early Discovery of Freud by the British General Public," *Social History of Medicine* 3, no. 2 (1990): 220.

151. See J. D. Sutherland, "Editorial Note" and "Editor's Note," in *Three Essays on the Theory of Sexuality*, by Sigmund Freud (New York: Basic Books, 1975), vii, ix; Patrick Joseph Mahony, "'A Child Is Being Beaten': A Clinic, Historical, and Textual Study," in *On Freud's "A Child Is Being Beaten,"* edited by Ethel Spector Person (New Haven, CT: Yale University Press, 1997), 48–49.

152. Graves and Hodge, *The Long Week-End*, 92.

153. Jonathan Rose, *The Intellectual Life of the British Working Classes*, 139.

154. Rapp, "The Early Discovery of Freud by the British General Public," 220.

155. Havelock Ellis, "The Art of Love," in *Studies in the Psychology of Sex*, vol. 2 (New York: Random House, 1936), 508.

156. Chesser, *Love without Fear*, 9.

157. Florence G. F., London, August 22, 1918, PP/MCS/box 14/A.87.

158. According to Robert Graves and Alan Hodge, the textbooks for homosexuality were Edward Carpenter's "bright little volume" *The Intermediate Sex*, which posited homosexuality as the third sex, and Havelock Ellis's massive *The Psychology of Sex*. Graves and Hodge, *The Long Week-End*, 90.

159. Jonathan Rose, *Intellectual Life of the British Working Classes*, 210.

160. Quoted in ibid.

161. Mrs. W.H.D., Liverpool, October 26, 1920, PP/MCS/A.72.

162. Fisher, *Birth Control, Sex, and Marriage in Britain*, 26–75.

CHAPTER 2

1. Marie Stopes, *Married Love* (1918; reprint, Oxford: Oxford University Press, 2004), 107.

2. For a statistical analysis of a sample of the correspondence, see Christopher Stopes-Roe's Statistical Appendix, in Ruth Hall, ed., *Dear Dr. Stopes* (London: Deutsch, 1978), 215–218. Most scholars see these correspondents as overwhelmingly middle class, however, working-class people wrote to her as well. Stopes's book *Mother England* is almost entirely composed of working-class requests for information and assistance. Even after World War II, the middle classes turned to Stopes for information. A survey by

Mass-Observation from 1949 found that just over half of respondents of the middle-class National Panel mentioned books as a source of information about sexuality. The most frequently mentioned writers were Marie Stopes and Havelock Ellis. See Chapter 1 for further discussion.

3. June Rose, *Marie Stopes and the Sexual Revolution* (London: Faber and Faber, 1992), 138–139.

4. Many of her materials went to the British Library, but the library was less interested in the thousands of letters from readers. Eventually, the Stopes family negotiated their deposit to the Wellcome Library. The Wellcome Library holds more than three hundred files of these papers but could offer no exact figures on the number of letters. Claire Davey suggests the figure of ten thousand. Claire Davey, "Birth Control in Britain during the Interwar Years: Evidence from the Stopes Correspondence," *Journal of Family History* 13, no. 3 (1988): 332. Though the letters remain partially closed to protect the confidentiality of the writers, the library allows researchers to use them as long as anonymity and confidentiality are maintained. These letters are archived at the Wellcome Library, Papers of Marie Carmichael Stopes (PP/MCS). To maintain anonymity, I have used only last initials, but I have specified location and date where available so that researchers can locate the document in the archives. Other sources of letters to Stopes are also available. Stopes herself reprinted letters sent to her in 1926 to create *Mother England*. Marie Stopes, *Mother England: A Contemporary History* (London: Bale, 1929). Ruth Hall edited *Dear Dr. Stopes*, a collection of letters from the years 1918–1928. These three bodies of letters provide a wealth of information, though not without certain problems.

5. R. Hall, *Dear Dr. Stopes*, 9; Lesley Hall, *Hidden Anxieties: Male Sexuality, 1900–1950* (Cambridge, UK: Polity Press, 1991), 11.

6. See, for example, Kate Fisher, *Birth Control, Sex, and Marriage in Britain, 1918–1960* (Oxford: Oxford University Press, 2006); Davey, "Birth Control in Britain during the Interwar Years," 329–345; Angus McLaren, *A History of Contraception* (Oxford: Blackwell, 1990); and Peter Neushul, "Marie C. Stopes and the Popularization of Birth Control Technology," *Technology and Culture* 39, no. 2 (1998): 245–272. For a broader history of the birth control movement in Britain, see Lucy Bland, *Banishing the Beast: Feminism, Sex and Morality* (London: Tauris Parke, 2001); Richard A. Soloway, *Birth Control and the Population Question in England, 1877–1930* (Chapel Hill: University of North Carolina Press, 1982); and Rosanna Ledbetter, *A History of the Malthusian League* (Columbus: Ohio State University, 1976).

7. As an advocate for spaced and desired births, Stopes was inundated with requests for information about abortion. Stopes claimed that she received twenty thousand pleas for information about abortion in a letter to the *Times*. Claire Davey that found 11 percent of letter writers attempted abortion as a form of birth control. Davey, "Birth Control in Britain during the Interwar Years," 333. For an overview of the history of legal regulation of abortion, see John Keown, *Abortion, Doctors, and the Law* (Cambridge: Cambridge University Press, 1988). For a discussion of family limitation that includes abortion, see Simon Szreter, *Fertility, Class and Gender in Britain, 1860–1940* (Cambridge: Cambridge University Press, 1996), pt. 4; and Wally Seccombe, *Weathering the Storm: Working-Class Families from the Industrial Revolution to the Fertility Decline* (London: Verso, 1993), chap. 5.

8. McLaren, *A History of Contraception*, 221.

9. For the ways that demographers and historians have debated the impact of birth control using Stopes's correspondence, see Deborah A. Cohen, "Private Lives in Public Spaces: Marie Stopes, the Mothers' Clinics and the Practice of Contraception,"

History Workshop Journal 35 (1993): 97; Szreter, *Fertility, Class and Gender in Britain, 1860–1940*, pt. 4; Wally Seccombe, *Weathering the Storm*; Wally Seccombe, "Starting to Stop: Working-Class Fertility Decline in Britain," *Past and Present* 126 (1990), 151–188; Robert Woods, "Debate: Working-Class Fertility Decline in Britain," *Past and Present* 134 (1992): 200–207; and Wally Seccombe, "Working-Class Fertility Decline in Britain: Reply," *Past and Present* 134 (1990): 207–211.

10. Lesley Hall, *Sex, Gender and Social Change in Britain since 1880* (New York: Palgrave Macmillan, 2000); June Rose, *Marie Stopes and the Sexual Revolution*; Hera Cook, *The Long Sexual Revolution: English Women, Sex, and Contraception, 1800–1975* (Oxford: Oxford University Press, 2005).

11. In this correspondence, Lesley Hall and Angus McLaren see evidence of the anxieties of modern life. Men in particular could not always force their bodies to follow the models of masculinity. Impotence, masturbation, and premature ejaculation haunted men and made them deeply aware of problematic demands of masculinity. Innumerable men wrote to Stopes and asked for ways to become the men that society demanded. Angus McLaren, *The Trials of Masculinity: Policing Sexual Boundaries, 1870–1930* (Chicago: University of Chicago Press, 1997); L. Hall, *Hidden Anxieties*.

12. Lesley Hall, "Uniting Science and Sensibility: Marie Stopes and the Narratives of Marriage in the 1920s," in *Rediscovering Forgotten Radicals: British Women Writers, 1889–1939*, edited by Angela Ingram and Daphne Patai (Chapel Hill: University of North Carolina Press, 1993), 118–136; Ellen Martha Holtzman, "Marriage, Sexuality, and Contraception in the British Middle Class, 1918–1939: The Correspondence of Marie Stopes" (Ph.D. diss., Rutgers University, 1982).

13. This study does not pretend to randomness or statistical representativeness. To write this chapter, I examined roughly three quarters of the letters held at the Wellcome Library. The letters have been alphabetized by the archive, which effectively randomized them. They have then been organized in files and those files in boxes. I read the first half of the letters to get a clear sense of the materials and then read every third box. I have supplemented these sources with materials published in Stopes's *Mother England* and R. Hall's *Dear Dr. Stopes*.

14. Marcus Collins, *Modern Love: Personal Relationships in Twentieth–Century Britain* (Newark: University of Delaware Press, 2003).

15. Fisher, *Birth Control, Sex, and Marriage in Britain*, chap. 5.

16. Collins, *Modern Love*, 98.

17. The working class also began to control fertility, though not all of those who practiced it used the model of compassionate marriage to justify the practice. Instead, an intense public debate about the meaning of marriage contributed to the burgeoning of models that began to shape people's practices and self-conceptions. See Fisher, *Birth Control, Sex, and Marriage in Britain*, 233n207.

18. See Bland, *Banishing the Beast*; Soloway, *Birth Control and the Population Question in England*.

19. Robert Graves and Alan Hodge, *The Long Week-End: A Social History of Great Britain* (1940; reprint, New York: Norton, 1994), 103.

20. An astonishing array of articles appeared in British journals between 1900 and 1914. See, for example, "Eugenics and Statecraft," *British Medical Journal* 2, no. 2438 (1907): 759–760; "Eugenics and Divorce," *British Medical Journal* 1, no. 2574 (1910): 1075; "Psychology and Eugenics," *British Medical Journal* 2, no. 2759 (1913): 1321; and "Eugenics from the Obstetrical Standpoint," *British Medical Journal* 2, no. 2741 (1913): 103.

21. Christina Hauck, "Abortion and Individual Talent," *ELH* 70, no. 1 (2003): 227.

22. Battles over the political implications of eugenics have been legion. Questions about whether eugenicists were left wing or right wing, authoritarian or populist, feminist or misogynist, and so forth have enlivened the historiography of the topic. See, for example, Greta Jones, "Eugenics and Social Policy between the Wars," *Historical Journal* 25, no. 3 (1982): 717–728; and Michael Freedman, "Eugenics and Progressive Thought," *Historical Journal* 22, no. 3 (1979): 645–671. See also Frank Dikotter, "Recent Perspectives on the History of Eugenics," *American Historical Review* 103, no. 2 (1998), 467–478; and Ann Taylor Allen, "Feminism and Eugenics in Germany and Britain, 1900–1940: A Comparative Perspective," *German Studies Review* 23, no. 3 (2000): 477–505.

23. Soloway, "The Galton Lecture, 1996: Marie Stopes, Eugenics and the Birth Control Movement," in *Marie Stopes and the English Birth Control Movement*, edited by Robert Peel (London: Galton Institute, 1997), 54.

24. John Macnicol, "Eugenics and the Campaign for Popular Sterilization in Britain between the Wars," *Social History of Medicine* 2, no. 2 (1989): 147–169. Throughout the 1920s and 1930s, disagreements among eugenicists and birth controllers continued to create tensions, first about the implications of birth control of the fit and then about voluntary sterilization for the unfit. Allen, "Feminism and Eugenics in Germany and Britain, 1900–1940," 498; Donald MacKenzie, "Eugenics in Britain," *Social Studies of Science* 6, nos. 3/4 (1976): 518–519.

25. Cohen, "Private Lives in Public Spaces," 101.

26. Soloway, "The Galton Lecture: Marie Stopes, Eugenics and the Birth Control Movement," 55.

27. Even Aldous Huxley, widely credited with satirizing such scientific approaches to social problems in *Brave New World*, saw the "unfit" as the greatest danger to the British race. According to Joanne Woiak, Aldous Huxley wrote *Brave New World* not to parody or predict but to articulate his concerns about eugenics. In a personal letter to Glyn Roberts, Huxley stated that "about 99.5% of the entire population of the planet are as stupid and philistine . . . as great masses of the English. The important thing, it seems to me, is not to attack the 99.5% . . . but to try to see that the 0.55 survives, keeps its quality up to the highest possible level, and if possible, dominates the rest." Joanne Woiak, "Designing a Brave New World: Eugenics, Politics, and Fiction," *Public Historian* 29, no. 3 (2007): 105.

28. June Rose, *Marie Stopes and the Sexual Revolution*, 291.

29. See, for example, Clare Debenham, "Mrs. Elsie Plant—Suffragette, Socialist and Birth Control Activist," *Women's History Review* 19, no. 1 (2010): 152.

30. Stopes, *Married Love*, 103.

31. Jane Lewis, "The Ideology and Politics of Birth Control in Inter-war England," *Women's Studies International Quarterly* 2 (1979): 33–48; see also Susanne M. Klausen, *Race, Maternity, and the Politics of Birth Control in South Africa, 1910–1939* (New York: Palgrave Macmillan, 2005).

32. Marie Stopes, *Wise Parenthood: A Practical Sequel to Married Love*, 16th ed. (London: Putnam, 1931); Marie Stopes, *Radiant Motherhood* (New York: Putnam, 1921).

33. Marie Stopes, *Enduring Passion* (Garden City, NY: Blue Ribbon Books, 1931); Marie Stopes, *Change of Life in Men and Women* (New York: Putnam, 1936).

34. Marie Stopes, *The Human Body* (Garden City, NY: Blue Ribbon Books, 1926).

35. According to "Courtship and Mating in an Urban Community," a paper that was read before the Eugenics Society in 1946, the younger generation had new expectations of sex in marriage. Supposedly, middle-aged couples were embarrassed and uninformed, incapable of talking about sex with their spouses. Older men seemed satisfied with sexual

relations, while women were resigned rather than pleased, according to the report. In comparison, the younger generation had different expectations and understandings of sexuality. According to Woodside's analysis, "Among younger married couples it is noticeable that the more intelligent are aware of sex as a source of mutual satisfaction, and are able to discuss it with each other." Moya Woodside, "Courtship and Mating in an Urban Community," *Eugenics Review* (April 1946): 36, Mass-Observation Archive.

36. Stopes, *Married Love*, 106.

37. L. Hall, "Uniting Science and Sensibility," 118–136.

38. Stopes, *Married Love*, 18.

39. Roy Porter and Lesley Hall, *Facts of Life: The Creation of Sexual Knowledge in Britain, 1650–1950* (New Haven, CT: Yale University Press, 1995), 209.

40. Ruth Hall nicely divides the letters she edits into such categories as "The Lower Classes," "The Upper Classes," "The Clergy," "The Medical Profession," and "Overseas." R. Hall, *Dear Dr. Stopes*.

41. A.J.C. Esquire, London, August 7, 1918, PP/MCS/A.50.

42. H. Cook, *The Long Sexual Revolution*, 168–172. Also evidencing Cook's claims are the first results of the Mass-Observation study of sexuality. Of the first five hundred interviews, reviewers found that 80 percent of the populations received no formal instruction. Part B: The Mechanics of Sex, Chapter 2: The Facts of Life, circa 1948, Mass-Observation Archive.

43. Arthur B., Rhine Army, August 19, 1919, PP/MCS/A.48.

44. Mrs. W.H.D., Liverpool, October 26, 1920, PP/MCS/A.72.

45. Stanley G., Stockport, n.d., circa 1933, PP/MCS/A.98.

46. John H., Bath, July 1919, PP/MCS/A.121.

47. Melvin A., Derby, February 17, 1919, PP/MCS/A.3.

48. Mr. T.C.N., Cambridge, September 9, 1922, PP/MCS/A.190.

49. Mr. and Mrs. A., Manchester, May 9, 1925, PP/MCS/A.14.

50. Stopes reply to Mr. and Mrs. A., Manchester, May 12, 1925, PP/MCS/A.14.

51. Samuel A., Hull, September 17, 19—, PP/MCS/A.2.

52. Captain J.W.B., Third Army Headquarters, France, October 1919, PP/MCS/A.31.

53. Captain E.H.B., School of Artillery, Salisbury Plan, March 5, 1923, PP/MCS/A.26.

54. Mr. M.F.D., Horeford, n.d., PP/MCS/A.69.

55. Judy Giles, *Women, Identity and Private Life in Britain, 1900–50* (New York: St. Martin's Press, 1995), 37.

56. Barbara Harrison, "Women and Health," in *Women's History: Britain, 1850–1945*, edited by June Purvis (New York: St. Martin's Press, 1995), 165.

57. Stopes, *Mother England*, 8.

58. Ibid., 2–3.

59. H.G.B., Transvaal, South Africa, September 20, 1929, PP/MCS/A.41.

60. Mrs. Edith B., Surrey, March 3, 1939, PP/MCS/A.20.

61. Margaret W., Larksfield, [*illegible*], June 18, 1935, PP/MCS/A.238.

62. Quoted in June Rose, *Marie Stopes and the Sexual Revolution* (London: Faber and Faber, 1992), 135.

63. Ibid., 253.

64. Second Lieutenant Alex B., Welsh Regiment, n.d., PP/MCS/A.31.

65. Major A.L.F., Italian Expeditionary Force, January 4, 1919, PP/MCS/A.86.

66. John C. A., Y.M.C.A. Students' Hostel, London, n.d., PP/MCS/A.10.

67. T. S. Follis, Esq., Whetstone, June 8, 1926, PP/MCS/A.89.

68. Mrs. E. B. Essex, July 14, 1925, PP/MCS/A.23.

69. H.M.B., Headington Orthopaedic Hospital, Oxford, May 29, 1921, PP/MCS/A.32.

70. Despite the rhetoric of a hero's welcome, the state made it hard to feel like a man when pensions for disabled men garnered less than an unskilled worker would make in a week. Disability pension rates began at 25 shillings a week, with a per-child allowance of 2 shillings 6 pence. Complicating the matter were problems that presented themselves well after the war, such as long-term mental illness and lung ailments. Disability pensions became harder to get for such ailments, not only because of the hidden nature of the affiliations but also because of the growing financial pressures after 1929 and the financial collapses of the Great Depression. Gerald DeGroot, *Blighty: British Society in the Era of the Great War* (London: Longman, 1996), 258. For discussions of sexuality and trauma, see Jason Crouthamel, "Male Sexuality and Psychological Trauma: Soldiers and Sexual Disorder in World War I and Weimar Germany," *Journal of the History of Sexuality* 17, no. 1 (2008): 60–84.

71. B. Wilmot A., Royal Citadel, Plymouth, December 31, 1939, PP/MCS/A.9.

72. Stopes, *Mother England*, v.

73. R. Hall, *Dear Dr. Stopes*, 128.

74. R.B., leading telegraphist, Wei-Hai-Wei, China, July 28, 1921, PP/MCS/A.44.

75. Mrs. Mabel G., Newcastle, April 17, 1921, PP/MCS/A.105.

76. E.E.A.T., Huddersfirth(?), November 3, 1921, PP/MCS/A.229.

77. Mrs. G., North Devon, January 18, 1932, PP/MCS/A.104.

78. R. Hall, *Dear Dr. Stopes*, 99.

79. Mr. H.F.R., Archery Road [London], June 3, 1919, PP/MCS/A.206.

80. Dr. Jane Lorimer Hawthorne wrote to Stopes about such dangers. She had seen a refined woman "of 38 years who had never been personally interested in sex matters, nor had any love affairs." However, Hawthorne continued, she was "'psychoanalyzed' a month or two ago—and was evidently roused to such an extent that she is now in a state of acute misery trying to fight and subdue this excess of feeling." R. Hall, *Dear Dr. Stopes*, 92.

81. Mr. T.C.N., Cambridge, September 21, 1922, PP/MCS/A.190.

82. Dorothy W. H., February 16, 1923, PP/MCS/A.121.

83. Frank C. B., Belfast, December 7, 1939, PP/MCS/A.17.

84. R. Hall, *Dear Dr. Stopes*, 146.

85. Mrs. D.J.E.E., n.d., Transvaal, South Africa, PP/MCS/A.82.

86. Daisy E. H., Wallasey, Cheshire, February 7, 1930, PP/MCS/A.118.

87. Mrs. A. G., Sheffield, June 1, 1921, PP/MCS/A.104.

88. Winifred B., Cricklewood, September 18, 1922, PP/MCS/A.38.

89. Kenneth A., Manchester, July 18, 1918, PP/MCS/A.15.

90. Marie Stopes, *Wise Parenthood: A Practical Sequel to Married Love*, 16th ed. (London: Putnam, 1931), 27.

91. Jocylen B., Hampstead, November 2, 1920, PP/MCS/A.42.

92. L.G., Essex, October 15, 1937, PP/MCS/A.107.

93. Eric G., London, March 18, 1929, PP/MCS/A.107.

94. D. H. Lawrence, *Lady Chatterley's Lover* (1928; reprint, London: Penguin, 2006), 138.

CHAPTER 3

1. Betty, "The Thrills of Freedom," *London Life*, November 1, 1930, p. 20.

2. G. Latimer, "Appeal to 'Silent Readers,'" *London Life*, August 24, 1935, p. 26.

3. The British Library houses the largest run of *London Life*, with copies from 1918 until 1960 with only a few missing issues and some mutilations. The Kinsey Institute holds an 1879 issue and then its run begins again in 1927 and continues sporadically until 1958. The run at the Kinsey has roughly three hundred issues. Also noteworthy are the existence of clipping files such as the one held at California State University, Northridge, Special Collections. Private clipping files, though harder to find, exist as well, and private collectors can be extremely generous with their collections.

4. Edward Shorter, *Written in the Flesh* (Toronto: University of Toronto Press, 2005), 223.

5. David Kunzle, *Fashion and Fetishism: Corsets, Tight-Lacing, and Other Forms of Body-Sculpture* (Stroud, UK: Sutton, 2004).

6. Valerie Steele, *The Corset: A Cultural History* (New Haven, CT: Yale University Press, 2001); Robert Bienvenu, "The Development of Sadomasochism as a Cultural Style in the Twentieth-Century United States" (Ph.D. diss., Indiana University, 1998).

7. According to David Kunzle, *London Life*'s papers were obliterated in the blitz in 1941. Kunzle, *Fashion and Fetishism*, 212–213.

8. Quoted in Lucy Bland, "Trials and Tribulations of Edith Thompson: The Capital Crime of Sexual Incitement in 1920s England," *Journal of British Studies* 47, no. 3 (2008): 635.

9. Jennifer Scanlon, *Inarticulate Longings: The Ladies' Home Journal, Gender, and the Promises of Consumer Culture* (New York: Routledge, 1995), 13.

10. Kirsten McKenzie, "Being Modern on a Slender Income: 'Picture Show' and 'Photoplayer' in Early 1920s Sydney," *Journal of Women's History* 22, no. 4 (2010): 117.

11. Gail Reekie, "Decently Dressed? Sexualized Consumerism and the Working Woman's Wardrobe 1918–1923," *Labour History*, no. 61 (1991): 52.

12. Bland, "Trials and Tribulations of Edith Thompson," 644.

13. My assessment of the publishing history of these magazines comes from my study of the physical copies of these publications at the British Library and from information garnered from *The Newspaper Press Directory*, *The Advertiser's Annual*, and *Willing's Press Guide*.

14. *New Fun* 6, no. 77 (January 3, 1914): n.p.

15. *Fun*, no. 71 (March 3, 1917): n.p.

16. "Alleged Obscene Picture," *The Times*, February 17, 1917, p. 5, col. F.

17. Peter Farrer, *Confidential Correspondence on Cross Dressing Part II, 1916–1920* (Liverpool, UK: Karn, 1998), 16.

18. Pulp magazines were defined by the wood-pulp paper on which they were printed and offered a lot of printed matter for the money. Erin A. Smith, "How the Other Half Read: Advertising, Working-Class Readers, and Pulp Magazines," *Book History* 3 (2000): 205.

19. "Thrilling Feats of One-Legged Aquatic Champion," *London Life*, March 2, 1929, p. 11.

20. G. Latimer, "Appeal to 'Silent Readers,'" p. 26.

21. See, for example, *London Life*, April 5, 1924, p. 15, and *London Life*, June 1, 1940, p. 21.

22. Air mail between Britain and Australia began during the 1930s. Leigh Edmonds, "Australia, Britain and the Empire Transport Scheme, 1934–38," *Journal of Transport History* 20, no. 2 (1999): 91–106.

23. A. Signaller, R.C.S., Jusselpore, India, "Soldier's Views on 'London Life,'" *London Life*, February 12, 1927, p. 27.

24. Billy and George, "An Appreciation from India," *London Life*, February 12, 1927, p. 27.

25. F.C.S., *London Life*, April 4, 1936, p. 24.

26. Rip Van Winkle, Burma, "Beauty in Burma," *London Life*, May 9, 1931, p. 30.

27. Anthony Quinn, e-mail communication, November 17, 2011.

28. The magazine listed its distributors. The February 12, 1927, issue of *London Life* stated the following: "Printed and Published for the Proprietors, the New Picture Press, Ltd, 7a Wine Office Court, Fleet Street, E.C. 4. Sole Agents for Australasia: Gordon and Gotch (Australasia), Ltd, South Africa: The Central News Agency Ltd." For histories of these organizations, see their websites, which both tell rags-to-riches stories of poor news agents becoming wholesalers.

29. An Australian Sheep Farmer, "Stop This High Boot Horror!" *London Life*, July 4, 1936, p. 23; S.J.F., "Proud of His Modern Sweetheart," *London Life*, July 5, 1930, p. 26.

30. Rita, "A Hint Passed On," *London Life*, August 29, 1931, p. 46; Glove Lover, "Shoulder-Length Gloves," *London Life*, August 29, 1931, p. 42.

31. The Publisher, "Notice to Newsagents," *London Life*, December 2, 1939, p. 4.

32. Shorter, *Written in the Flesh*, 223.

33. Steele, *The Corset*, 90.

34. D.S.F. Harris (Bristol), "Answers to Correspondents," *London Life*, December 6, 1930, p. 27.

35. One of a Sporty Trio, "'London Life' Brings Happiness," *London Life*, August 29, 1931, p. 44.

36. *London Life*, February 12, 1927, pp. 26–27.

37. "Answers to Correspondents," *London Life*, May 12, 1928.

38. Corduroy and Velvet, "Corduroy and Corsets," *London Life*, December 9, 1935, p. 24.

39. One-Legged Monopede, "A Cheery Souled Monopede," December 14, 1935, p. 26.

40. Molly Kramer, "American Lady Emulates 'Sporty Wife,'" *London Life*, February 15, 1930, p. 26.

41. Bozo, "Questions for Corset Wearer," and Inquisitive, "Doubts High-Heeler's Bona-Fides," *London Life*, November 28, 1931, p. 77.

42. Editor, "Two Queries Answered," *London Life*, February 15, 1936, n.p.

43. Laurence Lenton, "Interesting Experiences of a Corset Maker," *London Life*, January 5, 1929, p. 26.

44. Freda, "What I Like in 'London Life,'" *London Life*, January 3, 1931, p. 27.

45. The Scribe, "What We Think of 'London Life,'" *London Life* (double issue), August 29, 1931, p. 46.

46. Mirabella, "Astounding Revelations of a Voo-Doo Votary," *London Life*, March 4, 1933, p. 23.

47. Fed Up, Quetta, N.W.F. India, "Soldier on English and Indian Girls," *London Life*, October 15, 1927, p. 31.

48. Rip Van Winkle, "Beauty in Burma," p. 30.

49. The Mac Kid, "Smart Ski-ing Rig-Out," *London Life*, February 15, 1930, p. 26.

50. Harry Oosterhuis, *Stepchildren of Nature: Krafft-Ebing, Psychiatry, and the Making of Sexual Identity* (Chicago: University of Chicago Press, 2000), 60–61.

51. Ibid., 45; Renate Hauser, "Krafft-Ebing's Psychological Understanding of Sexual Behavior," in *Sexual Knowledge, Sexual Science*, edited by Roy Porter and Mikulas Teich (Cambridge: Cambridge University Press, 1992), 222–223.

52. Ivan Bloch, *A History of English Sexual Morals* (London: Francis Aldor, 1936), 456–457.

53. Henry Kripps, *Fetish: An Erotics of Culture* (Ithaca, NY: Cornell University Press, 1999), 7–8.

54. Anne Summers, "The Correspondents of Havelock Ellis," *History Workshop Journal* 32 (1991): 174.

55. Havelock Ellis, "Erotic Symbolism," in *Studies in the Psychology of Sex*, vol. 2 (New York: Random House, 1942), 20.

56. Kenneth Walker, *Physiology of Sex* (New York: Penguin, 1945), 144–159.

57. Eustace Chesser, *Love without Fear* (New York: Signet Books, 1947), 64–65.

58. Martin Pugh, *We Danced All Night: A Social History of Britain between the Wars* (London: Vintage Books, 2005), 181–183.

59. Adrian Bingham, *Family Newspapers? Sex, Private Life, and the British Popular Press, 1918–1978* (Oxford: Oxford University Press, 2009).

60. Bland, "Trials and Tribulations of Edith Thompson," 644.

61. Troubled, "Are Girls Fit for Freedom?" *London Life*, February 27, 1926, p. 23.

62. In the column, the writer suggested that the two girls were "chums," but they signed their letter with the same last name. Marie and Doris Ilkley, "Wrestling for Girls," *London Life*, August 11, 1923, p. 4.

63. Muscular Miss, "Self-Defense for Girls," *London Life*, May 30, 1931, p. 43.

64. Freda H., "How a Girl Punished a Bully," *London Life*, December 1, 1923, p. 6.

65. Photograph, *London Life*, October 4, 1930, p. 8.

66. M.G.C., "Wrestling Girl Defeats Soldier," *London Life*, November 1, 1930, p. 27.

67. Harold L. Weston, "Wonderful Women Wrestlers," *London Life*, December 22, 1923.

68. Gymn, "Woman's Superior Strength," *London Life*, August 17, 1929, p. 26.

69. "Talk of the Town," *London Life*, March 2, 1929, p. 2.

70. Leigh Summers, *Bound to Please: A History of the Victorian Corset* (New York: Berg, 2001), 210–211.

71. Ibid., 200.

72. Quoted in Cheryl Buckley and Hillary Fawcett, *Fashioning the Feminine: Representation and Women's Fashion from the Fin de Siècle to the Present* (London: Tauris, 2002), 87.

73. The Dresser, "Fashions, Fads and Fancies," September 22, 1928, p. 15.

74. Madeline Alverez, "Figure Training throughout the Ages," *London Life*, January 27, 1934, p. 21.

75. C.H., "Wasp-Like Waists," and Staylace, "Historical Tight-Lacers," *London Life*, April 19, 1924, p. 15.

76. Corset, "The Wasp-Waist Cult," *London Life*, January 2, 1926, p. 15.

77. "Wasp Waists on the Continent," *London Life*, January 31, 1931, pp. 50–51.

78. "Dora the Dominant," *London Life*, January 31, 1931, p. 40.

79. A.D.T., "Victorian Figure Training," *London Life*, May 30, 1931, p. 42.

80. Elsie J., "A Defense of the Wasp Waist," *London Life*, November 12, 1927, p. 31.

81. Six Inch Heels, "The Lure of Lingerie," *London Life*, July 5, 1930, p. 26.

82. A.C.B., "The Appeal of Complete Weakness," *London Life*, January 3, 1931, p. 26.

83. The Dresser, "High Legged Boots," *London Life*, September 22, 1928, p. 15.

84. K.P., "If That Is Pleasure, What Is Pain?" *London Life*, December 6, 1930, p. 26.

85. "London Life League" (newsletter), no. 3 (July 1984).

86. "London Life League" (newsletter), no. 4 (October 1984).

87. Copies of these letters and stories are available at http://www.overground.be/londonLife/. These stories and letters appear to have come from someone's clipping file. The website thanks an anonymous friend for the scans or copies. I checked the accuracy of the stories against copies of *London Life* at the Kinsey Institute and found the transcriptions accurate. There may be additional stories in the pages of *London Life*; however, most of the stories about amputees seem to have been transcribed.

88. "Marvellous Feats of One-Legged Dancers," *London Life*, July 26, 1924, pp. 10–11.

89. *London Life*, October 4, 1924, p. 14.

90. Wallace Stortt, "The Scarlet Slipper," *London Life*, August 28, 1926, pp. 16–18.

91. Ibid.

92. Wallace Stortt, "The Fascination of the One-Legged Girl," *London Life*, October 27, 1928, pp. 18–19.

93. Wallace Stortt, "The Confessions of a One-Legged Bride," *London Life*, July 26, 1930, pp. 16–17, 20–21, 24–25.

94. Wallace Stortt, "The Strange Experiences of a Lover," *London Life*, April 29, 1933, pt. 2, pp. 30–32.

95. Wallace Stortt, "Dr. Nicholas," *London Life*, December 8, 1928, pp. 18–19, 22–23, 26–27, 30–31, 34.

96. Wallace Stortt, "The Strange Experiences of a Lover," *London Life*, January 28, 1933, pp. 12–14.

97. Stortt, "Dr. Nicholas," 18–19, 22–23, 26–27, 30–31, 34.

98. Wallace Stortt, "The Strange Quest of Anthony Drew," *London Life*, August 31, 1929, pp. 31, 36, 37, 40, continued on August 31, 1940, pp. 10, 27–34, 39–40.

99. "One Legged but High-Heeled," *London Life*, August 22, 1925, p. 15.

100. "Only a One-Legged Girl," *London Life*, October 6, 1928, p. 26.

101. Legless, "Why the Limbless Are Interested in Life," *London Life*, May 11, 1935, p. 23.

102. One and a Half, "Making the Most of Misfortune," *London Life*, November 12, 1932, p. 24.

103. A New Monopede, "A Little Advice Wanted," *London Life*, November 24, 1934, p. 48.

104. L.N., "Advice Wanted," *London Life*, December 8, 1934, p. 23.

105. L.N., "Advice Wanted," *London Life*, February 23, 1935, p. 9.

106. L.N., "Where Were Her Sympathizers?" *London Life*, June 22, 1935, p. 20.

107. "A Welcome Criticism," *London Life*, August 22, 1931, p. 11.

108. Crippled Girl, "Advice to Monopedes," *London Life*, October 19, 1935, p. 24.

109. "A Reply to 'Forward Minx,'" *London Life*, September 12, 1931, p. 27.

110. Monopede Admirer, "Monopede Psychology," *London Life*, November 9, 1935, p. 22.

111. Husband of Single-Heel, "The Penalty of a Leg," *London Life*, December 21, 1935, p. 23.

112. Magpie S., "A Definition," *London Life*, April 25, 1936, p. 9.

113. This problem of how to model oneself is central to an understanding of the history of disability. See, for example, David Gerber, "Anger and Affability: The Rise and Representation of a Repertory of Self-Presentation Skills in a World War II Disabled Veteran," *Journal of Social History* 27, no. 1 (Autumn 1993): 5–27.

114. Seth Koven, "Remembering and Dismemberment: Crippled Children, Wounded Soldiers, and the Great War in Great Britain," *American Historical Review* 99, no. 4 (1994): 1169.

115. Joanna Bourke, *Dismembering the Male: Men's Bodies, Britain and the Great War* (Chicago: University of Chicago Press, 1996), 33.

116. Koven, "Remembering and Dismemberment," 1186.

117. Maria Tatar, *Lustmord: Sexual Murder in Weimar Germany* (Princeton, NJ: Princeton University Press, 1995).

118. Suzannah Biernoff, "The Rhetoric of Disfigurement in First World War Britain," *Social History of Medicine* 24, no. 3 (2011): 667.

119. Modris Eksteins, *Rites of Spring: The Great War and the Birth of the Modern Age* (New York: Anchor Books, 1989), 297.

120. "A Happy Couple," *London Life*, June 27, 1931, p. 25.

121. Gladys, "Advice to Monopedes," *London Life*, May 13, 1933, p. 22.

122. Quoted in Koven, "Remembering and Dismemberment," 1168.

123. A One-Legged but Not Deluded Girl, "I Contradict Wallace Stort [*sic*]," *London Life*, August 15, 1936, p. 24.

124. Louise Kaplan, *Cultures of Fetishism* (New York: Palgrave Macmillan, 2006), 22.

125. Kripps, *Fetish: An Erotics of Culture*, 7–8.

126. Single Leg, "Questions for Girls to Answer," *London Life*, October 19, 1935, p. 24.

127. Happy with One, "Happy One-Legged Mother and Wife," *London Life*, April 13, 1935, p. 22.

128. This idea is adapted from Lorraine Gamman and Merja Makinen, *Female Fetishism* (New York: New York University Press, 1994), 19.

129. One of a Sporty Trio, "'London Life' Brings Happiness," p. 44.

130. The writer makes use of the formula given to measure copy in newspapers and magazines. Experienced, "Filing Your Cuttings," *London Life*, November 25, 1939, p. 96.

131. *London Life*, July 5, 1930.

132. "Doreen's Dainty Dress," *London Life*, January 31, 1931, p. 58.

133. The Scribe, "What We Think of 'London Life,'" *London Life*, August 29, 1931, p. 46.

134. M.E.J., "Uncorseted Beauty," *London Life*, October 4, 1930, p. 27.

135. One of a Sporty Trio, "'London Life' Brings Happiness," p. 44.

136. Betty, "The Thrills of Freedom," *London Life*, November 1, 1930, p. 20.

137. Wallace Stortt, "Wallace Stortt Replies to 'Forward Minx,'" *London Life*, September 26, 1931, p. 42.

138. Wallace Stortt, "The Strange Quest of Anthony Drew,'" *London Life*, December 21, 1929, pp. 21–28.

139. "Memoirs of a Lady Tattooist," *London Life*, January 3, 1931, p. 23.

140. J.B., "What Do You Think?" *London Life*, September 22, 1923.

141. Constatia, "Eager for Next Week's Stor[y]," *London Life*, December 2, 1939, p. 26.

CHAPTER 4

1. Letters from Mervyn Hyde, January 9, 1923, and January 7, 1923, Exhibit 3, National Archives (TNA), Public Records Office (PRO), Central Criminal Court (CRIM) 1/234.

2. There are few close studies of people engaged in the obscene book trades. Since the obscene book trade remained largely illegal until the 1960s and 1970s, few dealers, print-

ers, publishers, or authors documented their relations to the trade. Armand Coppens's *Memoirs of an Erotic Bookseller* (London: Luxor Press, 1969) offers one such portrait. Laura Kipnis, *Bound and Gagged* (New York: Grove Press, 1996), offers a fascinating portrayal of Hustler's Larry Flynt, and Clarissa Smith examines the magazine publishing industry in postwar Britain in *One for the Girls! The Pleasures and Practices of Reading Women's Porn* (Bristol, UK: Intellect Books, 2007). Memoirs of cross-dressers are also rare, though Catalina de Erauso, *Lieutenant Nun: Memoirs of a Basque Transvestite in the New World* (Boston: Beacon Press, 1996), introduced by Marjorie Garber, provides an account of one. However, the sexual identity of Catalina de Erauso remains open to question because the historical context and definitions of gender do not necessarily correspond to the present day. Furthermore, cross-dressing has meant any number of things; it sometimes indexed sodomite culture, as Randolph Trumbach demonstrates; it sometimes spoke to transsexuality, as the work of Joanne Meyerowitz illustrates; and it sometimes indicated a desire to surmount economic limitation, as Julia Wheelwright illustrates. See Randolph Trumbach, *Sex and Gender Revolution* (Chicago: University of Chicago Press, 1998); Joanna Meyerowitz, *How Sex Changed: A History of Transsexuality in America* (Cambridge, MA: Harvard University Press, 2002); and Julia Wheelwright, *Amazons and Military Maids* (London: Pandora Books, 1990).

3. William Storey, "Big Cats and Imperialism: Lion and Tiger Hunting in Kenya and Northern India, 1898–1930," *Journal of World History* 2, no. 2 (1991): 138, 144.

4. David Arnold, "The Police and Colonial Control in South India," *Social Scientist* 4, no. 12 (1976): 5.

5. Paul Deslandes, "Competitive Examinations and the Culture of Masculinity in Oxbridge Undergraduate Life, 1850–1920," *History of Education Quarterly* 42, no. 4 (2002): 558.

6. Ibid., 564; George Orwell's well-documented struggles, including the humiliation of needing a scholarship to go to Eton and his family's economies from living on a colonial office pension, suggest that becoming a colonist was not so easy. See W. D. Rubinstein,"Education and the Social Origins of British Elites," *Past and Present* 112 (1986): 168–169; and Alok Rai, "Colonial Fictions: Orwell's 'Burmese Days,'" *Economic and Political Weekly* 18, no. 5 (1983): PE49.

7. Robert Nye, "Western Masculinities in War and Peace," *American Historical Review* 112, no. 2 (2007): 423.

8. War records for Mervyn Hyde, TNA, PRO, War Office (WO) 339/14462.

9. Richard A. Soloway, *Democracy and Degeneration: Eugenics and the Declining Birthrate in Twentieth-Century Britain* (Chapel Hill: University of North Carolina Press, 1990), 41. See also Jay Winter, "Military Fitness and Civilian Health in Britain during the First World War," *Journal of Contemporary History* 15, no. 2 (April 1980): 211–244.

10. For an overview of the Western Front, see Jay Winter and Blaine Baggett, *The Great War and the Shaping of the Twentieth Century* (New York: Penguin, 1996); and Jay Winter and Antoine Prost, *The Great War in History: Debates and Controversies, 1914 to the Present* (Cambridge: Cambridge University Press, 2005).

11. See Tracey Loughran, "Shell Shock and Psychological Medicine in First World War Britain," *Social History of Medicine* 22, no. 1 (2009): 79–95; and Edgar Jones and Simon Wessely, "The Impact of Total War on the Practice of British Psychiatry," in *The Shadows of Total War: Europe, East Asia, and the United States, 1919–1939*, edited by Roger Chickering and Stig Forster (Cambridge: Cambridge University Press, 2003).

12. Joanna Bourke, *Dismembering the Male: Men's Bodies, Britain, and the Great War* (Chicago: University of Chicago Press, 1996), 109; see also Scott Gelber, "A 'Hard-Boiled

Order': The Reeducation of Disabled WWI Veterans in New York City," *Journal of Social History* 39, no. 1 (2005): 168.

13. See Peter Barham, *Forgotten Lunatics of the Great War* (New Haven, CT: Yale University Press, 2004), chap. 10; and Gerald DeGroot, *Blighty: British Society in the Era of the Great War* (London: Longman, 1996), 258.

14. See, for example, Gabriel Koureas, *Memory, Masculinity and National Identity in British Visual Culture, 1914–1930* (Aldershot, UK: Ashgate, 2007), 126–133.

15. Ibid., 126.

16. Ibid.

17. As Matthew Thomson makes clear, histories of psychology in Britain have focused on the reception of Freudian and psychoanalytic theory. Matthew Thomson, *Psychological Subjects: Identity, Culture, and Health in Twentieth-Century Britain* (Oxford: Oxford University Press, 2006), 2. For example, see Dean Rapp, "The Early Discovery of Freud by the British General Educated Public, 1912–1919" *Social History of Medicine* 3, no. 2 (1990): 217–243. This material makes fascinating reading, but it does not illuminate the broader complexities of how soldiers' mental and emotional difficulties returning to civilian life played out in a society that saw little salience in psychological thinking. As a result, Britain saw trauma in terms of values, rather than psychology. See, for example, Thomson's discussion of sex and psychology in *Psychological Subjects*, 100–103. Divisions within the psychoanalytic community over the sexual content of Freud's theories heightened the difficulty in discussing soldiers' problems. See Suzanne Raitt, "Early British Psychoanalysis and the Medico-psychological Clinic," *History Workshop Journal* 58 (2004): 71. The historiography continues to ignore the issue of sexuality and instead treats "shell shock" as a predecessor of "battle fatigue" and other battle-related ailments.

18. Supposedly, men and women had two different sets of experiences, as the war divided the world into home front and war front, the two based in mutual incomprehension and mistrust. See Paul Fussell, *The Great War and Modern Memory* (Oxford: Oxford University Press, 1975); and Eric J. Leed, *No Man's Land: Combat and Identity in World War I* (Cambridge: Cambridge University Press, 1979). As the rush to battle in 1914 settled into a steady grinding war, the passivity of the war encouraged a new misogyny based on a belief about women's safety against men's losses. Men suffered from an enforced passivity that they thought women on the home front could neither understand nor alleviate. James S. Campbell, "'For You May Touch Them Not': Misogyny, Homosexuality, and the Ethics of Passivity in First War Poetry," *ELH* 64, no. 3 (1997): 823–842. People retained this belief despite the fact that women worked as drivers, nurses, and prostitutes at the front and the gender separation of men and women was never quite so clear as the press made it out to be. Margaret Vining and Barton C. Hacker, "From Camp Follower to Lady in Uniform: Women, Social Class and Military Institutions before 1920," *Contemporary European History* 10, no. 3 (2001): 353–373.

19. K. Craig Gibson, "Sex and Soldiering in France and Flanders: The British Expeditionary Force along the Western Front," *International Historical Review* 23, no. 3 (2001): 536.

20. Queenie, "A Convert from the Army," June 12, 1920, in Peter Farrer, ed., *Confidential Correspondence on Cross Dressing Part II, 1916–1920* (Liverpool, UK: Karn, 1998), 219.

21. J.E.H., "Macedonia's Leading Lady," November 23, 1918, in Farrer, *Confidential Correspondence on Cross Dressing Part II, 1916–1920*, 124.

22. See, for example, archived photographs of female impersonators such as Lt. Rider, "Female Impersonator of the Maple Leaves," September 1917, Canadian First

World War Official Exchange Collection, CO2013, Imperial War Museum, London, available at http://www.iwm.org.uk/collections/item/object/205194032. See also David A. Boxwell, "The Follies of War: Cross-Dressing and Popular Theater on the British Front Lines, 1914–18," *Modernism/Modernity* 9, no. 1 (2002): 1–20.

23. Sapper, "An Enthusiast," September 2, 1916, in Farrer, *Confidential Correspondence on Cross Dressing Part II, 1916–1920*, 51–52.

24. Tight Lacing Mad, "A Bit Kinky," September 30, 1916, in Farrer, *Confidential Correspondence on Cross Dressing Part II, 1916–1920*, 54.

25. Petite Taille, "From an Obvious Enthusiast," December 23, 1916, in Farrer, *Confidential Correspondence on Cross Dressing Part II, 1916–1920*, 64–65.

26. H.C., "An Effeminate Tommy," February 8, 1919, in Farrer, *Confidential Correspondence on Cross Dressing Part II, 1916–1920*, 138.

27. Petite Taille, "From an Obvious Enthusiast," December 23, 1916, in Farrer, *Confidential Correspondence on Cross Dressing Part II, 1916–1920*, 64–65.

28. Alison Oram, *Her Husband Was a Woman! Women's Gender-Crossing in Modern British Culture* (London: Routledge, 2007), 4.

29. George Chauncey, *Gay New York: Gender, Urban Culture, and the Making of the Gay Male World, 1890–1940* (New York: Basic Books, 1994), 11–16.

30. Laura Doan, *Fashioning Sapphism: The Origins of Modern English Lesbian Culture* (New York: Columbia University Press, 2001), 30.

31. Matt Houlbrook, *Queer London: Perils and Pleasures in the Sexual Metropolis, 1918–1957* (Chicago: University of Chicago Press, 2006), 7.

32. On the history of cross-dressing in the modern West, see Marjorie Garber, *Vested Interests: Cross Dressing and Cultural Anxiety* (New York: Routledge, 1992); and Vern L. Bullough and Bonnie Bullough, *Cross Dressing, Sex, and Gender* (Philadelphia: University of Pennsylvania Press, 1993).

33. Garber, *Vested Interests*, 37.

34. William Roughhead, *Bad Companions* (New York: Duffield and Green, 1931), 147–184; Clarence Joseph Bulliet, *Venus Castina* (1928; reprint, New York: Bonanza Books, 1956). See also James Vernon, "'For Some Queer Reason': The Trials and Tribulations of Colonel Barker's Masquerade in Inter-war Britain," *Signs* 26 (2000): 37–62.

35. For a fascinating discussion of bobbed hair in the French context, see Mary Louise Roberts, "Samson and Delilah Revisited: The Politics of Women's Fashions in 1920s France," *American Historical Review* 98, no. 3 (1993): 657–684. See also Joanna Bourke, "The Great Male Renunciation: Men's Dress Reform in Inter-war Britain," *Journal of Design History* 9, no. 1 (1996): 23–33; and Barbara Burman, "Better and Brighter Clothes: The Men's Dress Reform Party, 1929–1940," *Journal of Design History* 8, no. 4 (1995): 275–290. Experimentation took a variety of forms, including nudism and sunbathing. In Britain, the nudist movement came to the attention of authorities when Harold Hubert Vincent held up a "big card upon which was printed in big letters 'throw away your clothes.'" Metropolitan Police Report, Marylebone Lane Station, "D" Division, September 6, 1924, TNA, PRO, Metropolitan Police Department (MEPO) 3/946.

36. Angus McLaren, "National Responses to Sexual Perversion: The Case of Transvestitism," in *Sexual Cultures in Europe*, edited by Franz X. Eder, Lesley Hall, and Gert Hekma (Manchester, UK: Manchester University Press, 1999), 122.

37. Wheelwright, *Amazons and Military Maids*.

38. See Garber, *Vested Interests*; Anne McClintock, *Imperial Leather: Race, Gender, and Sexuality in the Colonial Context* (New York: Routledge, 1995); and Angus McLaren,

"Smoke and Mirrors: Willy Clarkson and the Role of Disguises in Inter-war England," *Journal of Social History* 40, no. 3 (Spring 2007): 597–598.

39. Peter Farrer has spent decades chasing down these sources and republishing them as editor of a series of volumes. The most relevant to this chapter are *Confidential Correspondence on Cross Dressing, 1911–1915* (Liverpool, UK: Karn, 1997); *Confidential Correspondence on Cross Dressing Part II, 1916–1920*; *Cross Dressing between the Wars: Selections from London Life, 1923–1933* (Liverpool, UK: Karn, 2000); and *Cross Dressing between the Wars: Selections from London Life, 1934–1941* (Liverpool, UK: Karn, 2006).

40. Few women wrote letters about cross-dressing in these magazines. Instead, the magazines printed articles about cross-dressed women; the "News of the World" column, for example, detailed the case of William Sidney Holton, who dressed as a man for twenty years. Other articles, such as "Scientists Seeking to Solve the Secrets of Sex," examined women who became men because of glandular secretions. "Scientists Seeking to Solve the Secrets of Sex," *London Life*, May 21, 1932, p. 23. Another article in *London Life* blamed the war for the rise of masculine women, although the publication date in 1929, more than a decade after the war's end, suggests a more complicated relationship between the war and such cross-dressing. According to the article, "One of the strangest results of the Great War has been the growing masculinity of women." According to Mrs. Winifred Broom, a correspondent for the *Sunday Chronicle*, "They used to be a type that were few and far between." "Now," she continued, "you find dozens of them in every large city. They are really like 'he-women,' and often wear a man's collar and tie. I have even found them wearing jackets like a man. Short-cropped hair and a masculine way of talking complete their make-up. They have no time for men, and are generally to be seen in the company of girl friends." "Extraordinary Masquerades by 'He-Girls,'" *London Life*, November 3, 1928, pp. 11–14. Such articles maintained the spectacle of female-to-male transformations even in the relative absence of letters that discussed women dressing as men in the correspondence columns. Perhaps the relaxation of women's dress standards allowed women to adopt more masculine styles without explicitly cross-dressing.

41. Letters and stories about men dressing in corsets had a long and well-documented tradition in the ephemeral trades, such as the infamous corset correspondence of the *Englishwoman's Domestic Magazine* from the 1860s. Margaret Beetham, "'Natural but Firm': The Corset Correspondence in *The Englishwoman's Domestic Magazine*," *Women: A Cultural Review* 2, no. 2 (1991): 163–167.

42. A Would-Be Alice, "Effeminacy," May 10, 1919, in Farrer, *Confidential Correspondence on Cross Dressing Part II, 1916–1920*, 178.

43. Tommy, "Effeminate Men," July 7, 1917, in Farrer, *Confidential Correspondence on Cross Dressing Part II, 1916–1920*, 74.

44. J.P., "Corsets," June 24, 1916, in Farrer, *Confidential Correspondence on Cross Dressing Part II, 1916–1920*, 36.

45. M.P., "Feminine Kinks," January 5, 1918, in Farrer, *Confidential Correspondence on Cross Dressing Part II, 1916–1920*, 84.

46. A Womanly Man, "Effeminacy," January 26, 1918, in Farrer, *Confidential Correspondence on Cross Dressing Part II, 1916–1920*, 85.

47. Badly Kinked, "A Fitting Nom de Plume," January 13, 1917, in Farrer, *Confidential Correspondence on Cross Dressing Part II, 1916–1920*, 68.

48. Waiting to Be Breeched, "One Who Wishes to Wear Trousers," August 26, 1916, in Farrer, *Confidential Correspondence on Cross Dressing Part II, 1916–1920*, 51.

49. Teddy, "Dressing Up," September 7, 1918, in Farrer, *Confidential Correspondence on Cross Dressing Part II, 1916–1920*, 114.

50. Corset Lover, "Why Was I Not Born a Girl?" December 14, 1918, in Farrer, *Confidential Correspondence on Cross Dressing Part II, 1916–1920*, 131.

51. Shy, "Corsets for Men," August 4, 1917, in Farrer, *Confidential Correspondence on Cross Dressing Part II, 1916–1920*, 75.

52. Effeminate, "Effeminacy," April 15, 1919, in Farrer, *Confidential Correspondence on Cross Dressing Part II, 1916–1920*, 145.

53. Interested, "Another Corset Fancier," March 23, 1918, in Farrer, *Confidential Correspondence on Cross Dressing Part II, 1916–1920*, 92.

54. Divine Wasp, "Tight Lacing and Corsets for Men," February 16, 1918, in Farrer, *Confidential Correspondence on Cross Dressing Part II, 1916–1920*, 87.

55. Magnus Hirschfeld, *Transvestites: The Erotic Drive to Cross-Dress* (1928; reprint, Buffalo, NY: Prometheus Books, 1991).

56. Sexual inversion had been used as a concept by J. A. Symonds in his essay *A Problem in Greek Ethics* and then developed further in Ellis and Symonds's volume *Sexual Inversion*. Inversion implied having the wrong soul in one's body, and Ellis saw any number of categories of desire as deriving from this alignment. For a fuller discussion, see Heike Bauer, *English Literary Sexology: Translations of Inversion, 1860–1930* (Basingstoke, UK: Palgrave Macmillan, 2009).

57. Havelock Ellis, "Eonism," in *Studies in the Psychology of Sex*, vol. 2 (New York: Random House, 1937), 13.

58. Quoted in Bauer, *English Literary Sexology*, 119.

59. Radclyffe Hall, *The Well of Loneliness* (1928; reprint, New York: Anchor Books, 1990), 106.

60. Bauer, *English Literary Sexology*, 118.

61. Doan, *Fashioning Sapphism*, 163.

62. Jay Prosser, "'Some Primitive Thing Conceived in a Turbulent Age of Transition': The Transsexual Emerging from *The Well*," in *Palatable Poison*, edited by Laura Doan and Jay Prosser (New York: Columbia University Press, 2001), 129–144, 130; Jay Prosser, "Transsexuals and the Transsexologists: Inversion and the Emergence of Transsexual Subjectivity," in *Sexology in Culture: Labeling Bodies and Desires*, edited by Lucy Bland and Laura Doan (Cambridge, UK: Polity Press, 1998), 116–131.

63. Meyerowitz, *How Sex Changed*, 16–21.

64. One reader, for example, plugged reading Hirschfeld's work in German. Reader, "A Psychological Reason," November 7, 1936, in Farrer, *Cross Dressing between the Wars, 1934–1941*, 90–92. See also Interested in Impersonating, "The Art of Acting," *London Life*, June 15, 1940, pp. 202–204.

65. A frequent contributor to *London Life* calling himself "The Brother of the Shadow" claimed training as a psychologist (though the quality of his analysis throws suspicion onto his credentials). Pulling cases from his "files," he analyzed sexual problems, including cross-dressing. In one letter, "The Brother of the Shadow" suggests that Allan, a cross-dresser, should fight off effeminacy until the third sex was legally recognized. Brother of the Shadow, "Letters from My Case-Book," *London Life*, January 27, 1940, p. 15.

66. Letters from Mervyn Hyde, January 7, 1923, Exhibit 3, TNA, PRO, CRIM1/234.

67. Letter from C. Benbow to T. Cockcroft, March 6, 1923, Exhibit 3, TNA, PRO, CRIM1/234.

68. Sentences, May 30, 1923, nos. 18 and 19, p. 5, TNA, PRO, CRIM9/69.

69. Statement of Cyril Benbow, April 18, 1923, Exhibit 42, TNA, PRO, CRIM1/234.

70. H. G. Cocks, "'Peril in the Personals: The Dangers and Pleasures of Classified Advertising in Early Twentieth-Century Britain," *Media History* 10, no. 1 (2004): 9.

71. Letters from Mervyn Hyde, January 13, 1923, Exhibit 3, TNA, PRO, CRIM1/234.

72. Ibid., January 21, 1923.

73. Ibid., January 23, 1923.

74. Addresses provided by Hyde, n.d., 7, Exhibit 3, TNA, PRO, CRIM1/234.

75. Ibid., n.d., 10.

76. Angus McLaren, *Sexual Blackmail: A Modern History* (Cambridge, MA: Harvard University Press, 2002).

77. Testimony of Oliver Burchett Clarence, May 18, 1923, TNA, PRO, CRIM1/234.

78. Articles found in trunk, Exhibit 79, TNA, PRO, CRIM1/234.

79. Gail Reekie, "Decently Dressed? Sexualized Consumerism and the Working Woman's Wardrobe 1918–1923," *Labour History*, no. 61 (1991): 52.

80. Exhibit 82, p. 110, TNA, PRO, CRIM1/234.

81. Ibid., pp. 103, 111.

82. Exhibit 18, TNA, PRO, CRIM1/234.

83. Exhibit 80, TNA, PRO, CRIM1/234.

84. Quoted in Peter Mendes, *Clandestine Erotic Fiction in English, 1800–1930: A Bibliographical Study* (Aldershot, UK: Scolar Press, 1993), 289, 290.

85. H. S. Ashbee, *Index Librorum Prohibitorum* (1877; reprint, New York: Documentary Books, 1962), xl.

86. Mendes, *Clandestine Erotic Fiction in English*, 247.

87. Viscount Ladywood, *Gynecocracy* (1893; reprint, Lexington, KY: Ophir Books, 2007), 40.

88. Ibid., 42.

89. Progress (Boston, Mass.), "Earrings and Eyesight," January 28, 1933, in Farrer, *Cross Dressing between the Wars, 1923–1933*, 154–156.

90. W.J.R., "Pictures of Boys in Pinafores Wanted," *London Life*, January 28, 1933, p. 51.

91. Male, untitled, carbon copy of *New Fun*, July 10, 1913, Louise Lawrence Collection, Box 3, Series II, Manuscripts, Other Manuscripts, Folder 46, Kinsey Institute for Research in Sex, Gender, and Reproduction, Bloomington, IN.

92. Roy (or Rather) Violet, "Petticoat Punishment," carbon copy of *New Fun*, March 22, 1913, Louise Lawrence Collection, Box 3, Series II, Manuscripts, Other Manuscripts, Folder 46.

93. Daphne, "Pinafores as a Reforming Influence," December 31, 1932, in Farrer, *Cross Dressing between the Wars, 1923–1933*, 146–147.

94. Painted Beauty, "Pinafores for Boys," December 31, 1932, in Farrer, *Cross Dressing between the Wars, 1923–1933*, 147.

95. A Lover of Skirts, "When Girls All Wear Breeches," December 9, 1916, in Farrer, *Confidential Correspondence on Cross Dressing Part II, 1916–1920*, 60–61.

96. Mdme. Nita Berrouda, "The Coming Dominance of Woman," *London Life*, March 17, 1928, p. 26.

97. Submissive Husband, "Believes in Woman's Dominance," *London Life*, February 15, 1930, p. 22.

98. Hopeful, "Wanted—A Masculine Soul-Mate," *London Life*, November 1, 1930, pp. 26–27.

99. Enslave, "A Grim Outlook for Men," August 28, 1937, in Farrer, *Cross Dressing between the Wars, 1934–1941*, 103–105.

100. Statement by Thompson Cockcroft, May 18, 1923, TNA, PRO, CRIM1/234.

101. Statement by Ronald E. Matheson, May 18, 1923, TNA, PRO, CRIM1/234.

102. Letter from C. Benbow to R. E. Matheson, March 6, 1923, Exhibit 17, TNA, PRO, CRIM1/234.

103. Letter from John Stewart to C. Benbow, September 25, 1922, Exhibit 69, TNA, PRO, CRIM1/234.

104. Exhibit 82, p. 96, TNA, PRO, CRIM1/234.

105. Ibid., pp. 107–108.

106. Ibid., p. 111.

107. Ibid., p. 112.

108. Ibid., p. 106.

109. Ibid., p. 112.

110. Ibid., p. 111.

111. Ibid., p. 103.

112. Ibid., p. 109.

113. Ibid., p. 110.

114. Ibid., p. 112.

115. Sentences, May 30, 1923, nos. 18 and 19, p. 5, TNA, PRO, CRIM9/69.

116. List or Manifest of Alien Passengers, List 4, "S. S. Franconia," passengers sailing from Southhampton to New York, June 11, 1932, available from ancestry.co.uk.

117. List or Manifest of Alien Passengers, List 4, San Francisco, "S. S. Mariposa," passengers sailing from Sydney, Australia, August 21, 1935, available from ancestry.co.uk.

118. List or Manifest of Alien Passengers, List 7, New York, "S. S. Aquitania," passengers sailing from Southampton, March 25, 1939, available from ancestry.co.uk.

119. Sea Arrival Card, record for Mervyn James Hyde, December 18, 1960, UK Incoming Passenger Lists, 1878–1960, available from ancestry.co.uk; Mervyn Hyde, SS 094-30-1826, Social Security Death Index, Social Security Administration, available from ancestry.co.uk.

120. Divine Wasp, "Tight Lacing and Corsets for Men," February 16, 1918, in Farrer, *Confidential Correspondence on Cross Dressing Part II, 1916–1920*, 87.

CHAPTER 5

1. E. A. Cormack, Medical Officer, H.M. Prison, Brixon, April 12, 1937, National Archives (TNA), Public Records Office (PRO), Central Criminal Court (CRIM) 1/929.

2. Exhibit 2, p. 1, TNA, PRO, CRIM 1/929.

3. Exhibit 8, p. 4, TNA, PRO, CRIM 1/929.

4. Exhibit 11, pp. 8–9, TNA, PRO, CRIM 1/929.

5. Exhibit 18, pp. 20–21, TNA, PRO, CRIM 1/929.

6. Exhibit 8, p. 5, TNA, PRO, CRIM 1/929.

7. Exhibit 12, p. 11, TNA, PRO, CRIM 1/929.

8. Exhibit 11, p. 9, TNA, PRO, CRIM 1/929.

9. Exhibit 18, p. 21, TNA, PRO, CRIM 1/929.

10. Exhibit 18, p. 22, TNA, PRO, CRIM 1/929.

11. Exhibit 12, pp. 11–12, TNA, PRO, CRIM 1/929.

12. Exhibit 19, pp. 23–24, TNA, PRO, CRIM 1/929.

13. Happy Mother, "A Mother's Duty," *London Life*, February 15, 1930, p. 26.

14. Worried Mater, "Oh, What a Plague Is an Obstinate Daughter," *London Life*, December 6, 1930, p. 26.

15. Magistrate's Clerk's Office, from the Medical Officer, H. M. Prison, Brixton, April 12, 1937, TNA, PRO, CRIM1/929.

16. Letter from the Medical Officer, H. M. Prison, Brixton, to Magistrate's Clerk's Office, Croydon, April 12, 1937, TNA, PRO, CRIM1/929.

17. Statement by Henry Leslie, Detective Inspector of the "Z" Division, Metropolitan Police, Croydon, April 13, 1937, TNA, PRO, CRIM1/929.

18. Metropolitan Police Report, Croydon Station, August 1, 1938, TNA, PRO, CRIM1/929.

19. Ibid.

20. Copy of letter addressed to Miss Barbara Tresure [sic], Metropolitan Police, Croydon Station, posted April 11, 1938, TNA, PRO, CRIM1/929.

21. Metropolitan Police Report, Croydon Station, August 1, 1938, TNA, PRO, CRIM1/929.

22. Death Index, 1916–2000, 1956, January, February, March, database online, p. 411, from General Register Office, England and Wales Civil Registration Indexes, London England HMSO, and the Office of the National Stationers.

23. Letter from the Medical Officer, H. M. Prison, Brixton, to Magistrate's Clerk's Office, Croydon, April 12, 1937, TNA, PRO, CRIM1/929.

24. Cheryl Buckley and Hillary Fawcett, *Fashioning the Feminine: Representation and Women's Fashion from the Fin de Siècle to the Present* (London: Tauris, 2002), 115.

25. A pornographic novel played up these associations. Yvan Kermor, *Silk Stockings* (Paris: Libraire des Editions Modernes, 1940).

26. Jeremy Farrell, *Socks and Stockings* (London: Batsford, 1992), 60–61.

27. Farrell, *Socks and Stockings*, 75, 70.

28. Anthony Berkeley, *Silk Stocking Murders* (London: Penguin, 1941).

29. Quoted in Clara Henderson, "'When Hearts Beat like Native Drums': Music and the Sexual Dimensions of the Notions of 'Savage' and 'Civilized' in Tarzan and His Mate, 1934," *Africa Today* 48, no. 4 (2001): 108.

30. Home Office, "Confidential," April 8, 1938, TNA, PRO, Customs (CUST) 49/2334.

31. Ibid.

32. London Metropolitan Archives, Public Morality Council Papers, A/PMC/207/1–121.

33. *High Heel Magazine: A Silk Stocking Publication* (January 1938): 33, Public Morality Council Papers, A/PMC/207/1–121, London Metropolitan Archives.

34. See Lisa Z. Sigel, *Governing Pleasures: Pornography and Social Change in England, 1815–1914* (New Brunswick, NJ: Rutgers University Press, 2000), 58–63; and H. S. Ashbee, *Centuria Librorum Absconditorum* (1879; reprint, New York: Documentary Books, 1962), 442–474.

35. H.C.G. Matthew, *Gladstone* (Oxford: Clarendon Press, 1997), 90–95.

36. For example, *Nell in Bridewell* was a translation of a nineteenth-century German exposé about women's prisons. Carrington reprinted it as part of the Society of British Bibliophiles series with a new title and a cover that featured a naked woman under the lash. W. Reinhard, *Nell in Bridewell* (Paris: Society of British Bibliophiles [Charles Carrington], 1900).

37. TNA, PRO, Metropolitan Police Department (MEPO) 3/938.

38. A. Cantab, *Two Flappers in Paris* (1920; reprint, New York: Grove Press, 1969). See Peter Mendes, *Clandestine Erotic Fiction in English, 1800–1930* (Aldershot, UK: Scolar Press, 1993), 404.

39. Sensible but Loving Ma, "A Mother of Daughters," *London Life*, July 25, 1925, p. 23.

40. Troubled, "Are Girls Fit for Freedom?" *London Life*, February 27, 1926, p. 23.

41. Docteur Ruba, "The Pleasure of Pain," *London Life*, July 17, 1926, p. 15.

42. Satisfied, "Paddling" *London Life*, September 26, 1936, p. 22.

43. HAROLDEO, "The Modern Child," *London Life*, February 15, 1941, in Peter Farrer, ed., *Cross Dressing between the Wars, 1934–1941*, 253–254.

44. The Sheik, "Can You Answer These Questions?" *London Life*, October 18, 1924, p. 21.

45. Polly, "Tight Laced Wife," *London Life*, November 1, 1930, p. 22.

46. Bas De Soie, "The Charm of Silk Stockings," *London Life*, December 6, 1930, p. 27.

47. Six Inch Heels, "The Allure of Lingerie," *London Life*, July 5, 1930, p. 26.

48. Ian Gibson, *The English Vice: Beating, Sex and Shame in Victorian England and After* (London: Duckworth Press, 1978), chaps. 2 and 3; Colette Colligan, "Anti-abolition Writes Obscenity: The English Vice, Transatlantic Slavery, and England's Obscene Print Culture," in *International Exposure: Perspectives on Modern European Pornography, 1800–2000*, edited by Lisa Z. Sigel (New Brunswick, NJ: Rutgers University Press, 2005), 67–99.

49. They also shared a basic emotive structure. Joseph Mercurio, in his examination of caning in New Zealand schools, labels the relationship created by caning and corporal punishment as one of subjection and submission. Joseph A. Mercurio, *Caning: Educational Rite and Tradition* (Syracuse, NY: Syracuse University Press, 1972), 19.

50. See, for example, Steven Pierce and Anupama Rao, eds., *Discipline and the Other Body: Correction, Corporeality, Colonialism* (Durham, NC: Duke University Press, 2006); in particular, Steven Pierce, "Punishment and the Political Body" in that volume.

51. Myra C. Glenn, "The Naval Reform Campaign against Flogging: A Case Study in Changing Attitudes toward Corporal Punishment, 1830–1850," *American Quarterly* 35, no. 4 (Autumn 1983): 409.

52. John Briggs, Christopher Harrison, Angus McInnes, and David Vincent, *Crime and Punishment in England: An Introductory History* (New York: St. Martin's Press, 1996).

53. Home Office, "Report of the Departmental Committee on Corporal Punishment" (London: HMSO, 1938), 1.

54. J. R. Dinwiddy, "The Early Nineteenth-Century Campaign against Flogging in the Army," *English Historical Review* 97, no. 383 (April 1982): 331.

55. I. Gibson, *The English Vice*, 178.

56. Ibid., chap. 3, 99–143.

57. Home Office, "Report of the Departmental Committee on Corporal Punishment," 3–6.

58. Statistical Branch, July 13, 1929, TNA, PRO, Home Office (HO) 45/14178.

59. Home Office, "Report of the Departmental Committee on Corporal Punishment," 149.

60. Corporal Punishment Returns, Acting Governor, Kenya to the Colonial Office, October 19, 1933, TNA, PRO, Colonial Office (CO) 533/434/12.

61. Analysis of cases of corporal punishment in Kenya for the year ending December 31, 1936, TNA, PRO, CO323/1399/3.

62. One of the last publicly sanctioned cases of caning girls on the posterior happened at a training school in 1923. Minutes, July 24, 1923, TNA, PRO, HO45/14545; letter to W. Clarke Hall, Esquire, January 3, 1924, TNA, PRO, HO144/17255.

63. "The Birching of Children," *British Medical Journal*, March 20, 1937, p. 619, TNA, PRO, HO144/21050.

64. George Benson and Edward Glover, "Corporal Punishment: An Indictment" (London: Howard League for Penal Reform, 1931), 6, TNA, PRO, HO45/17487.

65. Memorandum, December 1, 1936, TNA, PRO, CO533/483/14.

66. "Birch or No Birch," *Justice of the Peace and Local Government Review*, May 1, 1937, TNA, PRO, HO45/17489.

67. "Address for Overseas Prison Conference on Corporal Punishment," July 1936, TNA, PRO, HO45/17489.

68. Boys' schools received canes that were 33″ long and ⅜″ in diameter, the Boys' Reformatory School received the 36″ cane with a ⅜″ diameter, and the girls' schools received the "older and lighter 'industrial school' model." Memorandum and Addendum: Canes, January 1, 1933, TNA, PRO, HO144/17255.

69. According to a comprehensive report made in 1938, "The following are the actual specifications for birches manufactured in English prisons for use in administering corporal punishment to boys between ten and sixteen years:—overall length, 40 inches: length of handle, 15 inches: circumference of spray at the centre, 6 inches: total weight: 9 ounces. For boys under ten years of age there is a smaller birch." Home Office, "Report of the Departmental Committee on Corporal Punishment," 16.

70. The cat was "composed of nine lengths of fine whipcord, whipped at the end to prevent fraying, and attached to a short handle. Only one type of cat-o'-nine-tails is authorized, and the precise specifications are as follows:—length of handle 19-3/4 inches; weight of handle, covered with cloth, 6-3/4 ounces; weight of tails, 2-1/4 ounces; total weight, 9 ounces. As there seems to be some misapprehension of this point, we wish to emphasize the fact that the tails of the cat-o'-nine-tails now used in administering corporal punishment are of whip-cord, not leather, and are not knotted or weighted down in any way." Home Office, "Report of the Departmental Committee on Corporal Punishment," 52. See also Minutes, TNA, PRO, HO45/12907.

71. TNA, PRO, CO795/38/12.

72. For a description of the chicotte, see Adam Hochschild, *King Leopold's Ghost* (Boston: Houghton Mifflin, 1999), 120–123.

73. Home Office, "Report of the Departmental Committee on Corporal Punishment," 18.

74. See, for example, "Miss Coote's Confessions," a story that was serialized in *The Pearl*. Anonymous, *The Pearl* (1879; reprint, New York: Grove Press, 1968).

75. Home Office, "Report of the Departmental Committee on Corporal Punishment," 52–53.

76. Hermann Mannheim, "Review of the Report of the Departmental Committee on Corporal Punishment," *Modern Law Review* (June 1938): 54–56, 54–55.

77. Raymond L. Gard, *The End of the Rod: A History of the Abolition of Corporal Punishment in the Courts of England and Wales* (Boca Raton, FL: Brown Walker Press, 2009), 102.

78. Home Office, "Report of the Departmental Committee on Corporal Punishment," 32–33.

79. Arthur Osburn, "To Flog—or—Not to Flog?" 1930, 1, 3, TNA, PRO, HO45/14178. Osburn is identified in Paul Nash, "Training an Elite," *History of Education Quarterly* 1, no. 1 (1961): 19.

80. Letter to First Sea Lord, January 25, 1937, p. 4, TNA, PRO, HO144/21050.

81. Benson and Glover, "Corporal Punishment: An Indictment," 27, TNA, PRO, HO45/17487.

82. Ibid., 18.

83. Home Office, "Report of the Departmental Committee on Corporal Punishment," 1.

84. Gard also sees an enormous change in attitudes about corporal punishment in the interwar years among politicians and civil servants. He attributes this change in part to a different social background among officials, rather than an influence of psychological theory. See Gard, *The End of the Rod*, 105.

85. Colleen Lamos, "James Joyce and the English Vice," *Novel: A Forum on Fiction* 9, no. 1 (Autumn 1995): 29.

86. James Joyce, *Ulysses* (1922; reprint, New York: Vintage Books, 1990), 466–467.

87. Ibid., 468.

88. John M. Woolsey, "The Monumental Decision of the United States District Court Rendered December 6, 1933 by Hon. John M. Woolsey Lifting the Ban on *Ulysses*," appended to Joyce, *Ulysses*, xi.

89. Woolsey, "The Monumental Decision," xi–xii.

90. Indecent Pubns., "Ulysses"—Sale by W. G. Foyle Ltd., Home Office, September 22, 1936, TNA, PRO, LO2/30.

91. Exhibit 11, pp. 8–9, TNA, PRO, CRIM 1/929.

92. "Indecent Writings Found," Metropolitan Police Report, Criminal Investigations Department (CID), New Scotland Yard, October 15, 1921, Note 3, found September 14, 1921, TNA, PRO, MEPO3/380.

93. "Law Report, August 13, Court of Criminal Appeal," *The Times*, August 14, 1923, TNA, PRO, MEPO3/380.

94. "Indecent Writings Found," Metropolitan Police Report, CID, New Scotland Yard, October 15, 1921, Note 8, found October 7, 1921, TNA, PRO, MEPO.

95. TNA, PRO, MEPO3/380. See Metropolitan Police Report, CID, New Scotland Yard, June 29, 1921, for the allegations.

96. John Kucich, "Sadomasochism and the Magical Group: Kipling's Middle-Class Imperialism," *Victorian Studies* 46 no. 1 (2003): 57.

97. Carolyn Strange notes a paucity of research in the state's application of corporal punishment in the twentieth century. As she explains, "We have devoted comparatively little thought to modern penal violence." Carolyn Strange, "The 'Shock' of Torture: A Historiographical Challenge," *History Workshop Journal* 61 (2006): 140.

98. See, for example, Karen Halttunen, "Humanitarianism and the Pornography of Pain in Anglo-American Culture," *American Historical Review* 100, no. 2 (1995): 303–324.

CONCLUSION

1. Heine Sauge, "An Idea," *London Life*, September 18, 1937, p. 25.

2. "Confessions of a Lover of the Limbless," *London Life*, March 30, 1940, pp. 27–31, 43.

3. After being bombed out, the magazine went back to earlier roots as a "girlie" about-town magazine. It continued publication under that format for almost two decades before ceasing publication altogether.

4. For example, see League of Nations, Advisory Committee on Social Issues, "Summary of Annual Reports for 1942/1943 prepared by the Secretariat: Circulation of and Traffic in Obscene Publications," Geneva, November 15, 1944, p. 2; League of Nations, Advisory Committee on Social Issues, "Summary of Annual Reports for 1942/1943 prepared by the Secretariat: Circulation of and Traffic in Obscene Publications," Geneva, November 15, 1946, p. 2.

5. Flying Officer A.W.C., Officers Mess, RAF, Leighton Buzzard, Beds, December 26, 1941, Papers of Marie Carmichael Stopes PP/MCS/A.68.

6. John W.R.F., June 11, 1941, PP/MCS/A.86, and Stopes's reply, June 16, 1941.

7. Leicester City Police, "Table Shewing Offences Known to the Police," National Archives (TNA), Public Records Office (PRO), Home Office (HO) 45/25066; City of Sheffield Police, "Statistics Relative to Robbery with Violence," TNA, PRO, HO 45/25066; Leeds City Police, Criminal Investigations Department (CID), "Letter to Home Office" March 15, 1950, TNA, PRO, HO 45/25066.

8. Editor, *London Life League* (newsletter), no. 3 (July 1984).

9. The editor of the L3 newsletter notes the "distressing number of letters we have received lamenting, 'what was' or 'what might have been.'" *London Life League* (newsletter), no. 19 (Autumn 1988). By 1986, the newsletter had a formal feature called "Nostalgia Corner." *London Life League* (newsletter), no. 6 (April 1985): 8.

10. Amartya Sen, *Identity and Violence* (New York: Norton, 2006), xvi. In the body of his book, Sen suggests that the embrace of the multiple identities through which people can simultaneously conceptualize themselves may help dislodge that miniaturization.

Bibliography

PRIMARY SOURCES

Archives

California State Northridge, Harris/Wheeler Collection.

Imperial War Museum, Online Photography Collection, Great War.

Kinsey Institute for Research in Sex, Gender, and Reproduction, Department of Archives. David Kunzle Collection and Louise Lawrence Collection.

"London Life Clipping File" at OverGround. Available at http://www.overground.be/londonLife/.

London Metropolitan Archive, Public Morality Council Papers.

Mass-Observation Archive. Mass-Observation Archive at the University of Sussex Papers, microfilm, Adam Matthew Publications.

The National Archives (TNA) Public Records Office (PRO) materials are from Central Criminal Court (CRIM), Colonial Office (CO), Customs (CUST), Home Office (HO), Foreign Office (FO), Metropolitan Police Department (MEPO), Ministry of Health (MH), and War Office (WO).

Wellcome Library for the History of Medicine, Papers of Marie Carmichael Stopes (PP/MCS).

Magazines and Newspapers

Bits of Fun

British Medical Journal

Fun

Gay Book

Gymnos

Health and Efficiency

Health and Strength

High Heels

Illustrated Bits
London Life
London Life and Modern Society
London Life League newsletters (mimeographs)
Love Romances
Love Stories
The Man about Town
Movie Merry-Go-Round
New Fun
New Photo Fun
Nudelife
Paris Sex Appeal
Peg's Paper
Photo Bits
Photo Fun
Ranch Romances
Real Screen Fun
Reel Screen Humor
Screen Romances
Silk Stockings
Sun Bathing Review
The Times (London)

Books and Pamphlets

Anonymous. *The Pearl.* 1879. Reprint, New York: Grove Press, 1968.
Bell, Ralcy Husted. *Some Aspects of Adultery.* New York: Critic and Guide, 1921.
Berkeley, Anthony. *Silk Stocking Murders.* London: Penguin, 1941.
Bloch, Ivan. *A History of English Sexual Morals.* London: Francis Aldor, 1936.
Bulliet, Clarence Joseph. *Venus Castina.* 1928. Reprint, New York: Bonanza Books, 1956.
Cantab, A. *Two Flappers in Paris.* 1920. Reprint, New York: Grove Press, 1969.
Carrothers, W. A. *Emigration from the British Isles.* London: King, 1929.
Chesser, Eustace. *Love without Fear.* New York: Signet Books, 1947.
Christie, Agatha. "Death on the Nile." In *Poirot in the Orient.* 1937. Reprint, New York: Berkley Books, 2005.
———. "Murder in Mesopotamia." In *Poirot in the Orient.* 1936. Reprint, New York: Berkley Books, 2005.
Christie, May. *Love's Miracle.* New York: Grosset and Dunlap, 1930.
Cox, Harold. "The Peopling of the British Empire." *Foreign Affairs* 2, no. 1 (1923): 117–129.
Crisp, Quentin. *The Naked Civil Servant.* New York: Holt, Rinehart and Winston, 1977.
Ellis, Havelock. "Freud's Influence on the Changed Attitude toward Sex." *American Journal of Sociology* 45, no. 3 (November 1939): 309–317.
———. *Man and Woman.* Boston: Houghton Mifflin, 1929.
———. *Studies in the Psychology of Sex.* Vols. 1 and 2. New York: Random House, 1942.
Ernst, Morris. "Foreword." In *Studies in the Psychology of Sex,* by Havelock Ellis. New York: Random House, 1936.
Farrer, Peter, ed. *Confidential Correspondence on Cross-Dressing, 1911–1915.* Liverpool: Karn, 1997.
———, ed. *Confidential Correspondence on Cross-Dressing Part II, 1916–1920.* Liverpool, UK: Karn, 1998.

———, ed. *Cross Dressing between the Wars: Selections from London Life, 1923–1933.* Liverpool, UK: Karn, 2000.

———, ed. *Cross Dressing between the Wars: Selections from London Life, 1934–1941.* Liverpool, UK: Karn, 2006.

Freud, Sigmund. "A Child Is Being Beaten." In *On Freud's "A Child Is Being Beaten."* Edited by Ethel Spector Person. New Haven, CT: Yale University Press, 1997.

———. *Three Essays on the Theory of Sexuality.* New York: Basic Books, 1975.

Graves, Robert, and Alan Hodge. *The Long Week-End: A Social History of Great Britain.* 1940. Reprint, New York: Norton, 1994.

Hall, Radclyffe. *The Well of Loneliness.* 1928. Reprint, New York: Anchor Books, 1990.

Hirschfeld, Magnus. *Sexual History of the World War.* New York: Cadillac, 1941.

———. *Transvestites: The Erotic Drive to Cross-Dress.* 1928. Reprint, Buffalo, NY: Prometheus Books, 1991.

Home Office. "Report of the Departmental Committee on Corporal Punishment." London: HMSO, 1938.

Joyce, James. *Ulysses.* 1922. Reprint, New York: Vintage Books, 1990.

Kermor, Yvan. *Silk Stockings.* Illustrated by Edouard Bernard. Paris: Libraire des Editions Modernes, 1940.

Krafft-Ebing, Richard von. *Psychopathia Sexualis.* New York: Putnam, 1965.

Ladywood, Viscount [pseud.]. *Gynecocracy.* 1893. Reprint, Lexington, KY: Ophir Books, 2007.

Lawrence, David Herbert. "A Propos of *Lady Chatterley's Lover.*" In *Sex, Literature and Censorship.* New York: Viking Press, 1959.

———. *Lady Chatterley's Lover.* 1928. Reprint, London: Penguin, 2006.

League of Nations, Advisory Committee on Social Issues. "Summary of Annual Reports for 1942/1943 Prepared by the Secretariat: Circulation of and Traffic in Obscene Publications." Geneva, November 15, 1944.

Leavis, Q. D. *Fiction and the Reading Public.* 1932. Reprint, London: Pimlico, 2000.

Le Queux, William. *The Doctor of Pimlico.* London: Cassell, 1919.

Mannheim, Hermann. "Review of the Report of the Departmental Committee on Corporal Punishment." *Modern Law Review* (June 1938): 54–56.

Mass-Observation. *The Press and Its Readers.* London: Art and Technology, 1949.

Merrill, Frances, and Mason Merrill. *Among the Nudists.* New York: Knopf, 1931.

Orwell, George. "Boys Weeklies." In *The Collected Essays, Journalism and Letters of George Orwell,* vol. 1, *An Age Like This.* New York: Harcourt Brace, 1968.

Pedler, Margaret. *The Barbarian Lover.* New York: Grosset and Dunlap, 1923.

Reinhard, W. *Nell in Bridewell.* Paris: Society of British Bibliophiles [Charles Carrington], 1900.

Roughhead, William. *Bad Companions.* New York: Duffield and Green, 1931.

Shanahan, E. W. "Overpopulation, Emigration, Empire Development." *Economica,* no. 9 (1923): 215–223.

Stopes, Marie. *Change of Life in Men and Women.* New York: Putnam, 1936.

———. *Enduring Passion.* Garden City, NY: Blue Ribbon Books, 1931.

———. *The Human Body.* Garden City, NY: Blue Ribbon Books, 1926.

———. *Married Love.* 1918. Reprint, Oxford: Oxford University Press, 2004.

———. *Mother England: A Contemporary History.* London: Bale, 1929.

———. *Radiant Motherhood.* New York: Putnam, 1921.

———. *Wise Parenthood: A Practical Sequel to Married Love,* 16th ed. London: Putnam, 1931.

Tansley, A. G. *The New Psychology and Its Relation to Life.* London: Dodd, Mead, 1922.

Van de Velde, T. H. *Ideal Marriage.* New York: Random House, 1930.

Wadsley, Olive. *Possession.* London: Cassell, 1924.

Walker, Kenneth. *Diseases of the Male Organs of Generation.* London: Oxford Medical Publications, 1923.

———. *Physiology of Sex.* New York: Penguin, 1945.

Wallace, Edgar. *The Girl from Scotland Yard.* New York: Doubleday, 1926.

Woolf, Virginia. "Middlebrow." In *The Death of the Moth and Other Essays.* San Diego: Harcourt Brace, 1970.

Woolsey, John M. "The Monumental Decision of the United States District Court Rendered December 6, 1933 by Hon. John M. Woolsey Lifting the Ban on *Ulysses.*" Appended to *Ulysses*, by James Joyce. New York: Vintage Books, 1990.

Reference Sources

The Advertising Annual. London: Kingsway Press.

Ashbee, H. S. *Centuria Librorum Absconditorum.* 1879. Reprint, New York: Documentary Books, 1962.

———. *Index Librorum Prohibitorum.* 1877. Reprint, New York: Documentary Books, 1962.

Dictionary of National Biography. Oxford: Oxford University Press, online edition. Available at http://www.oxforddnb.com/.

Kearney, Patrick. *The Private Case.* London: Landesman, 1981.

Mendes, Peter. *Clandestine Erotic Fiction in English 1800–1930: A Bibliographical Study.* Aldershot, UK: Scolar Press, 1993.

Newspaper Press Directory. London: Mitchell.

Straight, Sheryl. The Erotica Bibliophile. Available at http://www.eroticabibliophile.com/index.php.

Willing's Press Guide. London: Willing Service, 1932.

SECONDARY SOURCES

Allen, Ann Taylor. "Feminism and Eugenics in Germany and Britain, 1900–1940: A Comparative Perspective." *German Studies Review* 23, no. 3 (2000): 477–505.

Anderson, Benedict. *Imagined Communities.* London: Verso, 1991.

Arnold, David. "The Police and Colonial Control in South India." *Social Scientist* 4, no. 12 (1976): 3–16.

Baggs, Chris. "How Well Read Was My Valley? Reading, Popular Fiction, and the Miners of South Wales, 1875–1939." *Book History* 4 (2001): 277–301.

Barham, Peter. *Forgotten Lunatics of the Great War.* New Haven, CT: Yale University Press, 2004.

Bartley, Paula. *Prostitution: Prevention and Reform.* London: Routledge, 1999.

Bauer, Heike. *English Literary Sexology: Translations of Inversion, 1860–1930.* Basingstoke, UK: Palgrave Macmillan, 2009.

Beetham, Margaret. "'Natural but Firm': The Corset Correspondence in *Englishwoman's Domestic Magazine.*" *Women: A Cultural Review* 2, no. 2 (1991): 163–167.

Bienvenu, Robert. "The Development of Sadomasochism as a Cultural Style in the Twentieth-Century United States." Ph.D. diss., Indiana University, 1998.

Biernoff, Suzannah. "The Rhetoric of Disfigurement in First World War Britain." *Social History of Medicine* 24, no. 3 (2011): 666–685.

Bingham, Adrian. *Family Newspapers? Sex, Private Life, and the British Popular Press, 1918–1978.* Oxford: Oxford University Press, 2009.

Bland, Lucy. *Banishing the Beast: Feminism, Sex and Morality.* London: Tauris Parke, 2001.

———. "Trials and Tribulations of Edith Thompson: The Capital Crime of Sexual Incitement in 1920s England." *Journal of British Studies* 47, no. 3 (2008): 624–648.

Bland, Lucy, and Laura Doan, eds. *Sexology in Culture: Labeling Bodies and Desires.* Chicago: University of Chicago Press, 1998.

Bloom, Clive. *Bestsellers: Popular Fiction since 1900.* Basingstoke, UK: Palgrave Macmillan, 2009.

Bourke, Joanna. *Dismembering the Male: Men's Bodies, Britain, and the Great War.* Chicago: University of Chicago Press, 1996.

———. "The Great Male Renunciation: Men's Dress Reform in Inter-war Britain." *Journal of Design History* 9, no. 1 (1996): 23–33.

Boxwell, David A. "The Follies of War: Cross-Dressing and Popular Theater on the British Front Lines, 1914–18." *Modernism/Modernity* 9, no. 1 (2002): 1–20.

Briggs, John, Christopher Harrison, Angus McInnes, and David Vincent. *Crime and Punishment in England: An Introductory History.* New York: St. Martin's Press, 1996.

Bristow, Joseph. "Symonds's History, Ellis's Heredity: Sexual Inversion." In *Sexology in Culture: Labeling Bodies and Desires,* edited by Lucy Bland and Laura Doan, 79–99. Chicago: University of Chicago Press, 1998.

Buckley, Cheryl, and Hillary Fawcett. *Fashioning the Feminine: Representation and Women's Fashion from the Fin de Siècle to the Present.* London: Tauris, 2002.

Bullough, Vern L., and Bonnie Bullough. *Cross Dressing, Sex, and Gender.* Philadelphia: University of Pennsylvania Press, 1993.

———. *Sexual Variance in Society and History.* New York: Wiley, 1976.

Burman, Barbara. "Better and Brighter Clothes: The Men's Dress Reform Party, 1929–1940." *Journal of Design History* 8, no. 4 (1995): 275–290.

Cameron, Laura, and John Forrester. "'A Nice Type of the English Scientist': Tansley and Freud." *History Workshop Journal,* no. 48 (Autumn 1999): 64–100.

Campbell, James S. "'For You May Touch Them Not': Misogyny, Homosexuality, and the Ethics of Passivity in First War Poetry." *ELH* 64, no. 3 (1997): 823–842.

Chauncey, George. *Gay New York: Gender, Urban Culture, and the Making of the Gay Male World, 1890–1940.* New York: Basic Books, 1994.

Cocks, H. G. *Nameless Offences: Homosexual Desire in the Nineteenth Century.* London: Tauris, 2003.

———. "'Peril in the Personals': The Dangers and Pleasures of Classified Advertising in Early Twentieth-Century Britain." *Media History* 10, no. 1 (2004): 3–16.

———. "Saucy Stories: Pornography, Sexology and the Marketing of Sexual Knowledge in Britain, c. 1918–70." *Social History* 29, no. 4 (November 2004): 465–484.

Cohen, Deborah A. "Private Lives in Public Spaces: Marie Stopes, the Mothers' Clinics and the Practice of Contraception." *History Workshop Journal* 35 (1993): 95–116.

Colligan, Colette. "Anti-abolition Writes Obscenity: The English Vice, Transatlantic Slavery, and England's Obscene Print Culture." In *International Exposure: Perspectives on Modern European Pornography, 1800–2000,* edited by Lisa Z. Sigel, 67–99. New Brunswick, NJ: Rutgers University Press, 2005.

Collins, Marcus. *Modern Love: Personal Relationships in Twentieth-Century Britain.* Newark: University of Delaware Press, 2003.

Cook, Hera. *The Long Sexual Revolution: English Women, Sex, and Contraception, 1800–1975.* Oxford: Oxford University Press, 2005.

Cook, Matt. *London and the Culture of Homosexuality, 1885–1914*. Cambridge: Cambridge University Press, 2003.

Coppens, Armand. *Memoirs of an Erotic Bookseller*. London: Luxor Press, 1969.

Crouthamel, Jason. "Male Sexuality and Psychological Trauma: Soldiers and Sexual Disorder in World War I and Weimar Germany." *Journal of the History of Sexuality* 17, no. 1 (2008): 60–84.

Crozier, Ivan. "Becoming a Sexologist: Norman Haire, the 1929 London World League for Sex Reform Congress, and Organizing Medical Knowledge about Sex in Interwar England." *Science History* 39 (2001): 299–329.

———. "Taking Prisoners: Havelock Ellis, Sigmund Freud, and the Construction of Homosexuality, 1897–1951." *Social History of Medicine* 13 (2000): 447–466.

Darnton, Robert. "Literary Surveillance in the British Raj: The Contradictions of Liberal Imperialism." *Book History* 2 (2001): 133–176.

Davey, Claire. "Birth Control in Britain during the Interwar Years: Evidence from the Stopes Correspondence." *Journal of Family History* 13, no. 3 (1988): 329–345.

Dawson, Graham. *Soldier Heroes: British Adventure, Empire and the Imagining of Masculinities*. London: Routledge, 1994.

Debenham, Clare. "Mrs. Elsie Plant—Suffragette, Socialist and Birth Control Activist." *Women's History Review* 19, no. 1 (2010): 145–158.

de Erauso, Catalina. *Lieutenant Nun: Memoirs of a Basque Transvestite in the New World*. Boston: Beacon Press, 1996.

DeGroot, Gerald. *Blighty: British Society in the Era of the Great War*. London: Longman, 1996.

de Jongh, Nicholas. *Politics, Prudery, and Perversions: The Censorship of the English Stage, 1901–1968*. London: Methuen, 2001.

Deslandes, Paul. "Competitive Examinations and the Culture of Masculinity in Oxbridge Undergraduate Life, 1850–1920." *History of Education Quarterly* 42, no. 4 (2002): 544–578.

———. *Oxbridge Men: British Masculinity and the Undergraduate Experience, 1850–1920*. Bloomington: University of Indiana Press, 2005.

Dikotter, Frank. "Recent Perspectives on the History of Eugenics." *American Historical Review* 103, no. 2 (1998): 467–478.

Dinwiddy, J. R. "The Early Nineteenth-Century Campaign against Flogging in the Army." *English Historical Review* 97, no. 383 (April 1982): 308–331.

Doan, Laura. *Fashioning Sapphism: The Origins of Modern English Lesbian Culture*. New York: Columbia University Press, 2001.

Edmonds, Leigh. "Australia, Britain and the Empire Transport Scheme, 1934–38." *Journal of Transport History* 20, no. 2 (1999): 91–106.

Eksteins, Modris. *Rites of Spring: The Great War and the Birth of the Modern Age*. New York: Anchor Books, 1989.

Eliot, Simon. "Hotten: Rotten: Forgotten? An Apologia for a General Publisher." *Book History* 3 (2000): 61–93.

Farrell, Jeremy. *Socks and Stockings*. London: Batsford, 1992.

Felski, Rita. "Introduction." In *Sexology in Culture: Labeling Bodies and Desires*, edited by Lucy Bland and Laura Doan, 1–8. Chicago: University of Chicago Press, 1998.

Fields, Jill. "'Fighting the Corsetless Evil': Shaping Corsets and Culture, 1900–1930." *Journal of Social History* 33, no. 2 (1999): 355–384.

Fisher, Kate. *Birth Control, Sex, and Marriage in Britain, 1918–1960*. Oxford: Oxford University Press, 2006.

Foucault, Michel. *The History of Sexuality*. Vol. 1, *An Introduction*. New York: Vintage Books, 1990.

Francis, Martin. "The Domestication of the Male? Recent Research on Nineteenth- and Twentieth-Century British Masculinity." *Historical Journal* 45, no. 3 (2002): 637–652.

Freedman, Michael. "Eugenics and Progressive Thought." *Historical Journal* 22, no. 3 (1979): 645–671.

Fussell, Paul. *The Great War and Modern Memory*. Oxford: Oxford University Press, 1975.

Gamman, Lorraine, and Merja Makinen. *Female Fetishism*. New York: New York University Press, 1994.

Garber, Marjorie. *Vested Interests: Cross Dressing and Cultural Anxiety*. New York: Routledge, 1992.

Gard, Raymond L. *The End of the Rod: A History of the Abolition of Corporal Punishment in the Courts of England and Wales*. Boca Raton, FL: Brown Walker Press, 2009.

Gelber, Scott. "A 'Hard-Boiled Order': The Reeducation of Disabled WWI Veterans in New York City." *Journal of Social History* 39, no. 1 (2005): 161–180.

Geppert, Alexander C. T. "Divine Sex, Happy Marriage, Regenerated Nation: Marie Stopes's Marital Manual *Married Love* and the Making of a Best-Seller, 1918–1955." *Journal of the History of Sexuality* 8, no. 3 (1998): 389–433.

Gerber, David. "Anger and Affability: The Rise and Representation of a Repertory of Self-Presentation Skills in a World War II Disabled." *Journal of Social History* 27, no. 1 (Autumn 1993): 5–27.

Gibson, Ian. *The English Vice: Beating, Sex and Shame in Victorian England and After*. London: Duckworth Press, 1978.

Gibson, K. Craig. "Sex and Soldiering in France and Flanders: The British Expeditionary Force along the Western Front." *International Historical Review* 23, no. 3 (2001): 535–579.

Gilbert, Sandra, and Susan Gubar. *No Man's Land*. New Haven, CT: Yale University Press, 2002.

Giles, Judy. *Women, Identity and Private Life in Britain, 1900–50*. New York: St. Martin's Press, 1995.

Glenn, Myra C. "The Naval Reform Campaign against Flogging: A Case Study in Changing Attitudes toward Corporal Punishment, 1830–1850." *American Quarterly* 35, no. 4 (Autumn 1983): 407–425.

Gullace, Nicoletta F. "White Feathers and Wounded Men: Female Patriotism and the Memory of the Great War." *Journal of British Studies* 36 (1997): 178–206.

Hall, Catherine. "Culture and Identity in Imperial Britain." In *The British Empire: Themes and Perspectives*, edited by S. E. Stockwell, 199–217. Malden, MA: Blackwell, 2008.

Hall, Lesley. "The English Have Hot Water Bottles." In *Sexual Knowledge, Sexual Science*, edited by Roy Porter and Mikulas Teich, 350–366. Cambridge: Cambridge University Press, 1994.

———. *Hidden Anxieties: Male Sexuality, 1900–1950*. Cambridge, UK: Polity Press, 1991.

———. "Review of *Marie Stopes and the Sexual Revolution*." *Medical History* 37, no. 2 (1993): 218–219.

———. *Sex, Gender and Social Change in Britain since 1880*. New York: Palgrave Macmillan, 2000.

———. "Uniting Science and Sensibility: Marie Stopes and the Narratives of Marriage in the 1920s." In *Rediscovering Forgotten Radicals: British Women Writers, 1889–1939*, edited by Angela Ingram and Daphne Patai, 118–136. Chapel Hill: University of North Carolina Press, 1993.

Hall, Ruth, ed. *Dear Dr. Stopes*. London: Deutsch, 1978.

Halperin, David M. *How to Do the History of Homosexuality*. Chicago: University of Chicago Press, 2002.

Halttunen, Karen. "Humanitarianism and the Pornography of Pain in Anglo-American Culture." *American Historical Review* 100, no. 2 (1995): 303–324.

Hansen, Randall. *Citizenship and Immigration in Post-war Britain: The Institutional Origins of a Multicultural Nation*. Oxford: Oxford University Press, 2000.

Harrison, Barbara. "Women and Health." In *Women's History: Britain, 1850–1945*, edited by June Purvis, 157–192. New York: St. Martin's Press, 1995.

Hau, Michael. *The Cult of Health and Beauty in Germany: A Social History 1890–1930*. Chicago: University of Chicago Press, 2003.

Hauck, Christina. "Abortion and Individual Talent." *ELH* 70, no. 1 (2003): 223–266.

Hauser, Renate. "Krafft-Ebing's Psychological Understanding of Sexual Behavior." In *Sexual Knowledge, Sexual Science*, edited by Roy Porter and Mikulas Teich, 210–227. Cambridge: Cambridge University Press, 1994.

Heath, Deana. *Purifying Empire: Obscenity and the Politics of Moral Regulation in Britain, India and Australia*. Cambridge: Cambridge University Press, 2010.

Heathorn, Stephen. "The Mnemonic Turn in the Cultural Historiography of Britain's Great War." *Historical Journal* 48, no. 4 (2005): 1103–1124.

Henderson, Clara. "'When Hearts Beat like Native Drums': Music and the Sexual Dimensions of the Notions of 'Savage' and 'Civilized' in Tarzan and His Mate, 1934." *Africa Today* 48, no. 4 (2001): 91–124.

Hindmarch-Watson, Katie. "Lois Schwich, The Female Errand Boy." *GLQ: A Journal of Lesbian and Gay Studies* 14, no. 1 (2008): 69–98.

Hochschild, Adam. *King Leopold's Ghost*. Boston: Houghton Mifflin, 1999.

Hoffman, Brian. "'A Certain Amount of Prudishness': Nudist Magazines and the Liberalisation of American Obscenity Law, 1947–58." *Gender and History* 22, no. 3 (2010): 708–732.

Holland, Robert. "The British Empire and the Great War." In *The Oxford History of the British Empire: The Twentieth Century*. Oxford: Oxford University Press, 1999.

Holtzman, Ellen Martha. "Marriage, Sexuality, and Contraception in the British Middle Class, 1918–1939: The Correspondence of Marie Stopes." Ph.D. diss., Rutgers University, 1982.

Houlbrook, Matt. *Queer London: Perils and Pleasures in the Sexual Metropolis, 1918–1957*. Chicago: University of Chicago Press, 2006.

———. "Sexing the History of Sexuality." *History Workshop Journal* 60 (2005): 216–222.

Howell, Phillip. *Geographies of Regulation*. Cambridge: Cambridge University Press, 2009.

Hunnings, Neville March. *Film Censors and the Law*. London: Allen and Unwin, 1967.

Hyam, Ronald. *Britain's Declining Empire: The Road to Decolonization, 1918–1968*. Cambridge: Cambridge University Press, 2007.

———. *Britain's Imperial Century, 1815–1914: A Study of Empire and Expansion*. New York: Palgrave Macmillan, 2002.

Jackson, Louise A. *Child Sexual Abuse in Victorian England*. New York: Routledge, 2000.

Jones, Edgar, and Simon Wessely. "The Impact of Total War on the Practice of British Psychiatry." In *The Shadows of Total War: Europe, East Asia, and the United States,*

1919–1939, edited by Roger Chickering and Stig Forster, 129–148. Cambridge: Cambridge University Press, 2003.

Jones, Greta. "Eugenics and Social Policy between the Wars." *Historical Journal* 25, no. 3 (1982): 717–728.

Joseph, Tiffany. "'Non-combatant's Shell-Shock': Trauma and Gender in F. Scott Fitzgerald's 'Tender Is the Night.'" *NWSA* 15, no. 3 (2003): 64–81.

Kaplan, Louise. *Cultures of Fetishism.* New York: Palgrave Macmillan, 2006.

Kellman, Steven. "James Joyce for Ordinary Blokes?" *Chronicle of Higher Education*, September 21, 2009. Available at http://chronicle.com/article/James-Joyce-for-Ordinary/48427/.

Kendrick, Walter. *The Secret Museum: Pornography in Modern Culture.* New York: Viking Press, 1987.

Kent, Susan Kingsley. *Gender and Power in Britain, 1640–1990.* London: Routledge, 1999.

———. *Making Peace: The Reconstruction of Gender in Interwar Britain.* Princeton, NJ: Princeton University Press, 1993.

Keown, John. *Abortion, Doctors, and the Law.* Cambridge: Cambridge University Press, 1988.

Kipnis, Laura. *Bound and Gagged.* New York: Grove Press, 1996.

Klausen, Susanne M. *Race, Maternity, and the Politics of Birth Control in South Africa, 1910–39.* New York: Palgrave Macmillan, 2005.

Koureas, Gabriel. *Memory, Masculinity and National Identity in British Visual Culture, 1914–1930.* Aldershot, UK: Ashgate, 2007.

Koven, Seth. "Remembering and Dismemberment: Crippled Children, Wounded Soldiers, and the Great War in Great Britain." *American Historical Review* 99, no. 4 (1994): 1167–1202.

———. *Slumming.* Princeton, NJ: Princeton University Press, 2006.

Kripps, Henry. *Fetish: An Erotics of Culture.* Ithaca, NY: Cornell University Press, 1999.

Kucich, John. "Sadomasochism and the Magical Group: Kipling's Middle-Class Imperialism." *Victorian Studies* 46, no. 1 (2003): 33–68.

Kunzel, Regina. "Pulp Fiction and Problem Girls: Reading and Rewriting Single Pregnancy in Postwar United States." *American Historical Review* 100, no. 5 (1995): 1465–1487.

Kunzle, David. *Fashion and Fetishism: Corsets, Tight-Lacing, and Other Forms of Body-Sculpture.* Stroud, UK: Sutton, 2004.

Ladenson, Elisabeth. *Dirt for Art's Sake: Books on Trial from Madame Bovary to Lolita.* Ithaca, NY: Cornell University Press, 2007.

Lamos, Colleen. "James Joyce and the English Vice." *Novel: A Forum on Fiction* 9, no. 1 (Autumn 1995): 19–26.

Laqueur, Thomas. *Solitary Sex: A Cultural History of Masturbation.* New York: Zone Books, 2003.

Larkin, Emma. "The Self-Conscious Censor: Censorship in Burma under the British, 1900–1939." *Journal of Burma Studies* 8 (2003): 64–101.

Ledbetter, Rosanna. *A History of the Malthusian League.* Columbus: Ohio State University, 1976.

Leed, Eric J. *No Man's Land: Combat and Identity in World War I.* Cambridge: Cambridge University Press, 1979.

Levene, Alysa, Samantha Williams, and Thomas Nutt, eds. *Illegitimacy in Britain, 1700–1920.* New York: Palgrave Macmillan, 2005.

Levine, Caroline. "Propaganda for Democracy: The Curious Case of *Love on the Dole*." *Journal of British Studies* 45 (October 2006): 846–874.

Levine, Philippa. "States of Undress: Nakedness and the Colonial Imagination." *Victorian Studies* 50, no. 2 (2008): 189–219.

Lewis, Jane. "The Ideology and Politics of Birth Control in Inter-war England." *Women's Studies International Quarterly* 2 (1979): 33–48.

Logan, Peter. *Nerves and Narratives: A Cultural History of Hysteria in 19th-Century British Prose*. Berkeley: University of California Press, 1997.

Loughran, Tracy. "Shell Shock and Psychological Medicine in First World War Britain." *Social History of Medicine* 22, no. 1 (2009): 79–95.

Louis, William Roger, ed. *The Oxford History of the British Empire*. Oxford: Oxford University Press, 2001.

Mabro, Judy. *I Ban Everything: Free Speech and Censorship at Oxford*. Oxford: Ruskin College Library, 1985.

MacKenzie, Donald. "Eugenics in Britain." *Social Studies of Science* 6, no. 3/4 (1976): 499–532.

Mackenzie, John M. "The Imperial Pioneer and Hunter and the Masculine Stereotypes in Late Victorian and Edwardian Times." In *Manliness and Morality*, edited by J. A. Mangan and James Walvin, 176–198. Manchester, UK: Manchester University Press, 1987.

———. *Propaganda and Empire: The Manipulation of British Public Opinion 1880–1960*. Manchester, UK: Manchester University Press, 1984.

Macnicol, John. "Eugenics and the Campaign for Popular Sterilization in Britain between the Wars." *Social History of Medicine* 2, no. 2 (1989): 147–169.

Mahony, Patrick Joseph. "'A Child Is Being Beaten': A Clinical, Historical, and Textual Study." In *On Freud's "A Child Is Being Beaten,"* edited by Ethel Spector Person, 47–66. New Haven, CT: Yale University Press, 1997.

Marshik, Celia. *British Modernism and Censorship*. Cambridge: Cambridge University Press, 2006.

———. "History's 'Abrupt Revenges': Censoring War's Perversions in *The Well of Loneliness* and *Sleeveless Errand*." *Journal of Modern Literature* 26, no. 2 (2002–2003): 145–159.

Matthew, H.C.G. *Gladstone*. Oxford: Clarendon Press, 1997.

McClintock, Anne. *Imperial Leather: Race, Gender, and Sexuality in the Colonial Context*. New York: Routledge, 1995.

McKenzie, Kirsten. "Being Modern on a Slender Income: 'Picture Show' and 'Photoplayer' in Early 1920s Sydney." *Journal of Women's History* 22, no. 4 (2010): 114–136.

McKibbin, Ross. *Classes and Cultures: England, 1918–1951*. Oxford: Oxford University Press, 2000.

———. "Introduction." In *Married Love*. 1918. Reprint, Oxford: Oxford University Press, 2004.

McLaren, Angus. *Birth Control in Nineteenth-Century England*. New York: Holmes and Meier, 1978.

———. *A History of Contraception*. Oxford: Blackwell, 1990.

———. "National Responses to Sexual Perversion: The Case of Transvestitism." In *Sexual Cultures in Europe*, edited by Franz X. Eder, Lesley Hall, and Gert Hekma, 121–138. Manchester, UK: Manchester University Press, 1999.

———. *Sexual Blackmail: A Modern History*. Cambridge, MA: Harvard University Press, 2002.

———. "Smoke and Mirrors: Willy Clarkson and the Role of Disguises in Inter-war England." *Journal of Social History* 40, no. 3 (2007): 597–618.

———. *The Trials of Masculinity: Policing Sexual Boundaries, 1870–1930.* Chicago: University of Chicago Press, 1997.

———. *Twentieth-Century Sexuality.* Oxford: Blackwell, 1999.

Melman, Billie. *Women and the Popular Imagination in the Twenties: Flappers and Nymphs.* New York: Palgrave Macmillan, 1988.

Mercurio, Joseph A. *Caning: Educational Rite and Tradition.* Syracuse, NY: Syracuse University Press, 1972.

Meyerowitz, Joanna. *How Sex Changed: A History of Transsexuality in America.* Cambridge, MA: Harvard University Press, 2002.

Mort, Frank. *Capital Affair: London and the Making of the Permissive Society.* New Haven, CT: Yale University Press, 2010.

Mullin, Katherine. *James Joyce, Sexuality, and Social Purity.* Cambridge: Cambridge University Press, 2003.

Nash, Paul. "Training an Elite." *History of Education Quarterly* 1, no. 1 (1961): 14–21.

Neushul, Peter. "Marie C. Stopes and the Popularization of Birth Control Technology." *Technology and Culture* 39, no. 2 (1998): 245–272.

Noyes, John K. *The Mastery of Submission.* Ithaca, NY: Cornell University Press, 1997.

Nye, Robert. "Western Masculinities in War and Peace." *American Historical Review* 112, no. 2 (2007): 417–438.

Oosterhuis, Harry. *Stepchildren of Nature: Krafft-Ebing, Psychiatry, and the Making of Sexual Identity.* Chicago: University of Chicago Press, 2000.

Oram, Alison. *Her Husband Was a Woman! Women's Gender-Crossing in Modern British Culture.* London: Routledge, 2007.

Parkes, Adam. *Modernism and the Theater of Censorship.* Oxford: Oxford University Press, 1996.

Pierce, Steven, and Anupama Rao, eds. *Discipline and the Other Body: Correction, Corporeality, Colonialism.* Durham, NC: Duke University Press, 2006.

Plock, Vike Martina. "A Feat of Strength in 'Ithaca': Eugen Sandow and Physical Culture in 'Joyce's Ulysses.'" *Journal of Modern Literature* 30, no. 1 (2006): 129–139.

Pollnitz, Christopher. "The Censorship and the Transmission of D. H. Lawrence's *Pansies*: The Home Office and the 'Foul-Mouthed Fellow.'" *Journal of Modern Literature* 28, no. 3 (2005): 44–71.

Porter, Bernard. *The Lion's Share: A Short History of British Imperialism, 1850–2004.* London: Longman, 2004.

Porter, Roy, and Lesley Hall. *The Facts of Life: The Creation of Sexual Knowledge in Britain, 1650–1950.* New Haven, CT: Yale University Press, 1995.

Porter, Roy, and G. S. Rousseau. *Sexual Underworlds of the Enlightenment.* Chapel Hill: University of North Carolina Press, 1988.

Price, Richard. "One Big Thing: Britain, Its Empire, and Their Imperial Culture." *Journal of British Studies* 45, no. 3 (2006): 602–627.

Prosser, Jay. "'Some Primitive Thing Conceived in a Turbulent Age of Transition': The Transsexual Emerging from *The Well*." In *Palatable Poison*, edited by Laura Doan and Jay Prosser, 129–144. New York: Columbia University Press, 2001.

———. "Transsexuals and the Transsexologists: Inversion and the Emergence of Transsexual Subjectivity." In *Sexology in Culture: Labeling Bodies and Desires*, edited by Lucy Bland and Laura Doan, 116–131. Chicago: University of Chicago Press, 1998.

Pugh, Martin. *We Danced All Night: A Social History of Britain between the Wars*. London: Vintage Books, 2009.

Rai, Alok. "Colonial Fictions: Orwell's 'Burmese Days.'" *Economic and Political Weekly* 18, no. 5 (1983): PE47–52.

Raitt, Suzanne. "Early British Psychoanalysis and the Medico-psychological Clinic." *History Workshop Journal* 58 (2004): 63–85.

Rapp, Dean. "The Early Discovery of Freud by the British General Educated Public, 1912–1919." *Social History of Medicine* 3, no. 2 (1990): 217–243.

Reekie, Gail. "Decently Dressed? Sexualized Consumerism and the Working Woman's Wardrobe 1918–1923." *Labour History*, no. 61 (1991): 42–56.

Richards, Jeffrey. "Controlling the Screen: The British Cinema in the 1930s." *History Today* 33 (1983): 11–17.

Roberts, Mary Louise. *Civilization without Sexes*. Princeton, NJ: Princeton University Press, 1994.

———. "Samson and Delilah Revisited: The Politics of Women's Fashions in 1920s France." *American Historical Review* 98, no. 3 (1993): 657–684.

Robertson, James C. *The British Board of Film Censors: Film Censorship in Britain, 1896–1950*. London: Taylor and Francis, 1985.

Roper, Michael. "Between Manliness and Masculinity: The 'War Generation' and the Psychology of Fear in Britain, 1914–1950." *Journal of British Studies* 44, no. 2 (2005): 342–362.

Rose, Jonathan. *The Intellectual Life of the British Working Classes*. New Haven, CT: Yale University Press, 2001.

Rose, June. *Marie Stopes and the Sexual Revolution*. London: Faber and Faber, 1992.

Ross, Chad. *Naked Germany: Health, Race and the Nation*. Oxford: Oxford University Press, 2005.

Rubinstein, W. D. "Education and the Social Origins of British Elites." *Past and Present* 112 (1986): 163–207.

Rush, Anne Spry. *Bonds of Empire: West Indians and Britishness from Victoria to Decolonization*. Oxford: Oxford University Press, 2011.

Sacks, Oliver. *The Man Who Mistook His Wife for a Hat and Other Clinical Tales*. New York: Touchstone Books, 1998.

Scanlon, Jennifer. *Inarticulate Longings: The Ladies' Home Journal, Gender, and the Promises of Consumer Culture*. New York: Routledge, 1995.

Schechtman, Marya. *The Constitution of Selves*. Ithaca, NY: Cornell University Press, 1996.

Seccombe, Wally. "Starting to Stop: Working-Class Fertility Decline in Britain." *Past and Present* 126 (1990): 151–188.

———. *Weathering the Storm: Working-Class Families from the Industrial Revolution to the Fertility Decline*. London: Verso, 1993.

———. "Working-Class Fertility Decline in Britain: Reply." *Past and Present* 134 (1992): 207–211.

Sen, Amartya. *Identity and Violence*. New York: Norton, 2006.

Shorter, Edward. *Written in the Flesh*. Toronto: University of Toronto Press, 2005.

Sieveking, Paul. *Man Bites Man*. London: Landesman, 1981.

Sigel, Lisa Z. "Censorship in Inter-war Britain: Denial, Publicity, and the Extension of the Liberal State." *Journal of Social History* 45, no. 1 (2011): 65–83.

———. "Filth in the Wrong People's Hands: Postcards and the Expansion of Pornography in Britain and the Atlantic World." *Journal of Social History* 33, no. 4 (2000): 859–885.

———. *Governing Pleasures: Pornography and Social Change in England, 1815-1914.* New Brunswick, NJ: Rutgers University Press, 2002.

Slade, Joseph. "Eroticism and Technological Regression: The Stag Film." *History and Technology* 22, no. 1 (March 2006): 27-52.

Smith, Clarissa. *One for the Girls! The Pleasures and Practices of Reading Women's Porn.* Bristol, UK: Intellect Books, 2007.

Smith, Erin A. "How the Other Half Read: Advertising, Working-Class Readers, and Pulp Magazines." *Book History* 3 (2000): 204-230.

Soloway, Richard A. *Birth Control and the Population Question in England, 1877-1930.* Chapel Hill: University of North Carolina Press, 1982.

———. *Democracy and Degeneration: Eugenics and the Declining Birthrate in Twentieth-Century Britain.* Chapel Hill: University of North Carolina Press, 1990.

———. "The Galton Lecture: Marie Stopes, Eugenics and the Birth Control Movement." In *Marie Stopes, Eugenics and the English Birth Control Movement,* edited by Robert Peel, 49-76. London: Galton Institute, 1997.

Souhami, Diana. *The Trials of Radclyffe Hall.* New York: Doubleday, 1999.

Steele, Valerie. *The Corset: A Cultural History.* New Haven, CT: Yale University Press, 2001.

St. John-Stevas, Norman. *Obscenity and the Law.* London: Seeker and Warburg, 1956.

Stockwell, S. E., ed. *The British Empire: Themes and Perspectives.* Malden, MA: Blackwell, 2008.

Storey, William. "Big Cats and Imperialism: Lion and Tiger Hunting in Kenya and Northern India, 1898-1930." *Journal of World History* 2, no. 2 (1991): 135-173.

Strange, Carolyn. "The 'Shock' of Torture: A Historiographical Challenge." *History Workshop Journal* 61 (2006): 135-152.

Strawson, Galen. "Against Narrativity." *Ratio* 17 no. 4 (2004): 428-452.

Summers, Anne. "The Correspondents of Havelock Ellis." *History Workshop Journal* 32 (1991): 167-183.

Summers, Leigh. *Bound to Please: A History of the Victorian Corset.* New York: Berg, 2001.

Sutherland, J. D. "Editorial Note" and "Editor's Note." In *Three Essays on the Theory of Sexuality,* by Sigmund Freud.New York: Basic Books, 1975.

Szreter, Simon. *Fertility, Class and Gender in Britain, 1860-1940.* Cambridge: Cambridge University Press, 1996.

Tatar, Maria. *Lustmord: Sexual Murder in Weimar Germany.* Princeton, NJ: Princeton University Press, 1995.

Thompson, Anthony Hugh. *Censorship in Public Libraries in the United Kingdom during the Twentieth Century.* Epping, UK: Bowker, 1975.

Thompson, E. P. *The Making of the English Working Class.* New York: Pantheon Books, 1964.

Thomson, Matthew. *Psychological Subjects: Identity, Culture, and Health in Twentieth-Century Britain.* Oxford: Oxford University Press, 2006.

Tilly, Louise, and Joan Scott. *Women, Work, and Family.* New York: Routledge, 1987.

Tinkler, Penny. "Women and Popular Literature." In *Women's History: Britain, 1850-1945,* edited by June Purvis, 131-156. New York: St. Martin's Press, 1995.

Toepfer, Karl. *Empire of Ecstasy: Nudity and Movement in German Body Culture, 1910-1935.* Berkeley: University of California Press, 1997.

Toon, Elizabeth, and Janet Golden. "'Live Clean, Think Clean, and Don't Go to Burlesque Shows': Charles Atlas as Health Advisor." *Journal of the History of Medicine and Allied Sciences* 57, no. 1 (January 2002): 39-60.

Trumbach, Randolph. *Sex and Gender Revolution.* Chicago: University of Chicago Press, 1998.

Vernon, James. "'For Some Queer Reason': The Trials and Tribulations of Colonel Barker's Masquerade in Inter-war Britain." *Signs* 26 (2000): 37–62.

Vining, Margaret, and Barton C. Hacker. "From Camp Follower to Lady in Uniform: Women, Social Class and Military Institutions before 1920." *Contemporary European History* 10, no. 3 (2001): 353–373.

Walkowitz, Judith R. *Prostitution and Victorian Society.* Cambridge: Cambridge University Press, 1982.

Warren, Allen. "Popular Manliness: Baden Powell, Scouting and the Development of Manly Character." In *Manliness and Morality,* edited by J. A. Mangan and James Walvin, 199–219. Manchester, UK: Manchester University Press, 1987.

Waters, Chris. "Distance and Desire in the New British Queer History." *GLQ: A Journal of Lesbian and Gay Studies* 14, no. 1 (2008): 139–155.

———. "Havelock Ellis, Sigmund Freud and the State: Discourses of Homosexual Identity in Interwar Britain." In *Sexology in Culture: Labeling Bodies and Desires,* edited by Lucy Bland and Laura Doan, 165–179. Chicago: University of Chicago Press, 1998.

Waugh, Thomas. *Hard to Imagine: Gay Male Eroticism in Photography and Film from Their Beginnings to Stonewall.* New York: Columbia University Press, 1996.

Weber, Eugen. *Peasants into Frenchmen: The Modernization of Rural France.* Palo Alto, CA: Stanford University Press, 1976.

Wee, Allison. "Trials and Eros: The British Home Office v. Indecent Publications, 1857–1932." Ph.D. diss., University of Minnesota, 2003.

Weeks, Jeffrey. "Queer(y)ing the 'Modern Homosexual.'" Paper presented at the British Queer History Conference, Montreal, McGill University, October 14, 2010.

Wheelwright, Julia. *Amazons and Military Maids.* London: Pandora Books, 1990.

Winter, Jay. *The Great War and the British People.* Cambridge, MA: Harvard University Press, 1986.

———. "Military Fitness and Civilian Health in Britain during the First World War." *Journal of Contemporary History* 15, no. 2 (April 1980): 211–244.

———. *Sites of Memory, Sites of Mourning: The Great War in European Cultural History.* Cambridge: Cambridge University Press, 1995.

Winter, Jay, and Blaine Baggett. *The Great War and the Shaping of the Twentieth Century.* New York: Penguin, 1996.

Winter, Jay, and Antoine Prost. *The Great War in History: Debates and Controversies, 1914 to the Present.* Cambridge: Cambridge University Press, 2005.

Woiak, Joanne. "Designing a Brave New World: Eugenics, Politics, and Fiction." *Public Historian* 29, no. 3 (2007): 105–129.

Woods, Robert. "Debate: Working-Class Fertility Decline in Britain." *Past and Present* 134 (1992): 200–207.

Zweiniger-Bargielowska, Ina. "Building a British Superman: Physical Culture in Interwar Britain." *Journal of Contemporary History* 41, no. 4 (2006): 595–610.

Index

Page numbers in italics refer to illustrations.

abortion/negative eugenics, 47, 49, 201n7

advertising: in consumer culture, 77–78, 178; in magazines, 24, 29, 79–80, 83, *116*; in newspapers, 148

The Advertising Annual, 79

Alexander, Sally, 89

All Quiet on the Western Front, 103

amputees/amputation, 98–106, 111, *121*; in artists' portrayals, 103, 105; and clipping files, 100–101; cosmetic/voluntary, 100, 102–104, 176; and fetishism, 99, 101, 104; in *Lady Chatterley's Lover*, 74, 103; and memory, 102–103; popularity of, in *London Life*, 77, 98, *121*; transcription of letters about, 209n87; among war wounded, 63, 101–103, 105; and women as fantasy agents, 99–100, 104, 105. *See also* disability; Stortt, Wallace

anonymity, 76, 84–85, 92, 111

archbishop of Canterbury, 1

Ashbee, H. S., 160

Australia, 11, 14, 21–22, 26, 68, 81; letter writers from, 206n22. *See also* Empire, British

The Awful Disclosures of Maria Monk, 24

Bad Companions, 132

The Barbarian Lover (Pedler), 31

Bauer, Heike, 136

BD/SM, 143–144, 150, 167. *See also* sadomasochism

"beefcake" imagery, 28

Benbow, Cyril, 138–140, 141, 147, 149

Berkeley, Anthony, 159

Bienvenu, Robert, 78

Biernoff, Suzannah, 103

Binet, Alfred, 87

birth control: and abortion, 47, 201n7; ads for, 24, 29, 80, 83; condoms, 180; in 1880s and 1890s, 48; eugenics and, 36, 48–49, 182, 203n24; learning about, 19; letters about, 46–47, 60, 64, 65; Stopes's promotion of, 36, 48–50; working women's desire for, 64, 202n17

birth rates, 48–49

Bits of Fun, 9, 30, 79, 130, 132, 150, 151, 155, 182, 187–188n35

Bland, Lucy: on books offering language, characters, narrative, 18, 78; on concerns about popular culture, 4; on interwar issues, 13; on modern-girl image, 89

Bloch, Ivan, 40, 88

"Bloody Code," 163. *See also* corporal punishment

bodybuilding photos, 28–29

body modification: hair removal, 141, 149; heel drill, 126, 138, 179, 181; piercing, 87, *119*; tattoos, 30, 37, 88, *119*, 145–146. *See also* corsets

booksellers: on Charing Cross Road, 23–24, 139; of illicit books, 20, 192n26; of legal

booksellers (*continued*)
 books, 20, 44; versus news agents, 25–26, 45, 81; of obscene goods, 21–22; as a way to distribute knowledge, 20, 23. *See also* Benbow, Cyril; Carrington, Charles (Paul Ferdinando); distribution patterns
Borstal system, 162–163, 173
boxing/wrestling, 89–92. *See also* modern girls; modernity/modern life
Brave New World (Huxley), 203n27
British Maternal and Child Health Act (1918), 49
British Museum Library, 20, 36, 178, 198n117
brow index of culture, 4, 191n13
Buckley, Cheryl, 93, 158
Bullough, Bonnie, 187n31
Bullough, Vern, 187n31
Burgess, Anthony, 34
Burma, 21, 80. *See also* Empire, British
Burton, Richard, 132

Cambridge Bookshop, 23. *See also* booksellers
Canada, 11, 14, 26, 68, 81, 189–190n62, 191n15. *See also* Empire, British
Carrington, Charles (Paul Ferdinando), 24, *114*
castration anxiety, 88, 104
celibacy, 42
censorship: and Charing Cross Road confiscations, 23–24; creating legal and illegal markets, 137; Customs and, 21–23, 25, *113*, 195; of films, 193–194n42; Foreign Office and, 22; and Hicklin definition of obscenity, 21, 36; history of, 20–26; Home Office and, 22, 159–160; and "kink," 86–87; and London Public Morality Council, 22, 193n41; patterns of, 86–87; of pornography, 22, 25; and shaping of sexual knowledge, 21–22, 26, 44, 78, 85–87; and treatment of scholarly works, 39, 41. *See also* distribution patterns; obscenity; pornography
Central News Agency (CNA), 26, 81
Ceylon, 21, 25. *See also* Empire, British
Chaddock, Charles Gilbert, 41
Change of Life in Men and Women (Stopes), 50
Charing Cross Road raid, 23–24. *See also* censorship
Charles and Company, 23–24, 83
Chauncey, George, 131
Chesser, Eustace, 37, 42, 88
A Child Is Being Beaten (Freud), 41, 169
Children: ideas about, 50, 104; longings for, 62; and sexual knowledge, 35, 52; whipping of, 162, 164, 166
Children and Young Person's Act (1932), 164
China, 64–65, 80

chorus lines and revue girls, 29, 160. *See also* Windmill Theatre
Christie, Agatha, 30, 31
Christie, May, 30, 32
classification of sexual disorders, 41, 87
clipping files, 106–107, 180–181
clitoral stimulation, 38, 53–54
Cocks, Harry, 8, 138
coitus interruptus, 55
Colligan, Colette, 162
Colonial Office, 152, 165–166
Commonwealth, 68, 152, 165–166
community: of cross-dressers, 146–149; of fetishists, 24, 109; fictive, 108–109, 111; formation of, 108–109; of *London Life* readers, 83, 106–111 (*see also* London Life League [L3]); and Mr. Hyde, 137–140, 146–149
compassionate marriage ideal, 48, 202n17
complementarity of gender, 144–145. *See also* gender roles
condoms, 180. *See also* birth control
"Confessions of a Lover of the Limbless" (Stortt), 176–177
consciousness and sexuality, 170–173
consumer culture: and economy, 89; and the empire, 14–15; and goods, 87, 111, 179; and pleasures, 92, *124*, 176–179; publishing as an aspect of, 77–78, 87, 178; and women, 11–12, 89
Cook, Hera, 18
Cook, Matt, 8
corporal punishment: birching, 143, 162, 164, 166–167, 170; and boys, 143, 162, 164, 166–167; and cat-o'-nine-tails, 161, 166; in correspondence, 153–158, 171; and the empire, 9, 15, 152–153; and Frederick Holeman, 153–158; and girls, 153–158, 161, 173; history of, 160, 163–165; and knickers, 153–154, 156, 158–159, 173; and perversion, 153, 167–169; and prison-manufactured canes, 165–166; in prisons, 153, 162–163, 165–169; as sadism, 167–168; for sex crimes, 162–169; and sexual pleasure, 162–169; standardization of, 152–153, 165–166; and stockings, 153–154, 156, 158–160, 173; triangle for, 166–167; and "whipping returns," 165. *See also A Child Is Being Beaten* (Freud); flagellation, sexual; whipping and caning
correspondence: and anonymity, 76, 84–85, 92, 111; columns for, 76–77, 81–85, 88–94, 101; and community, 106–110; in *London Life*, 76–77, 81–85, 88–94, 101; poison pen letters, 171–172; and veracity, 81–84, 150; during the war, 180

corsets: ads for, 30, 80, 83, *116*; and body modification, 78; and boxing, 90, 98; depicted in
pornography, 93; dominance and submission and, 95–97; in Edwardian era, 93; Ellis
on bipedalism and, 40; in fashion, 93–94;
and fetishism, 94–97; and figure training,
92–98; and health movement, 67, 69, 93; and
"heel-Hitler," *124*, 175–176; and L3 (London
Life League), 97, 181–182; in *London Life*,
94; and men, 30, 97, *123*, 129–131, 134, 137,
214n41; and nostalgia, 77, 97–98; not subject to censorship, 87; as part of script, 179;
post–World War II, 181; and women, 40, 69,
92–98. *See also Bits of Fun*; cross-dressing;
Hyde, Mervyn; "kink"; *London Life*; *Photo
Bits (Photo Fun/New Photo Fun)*
cosmetic/voluntary amputation, 100, 102–104,
176. *See also* amputees/amputation
country life as modern ideal, 67–69
couples as foundational, 37, 42, 50, 66
"Courtship and Mating in an Urban Community" (Woodside), 203–204n35
Criminal Law Amendment Act (1885), 163
Crisp, Quentin, 2
cross-dressing: among active-duty soldiers,
129–131, 134; ads for male-sized high heels,
30, 83; of boys as punishment, 143–145;
cartoon on, *123*; for comic effect, 132; consumer goods for, 30, 83, 139–141; craving for,
134–135; in "dickie bird" cartoon, *122*; different meanings of, 150; erotics of, 137–146;
and gender economy, 150–151; in *The Girl
from Scotland Yard*, 32–33; in *Gynecocracy*,
8, 142–143; in half bride–half groom photo,
122; and the "kink," 133–134; as legally
obscene unless portrayed humorously, 22;
in *London Life*, 80, 134; by Mervyn Hyde,
125, 128, 140–142, 150; by Quentin Crisp, 2;
sexology on, 135; in Shakespeare, 131–132;
as showing aesthetic superiority, 133, 135;
treatment of, in ephemeral press, 80, 132,
134, 137, 214n41; and views toward effeminacy, 134–135; by women, 3–4, 32–33, 131,
135–136. *See also* corsets; humiliation
Crozier, Ivan, 39, 40
cunnilingus, 38
Cupboard collection, British Museum, 20, 36,
178, 198n117
Customs Act (1853, U.K.), 21, 23, 25. *See also*
censorship

Dear Dr. Stopes (Hall), 202n13
Death on the Nile (Christie), 31
Dell, Ethel M., 30–31, 33

dildos, 141, 151
disability: fetishism of, 100–105; open discussion of, 98; pensions for, 205n70; in war veterans, 61–62, 101–103, 125, 128; and women,
100–104, 106. *See also* amputees/amputation
distribution patterns: and access, 19, 25, 26; in
the empire, 21, 22; of explicit material, 14–
15, 19–26, 80–81, 137; of magazines, 26–30;
of novels, 30–35; overseas, 21, 22; of pornography, 22–25, 44, 180; of sexology, 35–43. *See
also* Benbow, Cyril; literacy; reading
Doan, Laura, 4, 8, 34, 131, 136
The Doctor of Pimlico (Le Queux), 31, 32
dominance and submission: and amputee fantasies, 105; and corseting, 95–97; and female
boxers/wrestlers, 90–92; and gender economy, 144–145; and memories of childhood,
143–144; and stylized invalidism, 95–97,
162. *See also* BD/SM; sadomasochism
dysgenics, 5, 70, 71. *See also* eugenics

Earl Lavender (Davidson), 148
economy of gender, 144–145. *See also* gender
roles
Edward VIII, 1
Eksteins, Modris, 12, 103
Ellis, Havelock, 3, 38; on couple as foundation,
42; on cross-dressing, 135; on foot-fetishism,
44, 88; and Freud, 199–200n143; on inversion and homosexuality, 43; personal life of,
43
Empire, British, 68, 152, 165–166; at its apex,
13; and "British race," 69, 72, 75, 76; circulation of goods in, 14; consciousness of
empire, 13; consumer culture in, 14–15; and
culture of imperialism, 13–15; eugenics in,
48–49, 69–70, 75; health and fitness movement in, 68–69; letters from across, 47; mail
order across, 24–25, 76, 77, 80–81, 180; obscenity suppression in, 21–22, 25–26, 85–86;
racial codes in, 84–85; spread of ideas from
and within, 2, 14–15, 26, 81; whipping penal-
ties in, 164, 166, 169; World War I deaths in,
11. *See also* Australia; Canada; India; New
Zealand; World War I
Enduring Passion (Stopes), 37, 50
England: as center of media market, 21–22, 80,
137; corporal punishment in, 15, 165, 166,
169, 174; English girls, 84–85; and explicit
goods, 3, 24; fashion in, 78; letters from, 2;
literacy in, 4; medical community in, 41;
and Mervyn Hyde, 126, 128, 139, 149; and
military men, 11; periodicals versus serious
literature in, 25, 27; physical fitness in, 68;

England (*continued*)
spread of Freud's ideas in 38, 42, 88, 129. *See also* Empire, British
Englishwoman's Domestic Magazine, 82, 148, 214n41
ephemeral press: circulation of, 110, 138, 160, 180–181; and circulation of outdated material, 25, 138, 146, 178; Cupboard collection inclusion of, 178, 198n117; defined, 44; impact of, on readers' sexual identity, 177; versus sexology, 110; shaped by readers' letters and stories, 111; treatment of cross-dressing in, 80, 132, 134, 137, 214n41; veracity of letters in, 81–84, 150. *See also* magazines
"Erotic Symbolism" (Ellis), 44
eugenics: and birth control, 36, 182, 203n24; and country lifestyle, 68; and epilepsy, 70; and Eugenics Society, 49; Huxley's views on, 203n27; levels of awareness of, in letters to Stopes, 69–72; political implications of, 203n22; positive and negative forms of, 49; racial advancement theories and, 49–50, 69–70; and social class, 49, 70; and sterilization, 203n24; Stopes's views on, 14, 48–50, 69–72, 75; and venereal disease, 70; and the working class, 49
Exhibition of Female Flagellants, 24
Extraordinary Women (Mackenzie), 23

face powder, 78, 125, 149
Family Doctor, 148
Farnell, Lewis R., 20
Farrer, Peter, 78, 187–188n35
fashion: ambiguous trends in 1920s, 132; in Edwardian era, 93; fashion calendar, 87; and flappers, 12, 161; in interwar era, 93, 141, 158–159; for men, 28–29, 80, 132; and modernity, 32, 93, 100; for women, 32, 78, 93, 132, 144–146. *See also* corsets; glamour magazines; lingerie; stockings
Fashion and Fetishism (Kunzle), 78
father's role in Victorian family, 48, 95
Fawcett, Hillary, 93, 158
Felski, Rita, 3
Female Flagellants or the History of the Rod, 24
femininity: changing ideas of woman and, 133–134; and clothes, 93, 97, 129–130, 133, 143; and corsets, 93, 97; and cross-dressing, 129–130, 133–134; and falling in love, 31; and masculinity, 34, 73, 90, 97, 133–134, 145, 151; and sexuality, 141, 143. *See also* complementarity of gender; flappers; masculinity; modern girls

feminism, 5, 11–12, 48
Féré, Charles Samson, 87–88
fetishism: and amputees, 98–106; and boxing/wrestling, 89–92; and clubs, 109; and fashion, 78, 80; in *London Life*, 88–89; London Life League on, 181; original meaning of term, 87; in sexology texts, 87–89. *See also* corsets; high heels; Stortt, Wallace
figure training, 90, 93–97. *See also* corsets; heel drill; high heels
film censorship in Britain, 193–194n42
Fisher, Kate, 18
fitness movement in Britain, 49–50, 69. *See also* health
flagellation, sexual, 24, *114*, 142, 160–162, 168–169. *See also* corporal punishment
flappers, 12, 154, 161. *See also* modern girls; modernity/modern life
flogging, 162–163, 168. *See also* corporal punishment; flagellation, sexual; whipping and caning
Foucault, Michel: on effect of censorship, 86–87; on sexology and identity formation, 2–3, 181; on sexuality as central category, 2; on the Victorian era, 93
fresh air, 14, 67–69, 72
Freud, Sigmund, 4, 38; British mistrust of work of, 40; and Ellis, 40, 199–200n143; on fetishism and castration anxiety, 88, 104; lay public knowledge of, 41–42; popularity of, 41; on sadomasochism, 43; sexological works of, 4, 41; Stopes on, 66
Fu Manchu, 14
Fussell, Paul, 12, 60
future: views of, 64–66, 75, 77–79; writing a new, 16, 72–74. *See also* modernity/modern life

Galsworthy, John, 104
Garber, Marjorie, 132
"garroting" panic, 163
Gay New York (Chauncey), 131
gender roles: ambiguity/fluidity in, 131, 133–134; closed economy of, 144–145, 150–151; female boxers/wrestlers and reversal of, 90–92; during interwar years, 89–90, 179; models of, 11, 95, 133–136; politics of, 90; as separate from sex, 151; transformations of, 77, 214n40. *See also* femininity; girls; masculinity; World War I
Gennert, Ricardo, 138, 139
Germany, 29, 63, 103, 175
Gibson, Ian, 162, 173
The Girl from Scotland Yard (Wallace), 31–33

girls: and clothes, 93; as conceptual categories, 12, 32, 84, 90, 93; and cross-dressing, 3–4, 32–33, 131, 135–136; as daughters, 32, 152, 153–158, 161; as degenerate, 157, 173; as flappers, 12, 154, 161; transgressions of, 12, 153; and whipping, 153–158, 161, 173. *See also* boxing/wrestling; femininity; gender roles; modern girls

Gladstone, William, 160

glamour magazines, 14, 26, 29–30, 77–79

Glasgow Medical Commissioner's Report, 127

Gone with the Wind film, 94

Gordon and Gotch, 26, 81

Graves, Robert, 33, 39–42

Great War. *See* World War I

The Great War and Modern Memory (Fussell), 60

Grey, Zane, 30

Gynecocracy, 8, 142–143, 146

hair: bobbed or cropped, 93, 213n35, 214n40; and fetishism, 88; removal of, 141, 149

Haire, Norman, 39

Hall, Catherine, 14

Hall, Lesley, 40, 42, 47

Hall, Radclyffe: cross-dressing and, 131, 135–136; readers of, 45; and sapphism/inversion, 1–2, 34, 131; and sexology, 135–136; writing of, 30, 41

Hall, Ruth, 47, 202n13

Halperin, David, 8

Handies Silk Stocking Revue magazine, 159

health: and British Maternal and Child Health Act (1918), 49; in the empire, 68; and eugenics, 5, 14, 49–50; *Health and Efficiency*, 15, 28, *114*; *Health and Strength*, 15, 28; and Health and Strength League, 15; height as an indicator of, 127; ill health, 57, 72–73, 85, 104; and loose clothing, 132; magazines about, 15, 28, *114*; and marital happiness, 38, 50, 54, 198n117; nudism and, 28–29, *114*; and physical fitness, 28–29, 68–69, 93; of the race, 49–50, 69–71; sexual health, 38, 54, 57, 64, 66–67, 180; and views of modernity, 65–68; and Women's Health Inquiry, 57

Heath, Deana, 21

heel drill, 126, 138, 179, 181. *See also* high heels

"heel-Hitler," *124*, 175–176

Henry-Hemyng, Philip, 79

Hicklin standard (1868, U.K.), 21, 36

high heels, 80, 83, *116–117, 124*, 125, 130; and amputee fetishism, 101, 104; in "heel-Hitler," *124*, 175–176; and helplessness, 96–97; *High Heel Magazine*, 160; in L3, 181; for men, 30,

141, 147; as part of script, 179. *See also* heel drill

Hirschfeld, Magnus, 20, 40, 43, 135–136

historians of sexuality, 8–9, 18, 93

history: conceptions of, 12, 16, 72, 77; historical consciousness, 111–112, 182; and Marie Stopes, 64; medical histories, 55, 57–58; natural history, 40; and nostalgia, 92–98, 182; sexual history, 64–72; war as, 59, 61, 63–64. *See also* modernity/modern life; Victorian age

A History of English Sexual Morals (Bloch), 40, 88

The History of Sexuality (Foucault), 93

A History of the Rod (or *The History of the Rod*), 24, 44, 142. *See also* whipping and caning

Hodge, Alan, 33, 39–42

Hoffman, Brian, 28

Holeman, Frederick, 152–158, 171, 173

Holtzman, Ellen, 47

Home Office: and corporal punishment, 165, 168–169; and enforcement of obscenity laws, 21–22, 160–161

homosexuality: concern about whipping to punish, 168–169; Ellis on, 40, 43; and emergence of modern sexual identities, 7–8; Hirshfeld on, 43; Krafft-Ebing on, 43; sophistication of work on history of, 187n34. *See also* lesbianism; queer; sexual inversion

Hong Kong, 21, 25. *See also* Empire, British

Houlbrook, Matt: on books offering language and characters, 18, 78; on historical record, 9; on identity of London, 8; on range of queer identities, 131

Howard League for Penal Reform, 165, 168–169

Hull, E. M., 30, 31

The Human Body (Stopes), 50

humiliation, 8, 91, 144–145, 150–151, 155, 161

Hyde, Mervyn: address book kept by, 137–140, 147–148; arrest of, 128; conviction and prison sentence of, 148–149; death of, 149; and erotics of cross-dressing, 137–146; neurosis diagnosis and dismissal, 128; and police testimony and list of confiscated items, 140–142; pre-enlistment physical results for, 127; prewar life of, 125–127; queer desires and networks of, 146–149; service of, in France, 127–128; and trade in magazines, 137–138

Ideal Marriage (Van de Velde), 38

Identity and Violence (Sen), 182

identity formation, 2, 6, 7, 47, 75, 182. *See also* self-creation; sexual identity

ignorance, 18, 35–36, 52–54, 64
illiteracy, 19, 179, 191n6. *See also* reading
impotence, 63, 70, 202n11
incorrigible rogue status, 163
India, 14, 21, 80, 126–127, 174. *See also* Empire, British
International Convention for the Suppression of the Circulation of and Traffic in Obscene Publications, 21
International Journal of Psycho-Analysis, 39
The Interpretation of Dreams (Freud), 41
interwar years, 10; and aftermath of war, 12, 87; and lead-up to World War II, 175–177; sexual and gender fluidity during, 8, 93, 131, 150–151, 181–182; as window of experimentation, 179
inversion. *See* sexual inversion

Jack the Ripper, 32
Jones, Ernest, 39, 128–129
Joyce, James: and stream of consciousness, 12, 170–171; *Ulysses*, 20, 30, 33–34, 170–171; and whipping, 170
Jung, Karl, 38
Justice of the Peace and Local Government Review, 165

Kellman, Steven, 33–34
Kenya, 21, 162, 164. *See also* Empire, British
"khaki fever," 12
"kink": cross-dressing as "the kink," *123*, 133–134, 150; inadvertent encouragement of, by censorship codes, 86–87; interpretation of term by L3 members, 181; meaning of, 7, 9, 123, 133; mutually exclusive subsections of, 109; as nearly universal, 109
Kinsey, Alfred, 40
Klein, Melanie, 39
Koven, Seth, 102–103
Krafft-Ebing, Richard von, 3; availability of books by, 20; British mistrust of work of, 40; classification of sexual disorders by, 41, 87; on fetishism, 87; Hall's use of works of, 41; on homosexuality, 43
Kripps, Henry, 104
Kucich, John, 173
Kunzel, Regina, 4, 187n34
Kunzle, David, 29, 78

Ladenson, Elisabeth, 34
Ladies Home Journal, 78
Lady Chatterley's Lover (Lawrence): censorship battle over, 197n99; effects of censorship on,

20, 30, 33; portrayal of disabled veterans in, 74, 103
Lamos, Colleen, 170
The Lamp in the Desert (Dell), 33
Lansbury, George, 20
Lawrence, D. H., 20, 30, 33, 74, 103
Lawrence, T. E., 132
League of Nations, 21, 25
Leavis, Q. D., 4
Lenton, Laurence, 14, 83
Le Queux, William, 30, 31, 32
lesbianism: censored unless portrayed humorously, 22; in D. H. Lawrence's works, 33; and modern sexual identity, 3, 8; sophistication of work on history of, 187n34. *See also* Hall, Radclyffe; homosexuality; sexual inversion; *The Well of Loneliness* (Hall)
letters: in archival records, 182, 201n4; in correspondence columns, 76–77, 81–85, 88–94, 101; and identity formation, 47, 75; narrative strategies in, 6, 47; as sources for sexology, 9–11; veracity of, 81–84, 150. *See also* letter writing; *London Life*; Stopes correspondence
letter writing: as a compulsion, 13, 77, 158, 177; to correspondence columns, 76–77, 81–85, 88–94, 101; and identity, 47, 75; to Marie Stopes, 73; during World War I, 10–11
Lewiss, Charles Arthur, 79
libraries, 20, 30–31
lingerie, 24, 84, 93, 108, 141, 160
L'Instinct Sexual (Féré), 88
literacy, 19, 179, 191n6. *See also* reading
Lombroso, Cesare, 87
London, 8, 14, 81
London Life, 76–77, *116–122*, *124*; advertising in, 24, 83; and body modification, 78; and boxing, 89–92, *114*; and censorship policies, 85–86; circulation and distribution of, 4, 29, 80–81, 110; collapse of, 177, 180; and community of readers, 83, 106–111; connection to historic moment of interwar years, 111; and corsets, 94; covers of, 79; editor as arbitrator, 111; editor response to letters, 82–83; editor tips on suitable photos for, 83; freedom of anonymity in, 84–85; history of, 78–79; layout of, 79–80; and letters as narration of identity, 110–111; letters/correspondence section of, 9, 81–85, 108–109; letters on amputee fetish in, 98–106, *121*; letters on cross-dressing in, 132–133; letters on punishing children in, 155, 161–162; letters ridiculing other writers in, 109, 111; letters with self-descriptions of reading in, 106–110;

letters with self-photos in, 83–84, *117–118*; and lingerie, 84, 87, 108; naive readers of, 101; pictures from Windmill Theatre in, 3, 29; "Talk of the Town" feature, 80; variety of sexual tastes articulated in, 112; veracity of letters in, 81–84, 150. *See also* Stortt, Wallace

London Life League (L3), 110, 181–182

London Public Morality Council, 22

London Workers Education Association, 33

Love's Miracle (Christie), 32

Love without Fear (Chesser), 37

The Lustful Turk, 142

"lust-murderers," 32, 41

Mackenzie, Compton, 23

magazines, *113–114*; censorship of, 26, 85–87, 137; circulation of outdated, 25, 138, 146, 178; in the colonies, 24–25, 76, 77, 80–81; and consumer culture, 77–78, 87, 178; glamour magazines, 14, 26, 29–30, 77–79; Hyde as go-between for, 138–140; intellectuals' criticism of, 25; in news agents' shops, 25–26, 159–160; for nudists, 28–29; postwar worldwide distribution of, 14–15; pulp magazines, 44, 78–79, 206n18; as research material, 9; seizure of, 186n13; sexual education and, 110, 177; "slick paper," 77, 79. *See also individual magazines, such as London Life*

Maiden Tribute of Modern Babylon scandal, 163

mail-order trade in banned material, 24–25, 137, 147, 149. *See also* Hyde, Mervyn

The Making of the English Working Class (Thompson), 2

The Man about Town, 27

Maori, 14

Marital Confidences, 23

marriage: compassionate marriage ideal, 48, 202n17; as mainstay of society, 37; model of modern, 48–51; as social good, 42. *See also* birth control

Married Love (Stopes), 4, 5; and abortion, 47; and archiving of correspondence, 47, 201n4; and birth control, 47, 64–65; and conceptions of men, 48, 50; and conceptions of women, 48, 50; historians' debates about, 47; and menopause, 46; model of modern marriage in, 48–51, 66; narrative strategies of, 47, 50–51; periodicity concept in, 39, 50; popularity of, 4, 36–37, 51; publication of, 36; request for reader letters in, 9, 46–47; sales of, 36–37, 51; and sexual advice correspondence, 5, 46–47; and sexual func-

tion, 61, 63; writing style of, 50–51. *See also* Stopes, Marie; Stopes correspondence

Marshik, Celia, 22–23

masculinity: and character, 127; and examinations, 92, 127; and sexuality, 11, 73; and World War I, 11, 74, 103, 127. *See also* cross-dressing; gender roles; men

masochism, 3, 40–41, 43; Krafft-Ebing on, 41; origin of term, 3; stress on gendered dimensions of, 43; viewed favorably by sexologists, 43. *See also* BD/SM; sadomasochism

Mass-Observation study, 35–36, 198n113

masturbation, 40, 53, 73

Mauritius, 21, 25. *See also* Empire, British

McKibbin, Ross, 19, 36

McLaren, Angus, 38, 47, 140, 187n31

medical history narrative, 57–58

medical texts. *See* sexology texts

Memoirs of a Woman of Pleasure, 160

men: corset wearing by, 30, *123*, 129–131, 134, 137, 214n41; effect of World War I on, 11, 59–64, 101–103, 125, 128–129; role of, in tight lacing, 95, 97; unemployment among, 89; use of scientific language by, 54–57

Mendes, Peter, 142

menstruation, 55, 68

middle class: and bias in Mass-Observation study, 36; and corsets, 93; difficulties attaining, 149; and family size, 179; and femininity, 133–134; influence of Stopes on, 37, 48, 200–201n2; and physical fitness movement, 69; reading materials aimed at, 31; and sadomasochism, 173

modern girls, 31–32, 65–66, 84, 89–90, 93, 100; and boxing, 89–92; flappers, 12, 154, 161; as metaphors, 90. *See also* gender roles; girls; modernity/modern life

modernity/modern life, 68, 70, 72, 105, 202n11; and bobbed hair, 213n35; and popular culture, 78, 89; as portrayed in *London Life*, 85; recognition and anonymity as states of, 111; and unemployment among men, 89; and the Victorian family, 48; views of, 65–69; and World War I, 189n58. *See also* history

Mother England (Stopes), 64, 200–201n2, 201n4, 202n13

motherhood: and cross-dressing, 134, 143–144; and dread of pregnancy, 64; and fetishism, 88, 95, 97, 114; memories of, 65, 72–73; and *Radiant Motherhood*, 50, 65, 75; and whipping, 152, 154, 155, 157, 161. *See also* birth control

Mothers Clinics, 49

Movie Merry-Go-Round, 28

Murder in Mesopotamia (Christie), 31
Must England Lose India? (Osburn), 168
mutual orgasm, 67
My Beautiful Mother, 147
My Married Life, 142

narrative(s): changes over time in, 177; construction of, in Stopes correspondence, 47, 54–58, 74; effect of anonymity on, 85–86; fragmentation in Holeman's, 171; historical truth of, 6–7; Hyde living his own, 126, 150; of illness, 57–58; letters as narration of identity, 4, 110–111; multidirectionality of, 5–6, 106, 111; reader criticism of erotic disability, 101; rewriting of, 177–179; Sacks on, 6; Schechtman on personhood and, 6; and shutting out of others' miseries, 182; Strawson on self-deception and, 6; structures of, in popular literature, 78; use of narrative tension in romance, 31–32; war as part of, 64, 103–104
National Archives, 9
National Vigilance Association, 22
Nell in Bridewell, 114
neurosis: definition of, 128; and Marie Stopes, 66; and Mr. Hyde, 128, 149–150; understanding of, 128, 130. *See also* shell shock
New Photo Fun. See Bits of Fun
The New Psychology and Its Relation to Life (Tansley), 38–39
news agents' shops, 25–26, 159–160. *See also* booksellers; mail-order trade in banned material
New Zealand, 26, 68, 219n49. *See also* Empire, British
nostalgia: corsets and, 92–98, 112, 181–182; and historical consciousness, 112, 182; sexuality and, 13, 92–98
novels: distribution of, 26, 30, 35; ideas of masculinity in, 31; ideas of modern girls in, 31–32; in libraries, 20, 30–31; mysteries, 31, 159; popular romances, 30, 45, 112; and sex education, 33–35; sex novels, 22. *See also* literacy; reading
nudity/nudism, 22, 27, 28–29, 96–97, 213n35

obscenity: in the British Museum Library, 20, 36, 178, 198n117; definitions of, 21; determining legality of, 21–22, 34, 37, 159–160; effect of, on the market, 86–87, 137; in the empire, 21, 24; Hicklin standard of, 21; prosecutions for, 23, 37, 39, 79, 148–149, 161, 171–172, 194n46. *See also* censorship
"One-legged Venus" (Stortt), 99

Oosterhuis, Harry, 87, 186n10
Oram, Alison, 3, 131
Order of St. Bridget, 148
Orwell, George, 25, 211n6
Osburn, Arthur, 168
Oxford University, 20, 127

Paris Sex Appeal, 27
"passing" and cross-dressing, 132
Paul Lane, 80
The Pearl, 160
Pedler, Margaret, 14, 30, 31
pedophilia, 147
penal reform, 155, 165, 168–169
periodicity: and Marie Stopes, 39, 50, 59–60, *115*; theory of, 50, *115*. *See also* rhythm, matching of sexual
"petticoat discipline," 142–143, 145
Photo Bits (*Photo Fun/New Photo Fun*), 9, 30, 79, *123*, 130, 132, 138
photographs, *113–122*; ads for, 80, 83; "art house photos," 79–80; distribution of obscene photos, 22–26; in *London Life*, 29–30, 76, 91, 94, 107–109, *119–122*; in magazines, 24, 27–30; by mail, 147; of Mr. Hyde, 128, 141, 150; of readers, 83–84, 108–109; self-comparisons to, 28–29
physical culture, 15; and physical fitness, 67–69, 127, 190n70; and physical fitness magazines, 28–29, *114*. *See also* health
Physiology of Sex (Walker), 38
piercing, 87, *119*
poison pen letters, 152–157, 171–173
police, 22–24, 127, 159–160, 166, 180; police files, 9, 126, 140–143, 148
popular culture sources of sexual knowledge: ephemera, 44, 177; magazines, 110, 177; novels, 33–35; versus sexology, 110
popularizers of sexology, 3, 35–43. *See also names of individuals*
popular science, 14, 19, 26, 44
pornography: censorship of, 22, 25, 86–87; circulation of, 24, 138, 146, 178; corsets depicted in, 93; cross-dressing depicted in, 150–151; distribution of, 22–25, 44, 180; feminist position on, 5; films depicting, 193–194n42; Hyde's collection of, 126, 138, 142, 150–151, 178; as obscene materials, 22, 138; porn wars, 5; reader-response analysis of, 5; and whipping, *114*, 160, 166–167, 174. *See also* Benbow, Cyril; Gennert, Ricardo; *names of specific works*
Porter, Roy, 40, 42, 187n31
Possession (Wadsley), 32, 33

Post Office (Protection) Act (1884, U.K.), 21
premarital sex, implications of term, 42
premature ejaculation, 56, 59–60, 180
press guides, 79
Princess Sophie de Bourbon, 132
Pro-Race cervical cap, 49
Prosser, Jay, 136
prostitution, 88, 154, 163–164, 180
psychology: in Great Britain, 42; and psycho-
analysis, 44, 66, 129; and psychoanalytical
community, 129; and responses to shell
shock, 128; sex psychology, 40–42, 129. *See
also* Freud, Sigmund
Psychopathia Sexualis (Krafft-Ebing), 87

queer: interpretation of term by L3 members,
181; queerness and sexuality, 78; queerness
as community, 8–9, 77–78, 109–110, 146–
149; queerness as culture, 131, 147; queer
scholars, 7–9; queer theory, 9; use of term
by Stortt, 100; use of term in self-stories, 7,
29–30
Quinn, Anthony, 81

racial advancement and eugenics, 49–50,
69–72
racial codes: in the empire, 84–85; in *London
Life* letters, 84–85; in Stopes's writings, 69–72
Radiant Motherhood (Stopes), 37, 50
Ranch Romances, 27–28
Rapp, Dean, 42
reading: of antiquated sexual materials, 20,
94, 146, 147, 182; and distribution of explicit
material, 14–15, 19–26, 80–81, 137; and
historical reader-response studies, 5; and
ignorance, 18, 36, 52; and literacy, 4, 18,
179; popularity of, in interwar years, 4–5;
practice of, versus results of, 5–6; seeking
out materials for, 178–179; self-descriptions
of, by *London Life* readers, 106–110; supplying language for self-understanding, 18; and
writing, 51, 106. *See also* ephemeral press;
magazines; *Married Love* (Stopes)
Rhodes, Stanislaus Matthew de, 142–143
rhythm, matching of sexual, 38, 46, 54, 59–60,
73. *See also* periodicity
Richter, Dorchen, 136
Rodiad (Coleman), 148
Roe, Humphrey Verdon, 36, 47, 59
Rohmer, Sax, 14, 30
romance: and idealism, 58–59, 68, 73, 112;
mixed with science, 51, 54–55, 58, 74; for
narrative tension, 31–32; versus sex, 20, 30,
34, 45. *See also* modernity/modern life

Rose, Jonathan, 5, 42, 45
Royden, Maude, 20
rubber: in condoms, 180; as fetish, 80, 86–87,
118
Russell, Bertrand, 20, 43

Sacher-Masoch, Leopold von, 41, 170
Sacks, Oliver, 6
sadism: in sexology, 43; and whipping, 165–
168. *See also* BD/SM; masochism; sadomasochism
sadomasochism, 3, 40–41, 43, 44–45
Sandow, Eugen, 15, 190n70
sapphist stereotypes, 8, 32–33
Scanlon, Jennifer, 78
"The Scarlet Slipper" (Stortt), 99
Schechtman, Marya, 6
science, language of, 51, 54–55, 58, 74
scripts, development of shared, 179
self-creation, 6–7, 47, 75, 178, 182. *See also*
identity formation
Sen, Amartya, 182
sex education, 19–20
sexology texts: on cross-dressing, 126, 131,
135–136; difficulties in obtaining, 4, 20; ex-
empt from obscenity laws, 22; fetishism in,
87–89; and identity formation, 2–3; library
availability of, 20, 44; popularizers of, 3,
36–39; scholarly works of, 39–43; sources
having greatest impact, 35; on transgender
and transsexual categories, 136
sex problem writers, 33
sexual assaults following World War II, 180
sexual cycles of arousal (Stopes). *See* periodicity; rhythm, matching of sexual
sexual desires, 8, 110–111, 128, 141, 179
sexual identity, 7; formation of, 2–3, 7, 47, 76,
78; as historical process, 13, 131, 177–178, 182;
"kink" as, 87, 150; married love as, 42, 47
sexual intercourse: curtailed discussions about,
21, 141; explicit display of, 22, 24–25; in letters, 58–64, 67–72; in obscene works, 22;
problems with, 58–64, 67–72; in sexological
accounts, 37
sexual inversion: and Chevalier d'Eon de
Beaumont, 135; and cross-dressing, 134;
Ellis on, 39, 43; and homosexuality, 135;
Radclyffe Hall and, 1–2, 34, 135–136; in sexology, 135; Stopes on, 43; Symonds on, 39.
See also cross-dressing; gender roles; queer
sexual knowledge: from ephemeral press, 44,
177; and ignorance, 18, 35–36, 52–54, 64;
from magazines, 110, 177; from novels,
33–35; versus sexology, 110

The Sexual Urge (Féré), 88
The Sheik (Hull), 31
shell shock, 11–12, 61–62, 128. *See also* disability; neurosis; World War I
Shorter, Edward, 78, 81
The Simple Tale of Susan Aked, 142
Simpson, Wallis, 1
simultaneous orgasm, 66–67
The Sins of the Cities of the Plain or Recollections of a Mary-Ann, 146
Slade, Joseph, 195n60
Sleeveless Errand, 22
Smith, Clarissa, 5
social class: and access to literature, 19; blurring of boundaries of, 13; and brow index of culture, 191n13; and eugenics, 49, 70; and identity formation, 2, 7; Mervyn Hyde and, 126–127, 147–148, 149; and queer culture, 147; and Stopes's readership, 46, 48, 200–201n2. *See also* middle class; working class
social historians, 8–9
Society, 138
soldiers: cross-dressing entertainment among, 129–131; sexual symptoms among, 128; shell shock and physical injury in, 11–12, 61–62, 101–103, 125, 128
Sophie de Bourbon, 132
South Africa, 14, 26, 68, 81. *See also* Empire, British
Spanking Stories, 44
The Spirit of Flagellation, 142
Steele, Valerie, 78, 81–82
sterilization, involuntary, 49–50
stockings, 44, 93, 158–162; and amputees, 101; and cross-dressing, 129, 130, 140, 143; popular culture and, 159–160, 162; and whipping, 153, 154
Stopes, Marie: availability of works of, 23; on clitoral stimulation, 54; and disinheriting of son, 49; eugenicist views of, 5, 14, 48–50, 69–72; feminist views of, 48–50; and focus on modern British couple, 37, 50; as influenced by Ellis, 39; opposition of, to psychoanalysis, 66; Oxford speaking engagement banned, 20; personal life of, 36, 43, 59; statements on history by, 64; writing style of, 50–51. *See also Married Love* (Stopes); Stopes correspondence
Stopes correspondence, 5–6, 9; on abortion, 47, 201n7; construction of sexual identity in writing of, 47; effects of war shown in, 59–64; and frustrations with not achieving ideal, 58–59; language of, patterned on Stopes's, 54–58; letter on continual arousal,

17; letter on pregnancy from public lavatory, 17; letters seeking "right way" to have sex, 53–54; quantity of letters in, 47; request for reader letters leading to, 9, 46–47; Stopes addressed as leading authority in, 57; use of medical history language in, 57–58; view of history and modernity in, 64–69; during World War II, 180; and writers' determination to overcome ignorance, 51–54
Stortt, Wallace, 98–101, 104, 109–110, 176–177. *See also* amputees/amputation
storytelling, 6–8, 12, 47, 88. *See also* identity formation; letter writing; narrative(s)
"The Strange Quest of Anthony Drew" (Stortt), 109
Strawson, Galen, 6–7
students, whipping of, 162–163, 219n49, 219n62
Studies in the Psychology of Sex (Ellis), 39–40, 42
subjectivity in stories of self, 7
submission: and amputee fantasies, 105; and female boxers/wrestlers, 90–92; and gender economy, 144–145; and memories of childhood, 143–144; and stylized invalidism, 95–97, 162. *See also* BD/SM; sadomasochism
Summers, Leigh, 93
surgery, sexual reassignment, 136
Swinburne, Algernon, 160
Symonds, John Addington, 39

Tansley, Arthur, 38
Tarzan, 159
tattoos, 30, 37, 88, *119*, 145–146. *See also* body modification
Teleny, 146
"temple of strange gods," 109–110
third-person narrative in self-descriptions, 56–57, 60
Thompson, Edith, 186n17
Thompson, E. P., 2
Three Contributions to the Theory of Sex (Freud), 41, 44
Three Essays on the Theory of Sexuality (Freud), 4, 44
toilet seats and pregnancy concerns, 17, 18
touch mania, 88
Transvestites (Hirschfeld), 135
trench warfare. *See* World War I
Two Flappers in Paris, 161

Ulysses (Joyce), 20, 30, 33–34, 170–171
Unwilling Passenger (Osburn), 168

Vagrancy Acts, 21, 163
Van de Velde, Theodoor H., 38, 43

venereal disease (VD), 70
Venus Castina, 132
"Venus in furs," 41, 170
Venus School Mistress, 160
veterans. *See* World War I
Victorian age: eroticization of, 93; lack of sex
    education in, 52; versus model of modernity,
    66; model of sexuality in, 48; sexual identity
    formation in, 2–3; Stopes's portrayal of,
    64–65
vocabulary of sexuality, 51
voluntary amputation, 100, 102–104, 176
voyeurism: definitions of, 3; as a result of cor-
    poral punishment, 168; and tableaux, 3, 24

Wadsley, Olive, 30, 32, 33
Wales, 25, 169, 174. *See also* Empire, British
Walker, Kenneth, 38, 43, 88
Wallace, Edgar, 30
Waters, Chris, 187n30
Waugh, Thomas, 28
Webb, Beatrice, 132
Weeks, Jeffrey, 42
Wellcome Library, 201n4
The Well of Loneliness (Hall), 2, 22, 30, 34, 41,
    45, 135
West, Mae, 94
West, Rebecca, 31
whipping and caning: birching, 143, 162, 164,
    166–167, 170; of boys, 143, 162, 164, 166–167;
    in British pornography, 160; and cat-o'-nine-
    tails, 166; of children, 143, 162, 164, 166–167;
    and consciousness, 170–173; as corporal
    punishment, 9, 15, 152–153, 163–169; erotic
    implications of, 153–157, 160, 162, 165–169,
    219n49; of girls, 153–158, 161, 173; history
    of, 160, 163–165; in Holeman's poison pen
    letters, 153–157; and knickers, 153–154, 156,
    158–159, 173; in navy, 163; and perversion,
    16, 153, 168–169; of prisoners, 152–153; and
    stockings 153–154, 156, 158–159, 173; and
    "whipping returns," 165; of women, *114*, 163.
    See also flagellation, sexual
white slave trade panic, 163
Willing's Press Guide, 79
Windmill Theatre, 3, 29
Wise Parenthood (Stopes), 37, 50, 70
Woiak, Joanne, 203n27

Wolfenden Report, 8
women, *114*, *116*, *119–121*; and access to
    obscene/explicit wares, 19; ban on whip-
    ping of, 163; as boxers/wrestlers, 90–92;
    cross-dressing by, 131–132, 214n40; with
    disabilities, 100–102; as embodiment of "the
    Race," 69–70; gaining suffrage, 11; and gen-
    der ambiguity, 133–134; gender roles before
    and after World War I, 11; and ignorance
    equated with purity, 18; and love as yielding,
    31; masculinization of, 214n40; and modern-
    girl image, 12, 31–32, 65–66, 84, 89–90, 100,
    154, 161; post–World War I denouncements
    of, 11–12; poverty's effects on, 57; use of
    medical history language by, 57–58; in views
    of Victorian family, 48
Women's Health Inquiry (1933), 57
Woolf, Virginia, 12
Woolsey, John, 170–171
working class: and access to literature, 19; and
    cross-dressing, 133; and eugenics, 49; and
    fertility control, 202n17; health of women
    in, 57; influence of Stopes on, 37, 49, 200–
    201n2; lack of sexual knowledg among, 51;
    Mervyn Hyde and, 147–149; queer culture
    and, 147–148; and self-identity, 7; Stopes's
    statements on, 64; unemployment and, 89
World War I: casualty figures from, 11; conse-
    quences of, 11; and cross-dressing in enter-
    tainment reviews, 129–131; and desire for
    birth control, 60, 65; different experiences
    of men and women in, 212n18; effect of, on
    self-identity and sexuality, 11, 59–64, 128–
    129; explicit material available during, 19; as
    history, 61; and ideas of masculinity, 11, 74,
    127, 130; increase in letter writing during,
    10–11; and Marie Stopes, 59; Second Battle
    of Ypres, 127; shell shock and physical injury
    in, 11–12, 61–62, 101–103, 125, 128; trench
    warfare in, 11–12; Western Front, 127. *See
    also* amputees/amputation; disability
World War II, 179–180
writing: and conceptions of sexuality, 9, 51,
    54–58, 65, 171; and identity, 47, 75; of letters,
    76–77, 81–85, 88–94, 101; new models of,
    12; practices for, 54–58; sexological, 35–40,
    43; styles of, 73–74, 172. *See also* correspon-
    dence; letters; letter writing

Lisa Z. Sigel is an Associate Professor in the Department of History at DePaul University. She is the author of *Governing Pleasures: Pornography and Social Change in England, 1815–1914,* and the editor of *International Exposure: Perspectives on Modern European Pornography, 1800–2000.*